Starting an Online Business For Dummies® 4th Edition

Cheat Sheet

Contact Information to Keep Close at Hand

Nobody runs a business alone. You need to know where to go for help if problems arise. Take a moment to jot down the following names and phone numbers/e-mail addresses so that you have them when you need them:

- ✔ Your ISP's technical support number (where to call if you can't connect or access your e-mail) and your Internet access account's username and password:

  _____

- ✔ Your Web hosting service's number (the company that posts your Web site on its server — may be the same as your ISP), plus your Web hosting service's username and password, your Domain Name Service server names and IP addresses:

  _____

  _____

- ✔ Your Web site designer's number (a friend or a firm that you hired to help you build your Web site):

- ✔ Your technical support contact (a neighbor, a toll-free computer support company, or a paid service):

  _____

- ✔ Your employees' or business partners' numbers:

  _____

  _____

  _____

- ✔ Your credit card network's number (where to call when you want to process a credit card order):

  _____

- ✔ Your accountant's number:

  _____

- ✔ Your lawyer's number:

  _____

- ✔ Your Internet service provider's (ISP's) access number (the number you usually dial to connect to the Internet):

  _____

- ✔ Other contacts:

  _____

  _____

Copyright © 2005 Wiley Publishing, Inc. All rights reserved.

Item 8334-4.

For more information about Wiley Publishing, call 1-800-762-2974.

For Dummies: Bestselling Book Series for Beginners

Starting an Online Business For Dummies, 4th Edition

Legal and Business Requirements

- ✔ **Decide what type of business you're going to be:** Are you going to be a sole proprietorship, a partnership, or are you going to incorporate?

- ✔ **Sales tax:** If your state requires sales tax, you are required to collect it from customers who live in the same state where your company has a physical presence.

- ✔ **Choose an accounting method:** You can either use cash-basis or accrual-basis accounting.

- ✔ **Choose an accounting period:** The calendar year is simple, but you can also choose a fiscal year.

- ✔ **Record your revenue:** Write down the amount you receive, the form of payment, the date, the name of the client, and the goods or services you provided in exchange for the payment.

- ✔ **Keep track of expenses:** Write down the date the expense occurred, the name of the person or company that received payment, and the type of expense incurred.

- ✔ **Be aware of local restrictions:** Some cities, towns, or counties have zoning restrictions preventing businesses from operating from homes, or requiring home-based businesses to pay licensing fees.

- ✔ **Research your trade name:** Do a search on the Internet followed by a trademark search on the U.S. Patent and Trademark Office's Web site (http://tess2.uspto.gov/bin/gate.exe?f=tess&state=arg32.1.1).

Referral List

Smart businesspeople build goodwill and develop loyalty by referring customers to other sources when they can't provide what is needed. Keep a list of the names, e-mail addresses, Web site URLs, or phone numbers of companies or individuals that you can personally recommend:

Name_____ Contact info._____

Name_____ Contact info._____

Name_____ Contact info._____

Name_____ Contact info._____

Name_____ Contact info._____

Web Site Checklist

You can put almost anything you want on your Web site, but following are some essential things that you need to be sure you include:

- ❑ Your contact information
- ❑ Your company name and logo, if you have one
- ❑ Your business mission statement
- ❑ Titles that match each Web page's contents
- ❑ <META> tags that help search services index your site
- ❑ Copyright notice
- ❑ Links to main areas of your business Web site
- ❑ Feedback form or guest book
- ❑ Endorsements from satisfied customers/clients
- ❑ Clear photos of your merchandise for sale
- ❑ Online order form
- ❑ A Frequently Asked Questions (FAQ) page
- ❑ Customer service information
- ❑ Payment options (credit card, check, escrow account)
- ❑ Shipping options (overnight, two-day, ground)

For Dummies: Bestselling Book Series for Beginners

Starting an Online Business

FOR DUMMIES®

4TH EDITION

by Greg Holden

WILEY

Wiley Publishing, Inc.

Starting an Online Business For Dummies®, 4th Edition

Published by
Wiley Publishing, Inc.
111 River Street
Hoboken, NJ 07030-5774
www.wiley.com

Copyright © 2005 by Wiley Publishing, Inc., Indianapolis, Indiana

Published by Wiley Publishing, Inc., Indianapolis, Indiana

Published simultaneously in Canada

For general information on our other products and services, please contact our Customer Care Department within the U.S. at 800-762-2974, outside the U.S. at 317-572-3993, or fax 317-572-4002.

For technical support, please visit www.wiley.com/techsupport.

Wiley also publishes its books in a variety of electronic formats. Some content that appears in print may not be available in electronic books.

Library of Congress Control Number: 2005920578

ISBN: 0-7645-8334-4

Manufactured in the United States of America

10 9 8 7 6 5 4 3 2

4B/RW/QS/QV/IN

WILEY

About the Author

Greg Holden started a small business called Stylus Media, which is a group of editorial, design, and computer professionals who produce both print and electronic publications. The company gets its name from a recording stylus that reads the traces left on a disk by voices or instruments and translates those signals into electronic data that can be amplified and enjoyed by many. He has been self-employed for the past ten years. He is an avid user of eBay, both as a buyer and seller, and he recently started his own blog.

One of the ways Greg enjoys communicating is through explaining technical subjects in nontechnical language. The first edition of *Starting an Online Business For Dummies* was the ninth of his more than thirty computer books. He also authored *eBay PowerUser's Bible* for Wiley Publishing. Over the years, Greg has been a contributing editor of *Computer Currents* magazine, where he writes a monthly column. He also contributes to *PC World* and the University of Illinois at Chicago alumni magazine. Other projects have included preparing documentation for an electronics catalog company in Chicago and creating online courses on Windows 2000 and Microsoft Word 2000.

Greg balances his technical expertise and his entrepreneurial experience with his love of literature. He received an M.A. in English from the University of Illinois at Chicago and also writes general interest books, short stories, and poetry. Among his editing assignments is the monthly newsletter for his daughters' grade school.

After graduating from college, Greg became a reporter for his hometown newspaper. Working at the publications office at the University of Chicago was his next job, and it was there that he started to use computers. He discovered, as the technology became available, that he loved desktop publishing (with the Macintosh and LaserWriter) and, later on, the World Wide Web.

Greg loves to travel, but since his two daughters were born, he hasn't been able to get around much. He was able to translate his experiences into a book called *Karma Kids: Answering Everyday Parenting Questions with Buddhist Wisdom.* However, through the Web, he enjoys traveling vicariously and meeting people online. He lives with his family in an old house in Chicago that he has been rehabbing for — well, for many years now. He is a collector of objects such as pens, cameras, radios, and hats. He is always looking for things to take apart so that he can see how they work and fix them up. Many of the same skills prove useful in creating and maintaining Web pages. He is an active member of Jewel Heart, a Tibetan Buddhist meditation and study group based in Ann Arbor, Michigan.

Dedication

To my best friend Ann Lindner, who makes everything possible.

Author's Acknowledgments

One of the things I like best about this book is that it's a teaching tool that gives me a chance to share my knowledge — small business owner to small business owner — about computers, the Internet, and communicating your message to others in an interactive way. As any businessperson knows, most large-scale projects are a team effort.

While the online business landscape has changed since this book was first published, some basic principles remain the same. One is the fact that the most successful entrepreneurs also tend to be the ones who are the most generous with their time and experience. They taught me that the more helpful you are, the more successful you'll be in return.

I want to thank all those who were profiled as case studies, particularly John Moen of Graphic Maps, who pops up all through the book. Special recognition also goes to attorney David Adler (www.ecommerceattorney.com) for his assistance with Chapter 16. Thanks also go to Jeremy G. Alicandri of Simply Cheap.com; Ed Bryson of Yahoo! Small Business; Lucky Boyd of MyTexasMusic. com; Mike Holden of lp2cdsolutions; Kristin Lindner of Elephant of Joy; John Counsel of The Profit Clinic; Caroline Dauteuille, Jeffrey E. Edelheit, and Mike Gearhart of CMStat Corporation; Lars Hundley of Clean Air Gardening; Kimberly King; Mark Lauer of General Tool and Repair; Doug Laughter of The Silver Connection; Brennan Mulligan of Timbuk2 Designs; John Raddatz of SoftBear Shareware; Sarah-Lou Reekie of Alfresco; Michael Rosenberg of Health Decisions; Judy Vorfeld of Office Support Services; and Marques Vickers.

I would also like to acknowledge some of my own colleagues who helped prepare and review the text and graphics of this book and who have supported and encouraged me in other lessons of life. Thanks to Ann Lindner, whose teaching experience proved invaluable in suggesting ways to make the text more clear, and to my assistant Ben Huizenga.

For editing and technical assignments, I was lucky to be in the capable hands of the folks at Wiley Publishing: my project editor Nicole Sholly, my copy editor Jean Rogers, and technical editor Jim Kelly.

Thanks also to Neil Salkind and David and Sherry Rogelberg of Studio B, and to Terri Varveris of Wiley Publishing for helping me to add this book to the list of those I've authored and, in the process, to broaden my expertise as a writer.

Last but certainly not least, the future is in the hands of the generation of my two daughters, Zosia and Lucy, who allow me to learn from the curiosity and joy with which they approach life.

Publisher's Acknowledgments

We're proud of this book; please send us your comments through our online registration form located at www.dummies.com/register/.

Some of the people who helped bring this book to market include the following:

Acquisitions, Editorial, and Media Development

Project Editor: Nicole Sholly

Acquisitions Editor: Terri Varveris

Copy Editor: Jean Rogers

Technical Editor: Jim Kelly

Editorial Manager: Kevin Kirschner

Permissions Editor: Laura Moss

Media Development Specialist: Angela Denny

Media Development Manager: Laura VanWinkle

Media Development Supervisor:
Richard Graves

Editorial Assistant: Amanda Foxworth

Cartoons: Rich Tennant, www.the5thwave.com

Composition Services

Project Coordinator: Nancee Reeves

Layout and Graphics: Barry Offringa, Jacque Roth, Heather Ryan

Proofreaders: Leeann Harney, Jessica Kramer, TECHBOOKS Composition Services

Indexer: TECHBOOKS Composition Services

Publishing and Editorial for Technology Dummies

    Richard Swadley, Vice President and Executive Group Publisher

    Andy Cummings, Vice President and Publisher

    Mary Bednarek, Executive Acquisitions Director

    Mary C. Corder, Editorial Director

Publishing for Consumer Dummies

    Diane Graves Steele, Vice President and Publisher

    Joyce Pepple, Acquisitions Director

Composition Services

    Gerry Fahey, Vice President of Production Services

    Debbie Stailey, Director of Composition Services

Table of Contents

Part IV: Running and Promoting Your Online Business 227

Chapter 11: Easing the Shopping Experience 229

Chapter 12: Accepting Payments 247

Introduction

· ·

You've been thinking about starting your own business, but until now, it's been just a dream. After all, you're a busy person. You have a full-time job, whether it's running your home or working outside your home. Or perhaps you've been through some life-changing event and are ready to take off in a new direction. Then the economy took a turn for the worse, and you were understandably reluctant to make a big career change.

Well, I have news for you: *Now* is the perfect time to turn your dream into reality by starting your own online business. Individuals just like you are making money and enriching their lives by operating businesses online. The clock and your location are no longer limiting factors. Small business owners can now work any time of the night or day in their spare bedrooms, local libraries, or neighborhood coffee shops. And there are new ways of making money online, such as starting a blog or starting a full-time business on eBay, which are becoming more viable all the time.

If you like the idea of being in business for yourself, but you don't have a particular product or service in mind at the moment, relax and keep yourself open for inspiration. Many different kinds of commercial enterprises can hit it big on the Internet. Among the entrepreneurs I interviewed for this book are a woman who sells her own insect repellent, a mapmaker, a woman who provides office services for the medical community, a housewife who sells sweetener and coffee on eBay, a sculptor and painter, a young man who started selling electronics online at age 16, and several folks who create Web pages for other businesses. With the help of this book, you can start a new endeavor and be in charge of your own cyberbusiness, too.

You Can Do It!

What's that? You say you wouldn't know a merchant account, profit-and-loss statement, or clickthrough advertising rate if it came up to you on the street and introduced itself? Don't worry: The Internet (and this book) level the playing field, so a novice has just as good a chance at succeeding as MBAs who love to throw around business terms at cocktail parties.

The Internet is pretty much an accepted part of the business landscape these days. Whether you've been in business for 20 years or 20 minutes, the keys to success are the same:

- ✔ **Having a good idea:** If you have something to sell that people have an appetite for, and if your competition is slim, your chances of success are hefty.

- ✔ **Working hard:** When you are your own boss, you can make yourself work harder than any of your former bosses ever could. But if you put in the effort and persist through the inevitable ups and downs, you will be a winner.

- ✔ **Preparing for success:** One of the most surprising and useful things I discovered from the online businesspeople that I interviewed was that if you believe that you will succeed, you probably will. Believe in yourself and proceed as though you're going to be successful. Together with your good ideas and hard work, your confidence will pay off.

If you're the cautious type who wants to test the waters before you launch your new business on the Internet, let this book lead you gently up the learning curve. After you're online, you can master techniques to improve your presence. This book includes helpful hints for doing market research and reworking your Web site until you get the success you want. Even if you aren't among the lucky small business owners who make a fortune by connecting to the Net, the odds are very good that you will make new friends, build your confidence, and have fun, too.

The Water's Still Fine

When I first started revising this new edition in the fall of 2004, I was excited to find that new business opportunities were springing up again after some lean years. eBay is booming. Other well-known Web-based service providers like Yahoo!, PayPal, and Amazon.com are enabling entrepreneurs to start up new businesses. Bloggers are taking the Internet by storm, and some are making a regular source of income from their online diaries. Google and Overture are making it easier than ever to gain advertising revenue.

As the Web becomes more of a way of life and broadband Internet connections become widespread, doing business online becomes more of a real possibility. Still, you may have reasonable concerns about the future of e-commerce for the very entrepreneurs this book seeks to help — individuals who are starting their first businesses on the Web. Your fears will quickly evaporate when you read this book's case studies of my friends and colleagues who do business online. They're either thriving or at least treading water, and they enthusiastically encourage others to jump right in — the water's fine.

This is still a great time to start an online business. People who are getting into e-commerce today have advantages over those who started out three or four years ago. Simply put, both consumers and businesses are smarter. "There are more experts in the field so that it is easier to make things happen," says Sarah-Lou Reekie, an online entrepreneur I profile in Chapter 13. "The world is far more *au fait* and switched on to the Web. The percentage of people able to competently order is far higher. People aren't as nervous as they were to put through credit cards. After an amazingly short time, the Web has changed from an unknown and somewhat scary medium to something as easy as ABC for most users."

"I feel the best time to start an online business is when you are positioned to begin. I do not feel that there is an advantage/disadvantage to waiting for a 'better time' to start," says Mark Cramer, whose own online business and Web site are profiled in Bonus Chapter 1 on this book's Web site (located at www.dummies.com/go/onlinebusinessfd).

Where This Book Is Coming From

Online business isn't just for large corporations, or even just for small businesses that already have a storefront in the real world and simply want to supplement their marketability with a Web site.

The Internet is a perfect venue for individuals who want to start their own business, who like using computers, and who believe that cyberspace is the place to do it. You don't need much money to get started, after all. If you already have a computer and an Internet connection and can create your own Web pages (which this book will help you with), making the move to your own business Web site may cost only $100 or less. After you're online, the overhead is pretty reasonable, too: You may pay only $10 to $75 per month to a Web hosting service to keep your site online.

With each month that goes by, the number of Internet users increases exponentially. To be precise, in early 2004 Neilsen//NetRatings released data indicating that more than 74 percent of the U.S. population had access to the Internet at home. The Pew Internet & American Life Project reported that 39 percent of adults who surf the Internet do so with a broadband connection. We have now reached that critical mass where *most* people are using the Internet regularly for everyday shopping and other financial activities. The Internet is already becoming a powerhouse for small businesses.

So why wait to fall behind your competition? The goal of this book is to help you open your fledgling business on the Internet now. Let this book guide you through the following steps:

- ✔ Preparing a business plan, defining your target market, and setting goals
- ✔ Purchasing the hardware and software you need to run your business
- ✔ Making your Web pages content rich and interactive
- ✔ Reaching your customers through multiple marketplaces such as eBay, Yahoo!, Amazon.com, and your own Web site

    ✔ Marketing to customers around the world

    ✔ Creating a secure environment for shopping and receiving payments online

    ✔ Keeping your business records and observing legal requirements

How to Use This Book

Want to get an overview of the whole process of going online and be inspired by one man's online business success story? Zip ahead to Chapter 1. Want to find out how to accept credit card payments? Flip ahead to Chapter 12. Feel free to skip back and forth to chapters that interest you. I've made this book into an easy-to-use reference tool that you will be comfortable with, no matter what your level of experience with computers and networking. You don't have to scour each chapter methodically from beginning to end to find what you want. The Net doesn't work that way and neither does this book!

If you're just starting out and need to do some essential business planning, see Chapter 2. If you want to prepare a shopping list of business equipment, see Chapter 3. Chapters 4 through 10 are all about the essential aspects of creating and operating a successful online business, from organizing and marketing your Web site to providing effective online customer service and security. Later chapters get into advertising, legal issues, and accounting. The fun thing about being online is that continually improving and redoing your presentation is easy. So start where it suits you and come back later for more.

What This Book Assumes

This book assumes that you have never been in business before but that you're interested in setting up your own commercial site on the Internet. I also assume that you're familiar with the Internet, have been surfing for a while, and may even have put out some information of your own in the form of a home page.

It also assumes that you have or are ready to get the following:

    ✔ **A computer and a modem:** Don't worry, Chapter 2 explains exactly what hardware and software you need.

    ✔ **Instructions on how to think like a businessperson:** I spend a good amount of time in this book encouraging you to set goals, devise strategies to meet those goals, and do the sort of planning that successful businesspeople need to do.

✔ **Just enough technical know-how:** You don't have to do it all yourself. Plenty of entrepreneurs decide to partner with someone or hire an expert to perform design and technical work. This book can help you understand your options and give you a basic vocabulary so that you can work productively with the consultants you hire.

What's Where in This Book

This book is divided into six parts. Each part contains chapters that discuss stages in the process of starting an online business. There's also an Internet Directory that you can access through this book's Web site; it presents an up-to-date list of resources that are essential for any online businessperson.

Part 1: Strategies and Tools for Your Online Business

In Part I, I describe what you need to do and how you need to *think* in order to start your new online business. The first chapter follows the story about how a business started by a graphic artist-turned mapmaker has grown into an Internet success story. Subsequent chapters also present case studies profiling other entrepreneurs and describing how they started their online businesses. Within these pages is where I also describe the software that you need in order to create Web pages and perform essential business tasks, along with any computer upgrades that will help your business run more smoothly. You also discover how to choose a Web host and find exciting new ways to make money online.

Part 11: Establishing Your Online Presence

Even if you use an online service that isn't technically part of the Web, such as America Online, you need to create a Web site — a series of interconnected Web pages that everyone in cyberspace can view with a Web browser. As far as online business is concerned, the Web is where it's at. This part explains how to create a compelling and irresistible Web site, one that attracts paying customers around the world and keeps them coming back to make more purchases. This part also includes options for attracting and keeping customers, making your site secure, and updating and improving your online business.

Part III: Successful Online Business Models

Some of the most exciting new aspects of starting a business online are ways to generate sales revenue that don't involve setting up your own Web site from scratch. Instead of going it alone, you sign up with one of the many well-established business marketplaces on the Web that enables individuals just like you to create storefronts or sell individual items. You find out about creating storefronts on Amazon.com, Yahoo!, PayPal, and CafePress.com, among other venues. You also discover the ins and outs of starting a business on eBay, a marketplace that has changed lives and is quickly changing the landscape of online business.

Part IV: Running and Promoting Your Online Business

Your work doesn't end after you put your Web site online or start to make a few sales. In fact, what you do after you open your cyberdoors for business can make the difference between a site that says "Wow!" and one that says "Ho-hum." In this part, I describe cost-effective marketing and advertising techniques that you can do yourself to increase visibility and improve customer satisfaction. You discover how to make the shopping experience a smooth one for your customers, how to accept payments, and how to provide good customer service. You also find out about new ways to increase visibility with search services such as Google.

Part V: The Necessary Evils: Law and Accounting

This part delves into some less-than-sexy but essential activities for any online business. Find out about general security methods designed to make commerce more secure on the Internet. I also discuss copyrights, trademarks, and other legal concerns for anyone wanting to start a company in the increasingly competitive atmosphere of the Internet. Finally, you get an overview of basic accounting practices for online businesses and suggestions of accounting tools that you can use to keep track of your e-commerce activities.

Part VI: The Part of Tens

Filled with tips, cautions, suggestions, and examples, the Part of Tens presents many tidbits of information that you can use to plan and create your own business presence on the Internet, including ten hot new ways to make money on the Web.

An Online Feature: The Starting an Online Business For Dummies Internet Directory

If you're running your online business in your off hours or between other activities, you don't have time to scour the Web for help. Not to fear: You can find everything you need in this directory. It's a collection of links to Web sites and other Internet resources of special interest to individuals starting an online business — especially if you're working alone or at home and need to find people to help you. Access it at `www.dummies.com/go/onlinebusinessfd`. (On the Web site you'll also find Bonus Chapter 1, which details ten ways of ensuring online success.)

Conventions Used in This Book

In this book, I format important bits of information in special ways to make sure that you notice them right away:

- **In This Chapter lists:** Chapters start with a list of the topics that I cover in that chapter. This list represents a kind of table of contents in miniature.

- **Numbered lists:** When you see a numbered list, follow the steps in a specific order to accomplish a given task.

- **Bulleted lists:** Bulleted lists (like this one) indicate things that you can do in any order or list related bits of information.

- **Web addresses:** When I describe activities or sites of interest on the World Wide Web, I include the address, or Uniform Resource Locator (URL), in a special typeface like this: `http://www.wiley.com/`. Because the newer versions of popular Web browsers, such as Netscape Navigator and Microsoft Internet Explorer, don't require you to enter the entire URL, this book uses the shortened addresses. For example, if you want to connect to the Wiley Publishing site, you can get there by simply entering the following in your browser's Go To or Address box: `www.wiley.com`.

  Don't be surprised if your browser can't find an Internet address you type or if a Web page that's depicted in this book no longer looks the same. Although the sites were current when the book was written, Web addresses (and sites themselves) can be pretty fickle. Try looking for a missing site by using an Internet search engine. Or try shortening the address by deleting everything after the `.com` (or `.org` or `.edu`).

Icons Used in This Book

Starting an Online Business For Dummies, 4th Edition, also uses special graphical elements called *icons* to get your attention. Here's what they look like and what they mean:

This icon points out some technical details that may be of interest to you. A thorough understanding, however, isn't a prerequisite to grasping the underlying concept. Non-techies are welcome to skip items marked by this icon altogether.

This icon calls your attention to interviews I conducted with online entrepreneurs who provided tips and instructions for running an online business.

This icon flags practical advice about particular software programs or about issues of importance to businesses. Look to these tips for help with finding resources quickly, making sales, or improving the quality of your online business site. This icon also alerts you to software programs and other resources that I consider to be especially good, particularly for the novice user.

This icon points out potential pitfalls that can develop into more major problems if you're not careful.

This icon alerts you to facts and figures that are important to keep in mind as you run your online business.

We're in It Together

Improving communication is the whole point of this book. My goal is to help you express yourself in the exciting new medium of the Internet and to remind you that you're not alone. I'm a businessperson myself, after all. So I hope that you'll let me know what you think about this book by contacting me. Check out the *For Dummies* Web site at www.dummies.com. You're also welcome to contact me directly if you have questions or comments. Visit my personal Web page at www.gregholden.com or send e-mail to me at greg@gregholden.com.

Part I

Strategies and Tools for Your Online Business

The 5th Wave   By Rich Tennant

"As a Web site designer I never thought I'd say this, but I don't think your site has enough bells and whistles."

In this part . . .

What all does starting an online business involve? In this part, I answer that question with a brief overview of the whole process. The following chapters help you set your online business goals, draw up a blueprint for meeting those goals, and explore new ways to market your goods and services.

And just as dentists prepare their drills and carpenters assemble their tools, you need to gather the necessary hardware and software to keep your online business running smoothly. So, in this part, I discuss the business equipment that the online store owner needs and suggest ways that you can meet those needs even on a limited budget.

Let the step-by-step instructions and real-life case studies in this part guide you through the process of starting a successful business online.

Chapter 1

Opening Your Own Online Business in Ten Easy Steps

*S*tarting an online business is no longer a novelty. It's a fact of life for individuals and established companies alike. The good news is that e-commerce is here to stay and thriving once again. Not only that, but the steps required to conduct commerce online are well within the reach of individuals like you and me who have no prior business experience. New software and services make creating Web pages and transacting online business easier than ever. Even online businesses that were floundering a few years ago have figured out how to work smarter and more successfully. All you need is a good idea, a bit of start-up money, some computer equipment, and a little help from your friends.

One of my goals in this book is to be one of the friends who provides you with the right advice and support to get your business online and make it a success. In this chapter, I give you a step-by-step overview of the entire process of starting an online business.

Step 1: Identify a Need

"The best of anything hasn't been done yet," says John Moen, the successful e-businessperson profiled in this chapter. "The Web isn't over. Someday someone is going to invent a better Wal-Mart, and there's going to be a bigger and better store. As the technology changes, someone is going to create a business online that makes people say, 'Holy cow, that's cool.'"

E-commerce and the Web have been around for a decade now. But new products and ways to sell them are being identified all the time. Think of the things that didn't exist when the first Web sites were created: MP3s, wireless modems, DVDs, eBay. Consider my brother Mike: As I write this book, I am helping him create his own online business, lp2cdsolutions, Inc. Like many entrepreneurs, he reached a simple conclusion: "If I want this product so badly, I bet a lot of other people do, too." What he wanted was to convert his scratchy old records to clean and repackaged CDs. He spent thousands of dollars on computer hardware and software, and he got really good at audio restoration. Now he wants to make money by doing the same for others. Will he succeed because he has me to help him? I don't think success is guaranteed. It depends on you — your energy, dedication, and enthusiasm. You follow the progress of his site in this and subsequent chapters.

Your first job, accordingly, is to get in touch with your market (the people who'll be buying your stuff or using your services) and determine how you can best meet its needs. After all, you can't expect Web surfers to patronize your online business unless you identify services or items that they really need.

A hotbed of commerce

Statistically, the Internet is a hotbed of commerce — and it just keeps getting hotter. Listen to what the experts are saying:

✔ **BizRate** (www.bizrate.com) reported that online shoppers spent $8.6 billion during the 2003 Christmas season, 24 percent more than the year before. The top categories in terms of sales were computer hardware, electronics, and entertainment. However, the categories that saw the strongest growth were food and wine (up 58 percent over the year before), gifts and flowers (up 56 percent), and apparel (up 38 percent).

✔ **Statistics Canada** (www.statcan.ca), the Canadian government's central statistical agency, recently reported that e-commerce sales in Canada in 2003 rose for the fourth year in a row, jumping 40 percent from $13.7 billion in 2002 to $19.1 billion in 2003.

✔ **eMarketer** (www.emarketer.com/Report.aspx?b2c_us_jul04) cites The U.S. Department of Commerce's numbers indicating that e-commerce sales in the U.S. reached $56 billion in 2003, compared with $44.3 billion in 2002. Nearly one-third of 2003 sales occurred in the holiday shopping season in the fourth quarter.

✔ **Jupiter Research** (www.jupiterresearch.com) predicts that online sales of apparel and accessories, excluding shoes and jewelry, will reach $7.5 billion in 2004, from $6.2 billion the previous year. By 2008, the number should hit $12 billion, accounting for 4.9 percent of all apparel sales.

Check out the *Starting an Online Business For Dummies*, 4th Edition, Internet Directory on this book's Web site (located at www.dummies.com/go/onlinebusinessfd) for links to sites where you can gather fast facts and background information on doing business online.

Getting to know the marketplace

The Internet is a worldwide, interconnected network of computers to which people can connect either from work or home, and through which people can communicate via e-mail, receive information from the Web, and buy and sell items by using credit cards or other means.

Many people decide to start an online business with little more than a casual knowledge of the Internet. But when you decide to get serious about going online with a commercial endeavor, it pays to get to know the environment in which you plan to be working.

One of your first steps should be to find out what it means to do business online and to determine the best ways for you to fit into the exploding field of electronic commerce. For example, you need to realize that the Internet is a personal place; that customers are active, not passive, in the way they absorb information; and that the Net was established within a culture of people sharing information freely and helping one another.

Some of the best places to find out about the culture of the Internet are the newsgroups, chat rooms, and bulletin boards where individuals gather and exchange messages online. Visiting discussion forums devoted to topics that interest you personally can be especially helpful, and you're likely to end up participating. Also visit commerce Web sites, such as eBay, Amazon.com, or other online marketplaces, and take note of ideas and approaches that you may want to use.

"Cee-ing" what's out there

The more information you have about the "three Cs" of the online world, the more likely you are to succeed in doing business online:

- ✔ **Competitors:** Familiarize yourself with other online businesses that already do what you want to do. Don't let their presence intimidate you. You're going to find a different and better way to do what they already do.

- ✔ **Customers:** Investigate the various kinds of customers who shop online and who might visit your site.

- ✔ **Culture:** Explore the special language and style people use when they communicate.

As you take a look around the Internet, notice the kinds of goods and services that tend to sell in the increasingly crowded, occasionally disorganized, and sometimes-complex online world. The things that sell best in cyberspace include four Cs:

- ✔ **Cheap:** Online items tend to be sold at a discount — at least, that's what shoppers expect.

- ✔ **Customized:** Anything that's hard-to-find, personalized, or unique sells well online.

- ✔ **Convenient:** Shoppers are looking for items that are easier to buy online than at a "real" store, such as a rare book that you can order in minutes from Amazon.com (`www.amazon.com`), or an electronic greeting card that you can send online in seconds (`www.greeting-cards.com`).

- ✔ **Content-rich:** Consumers go online to quickly read news stories that are available by subscription, such as newspapers and magazines, or that exist online only, such as Web logs *(blogs)* and electronic publications *(ezines)*.

Visit one of the tried-and-true indexes to the Internet, such as Yahoo! (`www.yahoo.com`), or the preeminent search service Google (`www.google.com`). Enter a word or phrase in the site's home page search box that describes the kinds of goods or services you want to provide online. Find out how many existing businesses already do what you want to do. Better yet, determine what they *don't* do, and set a goal of meeting that specialized need yourself.

Mapmaker locates his online niche

John Moen didn't know a thing about computer graphics when he first started his online business, Graphic Maps, in 1995. He didn't know how to write HyperText Markup Language (HTML), the set of instructions used to create Web pages. (Not too many people in 1995 did.) But he did know a lot about maps. And he heard that setting up shop on the Web was "the thing to do." He scraped together $300 in start-up costs, learned to create some simple Web pages without any photos (only maps and other graphics), and went online.

At first, business was slow. "I remember saying to my wife, 'You know what? We had ten page views yesterday.'" The Graphic Maps site (`www.graphicmaps.com`) was averaging about 30 page views per day when Moen decided to do something that many beginners may find counterproductive, even silly: He started giving away his work for free. He created some free art (called clip art) and made it available for people to copy. And he didn't stop there: He began giving away his knowledge of geography. He answered questions submitted to him by schoolchildren and teachers.

Soon, his site was getting 1,000 visits a day. Today, he reports, "We are so busy, we literally can't keep up with the demand for custom maps. Almost 95 percent of our business leads come from the Web, and that includes many international companies and Web sites. Web page traffic has grown to more than 3 million hits per month, and banner advertising now pays very well."

John now has six employees, receives many custom orders for more than $10,000, and has done business with numerous Fortune 500 companies. To promote his site, John gives away free maps for nonprofit organizations, operates a daily geography contest with a $100 prize to the first person with the correct answer, and answers e-mail promptly. "I feel strongly that the secret on the Web is to provide a solution for a problem, and for the most part, do it free," he suggests. "If the service is high quality, and people get what they want . . . they will tell their friends and all will beat a path to your URL, and then, and only then, will you be able to sell your products to the world, in a way you never imagined was possible."

Moen created a second site called worldatlas.com (www.worldatlas.com, as shown here) that is devoted to geography. That site generates revenue from popup and banner ads that other companies place there because so many people visit. "It is not unusual to have 20 million impressions on that site and hundreds of thousands of geography questions a month from teachers and students who need an answer to a geography question," says Moen.

When asked how he can spare the time to answer questions for free when he has so much paying business available, he responds: "How can you not? I normally work 12-hour, and sometimes 16- or 18-hour days. If some little kid, some student, comes home from school, and says, 'Grandpa, I need to find out what's the tallest mountain in North America,' and he does a search on Google that directs him to go to worldatlas.com, we will try to answer that question."

His advice for beginning entrepreneurs: "Find your niche and do it well. Don't try to compete with larger companies. For instance, I can't compete with Microsoft or Rand McNally, but I don't try to. Our map site, graphicmaps.com, is one of the few custom map sites on the Web. There is no software yet available today that will do automatic mapping for a client. If you need a map for a wedding or for your office, we can make you one. I fill some needs that they don't fill, and I learned long ago how to drive business to my site by offering something for free. The fact is that if you have good ideas and you search for clients, you can still do well on the Web."

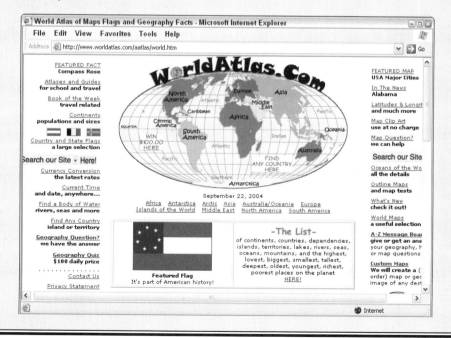

Figuring out how to do it better

After you take a look at what's already out there, the next step is to find ways to make your business stand out from the crowd. Direct your energies toward making your site unique in some way and providing things that others don't offer. The things that set your online business apart from the rest can be as tangible as half-price sales, contests, seasonal sales, or freebies. They can also involve making your business site higher in quality than the others. Maybe you can just provide better or more personalized customer service than anyone else.

What if you can't find other online businesses doing what you want to do? Lucky you! In electronic commerce, being first often means getting a head start and being more successful than latecomers, even if they have more resources than you do. (Just ask the owners of the online bookstore Amazon.com.) Don't be afraid to try something new and outlandish. It just might work!

Step 2: Determine What You Have to Offer

Business is all about identifying customers' needs and figuring out exactly what goods or services you're going to provide to meet those needs. It's the same both online and off. (Often, you perform this step before or at the same time that you scope out what the business needs are and figure out how you can position yourself to meet those needs, as I explain in the earlier section "Step 1: Identify a Need.")

To determine what you have to offer, make a list of all the items you have to put up for sale, or all the services that you plan to provide to your customers. Next, you need to decide not only what goods or services you can provide online, but also where you're going to obtain them. Are you going to create sale items yourself? Are you going to purchase them from another supplier? Jot down your ideas on paper and keep them close at hand as you develop your business plan.

The Internet is a personal, highly interactive medium. Be as specific as possible with what you plan to do online. Don't try to do everything; the medium favors businesses that do one thing well. The more specific your business, the more personal the level of service you can provide to your customers.

Step 3: Come Up with a Cyberbusiness Plan

The process of setting goals and objectives and then designing strategies for attaining them is essential when starting a new business. What you end up with is called a *business plan*. A good business plan applies not only to the start-up phase, but also to a business's day-to-day operation. It can also be instrumental in helping a small business obtain a bank loan.

Drawing up a business plan

To set specific goals for your new business, ask yourself these questions:

- ✔ Why do you want to start a business?
- ✔ Why do you want to start it online?
- ✔ What would *you* want to buy online?
- ✔ What would make you buy it?

These questions may seem simple. But many businesspeople never take the time to answer them. And only *you* can answer these questions for yourself. Make sure that you have a clear idea of where you're going so that you can commit to making your venture successful over the long haul. (See Chapter 2 for more on setting goals and envisioning your business.)

To carry your plan into your daily operations, observe these suggestions:

- ✔ Write a brief description of your company and what you hope to accomplish with it.
- ✔ Draw up a marketing strategy. (See Chapter 15 for tips.)
- ✔ Keep track of your finances. (See Chapter 17 for specifics.)

Consider using specialized software to help you prepare your business plan. Programs such as Business Plan Pro by Palo Alto Software (www.palo-alto.com) lead you through the process by asking you a series of questions as a way of identifying what you want to do. The program retails for $99.95. I also refer you to *Business Plans For Dummies,* 2nd Edition, by Paul Tiffany and Steven D. Peterson (Wiley).

If you set aside part of your home for business purposes, you are eligible for tax deductions. Exactly how much you can deduct depends on how much space you use. (For example, I have a nine-room house, and one room serves as my office, so I am able to deduct one-ninth of my utility bills and other housing costs. The deduction is based on floor space, but my office takes up about one-ninth of the total square footage in my house.) You can depreciate your computers and other business equipment, too. On the other hand, your municipality may require you to obtain a license if you operate a business in a residential area; check with your local authorities to make sure that you're on the up and up. You can find out more about tax and legal issues, including local licensing requirements, in Chapters 16 and 17 of this book.

Step 4: Assemble Your Equipment and Set Up Shop

One of the great advantages of opening a store on the Internet rather than on Main Street is money — or rather, the lack of it. Instead of having to rent a space and set up furniture and fixtures, you can buy a domain name, sign up with a hosting service, create some Web pages, and get started with an investment of only a few hundred dollars, or perhaps even less.

In addition to your virtual storefront, you also have to find a real place to do your business. You don't necessarily have to rent a warehouse or other large space. Many online entrepreneurs use a home office or perhaps a corner in a room where computers, books, and other business-related equipment reside.

Finding a host for your Web site

Although doing business online means that you don't have to rent space in a mall or open a real, physical store, you do have to set up a virtual space for your online business. You do so by creating a Web site and finding a company to host it. In cyberspace, your landlord is called a Web hosting service. A Web *host* is a company that, for a fee, makes your site available 24 hours a day by maintaining it on a special computer called a Web *server*.

A Web host can be as large and well known as America Online, which gives all its customers a place to create and publish their own Web pages. Some Web sites, such as Yahoo! GeoCities (geocities.yahoo.com) or Tripod (www.tripod.lycos.com), act as hosting services and provide easy-to-use Web site creation tools as well. When my brother decided to create his Web site, he signed up with a company called Webmasters.com, which charges him about $14.95 per month and offers many features, including the form shown in Figure 1-1 that enables you to create a simple Web page without having to type any HTML.

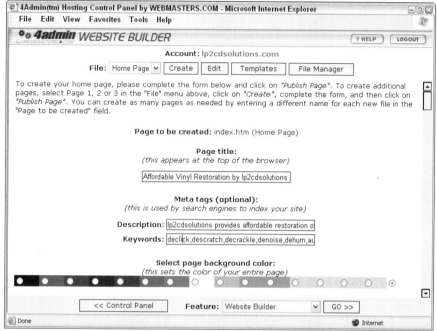

Figure 1-1:
Take the
time to
choose an
affordable
Web host
that makes it
easy for you
to create
and maintain
your site.

In addition, the company that gives you access to the Internet — your Internet service provider (ISP) — may also publish your Web pages. Make sure that your host has a fast connection to the Internet and can handle the large numbers of simultaneous visits, or *hits,* that your Web site is sure to get eventually. You can find a detailed description of Web hosting options in Chapter 3.

In Chapter 2, I describe two methods for selling your wares online that don't require a Web site — online classifieds and auctions. But most online businesses find that having a Web site is indispensable for generating and conducting sales. And hosts like America Online and Yahoo! make it easier than ever to create your own site, as I discuss in Chapter 3.

Assembling the equipment you need

Think of all the equipment you *don't* need when you set up shop online: You don't need shelving, a cash register, a parking lot, electricity, fire protection systems, a burglar alarm . . . the list goes on and on. You may need some of those for your home, but you don't need to purchase them especially for your online business.

For doing business online, your most important piece of equipment is your computer. Other hardware, such as scanners, modems, and monitors, are essential, too. You need to make sure that your computer equipment is up to snuff because you're going to be spending a lot of time online: answering e-mail, checking orders, revising your Web site, and marketing your product. Expect to spend anywhere between $1,000 and $6,000 for equipment, if you don't have any to begin with.

It pays to shop wisely and get the best setup you can afford up front so that you don't have to purchase upgrades later on. (For more suggestions on buying business hardware and software, see Chapter 2.)

Choosing business software

For the most part, the programs you need in order to operate an online business are the same as the software you use to surf the Internet. You do, however, need to have a wider variety of tools than you would use for simple information gathering.

Keeping track of your inventory

It's easy to overlook inventory and setting up systems for processing orders when you are just starting out. But as Lucky Boyd, an entrepreneur who started MyTexasMusic.com and other Web sites, pointed out to me, you need to make sure you have a "big vision" early in the process of creating your site. In his case, it meant having a site that could handle lots of visitors and make purchasing easy for them. In other cases, it might mean having sufficient inventory to meet demand.

Having too many items for sale is preferable to not having enough. "We operated on a low budget in the beginning, and we didn't have the inventory that people wanted," one entrepreneur commented. "People online get impatient if they have to wait for things too long. Make sure you have the goods you advertise. Plan to be successful."

Many online businesses keep track of their inventory by using a database that's connected to their Web site. When someone orders a product from the Web site, that order is automatically recorded in the database, which then produces an order for replacement stock.

In this kind of arrangement, the database serves as a so-called *back end* or *back office* to the Web-based storefront. This is a sophisticated arrangement that's not for beginners. However, if orders and inventory get to be too much for you to handle yourself, consider hiring a Web developer to set up such a system for you. If you're adventurous and technically oriented, you can link a database to a Web site by using a product such as FrontPage or Dreamweaver. For more information about these products and how they work, check out *FrontPage 2003 For Dummies*, by Asha Dornfest, and *Dreamweaver MX For Dummies*, by Janine Warner and Ivonne Berkowitz (both by Wiley).

Because you're going to be in the business of information *providing* now, as well as information gathering, you need programs such as the following:

- ✔ **A Web page editor:** These programs, which you may also hear called *Web page creation tools* or *Web page authoring tools,* make it easy for you to format text, add images, and design Web pages without having to master HTML.

- ✔ **Graphics software:** If you decide to create your business Web site yourself, rather than find someone to do it for you, you need a program that can help you draw or edit images that you want to include on your site.

- ✔ **Storefront software:** You can purchase software that leads you through the process of creating a full-fledged online business and getting your pages on the Web.

- ✔ **Accounting programs:** You can write your expenses and income on a sheet of paper. But it's far more efficient to use software that acts as a spreadsheet, helps you with billing, and even calculates sales tax.

Step 5: Find People to Help You

Conducting online business does involve relatively new technologies, but they aren't impossible to figure out. In fact, the technology is becoming more accessible all the time. Many people who start online businesses learn how to create Web pages and promote their companies by reading books, attending classes, or networking with friends and colleagues. Of course, just because you *can* do it all doesn't mean that you have to. Often, you're better off hiring help, either to advise you in areas where you aren't as strong or simply to help you tackle the growing workload — and help your business grow at the same time.

Hiring technical experts

Spending some money up front to hire professionals who can point you in the right direction can help you maintain an effective Web presence for years to come. Many businesspeople who usually work alone (myself included) hire knowledgeable individuals to do design or programming work that they would find impossible to tackle otherwise.

Don't be reluctant to hire professional help in order to get your business online. The Web is full of development firms that perform several related functions: providing customers with Web access, helping to create Web sites, and hosting sites on their servers. The expense for such services may be considerable at first. The programming involved in setting up databases, creating purchasing systems, and programming Web pages can run over $10,000 for particularly extensive Web sites, but they can pay off in the long term. Choose a designer carefully, and check out sites they've done before. Tell them your business plan, and spell out clearly what you want each page to do. Another area where you may want to find help is in networking and computer maintenance. You need to know how to do troubleshooting and find out how to keep your computers running. Find out if you have a computer expert in your neighborhood who is available on short notice.

If you do find a business partner, make sure that the person's abilities balance your own. If you're great at sales and public relations, for example, find a writer or Web page designer to partner with.

Gathering your team members

Many entrepreneurial businesses are family affairs. For example, a husband-and-wife team started Scaife's Butcher Shop in England, which has a successful Web site (www.jackscaife.co.uk). A successful eBay business, Maxwell Street Market, is run by a husband-and-wife team as well as family members and neighbors: The husband does the buying; the wife prepares sales descriptions; the others help with packing and shipping. John Moen found some retired teachers to help answer the geography questions that come into his worldatlas.com site. The convenience of the Internet means that these geography experts can log on to the site's e-mail inbox from their respective homes and answer questions quickly. (For more about John Moen and his Web site, see the "Mapmaker locates his online niche" sidebar, earlier in this chapter.)

Early on, when you have plenty of time to do planning, you probably won't feel a pressing need to hire others to help you. Many people wait to seek help when they have a deadline to meet or are in a financial crunch. Waiting to seek help is okay — as long as you realize that you *will* need help, sooner or later.

Of course, you don't have to hire family and friends, but you must find people who are reliable and can make a long-term commitment to your project. Keep these things in mind:

- ✔ Because the person you hire will probably work online quite a bit, pick someone who already exhibits experience with computers and the Internet.

- ✔ Online hiring practices work pretty much the same as those offline: You should always review a résumé, get at least three references, and ask for samples of the candidate's work.

- ✔ Pick someone who responds promptly and courteously and who provides the talents you need.

- ✔ If your only contact is by phone and e-mail, references are even more important.

Who are the people in your neighborhood?

Try to find an expert or helper right in your own neighborhood or town. In my own case, I work with a graphic designer who lives right around the corner from me, and he uses a consultant who lives across the street from him. Ask around your school or church, as well as other social venues. Your neighbors may be able to help you with various projects, including your online business . . . and your online business just may be able to help them, too.

Businesspeople who provide professional services also commonly recommend other consultants in the course of e-mail communications. Don't work in a vacuum. Participate in mailing lists and discussion groups online. Make contacts and strike up cooperative relationships with individuals who can help you.

Step 6: Construct a Web Site

Although you can make a living buying and selling full time on eBay, a Web site is still likely to be the focus of your online business. Fortunately, Web sites are becoming easier to create. You don't have to know a line of HTML in order to create an effective Web page yourself. Chapter 5 walks you through the specific tasks involved in organizing and designing Web pages. Also, see Chapter 6 for tips on making your Web pages content-rich and interactive.

Make your business easy to find online. Pick a Web address (otherwise known as a URL, or Uniform Resource Locator) that's easy to remember. You can purchase a short domain-name alias, such as www.company.com, to replace a longer one like www.internetprovider.com/~username/companyname/index.html. If the ideal dot-com (.com) name isn't available, you can choose one of the newer domain suffixes such as .biz. See Chapter 3 and Chapter 8 for more information on domain name aliases.

Make your site content-rich

The textual component of a Web site is what attracts visitors and keeps them coming back on a regular basis. The more useful information and compelling content you provide, the more visits your site will receive. By compelling content, I'm talking about words, headings, or images that induce visitors to interact with your site in some way. You can make your content compelling in a number of ways:

✔ Provide a call to action, such as "Click Here!" or "Buy Now!"

✔ Explain how the reader will benefit by clicking a link and exploring your site. ("Visit our News and Specials page to find out how to win 500 frequent flyer miles.")

✔ Briefly and concisely summarize your business and its mission.

✔ Scan or use a digital camera to capture images of your sale items (or of the services you provide) as I describe in Chapter 5, and post them on a Web page called Products.

Don't forget the personal touch when it comes to connecting with your customers' needs. People who shop online don't get to meet their merchants in person, so anything you can tell about yourself helps to personalize the process and put your visitors at ease. For example, one of Lucky Boyd's primary goals for his MyTexasMusic.com site is to encourage people to become members so they are more likely to visit on a regular basis. His photos of music fans (see Figure 1-2) personalize the site and remind visitors that they are members of a community of music lovers. Let your cybervisitors know that they're dealing with real people, not remote machines and computer programs.

Figure 1-2: Personalize your business to connect with customers online.

Peeking in on other businesses' Web sites — to pick up ideas and see how they handle similar issues — is a natural practice. In cyberspace, you can visit plenty of businesses that are comparable to yours from the comfort of your home office, and the trip takes only minutes.

Establishing a graphic identity

When you start up your first business on the Web, you have to do a certain amount of convincing. You need to convince customers that you are competent and professional. One factor that helps build trust is a graphic identity. A site with an identity looks a certain way. For example, take a look at Figure 1-3, as well as Figure 1-4 later in this chapter. Both pages are from the Graphic Maps Web site. Notice how each has the same white background, the same distinctive and simple logo, and similar heading styles. Using such elements consistently from page to page creates an identity that gives your business credibility and helps viewers find what they're looking for.

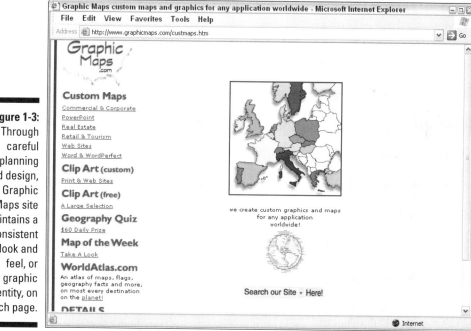

Figure 1-3: Through careful planning and design, the Graphic Maps site maintains a consistent look and feel, or graphic identity, on each page.

Step 7: Set Up a System for Processing Sales

Many businesses go online and then are surprised by their own success. They don't have systems in place for finalizing sales, shipping out purchased goods in a timely manner, and tracking finances and inventory.

An excellent way to plan for success is to set up ways to track your business finances and to create a secure purchasing environment for your online customers. That way, you can build on your success rather than be surprised by it.

Providing a means for secure transactions

Getting paid is the key to survival as well as success. When your business exists only online, the payment process is not always straightforward. Make your Web site a safe and easy place for customers to pay you. Provide different payment options and build customers' level of trust any way you can.

Although the level of trust among people who shop online is increasing steadily, some Web surfers are still squeamish about submitting credit card numbers online. And beginning businesspeople are understandably intimidated by the requirements of processing credit card transactions. In the early stages, you can simply create a form that customers have to print out and mail to you along with a check. (The Graphic Maps site is successful without having an online credit card system; clients phone in their orders.)

When you are able to accept credit cards, make your customers feel at ease by explaining what measures you're taking to ensure that their information is secure. Such measures include signing up for an account with a Web host that provides a *secure server,* a computer that uses software to encrypt data and uses digital documents called certificates to ensure its identity. (See Chapters 7 and 12 for more on Internet security and secure shopping systems.)

Becoming a credit card merchant

The words *electronic commerce* or *e-commerce* bring to mind visions of online forms and credit card data that is transmitted over the Internet. Do you have to provide such service in order to run a successful online business? Not necessarily. Being a credit card merchant makes life easier for your customers, to be sure, but it also adds complications and extra costs to your operation.

The traditional way to become a credit card merchant is to apply to a bank. Small and home-based businesses can have difficulty getting their applications approved. Alternatively, you can sign up with a company that provides electronic "shopping cart" services and credit card payments online to small businesses. See Chapter 12 for suggestions.

If you do get the go-ahead from a bank to become a credit card merchant, you have to pay it a *discount rate,* which is a fee (typically, 2 to 3 percent of each transaction). You sometimes have to pay a monthly premium charge of $10 to $25 as well. Besides that, you may need special software or hardware to accept credit card payments.

In the early stages of your business, you may find it easier to take orders over the phone. Remember that most of your customers probably don't have a second phone line for Internet access, however. They have to disconnect from the Internet to call and place their orders. Also invite them to send you an e-mail message that provides contact information and states what they want to order. Then if your business takes off, you can present your sales records to the bank and be more likely to get your merchant application approved. See Chapter 12 for more on electronic commerce options for your business.

To maximize your sales by reaching users who either don't have credit cards or don't want to use them on the Internet, provide low-tech alternatives, such as toll-free phone numbers and fax numbers, so that people can provide you with information by using more familiar technologies.

After much searching, Lucky Boyd signed up with a company called Goemerchant (www.goemerchant.com), which provides him with the payment systems that many online shoppers recognize when they want to make a purchase. First, there's a *shopping cart* — a set of pages that acts as an electronic "holding area" for items before they are purchased. Next, there's a secure way for people to make electronic purchases by providing online forms, where people can safely enter credit card and other personal information. The note stating that the payment area is protected by Secure Sockets Layer (SSL) encryption tells people that, even if a criminal intercepts their credit card data, he won't be able to read it.

Safeguarding your customers' personal information is important, but you also need to safeguard your business. Many online businesses get burned by bad guys who submit fraudulent credit card information. If you don't verify the information and submit it to your financial institution for processing, you're liable for the cost. Strongly consider signing up with a service that handles credit card verification for you in order to cut down on lost revenue. See Chapter 7 for more on these and other security issues.

Keeping your books straight

What does "keeping your books" mean, anyway? In the simplest sense, it means recording all financial activities that pertain to your business, including any expenses you incur, all the income you receive, as well as your equipment and tax deductions. The financial side of running a business also entails creating reports, such as profit-and-loss statements, that banks require if you apply for a loan. Such reports not only help meet financial institutions' needs, but also provide you with essential information about how your business is really doing at any given time.

You can record all this information the old-fashioned way, by writing it down in ledgers and journals, or you can use accounting software. (See Chapter 17 for some suggestions of easy-to-use accounting packages that are great for financial novices.). Because you're making a commitment to using computers on a regular basis by starting an online business, it's only natural for you to use computers to keep your books, too. Accounting software can help you keep track of expenses and provide information that may save you some headaches at tax time. And after you've saved your financial data on your hard drive, make backups so that you don't lose information you need to do business. See Chapter 7 for ways to back up and protect your files.

Step 8: Provide Personal Service

The Internet, which runs on wires, cables, and computer chips, may not seem like a place for the personal touch. But technology didn't actually create the Internet and all of its content; *people* did that. In fact, the Internet is a great place to provide your clients and customers with outstanding, personal customer service.

In many cases, customer service on the Internet is a matter of being available and responding quickly to all inquiries. You check your e-mail regularly; you make sure you respond within a day; you cheerfully solve problems and hand out refunds if needed. By helping your customers, you help yourself, too. You build loyalty as well as credibility among your clientele. For many small businesses, the key to competing effectively with larger competitors is by providing superior customer service. See Chapter 13 for more ideas on how you can do this.

Sharing your expertise

Your knowledge and experience are among your most valuable commodities. So you may be surprised when I suggest that you give them away for free. Why?

It's a "try before you buy" concept. Helping people for free builds your credibility and makes them more likely to pay for your services down the road.

When your business is online, you can easily communicate what you know about your field and make your knowledge readily available. One way is to set up a Web page that presents the basics about your company and your field of interest in the form of Frequently Asked Questions (FAQs). Another technique is to become a virtual publisher/editor and create your own newsletter in which you write about what's new with your company and about topics related to your work. See Chapter 13 for more on communicating your expertise through FAQs, newsletters, and advanced e-mail techniques.

My brother was skeptical when I recommended to him that he include a page full of technical information explaining exactly what equipment he uses and describing the steps involved in audio restoration. He didn't think anyone would be interested; he also didn't want to give away his "trade secrets." *Au contraire, mon frère!* People who surf the Internet gobble up all the technical details they can find. The more you wow them with the names and model numbers of your expensive equipment, not to mention the work you go through to restore their old records, the more they'll trust you. And trust will get them to place an order with you.

Making your site a go-to resource

Many *ontrepreneurs* (online entrepreneurs) succeed by making their Web sites not only a place for sales and promotion but also an indispensable resource, full of useful hyperlinks and other information, that customers want to visit again and again. For example, the Graphic Maps Web site, which I profile earlier in this chapter, acts as a resource for anyone who has a question about geography. To promote the site, John Moen gives away free maps for nonprofit organizations, operates a daily geography contest with a $100 prize to the first person with the correct answer (shown in Figure 1-4), and answers e-mail promptly. "I feel strongly that the secret on the Web is to provide a solution to a problem and, for the most part, to do it for free," he suggests.

The MyTexasMusic site (www.mytexasmusic.com) uses the concept of membership to strengthen connections with customers. The main purpose of the site is to make money by selling the works of Texas musicians, as well as tickets to concerts. But in order to make money, you need to give people a reason to visit your site on a regular basis.

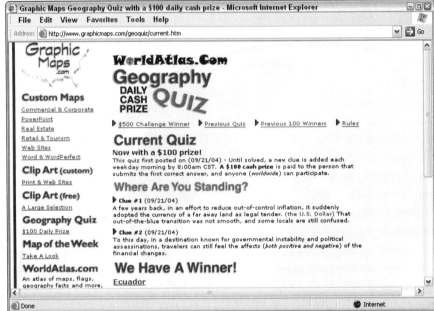

The site encourages music lovers and musicians to become members: They provide information about who they are and where they live, and they create their own username and password, so they can access special content and perform special functions on the site such as selling their own CDs or posting song clips online. For an online business, knowing the names and addresses of people who visit and who don't necessarily make purchases is a gold mine of information. The business can use the contact information to send members special offers and news releases; the more frequently contact is maintained, the more likely those casual shoppers will eventually turn into paying customers.

The concept of membership also builds a feeling of community among customers. By turning the e-commerce site into a meeting place for members who love Texas musicians, those members make new friends and have a reason to visit the site on a regular basis. Community building is one way in which commerce on the Web differs from traditional brick-and-mortar selling, and it's something you should consider, too.

Another way to encourage customers to congregate at your site on a regular basis is to create a discussion area. In Chapter 13, I show you how to provide a discussion page right on your own Web site.

Becoming a super e-mailer

E-mail is, in my humble opinion, the single most important marketing tool that you can use to boost your online business. Becoming an expert e-mail user increases your contacts and provides you with new sources of support, too.

The two best and easiest e-mail strategies are the following:

- ✔ Check your e-mail as often as possible.
- ✔ Respond to e-mail inquiries immediately.

Additionally, you can e-mail inquiries about comarketing opportunities to other Web sites similar to your own. Ask other online business owners if they will provide links to your site in exchange for you providing links to theirs. And always include a signature file with your message that includes the name of your business and a link to your business site. See Chapter 13 for more information on using e-mail effectively to build and maintain relations with your online customers.

Note: I'm encouraging you to use e-mail primarily for one-to-one communication. The Internet excels at bringing individuals together. Mailing lists and newsletters can use e-mail effectively for marketing, too. However, I'm *not* encouraging you to send out mass quantities of unsolicited commercial e-mail, a practice that turns off almost all consumers and that can get you in trouble with the law, too. You can read about a spammer who was sentenced to nine years in prison under the state of Virginia's anti-spam law at `www.pcworld.com/news/article/0,aid,118493,00.asp`.

Step 9: Alert the Media and Everyone Else

In order to be successful, small businesses need to get the word out to the people who are likely to purchase what they have to offer. If this group turns out to be only a narrow market, so much the better; the Internet is great for connecting to niche markets that share a common interest. (See Chapter 15 for more on locating your most likely customers on the Internet and figuring out how best to communicate with them.)

The Internet provides many unique and effective ways for small businesses to advertise, including search services, e-mail, newsgroups, electronic mailing lists, and more.

Listing your site with Internet search services

How, exactly, do you get listed on the search engines such as Yahoo! and Lycos? Frankly, it's getting more difficult. Many of the big search services charge for listings. But some let you contribute a listing for free, though there's no guarantee if or when you'll see your site included in their databases.

You can increase the chances that search services will list your site by including special keywords and site descriptions in the HTML commands for your Web pages. You place these keywords after a special HTML command (the <META> tag), making them invisible to the casual viewer of your site. Turn to Chapter 15 for details.

John Moen and Lucky Boyd have both created multiple Web sites for different purposes. One purpose is to reach different markets. Another is to improve rankings on search engines such as Google: by linking one site to several other sites, the site is considered more "popular" and its ranking rises. See Chapter 15 for more on this and other tips on getting listed by Internet search engines.

Reaching the entire Internet

Your Web site may be the cornerstone of your business, but if nobody knows it's out there, it can't help you generate sales. Perhaps the most familiar form of online advertising are *banner ads,* those little electronic billboards that seem to show up on every popular Web page that you visit.

But banner advertising can be expensive and may not be the best way for a small business to advertise online. In fact, the most effective marketing for some businesses hasn't been traditional banner advertising or newspaper/magazine placements. Rather, the e-marketers who run those businesses target electronic bulletin boards and mailing lists where people already discuss the products being sold. You can post notices on the bulletin boards where your potential customers congregate, notifying them that your services are now available. (Make sure the board in question permits such solicitation before you do so, or you'll chase away the very customers you want.)

This sort of direct, one-to-one marketing may seem tedious, but it's often the best way to develop a business on the Internet. Reach out to your potential customers and strike up an individual, personal relationship with each one.

Chapter 15 contains everything you need to know about advertising with mailing lists, newsgroups, and even traditional banner ads.

Step 10: Review, Revise, and Improve

For any long-term endeavor, you need to establish standards by which you can judge its success or failure. You must decide for yourself what you consider success to be. After a period of time, take stock of where your business is, and then take steps to do even better.

Taking stock

After 12 months online, Lucky Boyd took stock. His site was online, but he wasn't getting many page views. He redid the site, increased the number of giveaways, and traffic rose. Now, he wants to make music downloads available on his site; he's preparing to redo all of his Web pages with the Hypertext Preprocessor programming language (PHP).

HTML is a markup language: It identifies parts of a Web page that need to be formatted as headings, text, images, and so on. It can be used to include scripts, such as those written in the JavaScript language. But by creating his pages from scratch using PHP, Lucky Boyd can make his site more dynamic and easier to update. He can rotate random images, process forms, and compile statistics that track his visitors by using PHP scripts, for instance. He can design Web pages in a modular way so they can be redesigned and revised more quickly than with HTML, too.

When all is said and done, your business may do so well that you can reinvest in it by buying new equipment or increasing your services. You may even be in a position to give something back to nonprofits and those in need. The young founders of The Chocolate Farm (www.thechocolatefarm.com) set up a scholarship fund designed to bring young people from other countries to the United States to help them find out about free enterprise. Perhaps you'll have enough money left over to reward yourself, too — as if being able to tell everyone "I own my own online business" isn't reward enough!

Money is only one form of success. Plenty of entrepreneurs are online for reasons other than making money. That said, it *is* important from time to time to evaluate how well you're doing financially. Accounting software, such as the programs that I describe in Chapter 17, makes it easy to check your revenues on a daily or weekly basis. The key is to establish the goals you want to reach and develop measurements so that you know when and if you reach those goals.

Updating your data

Getting your business online now and then updating your site regularly is better than waiting to unveil the perfect Web site all at one time. In fact, seeing your site improve and grow is one of the best things about going online. Over time, you can create contests, strike up cooperative relationships with other businesses, and add more background information about your products and services.

Consider The Chocolate Farm, which is still owned and operated by Evan and Elise MacMillan of Denver, Colorado. The business was started when Elise was just 10 years old and Evan was 13. They began by selling chocolates with a farm theme, such as candy cows; these days, they focus more on creating custom chocolates — sweets made to order for businesses, many of which bear the company's logo. Evan, who manages the company's Web site, now updates it from his college dorm room in California. He and his sister oversee the work of 50 full- and part-time employees.

Businesses on the Web need to evaluate and revise their practices on a regular basis. Lucky Boyd studies reports of where visitors come from before they reach his site, and what pages they visit on the site, so he can attract new customers. Online business is a process of trial and error. Some promotions work better than others. The point is that it needs to be an ongoing process and a long-term commitment. Taking a chance and profiting from your mistakes is better than not trying in the first place.

Chapter 2

Choosing and Equipping Your New E-Business

In This Chapter

▶ Envisioning your own successful online business

▶ Understanding your options: sales, services, auctions, hike!

▶ Making your cybershop stand out from the crowd

▶ Obtaining or upgrading your computer hardware

▶ Assembling a business software suite

Starting your own online business is like rehabbing an old house — something I'm constantly doing. Both projects involve a series of recognizable phases:

✓ **The idea phase:** First, you tell people about your great idea. They hear the enthusiasm in your voice, nod their heads, and say something like, "Good luck." They've seen you in this condition before and know how it usually turns out.

✓ **The decision phase:** Undaunted, you begin honing your plan. You read books (like this one), ask questions, and shop around until you find just the right tools and materials. Of course, when the project is staring you down in your own workshop, you may start to panic, asking yourself whether you're really up for the task.

✓ **The assembly phase:** Still determined to proceed, you forge ahead. You plug in your tools and go to work. Drills spin, sparks fly, and metal moves.

✓ **The test-drive phase:** One fine day, out of the dust and fumes, your masterpiece emerges. You invite everyone over to enjoy the fruits of your labor. All of those who were skeptical before are now full of admiration. You get enjoyment from your project for years to come.

If rehabbing a house doesn't work for you, think about restoring an antique auto, planning an anniversary party, or devising a mountain-climbing excursion in Tibet. The point is that starting an online business is a project like any other — one that you can understand and accomplish in stages. Right now, you're at the first stage of launching your new cyberbusiness. Your creativity is working overtime. You have some rough sketches that only a mother could love.

This chapter helps you get from idea to reality. Your first step is to imagine how you want your business to look and feel. Then you can begin to develop and implement strategies for achieving your dream. You've got a big advantage over those who started new businesses a few years ago: You've got plenty of models to show you what works and what doesn't.

As you travel along the path from idea to reality, you must also consider properly equipping your online business — just like you would have to equip a traditional, brick-and-mortar business. One of the many exciting aspects of launching a business online, however, is the absence of much *overhead* (that is, operating expenses). Many non-cyberspace businesses must take out loans, pay rent, remodel their storefronts, pay license fees, and purchase store fixtures. In contrast, the primary overhead for an online business is computer hardware and software. Although it's great if you can afford top-of-the-line equipment, you'll be happy to know that the latest bells and whistles aren't absolutely necessary in order to get a business site online and maintain it effectively. But in order to streamline the technical aspects of connecting to the online world and creating a business Web site, some investment may be a wise and profitable idea.

Don't rush into signing a contract to host your online business. I've encountered experienced businesspeople who prepaid for a year's worth of Web hosting with nothing else yet in place. Be sure that you know your options and have a business strategy, no matter how simple, before you sign anything.

Mapping Out Your Online Business

How do you get to square one? Start by imagining the kind of business that is your ultimate goal. This is the time to indulge in some brainstorming. Envisioning your business is a creative way of asking yourself the all-important questions: Why do I want to go into business online? What are my goals? Table 2-1 illustrates some possible goals and suggests how to achieve them. By envisioning the final result you want to achieve, you can determine your online business goals.

Table 2-1	Online Business Models	
Goal	*Type of Web Site*	*What to Do*
Make big bucks	Sales	Sell items/gain paying advertisers
Gain credibility and attention	Marketing	Put your resume and samples of your work online
Promote yourself	Personal	Promote yourself so that people will hire you or want to use your goods or services
Turn an interest into a source of income	Hobby/special interest	Invite like-minded people to share your passion, participate in your site and generate traffic so that you can gain advertisers

Looking around

There's no need to feel that you have to reinvent the wheel. Your ultimate destination can be the best source of information on how to get there. Sometimes, spending just half an hour surfing the Net can stimulate your own mental network. Find sites with qualities you want to emulate. Throughout this book, I suggest good business sites you can visit to find good models to follow.

Because you are not unlike your target audience, your likes and dislikes have value. Keep a low-tech pencil and pad of paper handy each time you surf for ideas. Make a list as you go of what you find appealing and jot down notes on logos, designs, and text. That way, you'll have raw data to draw upon as you begin to refine what you yourself want to do.

Making your mark

The Web and other parts of the online world have undergone a population explosion. According to Internet Systems Consortium's Domain Survey (www.isc.org), in January 2004, 233.1 million computers that hosted Web sites were connected to the Internet, compared with 171.6 million the year before. Twenty percent of those computers host Web addresses that end with the commercial (.com) designation.

As an *ontrepreneur* (online entrepreneur), your goal is to stand out from the crowd — or to "position yourself in the marketplace," as business consultants like to say. Consider the following tried-and-true suggestions if you want your Web site to be a go-to place:

- **Pursue something you know well.** Experience adds value to the information that you provide. In the online world, expertise sells.

- **Make a statement.** On your Web site, include a mission statement that clearly identifies what you do, the customers you hope to reach, and how you're different from your competitors.

- **Give something away for free.** Giveaways and promotions are surefire ways to gain attention and develop a loyal customer base. In fact, there are entire Web sites devoted to providing free stuff online, like iWon (www.iwon.com) or WebStakes (www.webstakes.com). You don't have to give away an actual product; it can be words of wisdom based on your training and experience.

- **Find your niche.** Web space is a great place to pursue niche marketing. In fact, it often seems that the quirkier the item, the better it sells. Don't be afraid to target a narrow audience and direct all your sales efforts to a small group of devoted followers.

- **Do something you love.** The more you love your business, the more time and effort you're apt to put into it and, therefore, the more likely it is to be successful. Such businesses take advantage of the Internet's worldwide reach, which makes it easy for people with the same interests to gather at the same virtual location.

Scan through the list of *Inc.* magazine's (www.inc.com) Top 500 privately held companies, and you find many examples of businesses that follow all the aforementioned strategies. The 26-year-old CEO of the number 2 company for 2004, uSight (www.usight.com), almost closed his company in its second year before finding his niche: a do-it-yourself Web site application called uBuilder. Go Daddy (www.godaddy.com) switched from Web building software to domain name registration and became number 8 in 2004. High Point Solutions (www.highpt.com), the top-ranked company in *Inc.* magazine's 500 List for 2001, was started by two brothers who skipped college and began the business in their home in Sparta, New Jersey. The company focuses on a niche: helping a small but very satisfied group of corporate customers iron out the logistical details of buying network hardware. They find good prices on new and used equipment and deliver products fast.

Evaluating commercial Web sites

How is your business the same as others? How is it different than others? These are questions your customers will be asking, so you may as well start out by asking them also. Commercial Web sites — those whose Internet addresses end with .com or .biz — are the fastest-growing segment of the Net. This is the area you'll be entering, too. The trick is to be comfortable with the size and level of complexity of a business that's right for you. In general, your options are

- ✔ **A big commercial Web site:** The Web means big business, and plenty of big companies create Web sites with the primary goal of supplementing a product or business that's already well known and well established. Just a few examples are the Ragu Web site (`www.ragu.com`), the Pepsi World Web site (`www.pepsiworld.com`), and the Toyota Web site (`www.toyota.com`). True, these commercial Web sites were created by corporations with many thousands of dollars to throw into Web design, but you can still look at them to get ideas for your own site.

- ✔ **A mid-size site:** Many a small business of ten to twelve employees makes good use of the Web to provide customer service, disseminate information, and post a sales catalog. I describe many of these functions in my book *Small Business Internet For Dummies* (Wiley). Some features that mid-size companies use, such as a Frequently Asked Questions (FAQ) page or a sales catalog, may be useful to you. Look at the Golfballs.com site (`www.golfballs.com`) for good ideas.

- ✔ **A site that's just right:** There are no prerequisites for prior business experience that guarantee success on the Web. It's also fine to start out as a single person, couple, or family. In fact, the rest of this book is devoted to helping you produce a very fine homegrown entrepreneurial business. This chapter gets you off to a good start by examining the different kinds of businesses you can launch online and some business goals you can set for yourself.

Flavors of Online Businesses You Can Taste Test

If you're easily overstimulated, you may feel like you need blinders as you comb the Internet for ideas to give your online business a definite shape and form. Use the following brief descriptions of online businesses to create categories of interest and then zero in on the ones that will be most useful to you.

Selling consumer products

Leading Internet research firm Forrester Research (`www.clickz.com/stats/markets/retailing/article.php/3390571`) predicts that total e-commerce sales in the U.S. will grow from $144 billion in 2004 to $316 billion in 2010. The online marketplace is a great venue if you have products to sell (such as auto parts, antiques, jewelry, or food). The Web has always attracted those looking for unique items or something customized just for them. Consider taking your wares online if one or more of the following applies to you:

✔ Your products are high in quality.

✔ You create your own products; for example, you design dishes, make fudge, or sell gift baskets of wine.

✔ You specialize in some aspects of your product that larger businesses can't achieve. Perhaps you sell regional foods, such as Chicago deep-dish pizza or live lobsters from Maine.

Ice cream may not be good for my waistline, but I often go to the Web site of Ben and Jerry's (www.benjerry.com) just to drool. These guys are entrepreneurs just like you, and I like their Web site as well as their products. It focuses on the unique flavors and high quality of their ice cream, as well as their personalities and business standards.

So c'mon in; the water's fine. The key is to find your niche, as many small-but-successful businesses have done. Use your Web space to declare your love for your products (and, by implication, why your customers will love them, too).

Hanging out your professional services

Either through a Web site or through listings in indexes and directories, offering your professional services online can expand your client base dramatically. It also gives existing clients a new way to contact you: through e-mail. Here are just a few examples of professionals who are offering their services online:

✔ **Attorneys:** Immigration attorney Kevin L. Dixler is based in Chicago. Through his Web site (www.dixler.com), he can reach individuals around the world who want to come to the United States.

✔ **Psychotherapists:** Carole Killick, a music psychotherapist, has a simple, nicely designed Web site (www.eclipse.co.uk/pens/killick) that explains her work and the courses she teaches.

✔ **Physicians:** Dr. Peter J. Dorsen, a physician in Minneapolis, Minnesota, has a Web site (www.housecalldocs.com) that explains what he does that sets him apart from other doctors: His practice is based entirely on making "house calls."

✔ **Consultants:** Experts who keep their knowledge up-to-date and are willing to give advice to those with similar interests and needs are always in demand. Consultants in a specialized area often find a great demand for their services on the Internet. The Yahoo! consulting page is crowded with fields in which online consultants are available:

```
dir.yahoo.com/business_and_economy/business_to_business/
                consulting
```

We're busy people who don't always have the time to pore over the fine print. Short and snappy nuggets of information will draw customers to your site and make them feel as though they're getting "something for free." One way you can put forth this professional expertise is by starting your own online newsletter. You get to be editor, writer, and mailing-list manager. Plus, you get to talk as much as you want, network with tons of people who are interested enough in what you have to say to subscribe to your publication, and put your name and your business before lots of people. Judy Vorfeld (profiled in Chapter 6) puts out a regular newsletter called Communication Expressway that supplements her online business site (www.ossweb.com), as do Marques Vickers and many of the other online businesspeople I mention in this chapter.

Selling your expertise

The original purpose of the Internet was to share knowledge via computers, and information is the commodity that has fueled cyberspace's rapid growth. As the Internet and commercial online networks continue to expand, information remains key.

Finding valuable information and gathering a particular kind of resource for one location online can be a business in itself. People love to get knowledge they trust from the comfort of their own homes. For example, students and parents are eager to pay someone to help them sort through the procedures involved and the data required to apply for college. (See educational consultant Cornelia Nicholson's Web site, www.collegecounselor.com, for example.)

Other online businesses provide gathering points or indexes to more specific areas. Here are just a few examples:

- ✔ **Search engines:** Some businesses succeed by connecting cybersurfers with companies, organizations, and individuals that specialize in a given area. Yahoo! (www.yahoo.com) is the most obvious example. Originally started by two college students, Yahoo! has practically become an Internet legend by gathering information in one index so that people can easily find things online.

- ✔ **Links pages:** On her "Grandma Jam's I Love to Win" sweepstakes site, (www.grandmajam.com), Janet Marchbanks-Aulenta gathers links to current contests along with short descriptions of each one. Janet says her site receives as many as 22,000 visits per month, and generates income through advertising and affiliate links to other contest Web sites. She says she loves running her own business despite the hard work involved with keeping it updated. "The key to succeeding at this type of site is to build up a regular base of users that return each day to find new contests — the daily upkeep is very important," she says.

✔ **Personal recommendations:** The personal touch sells. Just look at About.com (`www.about.com`). This guide to the online world provides Web surfers with a central location where they can locate virtually anything. It works because real people do the choosing and provide evaluations (albeit brief) of the sites they list.

There are a number of ways that resource sites such as these can transform information into money. In some cases, individuals pay to become members; sometimes, businesses pay to be listed on a site; other times, a site attracts so many visitors on a regular basis that other companies pay to post advertising on the site. Big successes — such as About.com — carry a healthy share of ads and strike lucrative partnerships with big companies, as well.

Opportunities with technology or computer resources

What could be more natural than using the Web to sell what you need to get and stay online? The online world itself, by the very fact that it exists, has spawned all kinds of business opportunities for entrepreneurs:

✔ **Computers:** Some discount computer houses have made a killing by going online and offering equipment for less than conventional retail stores. Being on the Internet means that they save on overhead, employee compensation, and other costs, and they are able to pass those savings on to their customers.

✔ **Internet Service Providers:** These are the businesses that give you a dialup or direct connection to the Internet. Many ISPs, such as Netcom or UUNET, are big concerns. But smaller companies — such as YourNET Connection (`www.ync.net`), which is based in Schaumburg, Illinois, and offers free online Web training for its customers, are succeeding, as well.

✔ **Software:** Matt Wright is well known on the Web for providing free computer scripts that add important functionality to Web sites, such as processing information that visitors submit via online forms. Matt's Script Archive site (`worldwidemart.com/scripts`) now includes an advertisement for a book on scripting that he coauthored, as well as a Web postcard system for sale and an invitation to businesses to take out advertisements on his site.

Being a starving artist without the starving

Being creative no longer means you have to live out of your flower-covered van, driving from art fairs to craft shows. If you're simply looking for exposure and feedback on your creations, you can put samples of your work online. Consider the following suggestions for virtual creative venues (and revenues):

- ✔ **Host art galleries.** Thanks to online galleries, artists whose sales were previously limited to one region can get inquiries from all over the world. Art Xpo (`www.artxpo.com`) reports thousands of dollars in sales through its Web site and aggressive marketing efforts. The personal Web site created by artist Marques Vickers (`www.marquesv.com`), has received worldwide attention; see Figure 2-1. (The upcoming sidebar, "Painting a new business scenario," profiles Vickers' site.)

- ✔ **Publish your writing.** Blogs (Weblogs, or online diaries) are all the rage these days. The most successful are generating ad revenue. To find out how to create one yourself, check out Blogger (`www.blogger.com`).

- ✔ **Sell your music.** Singer-songwriter Michael McDermott sells his own CDs, videos, and posters through his online store (`www.michael-mcdermott.com`).

You can, of course, also sell all that junk that's been accumulating in your basement, as well as your relatives' and family members' junk, on eBay; see Chapter 10 for more information on this exciting business opportunity.

Figure 2-1:
A California artist created this Web site to gain recognition and sell his creative work.

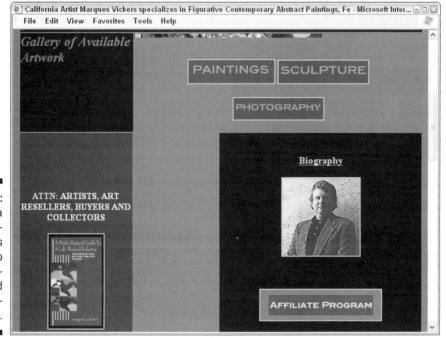

Marketing One-to-One to Your Customers

After you review Web sites that already conduct the sorts of business ventures that interest you, it's time to put your goals into action. First you develop marketing strategies that are well suited to expressing your unique talents and services. That will encourage customers to explore your business and place orders with you.

Does anyone still really believe that cyberspace is a place where millions of lonely, disconnected people interact without really getting to know one another? Your marketing strategy will debunk that myth. The fact is that online communities are often close-knit, long-standing groups of people who get to be great friends. The best way to promote your business is to communicate with people as individuals. The Web, newsgroups, and e-mail enable you to accomplish this goal in ways that other media can't match.

Painting a new business scenario

Marques Vickers is an artist based in Vallejo, California. Through his self-named Web site (www.marquesv.com), as well as 15–20 "mini-sites," he markets his own painting, sculpture, and photography, as well as his books on marketing and buying fine art online. He first went online in November 1999 and spends about 20 hours a week working on his various Web sites. His sites receive anywhere from 25,000 to 40,000 visits per month.

Q. What are the costs of running all your Web sites and doing the associated marketing?

A. Out of pocket expense is approximately $29 monthly for a Web site hosting and Internet access package. New domain name registrations and renewals probably add another $250 since I own more than 20 domain names.

Q. What would you describe as the primary goals of your online business?

A. My initial objective was to develop a personalized round-the-clock global presence in order to recruit sales outlets, sell directly to the public, and create a reference point for people to access and view my work. I also have an intuitive sense that an online Web site presence will be a marketing necessity for any future visual artist and a lifelong exposure outlet. Having an online presence builds my credibility as a fine artist and positions me to take advantage of the evolution of the fine arts industry, too.

Q. Has your online business been profitable financially?

A. Absolutely — but make no mistake, achieving sales volume and revenue is a trial-and-error process and involves a significant time commitment. I'm still perfecting the business model and it may require years to achieve the optimum marketing plan.

Q. How do you promote your site?

A. With the Internet, you are layering a collective web of multiple promotional sources. Experimentation is essential because recognition is not always immediate but may ultimately be forthcoming since postings in cyberspace are often stumbled across from unforeseen resources. I try multiple marketing outlets including paid ad positioning services such as Overture and Google, bartered advertising space, and reciprocally traded links. Some have had moderate success, some unforeseen and remarkable exposure. Unlike traditional advertising media that have immediate response times, the Internet may lag in its response. It is a long-term commitment and one that cannot be developed by short-term tactics or media blitzes.

Q. Do you create your Web pages yourself or do you work with someone to do that?

A. I'm too particular about the quality of content to subcontract the work out. Besides, I know what I want to say, how, and am capable of fashioning the design concepts I want to integrate.

The rectangular limitations of HTML design make color a very important component and the very minimal attention span of most Web viewers means that you'd better get to the point quickly and concisely. The more personalized, timely, and focused your content, the more reason an individual has to return to your Web site and ultimately understand your unique vision of what you're trying to create. A Web site is an unedited forum for telling your version of a story and a means for cultivating a direct support base.

Q. What advice would you give to someone starting an online business?

A. Don't hesitate one minute longer than necessary. Read substantially and from a diverse selection of sources on the subject. Subscribe to ezines on related subject matter and query the Webmasters of sites that impress you with their content. Go to informational seminars; ask questions. Experiment with marketing ideas and by all means, consider it a lifelong project. The Internet is continuing to evolve and the opportunities have never been more prevalent.

Focus on a customer segment

Old-fashioned business practices, such as getting to know your customers as individuals and providing personal service, are alive and well in cyberspace. Your number one business strategy, when it comes to starting your business online, sounds simple: Know your audience.

What's not so simple about this little maxim is that, in cyberspace, it takes some work to get to know exactly who your customers are. Web surfers don't leave their names, addresses, or even a random e-mail address when they visit your site. Instead, when you check the raw, unformatted records (or *logs*) of the visitors who have connected to you, you see pages and pages of what appears to be computer gobbledygook. You need special software to interpret the information, such as the program WebTrends.

How do you develop relationships with your customers?

- ✔ **Get your visitors to identify themselves.** Have them send you e-mail messages, place orders, enter contests, or provide you with feedback. (For more specific suggestions, see Chapter 6.)

- ✔ **Become an online researcher.** Find existing users who already purchase goods and services online that are similar to what you offer. Visit newsgroups that pertain to what you sell, search for mailing lists, and participate in discussions so that people can find out more about you.

- ✔ **Keep track of your visitors.** Count the visitors who come to your site and, more important, the ones who make purchases or seek out your services. Manage your customer profiles so that you can sell your existing clientele the items they're likely to buy.

- ✔ **Help your visitors get to know you.** Web space is virtually unlimited. Don't be reluctant to tell people about aspects of your life that don't relate directly to how you hope to make money. Consider Judy Vorfeld, who does Internet research, Web design, and office support. Her Web site (`www.ossweb.com`) includes the usual lists of clients and services; however, it also includes a link to her personal home page and a page that describes her community service work. (See Figure 2-2.)

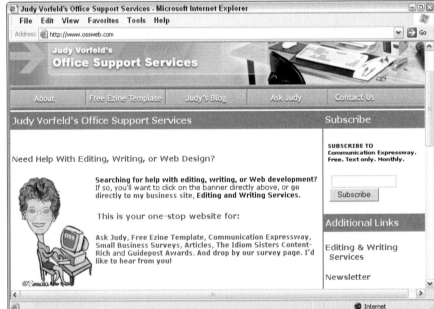

Figure 2-2:
Telling potential customers about yourself makes them more comfortable telling you about themselves.

I recommend doing your own Internet research so that you can find out more about the culture of the online world: how the most successful Web sites look and feel, and how many Web sites use a hip, techno-savvy tone when presenting information.

After you get to know your audience, job number two in your marketing strategy is to catch their attention. You have two ways to do this:

- **Make yourself visible.** In Web-space, the problem isn't so much that potential customers are surfing right past your site. Rather, your task is simply making them aware that your site exists at all. You do this by getting yourself included in as many indexes, search sites, and business listings as possible. Chapter 14 outlines some strategies for listing yourself with search engines, and Chapter 15 describes publicity options on other parts of the Web. You can also do a bit of self-promotion in your own online communications: John Counsel of the Profit Clinic (www.profit clinic.com) appends this interesting teaser, followed by a link to his Web site, to his e-mail messages:

  ```
  "90% of all small business owners are PRE-PROGRAMMED to
      FAIL. Are you one of them? Find out now with our Quick
              Quiz"
  ```

- **Make your site an eye-catcher.** Getting people to come to you is only half the battle. The other half is getting them to shop after they're there. Consider the importance of combining striking images with promotions, offering useful information, and providing ways for customers to interact with you. (See Chapters 5 and 6 for details.)

Boost your credibility

Marketing task number three is to transfer your confidence and sense of authority about what you do to anyone who visits you online. Convince people that you're an expert and a trustworthy person with whom to do business.

In this case, customers have reasons to be wary. The Web has been around only since the mid '90s, so everyone is a relative newcomer to online commerce and there are some who are dishonest. Here, too, you can do a quick two-step in order to market your expertise.

Document your credentials

Feature any honors, awards, or professional affiliations you have that relate to your online work. If you're providing professional or consulting services online, you might even make a link to your online résumé. Give details about how long you've been in your field and how you got to know what you know about your business.

If these forms of verification don't apply to you, all is not lost. Just move to the all-important technique that I describe next.

Convince with must-have information

Providing useful, practical information about a topic is one of the best ways to market yourself online. One of the great things about starting an online business is that you don't have to incur the design and printing charges to get a brochure or flyer printed. You have plenty of space on your online business site to talk about your sales items or services in as great detail as you want.

Most Internet service providers give you 20MB (megabytes, that is) or more of space for your Web pages and associated files. Because the average Web page occupies only 5 to 10K (that's kilobytes) of space not counting the space taken up by images and multimedia files, it'll take a long time before you begin to run out of room.

What, exactly, can you talk about on your site? Here are some ideas:

- ✔ Provide detailed descriptions and photos of your sale items.
- ✔ Include a full list of clients you have worked for previously.
- ✔ Publish a page of testimonials from satisfied customers.
- ✔ Give your visitors a list of links to Web pages and other sites where people can find out more about your area of business.
- ✔ Toot your own horn: Explain why you love what you do and why you're so good at it.

Ask satisfied customers to give you a good testimonial. All you need is a sentence or two that you can use on your Web site.

A site that contains compelling, entertaining content will become a resource that online visitors bookmark and return to on a regular basis. Be sure to update it regularly, and you will have fulfilled the dream of any online business owner.

Customer to customer contact: Everyone wins

A 16-year-old cartoonist named Gabe Martin put his cartoons on his Web site, called The Borderline. Virtually nothing happened. But when his dad put up some money for a contest, young Gabe started getting hundreds of visits and inquiries. He went on to create 11 mirror sites around the world, develop a base of devoted fans, and sell his own cartoon book.

Cybersurfers regularly take advantage of freebies online by, for example, downloading shareware or freeware programs. They get free advice from newsgroups, and they find free companionship from chat rooms and online forums. Having already paid for network access and computer equipment, they actually *expect* to get something for free.

Your customers will keep coming back if you devise as many promotions, giveaways, or sales as possible. You can also get people to interact through online forums or other tools, as I describe in Chapter 6.

In online business terms, anything that gets your visitors to click links and enter your site is good. Provide as many links to the rest of your site as you can on your home page. Many interactions that don't seem like sales do lead to sales, and it's always your goal to keep people on your site as long as possible.

See Chapters 5 and 6 for instructions on how to create hyperlinks and add interactivity to your Web site. For more about creating Web sites, check out *Creating Web Pages For Dummies,* 7th Edition, by Bud E. Smith and Arthur Bebak (Wiley).

Be a player in online communities

You may wait until the kids go off to school to tap away at your keyboard in your home office, but that doesn't mean that you really are alone. Thousands of home-office workers and entrepreneurs just like you connect to the Net every day and share many of the same concerns, challenges, and ups and downs as you.

Starting an online business isn't only a matter of creating Web pages, scanning photos, and taking orders. Marketing and networking are essential to making sure that you meet your goals. Participate in groups that are related either to your particular business or to online business in general. Here are some ways that you can make the right connections and get support and encouragement at the same time.

Be a newsgroupie

Newsgroups are discussion groups that occupy an extensive and popular part of the Internet called Usenet, as well as appear on America Online and other online services. Many large organizations such as universities and corporations run their own internal newsgroups, too.

Businesspeople tend to overlook newsgroups because of admonitions about *spam* (unsolicited messages sent by people trying to sell something to newsgroup participants who don't want it) and other violations of *Netiquette* (the set of rules that govern newsgroup communications). However, when you approach newsgroup participants on their own terms (not by spamming them but by answering questions and participating in discussions), newsgroups can be a wonderful resource for businesspeople. They attract knowledgeable consumers who are strongly interested in a topic — just the sorts of people who make great customers.

A few newsgroups (in particular, the ones with `biz` at the beginning of their names) are especially intended to discuss small business issues and sales. Here are a few suggestions:

- ✔ `misc.entrepreneurs`
- ✔ `biz.marketplace.discussion`
- ✔ `biz.marketplace.international.discussion`
- ✔ `biz.marketplace.services.discussion`
- ✔ `alt.business.home`
- ✔ `alt.business.consulting`
- ✔ `alt.business.franchise`
- ✔ `aol.commerce.general`

The easiest way to access newsgroups is to use Google's Web-based directory (`groups.google.com`). You can also use the newsgroup software that comes built into the two most popular Web browser packages, Netscape Communicator and Microsoft Internet Explorer. Each browser or newsgroup program has its own set of steps for enabling you to access Usenet. Use your browser's online help system to find out how you can access newsgroups.

Be sure to read the group's FAQ (frequently asked questions) page before you start posting. It's a good idea to *lurk before you post* — that is, simply read messages being posted to the group in order to find out about members' concerns before posting a message yourself. Stay away from groups that seem to consist only of get-rich-quick schemes or other scams. When you do post a message, be sure to keep your comments relevant to the conversation and give as much helpful advice as you can.

The most important business technique in communicating by either e-mail or newsgroup postings is to include a signature file at the end of your message. A *signature file* is a simple text message that newsgroup and mail software programs automatically add to your messages. A typical one includes your name, title, and the name of your company. You can also include a link to your business's home page. A good example is Judy Vorfeld's signature file, shown in Figure 2-3. (Chapter 13 tells how to create your own signature file.)

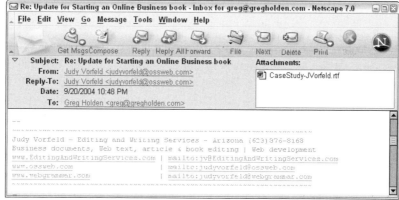

Be a mailing list-ener

A *mailing list* is a discussion group that communicates by exchanging e-mail messages between members who share a common interest and who have subscribed to join the list. Each e-mail message sent to the list is distributed to all the list's members. Any of those members can, in turn, respond by sending e-mail replies. The series of back-and-forth messages develops into discussions.

The nice thing about a mailing list is that it consists only of people who have subscribed to the list, which means that they really want to be involved and participate.

An excellent mailing list to check out is the Small and Home-Based Business Discussion List (`www.talkbiz.com/bizlist/index.html`). This list is *moderated,* meaning that someone reads through all postings before they go online and filters out any comments that are inappropriate or off-topic. Also, try searching the Topica directory of discussion groups (`www.lists.topica.com`). Click Small Business (under Choose from Thousands of Newsletters and Discussions) to view a page full of discussion groups and other resources for entrepreneurs.

The number of groups you join and how often you participate in them is up to you. The important thing is to regard every one-to-one-personal contact as a seed that may sprout into a sale, a referral, an order, a contract, a bit of useful advice, or another profitable business blossom.

It's not a newsgroup or a mailing list, but a Web site called iVillage.com (www.ivillage.com) brings women together by providing chat rooms where they can type messages to one another in real time, as well as message boards where they can post messages. (Men, of course, can participate, too.) Experts (and some who just claim to be experts) often participate in these forums. The work-from-home section (www.ivillage.com/work) is a good one for online entrepreneurs like you.

Add ways to sell and multiply your profits

Many successful online businesses combine more than one concept of what constitutes electronic commerce. Chapter 8 discusses ways to sell your goods and services on your Web site, but the Internet offers other venues for promoting and selling your wares.

Free income for your Web site

You can make money on your Web site without having anything to sell. Some sites will pay you for building your page with them or linking to them. You find out more in Chapter 4, but here are some quick suggestions:

- **We'll pay you to join:** Usually, you pay a membership fee to join something. But if you build your Web site on Tripod (www.tripod.lycos.com) and get enough visits, they'll pay you cash through a program called Builder Bucks.

- **Lucrative links:** If you become a member of Yahoo! GeoCities (www.geocities.yahoo.com) and locate your Web site there (see Chapter 3), you can join the Pages that Pay Affiliate Program, in which you make links to specified business Web sites. You receive commissions for each visitor who goes to the business's Web site from yours. Amazon.com (www.amazon.com) has had a similar program for years.

Selling through online classifieds

If you're looking for a quick and simple way to sell products or promote your services online without having to pay high overhead costs, consider taking out a classified ad in an online publication or a popular site like Craigslist (www.craigslist.org).

The classifieds work the same way online as they do in print publications: You pay a fee and write a short description along with contact information, and the publisher makes the ad available to potential customers. However, online classifieds have a number of big advantages over their print equivalents:

- ✓ **Audience:** Rather than hundreds or thousands who might view your ad in print, tens of thousands or perhaps even millions can see it online.

- ✓ **Searchability:** Online classifieds are often indexed so that customers can search for particular items with their Web browser. This makes it easier for shoppers to find exactly what they want, whether it's a Precious Moment figurine or a Martin guitar.

- ✓ **Time:** On the Net, ads are often online for a month or more.

- ✓ **Cost:** Some sites, such as Commerce Corner (`www.comcorner.com`), let you post classified ads for free.

On the downside, classifieds are often buried at the back of online magazines or Web sites, just as they are in print, so they're hardly well-traveled areas. Also, most classifieds don't make use of the graphics that help sell and promote goods and services so effectively throughout the Web.

Classifieds are an option if you're short on time or money. But don't forget that on your own online business site you can provide more details and not have to spend a cent.

Selling via online auctions

Many small businesses, such as antique dealerships or jewelry stores, sell individual merchandise through online auctions. eBay and other popular auction sites provide effective ways to target sales items at collectors who are likely to pay top dollar for desirable goodies. If you come up with a system for finding things to sell and for turning around a large number of transactions on a regular basis, you can even turn selling on eBay into a full-time source of income. See Chapter 10 for more about starting a business on eBay.

Easyware (Not Hardware) for Your Business

Becoming an information provider on the Internet places an additional burden on your computer and peripheral equipment. When you're "in it for the money," you may very well start to go online every day, and perhaps hours at a time, especially if you buy and sell on eBay. The better your computer setup, the more e-mail messages you can download, the more catalog items you can store, and so on. In this section, I introduce you to many upgrades you may need to make to your existing hardware configuration.

Some general principles apply when assembling equipment (discussed in this section) and programs (discussed in a subsequent section, "Software Solutions for Online Business") for an online endeavor:

- ✔ Look on the Internet for what you need. You can find just about everything you want to get you started.

- ✔ Be sure to pry before you buy! Don't pull out that credit card until you get the facts on what warranty and technical support your hardware or software vendor provides. Make sure that your vendor provides phone support 24 hours a day, 7 days a week. Also ask how long the typical turnaround time is in case your equipment needs to be serviced.

If you purchase lots of new hardware and software, remember to update your insurance by sending your insurer a list of your new equipment. Also consider purchasing insurance specifically for your computer-related items from a company such as Safeware (www.safeware.com).

The right computer for your online business

You very well may already have an existing computer setup that's adequate to get your business online and start the ball rolling. Or you may be starting from scratch and looking to purchase a computer for personal and/or business use. In either case, it pays to know what all the technical terms and specifications mean. Here are some general terms you need to understand:

- ✔ **Gigahertz (GHz) and megahertz (MHz):** This unit of measure indicates how quickly a computer's processor can perform functions. The central processing unit (CPU) of a computer is where the computing work gets done. In general, the higher the processor's internal clock rate, the faster the computer.

- ✔ **Random access memory (RAM):** This is the memory that your computer uses to temporarily store information needed to operate programs. RAM is usually expressed in millions of bytes, or megabytes (MB). The more RAM you have, the more programs you can run simultaneously.

- ✔ **Synchronous dynamic RAM (SDRAM):** Many ultrafast computers use some form of SDRAM synchronized with a particular clock rate of a CPU so that a processor can perform more instructions in a given time.

- ✔ **Double data rate SDRAM (DDR SDRAM):** This is a type of SDRAM that can dramatically improve the clock rate of a CPU.

- ✔ **Auxiliary storage:** This term refers to physical data-storage space on a hard drive, tape, CD-RW, or other device.

- ✔ **Virtual memory:** This is a type of memory on your hard drive that your computer can "borrow" to serve as extra RAM.

- ✔ **Network interface card (NIC):** You need this hardware add-on if you have a cable or DSL modem or if you expect to connect your computer to others on a network. Having a NIC usually provides you with Ethernet data transfer to the other computers. (*Ethernet* is a network technology that permits you to send and receive data at very fast speeds.)

The Internet is teeming with places where you can find good deals on hardware. A great place to start is the CNET Shopper.com Web site (`shopper.cnet.com`). Also visit the auction site uBid.com (`www.ubid.com`).

Processor speed

Computer processors are getting faster all the time. Don't be overly impressed by a computer's clock speed (measured in megahertz or even gigahertz). By the time you get your computer home, another, faster chip will already have hit the streets. Just make sure you have enough memory to run the types of applications shown in Table 2-2. (Note that these are only estimates, based on the Windows versions of these products that were available at the time of this writing.)

Table 2-2	Memory Requirements	
Type of Application	*Example*	*Amount of RAM Recommended*
Web browser	Internet Explorer	32MB
Web page editor	Macromedia Dreamweaver	128MB
Word processor	Microsoft Word	136MB (on Windows XP)
Graphics program	Paint Shop Pro	256MB
Accounting software	Microsoft Excel	8MB (if you are already running an Office application)
Animation/Presentation	Macromedia Flash	128MB

The RAM recommended for the sample applications in Table 2-2 adds up to a whopping 688MB. If you plan to work, be sure to get at least 512MB of RAM — more if you can swing it. Memory is cheap nowadays, and the newer PCs will allow you to install several GB (that's gigabytes) of RAM.

Hard drive storage

Random access memory is only one type of memory your computer uses; the other kind, *hard drive,* stores information, such as text files, audio files, programs, and the many essential files that your computer's operating system needs. Most of the new computers on the market come with hard drives that store many gigabytes of data. Any hard drive with a few gigabytes of storage space should be adequate for your business needs if you don't do a lot of graphics work. But most new computers come with hard drives that are 60GB or larger in size.

CD-RW/DVD±RW drive

Although a DVD and/or CD recordable drive may not be the most important part of your computer for business use, it can perform essential installation, storage, and data communications functions, such as installing software and saving and sharing data. A growing number of machines are now being made available with a *digital versatile disc* (DVD) drive. You can fit 4.7GB or more of data on a DVD±RW, compared with the 700MB or so that a conventional CD-RW can handle.

Be sure to protect your equipment against electrical problems that can result in loss of data or substantial repair bills. At the very least, make sure that your home office has grounded three-prong outlets and a *surge suppressor.* A common variety is a five- or six-outlet strip that has a protection device built in. Also consider the option of an uninterruptible power supply (UPS), which keeps devices from shutting off immediately in the event of blackouts. The PowerCard by Guardian On Board (www.guardian-ups.com) is available at most computer retail outlets, and costs about $149.

Building an online presence: It's an ongoing process

Judy Vorfeld, who is profiled in Chapter 6, needs to update her computer hardware regularly even though she works in the editorial field rather than a more technically oriented profession. As far as equipment goes, Judy estimates that each year she spends about $800 to $1,000 on computer hardware and $350 on software related to her business. She has two networked desktop computers, a Pentium 3 and Pentium 4, which she upgrades as needed. She has a CD/DVD burner on her main computer, and backs up her files on DVDs. Her 6-lb. laptop, which she uses whenever she travels, has a CD-RW/DVD-ROM drive, and 256 MB of RAM. For software, she uses the Web page editor Macromedia HomeSite to create Web pages, Paint Shop Pro to work with graphics, and Microsoft Word for most of her book editing.

Monitor

In terms of your online business, the quality or thinness of your monitor doesn't affect the quality of your Web site directly. Even if you have a poor-quality monitor, you can create a Web site that looks great to those who visit you. The problem is that you won't know how good your site really looks to customers who have high-quality monitors.

Flat-panel LCD (liquid crystal display) monitors continue to be a hot item, and they're becoming more affordable, too. You've got a real choice between a traditional CRT (cathode-ray tube) monitor and a flat LCD. Whether you choose flat or traditional, the quality of a monitor depends on several factors:

- **Resolution:** The resolution of a computer monitor refers to the number of pixels it can display horizontally and vertically. A resolution of 640 x 480 means that the monitor can display 640 pixels across the screen and 480 pixels down the screen. Higher resolutions, such as 800 x 600 or 1,024 x 768, make images look sharper but require more RAM in your computer. Anything less than 640 x 480 is unusable these days.

- **Size:** Monitor size is measured diagonally, as with TVs. Sizes such as 14 inches, 15 inches, and up to 21 inches are available. (Look for a 17-inch CRT monitor, which can display most Web pages fully, and which is now available for less than $200.)

- **Refresh rate:** This is the number of times per second that a video card redraws an image on-screen (at least 60 Hz [hertz] is preferable).

Keep in mind that lots of Web pages seem to have been designed with 17-inch or 21-inch monitors in mind. The problem isn't just that some users (especially those with laptops) have 15-inch monitors, but you can never control how wide the viewer's browser window will be. The problem is illustrated in the page from the Yale Style Manual, one of the classic references of Web site design (www.webstyleguide.com).

Computer monitors display graphic information that consists of little units called *pixels.* Each pixel appears on-screen as a small dot — so small that it's hard to perceive with the naked eye, unless you magnify an image to look at details close up. Together, the patterns of pixels create different intensities of light in an image, as well as ranges of color. A pixel can contain one or more bytes of binary information. The more pixels per inch (ppi), the higher a monitor's potential resolution. The higher the resolution, the closer the image appears to a continuous-tone image such as a photo. When you see a monitor's resolution described as 1,280 x 1,024, for example, that refers to the number of pixels that the monitor can display. *Dot pitch* refers to the distance between any two of the three pixels (one red, one green, and one blue) that a monitor uses to display color. The lower the dot pitch, the better the image resolution that you obtain. A dot pitch of 0.27 mm is a good measurement for a 17-inch monitor.

Fax equipment

A fax machine is an essential part of many home offices. If you don't have the funds available for a standalone machine, you can install software that helps your computer send and receive faxes. You have three options:

- ✔ You can install a fax modem, a hardware device that usually works with fax software. The fax modem can be an internal or external device.

- ✔ You can use your regular modem but install software that enables your computer to exchange faxes with another computer or fax machine.

- ✔ You can sign up for a service that receives your faxes and sends them to your computer in the body of an e-mail message. (For more information, see the "Fax Services" section of the Internet Directory on this book's Web site.)

I also recommend that you look into WinFax PRO by Symantec, Inc. (`www.symantec.com/winfax/index.html`). Your Windows computer needs to be equipped with a modem in order to send or receive faxes with WinFax.

If you plan to fax and access the Internet from your home office, you should get a second phone line or a direct connection, such as DSL or cable modem. The last thing a potential customer wants to hear is a busy signal.

Image capture devices

When you're ready to move beyond the basic hardware and on to a frill, think about obtaining a tool for capturing photographic images. (By *capturing*, I mean *digitizing* an image or, in other words, saving it in computerized, digital format.) Photos are often essential elements of business Web pages: They attract a customer's attention, they illustrate items for sale in a catalog, and they can provide before-and-after samples of your work. If you're an artist or designer, having photographic representations of your work is vital.

Including a clear, sharp image on your Web site greatly increases your chances of selling your product or service. You have two choices for digitizing: a scanner or digital camera. To decide which, read on.

Digital camera

Not so long ago, digital cameras cost thousands of dollars. These days, you can find a good digital camera made by a reputable manufacturer, such as Nikon, Fuji, Canon, Olympus, or Kodak, for $275–$600. You have to make an investment up front, but this particular tool can pay off for you in the long run. With the addition of a color printer, you can even print your own photos, which can save you a pile in photo lab costs.

A low-budget alternative

If you only want to get a computerized version of a photo on your Web without investing in any of the hardware that I mention here, not to worry. Just call your local photo shop or copy center. Many Kinko's Copies outlets, for example, provide computer services that include scanning photos. If you do your photo processing through Kodak, you can have the images placed online or on a CD. If you're a member of America Online, you can get your photos online through a program called "You've Got Pictures" and delivered to a location that you set up with AOL.

Wherever you go, be sure to tell the technician that you want the image to appear on the Web, so it should be saved in GIF or JPEG format. Also, if you have an idea of how big you want the final image to be when it appears online, tell that to the technician, too. The person can save the image in the size that you want so you don't have to resize it later in a graphics program.

Don't hesitate to fork over the extra dough to get a camera that gives you good resolution. Cutting corners doesn't pay when you end up with images that look fuzzy, but you can find many low-cost devices with good features. For example, the Canon PowerShot A20, which I spotted for $279, has a resolution of more than 2 megapixels — fine enough to print on a color printer and enlarge to a size such as 5 x 7 inches — and a zoom feature. *Megapixels* are calculated by multiplying the number of pixels in an image — for instance, when actually multiplied, 1,984 x 1,488 = 2,952,192 pixels or 2.9 megapixels. The higher the resolution, the fewer photos your camera can store at any one time because each image file requires more memory.

Online material is primarily intended to be displayed on computer monitors (which have limited resolution), so having super-high resolution images isn't critical for Web pages. Before being displayed by Web browsers, images must be compressed by using the GIF or JPEG formats. (See Chapter 5 for more scintillating technical details on GIF and JPEG.) Also, smaller and simpler images (as opposed to large, high-resolution graphics) generally appear more quickly on the viewer's screen. If you make your customers wait too long to see an image, they're apt to go to someone else's online store.

When shopping for a digital camera, look for the following features:

✔ The ability to download images to your computer via a FireWire or USB connection

✔ Bundled image-processing software

✔ The ability to download image files directly to a memory card that you can easily transport to a computer's memory card reader

✔ An included LCD screen that lets you see your images immediately

On the downside, because of optical filtering that's intended to reduce *color artifacts* — distortions of an image caused by limitations in hardware — photos taken with digital cameras tend to be less sharp than conventional 35mm photos. Correcting this problem in a graphics program can be time consuming. For high-quality close-ups on the cheap, try a scanner instead.

Digital photography is a fascinating and technical process, and you'll do well to read more about it in other books, such as *Digital Photography All-in-One Desk Reference For Dummies,* 2nd Edition, by David Busch or *Digital Photography For Dummies,* 4th Edition, by Julie Adair King (both by Wiley).

Scanners

Scanning is the process of turning the colors and shapes contained in a photographic print or slide into digital information (that is, bytes of data) that a computer can understand. You place the image in a position where the scanner's camera can pass over it, and the scanner turns the image into a computer document that consists of tiny bits of information called *pixels*. The type that I find easiest to use is a flatbed scanner. You place the photo or other image on a flat glass bed, just like what you find on a photocopier. An optical device moves under the glass and scans the photo.

The best news about scanners is that they've been around for a while, which, in the world of computing, means that prices are going down at the same time that quality is on the rise. The bargain models are well under $100, and I've even seen a couple priced as low as $49.95 after a rebate.

A type of scanner that has lots of benefits for small or home-based businesses is a multifunction device. You can find these units, along with conventional printers and scanners, at computer outlets. I have a multifunction device myself, in my home office. It sends and receives faxes, scans images, acts as a laser printer, and makes copies — plus it includes a telephone and answering machine. Now, if it could just make a good cup of espresso. . . .

For more detail about scanners, check out *Scanners For Dummies,* 2nd Edition, by Mark L. Chambers (Wiley).

Getting Online: Connection Options

After you purchase the computer hardware that you need, telephone bills are likely to be the biggest monthly expense you'll encounter in connection with your online business. At least, they are for me: I pay for local service, long-distance service, cell phone service, plus DSL service over my phone lines. It pays to choose your *telco* (telephone company) connection wisely.

A second phone line

Having a second line is pretty much a given if you plan to do business online regularly. A cell phone will work fine for business purposes if you don't want to pay your telephone company's fees for the extra land line. Because you'll be using your modem to dial the same one or two access numbers provided by your Internet service provider, confirm with your telco that your Internet access number is local so you don't end up paying long-distance fees.

Ask your telco about a *call pack* so you can call one number a lot for the same rate: 100 calls per month for a flat $10 fee, for example.

Beyond dialup

The best way to connect to the Internet is through a *direct line,* which means that, rather than be connected to the Internet for the length of your modem's phone call, you're connected all the time. Besides freeing up a phone line, a direct connection is typically light years faster than a dialup modem connection. Before you get your heart set on a high-speed Internet connection, check to see whether these options are available in your area.

Cable modem

Cable modem connections offer a really attractive way to get a high-speed connection to cyberspace. So go ahead and ask your local cable TV providers whether they provide this service. Turmoil erupted when the largest cable provider, @Home, ceased operations in early 2002. But other options, such as AT&T Broadband Internet (www.attbroadband.com) and EarthLink (www.earthlink.net/home/broadband/cable) provide high-speed Internet access through affiliations with cable TV providers in many parts of the country. In my neighborhood in Chicago, a company called RCN Chicago (rcnchicago.com) offers Internet access via cable modem for $45.95 plus a $75 installation fee that includes the cable modem device itself. AT&T Broadband Internet (www.attbroadband.com), however, offers similar service for $39.95.

The advantages of having a cable modem connection are many: It's a direct connection, it frees up a phone line, and it's super fast. Cable modems have the capacity to deliver 4 or 5MB of data per second. In reality, of course, the speed is going to be less than this because you're sharing access with other users. Plus, you have to purchase or lease the cable modem itself, pay an installation fee, and purchase an Ethernet card (if your computer doesn't already have one installed). But a cable modem is going to be far faster than a dialup connection.

You can find out which cable modem and DSL providers cover your area by using the Service Availability tool provided by Cable-Modem.net (www.cable-modem.net/gc/service_availability.html).

DSL

Wouldn't it be great if you could use conventional telephone lines to connect to the Internet all the time? Wouldn't it be even better if the connection were really fast — say, 100 times as fast as a 56 Kbps dialup modem?

If your telephone company offers its customers Digital Subscriber Line (DSL) connections, these aren't just pie-in-the-sky questions. DSLs "borrow" the part of your phone line that your voice doesn't use, the part that transmits signals of 3,000 Hz (hertz) or higher. DSLs can *upload* (send) data to another location on the Internet at 1.088 Mbps (megabits per second), and *download* (receive) data at more than twice that rate: 2.560 Mbps.

DSL comes in different varieties. Asymmetrical Digital Subscriber Line (ADSL) transmits information at different speeds depending on whether you're sending or receiving data. Symmetrical Digital Subscriber Line (SDSL) transmits information at the same speed in both directions. As DSL gets more popular, it becomes more widely available and the pricing drops. As I'm writing this, EarthLink DSL is available for $49.95 per month with free DSL modem and installation. Your local phone provider might offer DSL, too. In the Chicago area, Ameritech has a DSL option for $49 per month plus $99 to purchase the DSL modem.

Software Solutions for Online Business

One of the great things about starting an Internet business is that you get to use Internet software. As you probably know, the programs you use online are inexpensive (sometimes free), easy to use and install, and continually being updated.

Although you probably already have a basic selection of software to help you find information and communicate with others in cyberspace, the following sections describe some programs you may not have as yet and that will come in handy when you create your online business.

Don't forget to update your insurance by sending your insurer a list of new software (and hardware) or even by purchasing insurance specifically for your computer-related items from a company such as Safeware (www.safeware.com).

Anyone who uses firewall or antivirus software will tell you how essential these pieces of software are, for home or business use. Find out more about such software in Chapter 7 or in my book *Norton Internet Security For Dummies* (Wiley). See Chapter 17 for suggestions of accounting software — other important software you'll need.

Web browser

A *Web browser* is software that serves as a visual interface to the images, colors, links, and other content contained on the Web. The most popular such program is Microsoft Internet Explorer, with Netscape Navigator (part of the Communicator suite) coming in a distant second place.

Your Web browser is your primary tool for conducting business online, just as it is for everyday personal use. When it comes to running a virtual store or consulting business, though, you have to run your software through a few more paces than usual. You need your browser to

- Preview the Web pages you create
- Display frames, animations, movie clips, and other goodies you plan to add online
- Support some level of Internet security, such as Secure Sockets Layer (SSL), if you plan to conduct secure transactions on your site

In addition to having an up-to-date browser with the latest features, installing more than one kind of browser on your computer is a good idea. For example, if you use Microsoft Internet Explorer because that's what came with your operating system, be sure to download the latest copy of Netscape Navigator, as well. That way, you can test your site to make sure that it looks good to all your visitors.

Web page editor

HyperText Markup Language (HTML) is a set of instructions used to format text, images, and other Web page elements so that Web browsers can correctly display them. But you don't have to master HTML in order to create your own Web pages. Plenty of programs called *Web page editors* are available to help you format text, add images, make hyperlinks, and do all the fun assembly steps necessary to make your Web site a winner.

In many cases, Web page editors come with electronic storefront packages; QuickSite, which I discuss in Chapter 4, comes with Microsoft FrontPage Express. Sometimes, programs that you use for one purpose can also help you create Web documents: Microsoft Word has an add-on called Internet Assistant that enables you to save text documents as HTML Web pages, and Microsoft Office 98 and later (for the Mac) or Office 2000 or later (for Windows) enables you to export files in Web page format automatically.

Taking e-mail a step higher

You're probably very familiar with sending and receiving e-mail messages. But when you start an online business, you should make sure that e-mail software has some advanced features:

- ✔ **Autoresponders:** Some programs automatically respond to e-mail requests with a form letter or document of your choice.

- ✔ **Mailing lists:** With a well-organized address book (a feature that comes with some e-mail programs), you can collect the e-mail addresses of visitors or subscribers and send them a regular update of your business activities or, better yet, an e-mail newsletter.

- ✔ **Quoting:** Almost all e-mail programs let you quote from a message to which you're replying, so you can respond easily to a series of questions.

- ✔ **Attaching:** Attaching a file to an e-mail message is a quick and convenient way to transmit information from one person to another.

- ✔ **Signature files:** Make sure that your e-mail software automatically includes a simple electronic signature at the end. Use this space to list your company name, your title, and your Web site URL.

Both Outlook Express, the e-mail component of Microsoft Internet Explorer, and Netscape Messenger, which is part of the Netscape Communicator suite of programs, include most or all these features. Because these functions are all essential aspects of providing good customer service, I discuss them in more detail in Chapter 13.

Discussion group software

When your business site is up and running, consider taking it a step farther by creating your own discussion area right on your Web site. This sort of discussion area isn't a newsgroup as such; it doesn't exist in Usenet, and you don't need newsgroup software to read and post messages. Rather, it's a Web-based discussion area where your visitors can compare notes and share their passion for the products you sell or the area of service you provide.

Programs such as Microsoft FrontPage enable you to set up a discussion area on your Web site. See Chapter 13 for more information.

FTP software

FTP (File Transfer Protocol) is one of those acronyms you see time and time again as you move around the Internet. You may even have an FTP program that your ISP gave you when you obtained your Internet account. But chances are you don't use it that often.

In case you haven't used FTP yet, start dusting it off. When you create your own Web pages, a simple, no-nonsense FTP program is the easiest way to transfer them from your computer at home to your Web host. If you need to correct and update your Web pages quickly (and you will), you'll benefit by having your FTP software ready and set up with your Web site address, user-name, and password so that you can transfer files right away. See Chapter 3 for more about using File Transfer Protocol.

Image editors

You need a graphics-editing program either to create original artwork for your Web pages or to crop and adjust your scanned images and digital photographs. In the case of adjusting or cropping photographic image files, the software you need almost always comes bundled with the scanner or digital camera, so you don't need to buy separate software for that.

In the case of graphic images, the first question to ask yourself is, "Am I really qualified to draw and make my own graphics?" If the answer is yes, think shareware first. Three programs I like are Adobe Photoshop Elements (www.adobe.com), LView Pro by Leonardo Haddad Loureiro (www.lview.com), and Paint Shop Pro by Jasc, Inc. (www.jasc.com). You can download all these programs from the Web to use on a trial basis. After the trial period is over, you'll need to pay a small fee to the developer in order to register and keep the program. Photoshop Elements costs $99, LView Pro version 2001 costs $40; Paint Shop Pro costs $119 to download for Version 9 or $129 for a boxed version.

The ability to download and use free (and almost free) software from shareware archives and many other sites is one of the nicest things about the Internet. Keep the system working by remembering to pay the shareware fees to the nice folks who make their software available to individuals like you and me.

Instant messaging

You may think that MSN Messenger, AOL Instant Messenger, ICQ, and PalTalk are just for social "chatting" online, but instant messaging has its business applications, too. Here are a few suggestions:

✔ If individuals you work with all the time are hard to reach, you can use a messaging program to tell you if those people are logged on to their computers. This allows you to contact them the moment they sit down to work (provided they don't mind your greeting them so quickly, of course).

✔ You can cut down on long-distance phone charges by exchanging instant messages with far-flung colleagues.

✔ With a microphone, sound card, and speakers, you can carry on voice conversations through your messaging software.

MSN Messenger enables users to do file transfers without having to use FTP software or attaching files to e-mail messages.

Backup software

Losing copies of your personal documents is one thing, but losing files related to your business can hit you hard in the pocketbook. That makes it even more important to make backups of your online business computer files. Iomega Zip or Jaz drives (www.iomega.com) come with software that lets you automatically make backups of your files. If you don't own one of these programs, I recommend you get really familiar with the backup program included with Windows XP or look into Backup Exec by VERITAS Software Corporation (www.veritas.com).

Chapter 3

Selecting the Right Web Host and Design Tools

*Y*ou *can* sell items online without having a Web site. But do you really want to? Doing real online business without some sort of online "home base" is time consuming and inefficient. The vast majority of online commercial concerns use their Web sites as the primary way to attract customers, convey their message, and make sales. A growing number of ambitious capitalists use online auction sites such as eBay (`www.ebay.com`) to make money, but the auctioneers who depend on eBay for regular income often have their own Web pages, too.

The success of a commercial Web site depends in large measure on two important factors: Where it's hosted and how it's designed. These factors affect how easily you can create and update your Web pages, what special features such as multimedia or interactive forms you can have on your site, and even how your site looks. Some hosting services provide Web page creation tools that are easy to use but that limit the level of sophistication you can apply to the page's design. Other services leave the creation and design up to you. In this chapter, I provide an overview of your Web hosting options as well as different design approaches that you can implement.

Plenty of Web sites and CD-ROMs claim that they can have your Web site up and running online "in a matter of minutes" using a "seamless" process. The actual construction may indeed be quick and smooth — as long as you've done all your preparation work beforehand. This preparation work includes identifying your goals for going online, deciding what market you want to reach, deciding what products you want to sell, writing descriptions and capturing images of those products, and so on. Before you jump over to Yahoo! Small Business or Microsoft Small Business Center and start assembling your site, be sure that you've done all the groundwork that I discuss in Chapter 2, such as identifying your audience and setting up your hardware.

Getting the Most from Your Web Host

An Internet connection and a Web browser are all you need if you're primarily interested in surfing through cyberspace, consuming information, and shopping for online goodies. But when you're starting an online business, you're no longer just a consumer; you're becoming a provider of information and consumable goods. Along with a way to connect to the Internet, you need to find a hosting service that will make your online business available to your prospective customers.

A *Web hosting service* is the online world's equivalent of a landlord. Just as the owner of a building gives you office space or room for a storefront where you can hang your shingle, a hosting service provides you with space online where you can set up shop.

You can operate an online business without a Web site if you sell regularly on eBay. But even on eBay, you can create an About Me page or an eBay store; eBay itself is your host in both cases. (You pay a monthly fee to eBay in order to host your store. See Chapter 10 for more information.)

A Web host provides space on special computers called *Web servers* that are connected to the Internet all the time. Web servers are equipped with software that makes your Web pages visible to people who connect to them by using a Web browser. The process of using a Web hosting service for your online business works roughly like this:

1. **You decide where you want your site to appear on the Internet.**

   Do you want it to be part of a virtual shopping mall that includes many other businesses? Or do you want a standalone site that has its own Web address and doesn't appear to be affiliated with any other organization?

2. **You sign up with a Web host.**

   Sometimes you pay a fee. In some cases, no fee is required. In all cases, you're assigned space on a server. Your Web site gets an address, or *URL,* that people can enter in their browsers to view your pages.

3. **You create your Web pages.**

   Usually, you use a Web page editor to do this.

4. **After creating content, adding images, and making your site look just right, you transfer your Web page files (HTML documents, images, and so on) from your computer to the host's Web server.**

   You generally need special File Transfer Protocol (FTP) software to do the transferring. But many Web hosts will help you through the process by providing their own user-friendly software. (The most popular Web editors, such as Macromedia Dreamweaver, will let you do this, too.)

5. **You access your own site with your Web browser and check the contents to make sure that all the images appear and that any hypertext links you created go to the intended destinations.**

   At this point, you're open for business — visitors can view your Web pages by entering your Web address in their Web browser's Go To or Address box.

6. **You market and promote your site to attract potential clients or customers.**

Carefully choose a Web host because the host will affect which software you'll use to create your Web pages and get them online. The Web host also affects the way your site looks, and it may determine the complexity of your Web address. (See the "What's in a name?" sidebar later in this chapter for details.)

If you have a direct connection to the Internet such as a DSL line and are competent with computers (or if you have access to someone who is), you can host your own site on the Web. However, turning your own computer into a Web server is a lot more complicated than signing up with a hosting service. (Your ISP may not allow you to set up your own server anyway; check your user agreement first.) You need to install server software and set up a domain name for your computer. You'll also have to purchase a static IP address for your machine. (An *IP address* is a number that identifies every computer that's connected to the Internet, and that consists of four sets of numerals separated by dots, such as 206.207.99.1. A *static IP address* is one that doesn't change from session to session.) If you're just starting a simple home-based or part-time business, hosting your own Web site is probably more trouble than you care to handle, but you should be aware that it's an option. If you're interested in becoming a Webmaster, check out Speakeasy (www.speakeasy.net). This ISP encourages users to set up their own Web servers, and even offers two static IP address with a DSL line for $59.95 per month.

Finding a Web Server to Call Home

Hi! I'm your friendly World Wide Web real estate agent. Call me Virtual Larry. You say you're not sure exactly what kind of Web site is right for you, and you want to see all the options, from a tiny storefront in a strip mall to your own landscaped corporate park? Your wish is my command. Just hop into my 2005-model Internet Explorer, buckle your seat belt, and I'll show you around the many different business properties available in cyberspace.

Here's a road map of our tour:

- **Online Web-host-and-design-kit combos:** Yahoo! Small Business Merchant Solutions, Yahoo! GeoCities, and Microsoft Small Business Center (formerly called bCentral), among others.

- **America Online:** My FTP Place and Hometown AOL.

- **Electronic merchant CD-ROMs:** ShopSite and WebSite Complete, to name two.

- **eBay:** A site that lets its users create their own About Me Web pages and their own stores.

- **Auxiliary companies:** These folks do something that doesn't seem directly related to e-commerce, but they let you build a store online, like FedEx eCommerce Builder.

- **An online shopping mall:** You can rent a space in these virtual malls.

- **Your current Internet service provider (ISP):** Many ISPs are only too happy to host your e-commerce site — for an extra monthly fee in addition to your access fee.

- **Companies devoted to hosting Web sites full time:** These are businesses whose primary function is hosting e-commerce Web sites and providing their clients with associated software, such as Web page building tools, shopping carts, catalog builders, and the like.

The first four options combine Web hosting with Web page creation kits. Whether you buy these services or get to use them on the Web for free, you simply follow the manufacturer's instructions. Most of these hosting services enable you to create your Web pages by filling in forms; you never have to see a line of HTML code if you don't want to. Depending on which service you choose, you have varying degrees of control over how your site ultimately looks.

The last three options (ISPs, online malls, and full-time Web hosts) tend to be do-it-yourself projects. You sign up with the host, you choose the software, and you create your own site. However, the distinction between this category and the others is blurry. As competition between Web hosts grows keener, more and more companies are providing ready-made solutions that streamline the process of Web site creation for their customers. For you, the end user, this is a good thing: You have plenty of control over how your site comes into being and how it grows over time.

If you simply need a basic Web site and don't want a lot of choices, go with one of the kits. Your site may look like everyone else's and seem a little generic, but setup is easy and you can concentrate on marketing and running your business.

However, if you're the independent type who wants to control your site and have lots of room to grow, consider taking on a do-it-yourself project. The sky's the limit as far as the degree of creativity you can exercise and the amount of sweat equity you can put in (as long as you don't make your site so large and complex that shoppers have a hard time finding anything, of course). The more work you do, the greater your chances of seeing your business prosper.

Web site homesteading for free

Free Web hosting is still possible for small businesses. If you're on a tight budget and looking for space on a Web server for free, turn first to your ISP, which probably gives you server space to set up a Web site. You can also check out one of a handful of sites that provide customers with hosting space for no money down and no monthly payments, either. Rather than money, you pay in terms of advertising: You may have to look at ads or other things, but if you don't mind, here are some good deals you can enjoy:

✔ **Netfirms** (www.netfirms.com): This site places ads on your Web pages but gives you 25MB of server space where you can set up a business Web site for free and get CGI processing for your forms, too. CGI (Common Gateway Interface) provides a way for a Web server to interact with an application, such as a computer script, that receives the information from a form and processes it in a form that you can read easily.

✔ **Freeservers** (www.freeservers.com): In exchange for banner ads and popup ads, which you are required to display if you set up a Web site on one of its servers, and Freeservers Special Offers, which are sent to your e-mail address, this site gives you several tools. You have the choice of two free editors, add-ons (such as guest books and hit counters), and an online Web page building tool for creating your site — not to mention 12MB of server space.

You can find more free Web hosting services on Yahoo! here:

dir.yahoo.com/Business_and_
Economy/Business_to_Business/
Communications_and_Networking/
Internet_and_World_Wide_Web/
Network_Service_Providers/Hosting/
Web_Site_Hosting/Free_Hosting/

Be sure that the site you choose lets you set up for-profit business sites for free.

Installing software to build a Web site

A new class of Web sites has caught on to the concept of making things easy and affordable for would-be ontrepreneurs (online entrepreneurs). These sites act as both a Web host and a Web page creation tool. You connect to the site, sign up for service, and fill out a series of forms. Submitting the completed forms activates a script on the host site that automatically generates your Web pages based on the data you entered.

In this section, I show you how to set up a business Web site with Yahoo! Store, a popular "kit" service. Many such sites are available, and investigating all your options is always smart. Some other Web site creation packages are available at the following sites:

- ✔ **Yahoo! GeoCities** (`geocities.yahoo.com`): Yahoo! GeoCities is a popular spot for individuals who want to create home pages and full-fledged personal and business Web sites at a low cost. The site provides a free hosting option that requires users to display ads on the sites they create. If you want ad-free hosting, you can choose between GeoCities PLUS, which offers extra storage for a $10 setup fee plus a $4.95 per month hosting fee, or GeoCities PRO, which offers your own domain and e-mail for a $15 setup fee plus $8.95 per month.

- ✔ **AOL Hometown** (`hometown.aol.com`): America Online hosts this Web site where individuals can create their own Web pages for business or personal use. A "neighborhood" within AOL Hometown, called Business Park, is set aside for commercial sites, and an area within the Business Park area hosts home-based businesses. (See the upcoming section, "You've got business: Creating an AOL store," for more information.)

Suppose you have some music CDs, photos, or artwork that can be printed and sold on clothing. You've created the art or saved the photos as GIF or JPEG image files, and you want to place them on products you can sell to friends, family, or anyone who's interested. A popular service called CafePress (`www.cafepress.com`) makes it easy for you to create and sell such products online for free. The hard part is deciding what you want to sell, how best to describe your sales items, and how to promote your site. Getting your words and images online is remarkably straightforward:

1. **Connect to the Internet, start up your Web browser, and go to the CafePress Free Store page (`www.cafepress.com/cp/info/sell`).**

   The Sell Stuff Online — Free Store page appears in your browser window.

2. **Click the Start Selling Now button just beneath the introductory text.**

   The CafePress.com — Join page appears. Before creating a store, you need to register with CafePress.

3. **Assign yourself a username and password (if you haven't done so already). When you're done, click Join Now.**

   The New Member Survey page appears.

4. **Fill out the survey, and click Let's Start Selling!**

   The Open a Shop page appears.

5. **Click Open a Basic Shop.**

   The Welcome to CafePress.com Basic Shops! page appears.

6. **Under the Shop Information heading, enter a short ID that will be included in your store's URL and a name for your store. Fill out the rest of the options on the page if necessary, and click Submit when you're done.**

   The Welcome to CafePress.com Basic Shops! page appears. Click the URL supplied for your new store so you can see that, although it's empty, it really exists (see Figure 3-1).

7. **Close the new browser window that opened so you could inspect your page and return to the Welcome to CafePress.com Basic Shops! page. Click the Add Products to My Shop button at the bottom of the page.**

   The Your Account page appears.

8. **Under the heading Shop Management, click Products.**

   The Products page appears.

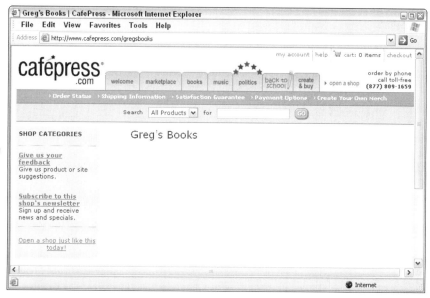

Figure 3-1:
Presto!
You've
opened your
store, which
you can now
fill with mer-
chandise.

9. **Click Add a Product.**

   The Choose a Product page appears, with a set of products you can personalize and sell in your store (see Figure 3-2).

   You can't sell just anything on CafePress.com: If you want to sell something other than a tote bag, license plate frame, book, or other products shown on the Choose a Product page, you'd better open a site with another Web host. But if you're just beginning with e-commerce and aren't sure what to sell, a CafePress.com store can be a good starting point.

10. **Click the box that contains the type of item you want to sell.**

    The Design Your Product Front page appears.

11. **Click Select Image.**

    The Media Basket page appears. This page is intended as a storage area — a place where you can store product images so that you can add them later when you want to put them up for sale.

12. **Click Add Image.**

    The Upload Image page appears, with an explanation you should read that describes the acceptable file formats.

13. **Click Browse.**

    The Choose File dialog box appears.

Figure 3-2: CafePress.com gives you a selection of items that you can personalize and sell online.

14. **Select the file you want to place on the front of the object, and click Open.**

    The path leading to the location of the image file on your computer appears in the Image file box.

15. **Check the I Agree to the Terms and Conditions Described Above box, and then click Upload.**

    An Uploading dialog box appears with a progress bar that describes the progress of the file transfer. When transfer is complete, the image appears in your Media Basket.

16. **Click Add image.**

    The image is added to the front of your product (see Figure 3-3).

17. **Click Next and follow the subsequent steps to add images to the back of the object and to add more objects to your online store.**

    Make sure that your logo or other image meets the height and other requirements for a CafePress.com store. Images must be 200 pixels in height (one inch equals approximately 72 pixels). Find out more by clicking the Need More Image Help? link, which appears on the product design pages as you're creating your store.

You can visit your new site by entering your own Web address, which takes the form `www.cafepress.com/storename` (where *storename* is the name you entered in Step 6).

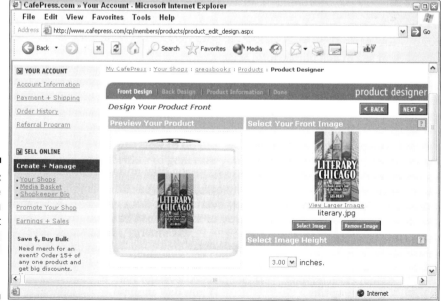

Figure 3-3: You save the items you want to print in a holding area called the Media Basket.

You've got business: Creating an AOL store

If you're one of the millions of folks who already have an account with America Online, it makes sense to consider setting up your online store with AOL as your host. Even if you don't have an account with AOL presently, you may want to sign up in order to create and publish a simple Web site. Plenty of entrepreneurs either started an online business with AOL and then moved on to another Web host, or continue to maintain their business Web sites on one of AOL's Web servers.

When you sign up for an account with America Online, you're entitled to 2MB of space for your own Web pages. That may not seem like a lot of room, but consider that the average Web page is only 5 to 10K in size. Even if each page contains images that are perhaps 10 to 20K in size, which still means you have room for 70 to 100 Web pages. Besides that, an account with AOL provides for seven separate usernames. Each username is entitled to 2MB of Web site space. In theory, at least, you have 14MB of space at your disposal. This is more than enough to accommodate most moderately sized Web sites.

If AOL is so great, why doesn't everyone publish Web sites with it? Well, AOL has its downsides, too. For one thing, its servers seem (to me, at least) to be noticeably slower than others, perhaps because of the sheer volume of users. AOL has had problems with members being unable to get online during busy times. And unless you pay AOL's flat monthly rate for unlimited access, you're liable to run up some sizable hourly access charges in the course of creating, revising, and maintaining your business site. Finally, there's a subtle but important difference between AOL and a Web host that's on the Internet: Even though it has its own Web sites, AOL isn't really part of the Internet. It's on its own online network. E-mail sent from an AOL user to someone on the Internet has to go through a computer connection called a *gateway*. If the gateway goes down or if some other aspect of AOL's operation experiences a problem, all AOL users are suddenly inaccessible from the Internet. Your business may be inaccessible to many potential customers for a time. Although AOL does seem to be getting more reliable, the fact that it's separate from the Internet is an important consideration to keep in mind if you're thinking about setting up shop there.

America Online presents several resources for customers who want to publish Web pages for their business or personal use. Some of these resources are accessible only through America Online, but because AOL is making an effort to branch out onto the Web itself, other resources are located on the Web, not within AOL.

Collectively, the AOL Web page publishing options are known as My Place or My FTP Space, as shown in Figure 3-4.

Figure 3-4:
My FTP
Space
and AOL
Hometown
are the
primary
resources
that AOL
offers
members
who want
to publish
their own
Web sites.

Within My FTP Space, you can find plenty of resources, including

- **1-2-3 Publish:** This is a service that performs roughly the same function as the Web page generators provided by Yahoo! GeoCities, CNET WebSite Builder, or Yahoo! Store. You fill out a form by using your AOL browser. The information on the form is presented in the form of a very rudimentary Web page. The information requested is personal, however, and not intended for business use. (AOL Keyword: 1-2-3 Publish.)

- **Easy Designer:** This is AOL's graphic Web page design tool for publishing sites on AOL Hometown (which I discuss in a later bullet). It lets you create and preview your own pages without having to master HTML. Versions are available for both Windows and Macintosh users.

- **Other Web page editors:** AOL also provides links to clip art shareware and commercial Web editors that you can download and use to create your business site.

- **My FTP Space:** This is the service that transfers Web pages you have already made to your directory on one of AOL's servers with FTP (File Transfer Protocol). My FTP Place doesn't create your Web pages for you, but you can use any Web page authoring tool to do that. (AOL Keyword: My FTP Space.)

✔ **AOL Hometown:** After you publish your Web site on AOL by using My FTP Space, you can add the site to the AOL online community on the Web. AOL Hometown (`hometown.aol.com`) is a "real" Web site on the Internet: It's not part of AOL's own domain the way My Place is. AOL Hometown is open to America Online members and other Internet users alike. AOL members who go through the extra effort of including their sites on AOL Hometown get double exposure: Their sites are accessible both within AOL (through My FTP Space) and on the Web itself (through AOL Hometown).

If you're an AOL customer and you want to start a home-based business for virtually nothing, you have two options: My FTP Space or AOL Hometown. Which one is best? AOL Hometown gives you more space (either 4MB or 12MB, depending on how many files you keep online). Getting your files online is also easier with AOL Hometown. With My FTP Space, you create the pages by using one of the AOL Web page tools or another Web editor. You then upload the files, following the instructions in the My FTP Space Help files. But if you use one of the AOL Web page creation tools (1-2-3 Publish or Easy Designer) to create your site, you can upload the files from within the same program.

To set up your site at AOL Hometown by using 1-2-3 Publish, follow these steps:

1. **Create a new screen name.**

   The first step is to pick a screen name for your site. This doesn't need to be the same as your usual AOL username. AOL lets you use as many as seven different screen names, and I recommend reserving one for your personal use and one for your business site. To create a new screen name, connect to AOL by using your master screen name, enter the keyword **Names**, and then follow the instructions for creating a new screen name.

   Your choice of screen name is important when you use My FTP Space as your Web site host. The screen name appears as part of your Web site URL. For example, if your business is called WidgetWorld, you might choose the screen name *widgets*. When you transfer your files online by using My FTP Place, you and your visitors can then access your site by using the URL `members.aol.com/widgets`.

2. **Go to** `hometown.aol.com/hmtwn123` **and start using 1-2-3 Publish by clicking the Your First Home Page link. (AOL Keyword: 1-2-3 Publish).**

   The Welcome page, entitled Get a Free Page in Minutes!, appears. A number of predesigned page templates appear on this page.

   You don't have to be using AOL software to use 1-2-3 Publish; you don't even have to be an AOL subscriber. If you're not a subscriber, you do have to sign up for a screen name, but it's free to do so. Go to `hometown.aol.com` to find out more.

3. **Click My Business Page to begin designing your Web page.**

   The My Business Page Template page appears.

4. **Choose a color and background for your page, and assign a name to the page by filling out this page's form; then click the Save this Page button.**

   A preview of your page appears.

5. **If you want to make changes, click Modify. When you're satisfied with your page's appearance, click Done.**

   When you click Done, a page appears with the message Congratulations — You've Got a Home Page! and a link to the site that you just created.

6. **Click the link to view your new Web site.**

It's as easy as that. If you ever want to edit your page, click the Edit My Page link that appears above any AOL Hometown page.

You don't have to use 1-2-3 Publish to create a Web site, but it's a great tool for beginners. More experienced users can create a complete Web site by using a Web editor. After you've completed your pages, go to AOL Hometown and click the Create link that appears above any page on the site. You'll go to a page entitled Create or Edit Pages. Click Upload to move your already created files to AOL Hometown, or click Add to add your pages to an AOL Hometown site that you've previously created.

Investigating electronic storefront software

All the other options that this chapter provides for publishing your business site are ones that you access and utilize online. Yet another option for creating a business site and publishing it online is to purchase an application that carries you through the entire process of creating an electronic storefront. The advantage is control: You own and operate the software and are in charge of the entire process (at least until the files get to the remote Web servers). The speed with which you develop a site depends on how quickly you master the process, not on the speed of your Internet connection.

Like hosting services such as Yahoo! Store, Tripod, and CNET WebBuilder, electronic storefront software is designed to facilitate the process of creating Web pages and to shield you from having to master HTML. Most storefront software provides you with predesigned Web pages, called *templates,* which you customize for your particular business. Some types of electronic storefront options go a step or two beyond the other options by providing you with shopping cart systems that enable customers to select items and tally the cost at checkout. They may also provide for some sort of electronic payment option, such as credit card purchases.

Usually, you purchase the software on floppy disk or CD-ROM, install the package like any other application, and follow a series of steps that detail the primary aspects of a business:

- ✔ **The storefront:** The Web pages that you create. Some packages, such as WebSite Complete, include predesigned Web pages that you can copy and customize with your own content.

- ✔ **The inventory:** You can stock your virtual storefront shelves by presenting your wares in the form of an online catalog or product list.

- ✔ **The delivery truck:** Some storefront packages streamline the process of transferring your files from your computer to the server. Instead of using FTP software, you publish information simply by clicking a button in your Web editor or Web browser.

- ✔ **The checkout counter:** Most electronic storefront packages give you the option to accept orders by phone, fax, or online with a credit card.

Besides providing you with all the software that you need to create Web pages and get them online, electronic storefronts instruct you on how to market your site and present your goods and services in a positive way. In addition, some programs provide you with a backroom for your business, where you can record customer information, orders, and fulfillment.

The problem with many electronic storefront packages is that they're very expensive — some cost $5,000 to $10,000 or more. They're not intended for individuals starting their own small businesses, but rather for large corporations that want to branch out to the Web. However, a few packages (two of which I describe in the following sections) provide a Ford-type alternative to the Rolls-Royce storefronts.

ShopSite

ShopSite, by ShopSite, Inc., isn't software that you purchase and install on your computer. Rather, you find a Web hosting service that runs ShopSite on its servers. You then set up an account with the host and use the ShopSite software over the Internet, using your Web browser. This kind of setup, which is called a *hosted application,* means you don't have to worry about having enough memory or hard drive space to run the program yourself. You also don't have to bother with updating or troubleshooting the software; that, too, is the hosting service's responsibility.

In order to find a hosting service that runs ShopSite, you go to the ShopSite Web site (www.shopsite.com) and scan a list of hosts. You pick a company and arrange for an account. Pricing varies depending on the host and the version of the service that you want. ShopSite comes in three varieties:

✔ **Starter:** Lets you create a catalog of only 15 items for sale and 5 Web pages.

✔ **Manager:** Gives you an unlimited number of pages, plus templates, themes, a shopping cart, and real-time credit card processing.

✔ **Pro:** Adds the ability to track inventory as products are purchased.

One host I saw was offering ShopSite Starter for $49 with its hosting packages, the Manager version for $74 per month, and the Pro version for $125 per month. Instead of renting the software on a monthly basis, you can also buy a life-time license. I saw ShopSite Lite advertised for $135, Manager for $495, and Pro for $1,295.

ecBuilder Pro

ecBuilder Pro, by Maximizer Software, Inc. (`www.ecbuilder.com`), is soft-ware that you purchase and install on your computer. You either download the program from its own Web site for $379 or purchase it on a CD-ROM for $399. The software makes it easy for you to create not only basic Web pages, but to also make a site searchable by keyword, to set up password-protected pages, and to set up a shopping cart.

If ecBuilder Pro seems expensive, you can sign up with a host that includes the software among the services it gives you for a monthly fee. Easyhosting (`www.easyhosting.com`) includes ecBuilder's shopping cart software with its Standard to Intermediate hosting packages, which range from $29.99 to $79.99 per month.

ecBuilder Pro comes with 40 templates and interactive wizards for creating Web sites; it works with Windows 95 or later.

Moving into an online mall

In addition to Web site kits, Internet service providers, and businesses that specialize in Web hosting, online shopping malls provide another form of Web hosting. You set up your site, either on your own or using special Web page authoring utilities that some malls provide. You pay a monthly fee, you transfer your files to the mall's Web site, and your store appears online. The basic steps are the same with an online mall as with any of the other hosting businesses that I mention in this chapter.

What's the difference, then, between a shopping mall that does Web hosting, an Internet service provider that does hosting, and a Web hosting service? Their names and the features they offer differ slightly, but the important thing to remember is that they all do essentially the same thing. After you open your virtual business on the Web, your customers can't always tell whether you're part of America Online, a mall, or a Web host such as EarthLink.

What *is* an online shopping mall, anyway? It's a collection of online businesses that are listed in a directory or index provided by a single organization. The directory may be a simple list of stores on a single Web page. For larger malls with a thousand stores or more, the online businesses are arranged by category and can be found in a searchable index.

CASE STUDY

Finding a host that makes your business dynamic

Whether you choose America Online or another ISP, which Web host you choose can have a big impact on how easy it is to get online and run your business successfully. Just ask Doug Laughter. He and his wife Kristy own The Silver Connection, LLC, which sells sterling silver jewelry imported from India, Asia, and Mexico. They began their endeavor when Kristy brought back some silver jewelry from Mexico. The Silver Connection went online in April 1998 at www.silver connection.com and is hosted by CrystalTech Web Hosting, Inc. (www.crystaltech.com).

Q. Why did you choose CrystalTech as your Web host?

A. CrystalTech is my second Web host. I didn't have any problems with my previous host, but the issue of changing Web hosts came down to the Web development technology I wanted to choose for my site. I settled on CrystalTech because it supported the Web Application Server that I chose, which was a Windows platform running Internet Information Server. I also wanted to use Microsoft Access or Microsoft SQL Server for my database solution to support the development of Active Server Pages (ASP).

Q. What makes CrystalTech such a good Web host?

A. What makes CrystalTech particularly good is that it gives its clients access to a Control Center that allows complete administrative control for the domain. Included in this are mail, FTP, and Domain Name System with automatic ODBC (Open Database Connectivity) for databases. A client also gets access to several utilities that analyze traffic

to your Web site. I also use the comprehensive knowledge base and online forums that carry on discussions about programming, Web site design, databases, networking, and other topics.

Q. What kinds of customer service features do you use that other business owners should look for?

A. One feature that CrystalTech is very good with is notification. If Web hosting or mail services will be offline for a certain amount of time, I receive an e-mail in advance specifying exactly what is going to happen and when. I have always been treated very well by tech support when I have needed to call.

Q. What kinds of questions should small business owners and managers ask when they're shopping around for a hosting service? What kinds of features should they be looking for initially?

A. I would first suggest considering how you want to develop your Web site. Today's e-commerce site needs to be dynamic in nature, so the business needs to research and determine what Web server application it will use. A Web server application consists of the following:

- ✔ **Server Side Technology:** Active Server Pages, ColdFusion, Java Server Pages, PHP

- ✔ **Database Solution:** Microsoft SQL Server, MS Access, MySQL, Oracle

- ✔ **Server Application:** IIS, Apache, iPlanet, Netscape Enterprise

- ✔ **Operating Platform:** Windows, UNIX

So the decision on how the e-commerce Web site will be developed and in what technology is a very key decision to make from the onset. Once this is decided, choose a Web host that supports your Web server application of choice.

Q. After the development platform is determined, what features should you look for?

A. Look for dedicated disk space for database applications. 250MB or 500MB of disk space might be fine for your Web site files, but throw in a highly developed Microsoft SQL Server relational database management system, and you'll be paying for some additional space.

Also ask about how much data transfer you can do in a given period, how many e-mail addresses are given with the domain, and whether there's an application that lets you control and administer your entire Web site. If you don't have your own shopping cart application, ask your host what it offers in this area. Specifically, find out what application it offers, how transactions are completed, and how credit card purchases are processed. Finally, make sure there's an application that can analyze traffic, such as WebTrends or SmarterStats, or Media House Services.

In theory, an online shopping mall helps small businesses by giving them additional exposure. A customer who shops at one of the mall's stores might notice other businesses on the same site and visit it, too. Some malls function as Web hosts that enable their customers to transfer Web page files and present their stores online, using one of the mall's Web servers. Other malls let people list their business in the mall with a hyperlink, even if the store is actually hosted by another company.

Perhaps the only thing that really distinguishes online malls from other hosting services is presentation:

- Some malls, such as Downtown Anywhere (`www.awa.com`), use the metaphor of a town square to organize their businesses. Stores are presented as being on particular streets; visitors browse the shops as though walking around the streets of a small town.

- Another online mall to look into is Microsoft bCentral Small Business Directory (`sbd.bcentral.com`), which gathers in one location a number of small businesses that are hosted by Microsoft Small Business Services. Microsoft, like its rival Yahoo! Small Business, no longer lets you test its Web page creation system for free. You must now pay a monthly fee to locate your business with the site permanently.

Consider joining an online mall if you find one that offers an attractive hosting package, particularly if it has Web page forms that will help you set up your site or create an online catalog quickly. But remember that to Web shoppers it doesn't matter who your host is; what's more important is that you develop compelling content for your site to attract customers and encourage sales.

Amazon.com doesn't look like an online mall, but it has instituted some opportunities for entrepreneurs to sell items on its site. If you don't want to create an entire storefront, you also have the option of selling items individually on the Amazon.com site. You pay fees to list items for sale and for completed sales as well. Find out more by going to the Amazon.com home page (`www.amazon.com`) and clicking the Sell Your Stuff link near the top of the page.

Turning to your ISP for Web hosting

People sometimes talk about Internet service providers (ISPs) and Web hosts as two separate types of Internet businesses, but that's not necessarily the case. Providing users with access to the Internet and hosting Web sites are two different functions, to be sure, but they may well be performed by the same organization.

In fact, it's only natural to turn to your own ISP first to ask about its Web hosting policies for its customers. Like John Raddatz (see the section Chapter 15), if you already go online with AOL, trying out its Web hosting facilities makes sense. If you have an Internet access account with the popular ISP EarthLink (`www.earthlink.net`), by all means, consider EarthLink as a Web host for your business site.

EarthLink has different Web hosting options depending on the kind of account you have. Like most ISPs, however, EarthLink provides Web space to its customers so that they can publish Web pages that are primarily personal in nature. Yes, you *can* publish a business Web site, and EarthLink won't complain or cancel your account. But it really suggests that business users "spring" for special business services that include oodles of Web space, support for forms and CGI scripts, and a "vanity" URL of the `www.company.com` variety.

EarthLink offers a StarterSite package ($19.95 per month plus $25 setup fee), which provides individual users with the following Web hosting options:

- 200MB of storage space
- 30 separate e-mail accounts for personal or family members' use
- Free CGI scripts that you can run to capture information submitted in a Web page form to either an e-mail message or a file that you can read
- Site Builder, the EarthLink Web page editing tool
- Urchin, a reporting service that analyzes traffic to your site
- The ability to create Web blogs
- A Web page URL that takes the form `www.earthlink.com/~username`

What should you look for in an ISP Web hosting account, and what constitutes a good deal? For one thing, price: A rate of $19.95 per month for unlimited access and 50 to 100MB (or even 200MB with StarterSite) of Web site space is a pretty good deal. Look for a host that doesn't limit the number of Web pages that you can create. Also find one that gives you at least one e-mail address with your account and that lets you add extra addresses for a nominal fee. Finally, look for a host that gives you the ability to include Web page forms on your site so that visitors can send you feedback.

What to expect from an ISP Web hosting service

The process of setting up a Web site varies from ISP to ISP. Here are some general features that you should look for, based on my experience with my own ISP:

- **Web page editor:** You don't necessarily need to choose a provider that gives you a free Web page editor. You can easily download and install the editor of your choice. I tend to use one of two programs, either Microsoft FrontPage or Macromedia Dreamweaver, to create Web pages. (I describe both programs later in this chapter.)

- **Password and username:** When my Web pages are ready to go online, I get to use the same username and password to access my Web site space that I use when I dial up to connect to the Internet. Although you don't need to enter a password to view a Web site through a browser (well, at least at most sites), you do need a password to protect your site from being accessed with an FTP program. Otherwise, anyone can enter your Web space and tamper with your files.

- **FTP software:** When I signed up for a hosting account, I received a CD-ROM containing a basic set of software programs, including a Web browser and an FTP program. FTP is the simplest and easiest-to-use software to transfer files from one location to another on the Internet. When I access my Web site space from my Macintosh, I use an FTP program called Fetch. From my PC, I use a program called WS-FTP. Cute FTP (www.cuteftp.com) is another program that many Web site owners use, which costs $39.95. Most FTP programs are available for free on the Internet or can be purchased for a nominal fee.

- **URL:** When you set up a Web site by using your ISP, you're assigned a directory on a Web server. The convention for naming this directory is ~username. The ~username designation goes at the end of your URL for your Web site's home page. However, you can (and should) register a shorter URL with a domain name registrar, such as Network Solutions. You can then "point" the domain name to your ISP's server so that it can serve as an "alias" URL for your site.

After you have your software tools together and have a user directory on your ISP's Web server, it's time to put your Web site together. Basically, when I want to create or revise content for my Web site, I open the page in my Web page editor, make the changes, save the changes, and then transfer the files to my ISP's directory with my FTP program. Finally, I review the changes in my browser.

What's the ISP difference?

What's the big difference between using a kit, such as Yahoo! Small Business, to create your site and using your own inexpensive or free software to create a site from scratch and post it on your ISP's server? It's the difference between putting together a model airplane from a kit and designing the airplane yourself. If you use a kit, you save time and trouble; your plane ends up looking pretty much like everyone else's, but you get the job done faster. If you design it yourself, you have absolute control. Your plane can look just the way you want. It takes longer to get to the end product, but you can be sure you get what you wanted.

On the other hand, three differences lie between an ISP-hosted site and a site that resides with a company that does *only* Web hosting, rather than provides Internet dialup access and other services:

  ✔ A business that does only Web hosting charges you for hosting services, whereas your ISP may not.

  ✔ A Web hosting service lets you have your own domain name (www.company.com), whereas an ISP may not. (Some ISPs require that you upgrade to a business hosting account in order to obtain the vanity address. See the "What's in a name?" sidebar for more about how Web hosting services offer an advantage in the domain-name game.)

  ✔ A Web hosting service often provides lots of frills, such as super-fast connections, one-button file transfers with Web editors such as Microsoft FrontPage, and tons of site statistics, as well as automatic backups of your Web page files.

To find out more about using a real, full-time Web hosting service, see the section, "Going for the works with a Web hosting service," later in this chapter.

Where to find an ISP

What if you don't already have an Internet service provider, or you're not happy with the one you have? On today's Internet, you can't swing a mouse without hitting an ISP. How do you find the one that's right for you? In general, you want to look for the provider that offers you the least expensive service with the fastest connection and the best options available for your Web site.

Bigger doesn't necessarily mean cheaper or better; many regional or local ISPs provide good service at rates that are comparable to the giants such as Verio or EarthLink. When you're shopping around for an ISP, be sure to ask the following types of questions:

✔ What types of connections do you offer?

✔ How many dialup numbers do you have?

✔ What is your access range? (Do you provide only local coverage, or regional or international coverage as well?)

✔ What type of tech support do you offer? Do you accept phone calls or e-mail inquiries around the clock or only during certain hours? Are real human beings always available on call or are clients sent to a phone message system?

Some Web sites are well known for listing ISPs by state or by the services they offer. Here are a few good starting points in your search for the ideal ISP:

✔ **The List:** This site lists about 8,000 ISPs. You can search the list by area code or by country code, or you can focus on the United States or Canada.

`thelist.internet.com`

✔ **Yahoo's List of Internet Access Providers:** This is a good source for directories of national and international ISPs.

`dir.yahoo.com/Business_and_Economy/Business_to_Business/`
`Communications_and_Networking/Internet_and_World_Wide_`
`Web/Network_Service_Providers/Internet_Service_Providers_`
`ISPs_/`

Going for the works with a Web hosting service

After you've had your site online for a while with a free Web host, such as AOL (which is free if you have an AOL account) or Yahoo! GeoCities, you may well decide that you need more room, more services (such as Web site statistics), and a faster connection that can handle many visitors at one time. In that case, you want to locate your online business with a full-time Web hosting service.

As the preceding sections attest, many kinds of businesses now host Web sites. But in this case, I'm defining *Web hosting service* as a company whose primary mission is to provide space on Web servers for individual, nonprofit, and commercial Web sites.

What to look for in a Web host

Along with providing lots of space for your HTML, image, and other files (typically, you get anywhere from 50 to 500MB of space), Web hosting services offer a variety of related services, including some or all the following:

- ✓ **E-mail addresses:** You're likely to be able to get several e-mail addresses for your own or your family members' personal use. Besides that, many Web hosts give you special e-mail addresses called *auto-responders*. These are e-mail addresses, such as `info@yourcompany.com`, that you can set up to automatically return a text message or a file to anyone looking for information.

- ✓ **Domain names:** Virtually all the hosting options that I mention in this chapter give customers the option of obtaining a short domain name, such as `www.mycompany.com`. But some Web hosts simplify the process by providing domain-name registration in their flat monthly rates.

- ✓ **Web page software:** Some hosting services include Web page authoring/ editing software, such as Microsoft FrontPage. Some Web hosting services even offer Web page forms that you can fill out online in order to create your own online shopping catalog. All you have to provide is a scanned image of the item you want to sell, along with a price and a description. You submit the information to the Web host, who then adds the item to an online catalog that's part of your site.

- ✓ **Multimedia/CGI scripts:** One big thing that sets Web hosting services apart from other hosts is the ability to serve complex and memory-intensive content, such as RealAudio sound files or RealVideo video clips. They also let you process Web page forms that you include on your site by executing computer programs called *CGI scripts*. These programs receive the data that someone sends you (such as a customer service request or an order form) and present the data in readable form, such as a text file, e-mail message, or an entry in a database. See Chapter 6 for more about how to set up and use forms and other interactive Web site features.

- ✓ **Shopping cart software:** If part of your reason for going online is to sell specific items, look for a Web host that can streamline the process for you. Most organizations provide you with Web page forms that you can fill out to create sale items and offer them in an online shopping cart, for example.

- ✓ **Automatic data backups:** Some hosting services automatically back up your Web site data to protect you against data loss — an especially useful feature because disaster recovery is important. The automatic nature of the backups frees you from the worry and trouble of doing it manually.

✔ **Site statistics:** Virtually all Web hosting services also provide you with site statistics that give you an idea (perhaps not a precisely accurate count, but a good estimate) of how many visitors you have received. Even better is access to software reports that analyze and graphically report where your visitors are from, how they found you, which pages on your site are the most frequently viewed, and so on.

✔ **Shopping and electronic commerce features:** If you plan to give your customers the ability to order and purchase your goods or services online by using their credit cards, be sure to look for a Web host that provides you with secure commerce options. A *secure server* is a computer that can encrypt sensitive data (such as credit card numbers) that the customer sends to your site. For a more detailed discussion of secure electronic commerce, see Chapter 7.

Having so many hosting options available is the proverbial blessing and curse. It's good that you have so many possibilities and that the competition is so fierce because that can keep prices down. On the other hand, deciding which host is best for you can be difficult. In addition to asking about the preceding list of features, here are a few more questions to ask prospective Web hosts about their services to help narrow the field:

✔ **Do you limit file transfers?** Many services charge a monthly rate for a specific amount of electronic data that is transferred to and from your site. Each time a visitor views a page, that user is actually downloading a few kilobytes of data in order to view it. If your Web pages contain, say, 1MB of text and images and you get 1,000 visitors per month, your site accounts for 1GB of data transfer per month. If your host allocates you less than 1GB per month, it will probably charge you extra for the amount you go over the limit.

✔ **What kind of connection do you have?** Your site's Web page content appears more quickly in Web browser windows if your server has a super-fast T1 or T3 connection. Ask your ISP what kind of connection *it* has to the Internet. If you have a DSL line, speeds differ depending on the ISP: You might get a fast 1.5MBps connection or a more common 684Kbps connection. Make sure you're getting the fastest connection you can afford.

✔ **Will you promote my site?** Some hosting services (particularly online shopping malls) help publicize your site by listing you with Internet search indexes and search services so that visitors are more likely to find you.

What's in a name?

Most hosts assign you a URL that leads to your directory (or folder) on the Web server. For example, my account with my ISP includes space on a Web server where I can store my Web pages, and the address looks like this:

`http://homepage.xo.com/~gholden`

This is a common form of URL that many Web hosts use. It means that my Web pages reside in a directory called `~gholden` on a computer named `homepage`. The computer, in turn,

resides in my provider's domain on the Internet: `xo.com`.

However, for an extra fee, some Web hosts allow you to choose a shorter domain name, provided that the one you want to use isn't already taken by another site. For example, if I'd paid extra for a full-fledged business site, my provider would have let me have a catchier, more memorable address, like this:

`www.gregholden.com`

Besides these, the other obvious questions that you would ask of any contractor apply to Web hosting services as well. These include questions like: "How long have you been in business?" and "Can you suggest customers who will give me a reference?"

The fact that I include a screen shot of a particular Web hosting service's site in this chapter or elsewhere in this book doesn't mean that I'm endorsing or recommending that particular organization. Shop around carefully and find the one that's best for you. Check out the hosts with the best rates and most reliable service. Visit some other sites that they host and e-mail the owners of those sites for their opinion of their hosting service.

Competition is tough among hosting services, which means that prices are going down. But it also means that hosting services may seem to promise the moon in order to get your business. Be sure to read the fine print and talk to the host before you sign a contract, and always get statements about technical support and backups in writing.

What's it gonna cost?

Because of the ongoing competition in the industry, prices for Web hosting services vary widely. If you look in the classified sections in the back of magazines that cover the Web or the whole Internet, you'll see adds for hosting services costing from $9.95 to $24.95 per month. Chances are, these prices are for a basic level of service: Web space, e-mail addresses, domain name, and software. This may be all you need.

The second level of service provides CGI script processing, the ability to serve audio and video files on your site, regular backups, and extensive site statistics, as well as consultants who can help you design and configure your site. This more sophisticated range of features typically runs from $20 per month up to $100 or more per month. At Hosting.com, for instance, you can conduct secure electronic commerce on your site as part of hosting packages that cost between $19.95 and $99.95 per month. MySQL database support starts at $59 per month.

Fun with Tools: Choosing a Web Page Editor

A woodworker has his or her favorite hammer and saw. A cook has an array of utensils and pots and pans. Likewise, a Web site creator has software programs that facilitate the presentation of words, colors, images, and multimedia in Web browsers.

A little HTML is a good thing — but just a little. Knowing HTML comes in handy when you need to add elements that Web page editors don't handle. Some programs, for example, don't provide you with easy buttons or menu options for adding <META> tags, which enable you to add keywords or descriptions to a site so that search engines can find them and describe your site correctly.

If you really want to get into HTML or to find out more about creating Web pages, read *HTML 4 For Dummies,* 4th Edition, by Ed Tittel and Natanya Pitts, or *Creating Web Pages For Dummies,* 6th Edition, by Bud Smith and Arthur Bebak (both by Wiley).

It pays to spend time choosing a Web page editor that has the right qualities. What qualities should you look for in a Web page tool, and how do you know which tool is right for you? To help narrow the field, I've divided this class of software into different levels of sophistication. Pick the type of program that best fits your technical skill.

For the novice: Use your existing programs

A growing number of word processing, graphics, and business programs are adding HTML to their list of capabilities. You may already have one of these programs at your disposal. By using a program with which you're already comfortable, you can avoid having to install a Web page editor.

Here are some programs that enable you to generate one type of content and then give you the option of outputting that content in HTML, which means that your words or figures can appear on a Web page:

- ✔ **Microsoft Word:** The most recent versions of the venerable word processing standby work pretty much seamlessly with Web page content. You can open Web pages from within Word and save Word files in Web page format.

- ✔ **Adobe PageMaker/Quark Xpress:** The most recent versions of these two popular page layout programs let you save the contents of a document as HTML — only the words and images are transferred to the Web, however; any special typefaces become generic Web standard headings.

- ✔ **Microsoft Office XP or 2003:** Word, Excel, and PowerPoint all give users the option of exporting content to Web pages.

- ✔ **WordPerfect and Presentations 12:** These two component programs within Corel's suite of tools let you save files as an HTML page or a PDF file that you can present on the Web. If you have chosen to present one slide per Web page, the program adds clickable arrows to each slide in your presentation so that viewers can skip from one slide to another.

Although these solutions are convenient, they probably won't completely eliminate the need to use a Web page editor. Odds are, you'll still need to make corrections and do special formatting after you convert your text to HTML.

For intermediate needs: User-friendly Web editors

If you're an experienced Web surfer and eager to try out a simple Web editor, try a program that lets you focus on your site's HTML and textual content, provides you with plenty of functionality, and is still easy to use. Here are some user-friendly programs that arc inexpensive (or, better yet, free), yet allow you to create a functional Web site.

The following programs don't include some of the bells and whistles you need to create complex, interactive forms, format a page using frames, or access a database of information from one of your Web pages. These goodies are served up by Web page editors that have a higher level of functionality, which I describe in the upcoming section for advanced commerce sites.

BBEdit

If you work on a Macintosh and you're primarily concerned with textual content, BBEdit is one of the best choices you can make for a Web page tool. It lives up to its motto: "It doesn't suck." BBEdit is tailored to use the Mac's highly visual interface, and version 8 will run on the Mac OS 10.3.5 or later. You can use Macintosh drag and drop to add an image file to a Web page in progress by dragging the image's icon into the main BBEdit window, for example. Find out more about BBEdit at the Bare Bones Software, Inc. Web site (www.barebones.com/products/bbedit/index.html).

Other good choices of Web editors for the Macintosh are Taco HTML Edit by Taco Software (www.tacosw.com) or PageSpinner by Optima System (www.optima-system.com).

Macromedia HomeSite

HomeSite is an affordable tool for Web site designers who feel at ease working with HTML code. However, HomeSite isn't just an HTML code editor. It provides a visual interface so that you can work with graphics and preview your pages layout. HomeSite also provides you with step-by-step utilities called *wizards* to quickly create pages, tables, frames, and JavaScript elements. A version of HomeSite is bundled with Macromedia Dreamweaver MX 2004, the latest version of the Dreamweaver Web site editor. HomeSite is also available as a standalone program that works with Windows 98 or later; find out more about it at www.macromedia.com/software/homesite.

Microsoft FrontPage Express

Microsoft doesn't support FrontPage Express anymore, but if you still use Windows 98 and you're on a tight budget, give it a try. The software comes bundled with Windows 98 and you don't have to do a thing to install it. Just choose Start⇨Programs⇨Internet Explorer⇨FrontPage Express to open FrontPage Express.

CoffeeCup HTML Editor

CoffeeCup HTML Editor, by CoffeeCup Software (www.coffeecup.com), is a popular Windows Web site editor that contains a lot of features for a small price ($49). You can begin typing and formatting text by using the CoffeeCup HTML Editor menu options. You can add an image by clicking the Insert Image toolbar button, or use the Forms toolbar to create the text boxes and radio buttons that make up an interactive Web page form. You can even add JavaScript effects and choose from a selection of clip art images that come with the software.

CoffeeCup HTML Editor doesn't let you explore database connectivity, add Web components, or other bonuses that come with a program like FrontPage or Dreamweaver. But it does have everything you need to create a basic Web page.

Netscape Composer

When I read reviews of Web page software, I don't often see Netscape Composer included in the list. But to me, it's an ideal program for an entrepreneur on a budget. Why? Let me spell it out for you: F-R-E-E.

Netscape Composer is the Web page editing and authoring tool that comes with Netscape 7.2 as well as earlier versions. All you have to do is download one of these packages from the Netscape Browser Central page (`channels.netscape.com/ns/browsers/default.jsp`), and Composer is automatically installed on your computer along with Navigator (the Netscape Web browser) and several other Internet programs.

With Composer, you can create sophisticated layout elements, such as tables (which I discuss further in Chapter 5), with an easy-to-use graphical interface. After you edit a page, you can preview it in Navigator with the click of a button. Plus, you can publish all your files by choosing a single menu item. If you already have Navigator installed, check out Composer right now!

For advanced commerce sites: Programs that do it all

If you plan to do a great deal of business online, or even to add the title of Web designer to your list of talents (as some of the entrepreneurs profiled in this book have done), it makes sense to spend some money up front and use a Web page tool that can do everything you want — today and for years to come.

The advanced programs that I describe here go beyond the simple designation of Web page editors. They not only let you edit Web pages but also help you add interactivity to your site, link dynamically updated databases to your site, and keep track of how your site is organized and updated. Some programs (notably, FrontPage) can even transfer your Web documents to your Web host with a single menu option. This way, you get to concentrate on the fun part of running an online business — meeting people, taking orders, processing payments, and the like.

Macromedia Dreamweaver

What's that you say? You can never hear enough bells and whistles? The cutting edge is where you love to walk? Then Dreamweaver, a Web authoring tool by Macromedia (www.macromedia.com), is for you. Dreamweaver is a feature-rich, professional piece of software.

Dreamweaver's strengths aren't so much in the basic features such as making selected text bold, italic, or a different size; rather, Dreamweaver excels in producing Dynamic HTML (which makes Web pages more interactive through scripts) and HTML style sheets. Dreamweaver has ample FTP (File Transfer Protocol) settings, and it gives you the option of seeing the HTML codes you're working within one window and the formatting of your Web page within a second, WYSIWYG window. The latest version, Dreamweaver MX 2004, is a complex and powerful piece of software. It lets you create Active Server pages, connect to the ColdFusion database, and contains lots of templates and wizards. Dreamweaver is available for both Windows and Macintosh computers; find out more at the Macromedia Web site (www.macromedia.com/software/dreamweaver).

Editors that'll flip your whizzy-wig

Web browsers are multilingual; they understand exotic-sounding languages such as FTP, HTTP, and GIF, among others. But one language browsers don't speak is English. Browsers don't understand instructions such as "Put that image there" or "Make that text italic." HyperText Markup Language, or HTML, is a translator, if you will, between human languages and Web languages.

If the thought of HTML strikes fear into your heart, relax. Thanks to modern Web page creation tools, you don't have to master HTML in order to create Web pages. Although knowing a little HTML does come in handy at times, you can depend on these special user-friendly tools to do almost all your English-to-HTML translations for you.

The secret of these Web page creation tools is their WYSIWYG (pronounced whizzy-wig) display. WYSIWYG stands for "What You See Is What You Get." A WYSIWYG editor lets you see on-screen how your page will look when it's on the Web, rather than force you to type (or even see) HTML commands like this:

```
<H1> This is a Level 1 Heading
     </H1>
<IMG SRC = "lucy.gif"> <BR>
<P>This is an image of
     Lucy.</P>
```

A WYSIWYG editor, such as CoffeeCup HTML Editor for Windows (www.coffeecup.com), shows you how the page appears even as you assemble it. Besides that, it lets you format text and add images by means of familiar software shortcuts such as menus and buttons.

Microsoft FrontPage

FrontPage (`www.microsoft.com/frontpage`) is a powerful Web authoring tool that has some unique e-commerce capabilities. For one thing, it provides you with a way to organize a Web site visually. The main FrontPage window is divided into two sections. On the left, you see the Web page on which you're currently working. On the right, you see a treelike map of all the pages on your site, arranged visually to show which pages are connected to each other by hyperlinks.

Another nice thing about FrontPage — something that you're sure to find helpful if you haven't been surfing the Web or working with Web pages for very long — is the addition of wizards and templates. The FrontPage wizards enable you to create a discussion area on your site where your visitors can post messages to one another. The wizards also help you connect to a database or design a page with frames. (See Chapter 5 for more about creating frames.)

If you want to create an e-commerce Web site hosted by Microsoft Small Business Center, you can download and install an auxiliary program FrontPage calls an add-in that enables you to create a sales catalog and upload the files to bCentral, all from within FrontPage.

Adobe GoLive

GoLive, a highly popular Web page tool by Adobe Systems Incorporated (`www.adobe.com/products/golive/main.html`), is an especially good choice if you want to exert a high level of control over how your Web page looks. It helps you make use of the latest HTML style-sheet commands that precisely control the positioning of text and images on a page.

GoLive (which is available in versions for Windows 2000 and XP and for the Macintosh OS X versions 10.2.4 through 10.3) is especially well integrated with Adobe Photoshop and Illustrator, two popular and sophisticated graphics programs. Like Dreamweaver, GoLive supports server technologies such as ASP, JSP, and PHP, which enable you to create active, dynamic Web sites. You can even create Web pages that are especially formatted for wireless devices, such as PDAs and Web-enabled cell phones.

Chapter 4

Exploiting New Ways to Build Business

*W*hen you open up shop on the Internet, you don't just begin to operate in isolation. The whole point of the Internet is interconnection. That plays out for businesses just as it does for individuals. Whether you realize it or not, you're not alone. You have access to thousands, even millions, of other businesses that are in the same situation you are — or that went through the same kinds of uncertainties you're encountering before they achieved success.

The fact that you're online means that you enjoy advantages over businesses operating solely in the brick-and-mortar marketplace. You can overcome the usual limitations of time and geography that previously would have limited how many potential customers you could actually reach. You can communicate using tools such as e-mail and blogging that don't have a counterpart in the offline world. Finally, you have access to services such as search engines that can help you find suppliers and do business research and marketing. This chapter provides you with a user friendly overview of the many new opportunities available to you when you start an online business, including tools, services, and opportunities for partnering so that you can advertise your new endeavor in ways that help you break through to success without breaking your budget.

Advantages of Doing Business Online

Sometimes, the key to success is simply being aware of all the opportunities that are available to you. The worst reason you can have for going online is a blind "everybody's doing it" mindset. Instead of focusing narrowly on one way of advertising or selling, take stock of all the aspects of online business that you can exploit. Then when you create your Web site, select a payment option, or set up security measures as described in succeeding chapters, and you'll do things right the first time around. The sections that follow describe some advantages you need to make part of your business plan.

Operating 24/7

One of the first reasons why entrepreneurs flocked to the Web was the ability to do business around the clock with customers across the globe. It still applies today: It may be 2 a.m. in your local time zone, but someone can still be making a purchase in London or Paris from your Web site or eBay Store across the globe where it's bright and early in the morning.

If you're just starting out and you're trying to reach the widest possible audience of consumers for your goods or services, be sure they are

- ✔ **Small:** That means they're easy to pack and easy to ship.
- ✔ **Something that people need and can use worldwide:** DVDs, CDs, computer products, action figures, and sports memorabilia will appeal to many.
- ✔ **Something that people can't find in their local area:** Many sites resell gourmet foodstuffs from their home region that can't easily be found overseas, for example.

Make sure that you appeal to a *small, niche segment* of individuals around the world. The things that tend to sell best online are things that people love and are passionate about — specialty items like gourmet foods, rare beers and wines, hard-to-find movies, old toys, and anything sold as a "limited edition."

See the section on marketing to a worldwide audience in Chapter 15 for suggestions on how to reach overseas consumers in their own languages, and how to observe trade rules and restrictions that may apply.

If you do sell DVDs online, be aware that DVD players are required to include codes that prevent the playback of DVDs in geographical regions where movies have not been released to video as yet. A disc purchased in one country might not play on a player purchased in another country. You need to pay attention to the codes assigned to the DVDs you sell so your customers will actually be able to play them.

Communicating with new tools

Nothing beats e-mail, in my opinion, for reaching customers in a timely and friendly way. I know all about the immediacy of talking to people over the phone. But phone calls can be intrusive, and most consumers are wary of anyone who wants to market to them with an unsolicited phone call that interrupts their daily activities. E-mail messages can come in at any time of the day or night, but they don't necessarily interrupt what the customers are doing. And if customers have already made a purchase from your company, they might welcome a follow-up contact by e-mail. And customers have the luxury of being able to respond to you at their own convenience. Not only that, but e-mail messages can contain links to products and services on your Web site, and even entire newsletters that inform whoppers of new product offerings.

One of the most popular online communications systems, Instant Messaging (IM), is useful for keeping in touch with business partners and co-workers. But it can be the kiss of death for approaching current or potential customers. Consumers are used to dropping everything to answer instant messages from friends. When they discover that it's a marketing message, they are going to be turned off and downright hostile.

Besides e-mail newsletters, what kinds of communications strategies work with online shoppers? The sections that follow give a few suggestions.

Giving away a free sample

I was in the grocery store the other day, looking at a hunk of cheese that cost $13.99 a pound, and wishing I could open up the package and taste-test that expensive curd before I plunked down the big bucks for it. The concept of the "free sample" is one that Web surfers love. Newspapers like the Chicago Tribune do it by making the first paragraph or two of archived articles available online; if you want to read the rest, you are asked to pay a nominal fee. Amazon.com makes brief excerpts of selected CD tracks available on its Web site so shoppers can listen to the music before deciding whether or not to buy the CD.

On the Internet, software producers have been giving away free samples for many years in the form of computer *shareware:* software programs that users can download and use for a specified period of time. After the time period expires, the consumers are asked (or required, if the program ceases to function) to pay a shareware fee if they want to keep the program. A tiny Texas company called id Software started giving away a stripped-down computer game on the Internet back in 1993, in the hope of getting users hooked on it so they would pay for the full-featured version. The plan worked, and since then more than 100,000 customers have paid as much as $40 for a full copy of the game, which is called Doom. id Software has gone on to create and sell many other popular games since.

Giving out discounts

One reason shoppers turn to the Internet is to save money. Thanks to sites such as Amazon.com, which routinely knock money off the list price of books and other media, shoppers are used to expecting some sort of discount from the Internet. They'll love it if you offer special "Internet only" prices on your Web site, or give them coupons to print out and take to your store, like the coupon provided by the tiny basement music store Schoolkids Records in Exile in Ann Arbor, Michigan (see Figure 4-1).

Figure 4-1:
Coupons, discounts, and Internet-only specials can drive customers to your brick-and-mortar store.

Giving customers the chance to talk back

The ability to interact with customers and give them the opportunity to actively participate in the way a company manufactures and markets its products is a relatively new and exciting trend. One company that's been putting customers in charge for many years is Timbuk2, the manufacturer of those tricolored bicycle shoulder bags you've probably seen around town. When I wrote an article about Timbuk2 a few years ago, the company let me design my own bag, which they shipped to me in a matter of a couple of days. You, too, can pick out colors, logos, and special features like cell phone holders for your shoulder bags through the company's Build Your Own Bag feature (`www.timbuk2.com/tb2/byob.t2`). As shown in Figure 4-2, you tell the company exactly what you want; you confirm the price; you pay online; and the bag is manufactured for you immediately on the factory floor.

A shoe designer named John Fluevog is doing the same thing as Timbuk2, only with footwear. He offers "open source footwear" through his entertaining Web site (`www.fluevog.com/files/os-1.html`). You pick the style and colors, send the form to Fluevog, and he manufactures the one-of-a-kind shoes just for you.

Figure 4-2: The Web enables manufacturers to put customers in charge of the design process.

A number of forward-looking companies are building their reputations by letting customers voice opinions and make suggestions online. The shoe and sporting apparel manufacturer Nike isn't exactly a small business, but it's taken a leading position in building community among its customers. Every week a live chat session is held for Nike customers. Discussion boards are also available; the site (www.nikechat.com) boasts more than 33,000 registered members and a total of 3.5 million messages posted.

Chat doesn't make sense unless you have a solid user base of at least several hundred regular users who feel passionately about your goods and services and are dedicated enough to want to type real-time messages to one another and to you. However, discussion groups are practical, even for small businesses; you can set them up with a discussion area through Microsoft FrontPage or on Yahoo! (groups.yahoo.com). Find out more about making your Web site more interactive in Chapter 6.

Taking advantage of micropayments' rebirth

Credit card payments make the Web a viable place for e-commerce. But the cost of the typical credit card transaction makes payments of less than $1 pointless. The popular payment service PayPal (www.paypal.com) charges 2.9 percent plus a 30-cent fee for each sale, which makes it impractical for content providers to sell something for, say, 20 or 30 cents. Such small transactions are known as *micropayments*. In the early dot-com days, the term "micropayment" was thrown around quite a bit, both by writers like me and by companies hoping they could induce Web surfers to pay small amounts of money for bits of online content. Many of those companies failed to find success and disappeared, in part because the process of setting up micropayments was cumbersome and highly technical.

Today, micropayment systems are attempting a comeback. A large percentage of Web surfers have high-speed broadband connections and are used to paying for content online. A system called BitPass brings small payments to more than 100 Web sites. There's much more content online, including articles, music clips, and cartoons, that could only be sold for small amounts of money. If your business involves text, music, art, or other kinds of content, you may be able to make a few cents for your work by using one of the following payment services:

✔ **Peppercoin:** This company (www.peppercoin.com) tackles the problem of credit card transaction costs by allowing customers to combine a number of small payments before the card is charged. The company says that for a 99-cent transaction, its fees amount to 10 cents or less.

- ✔ **Yaga:** This company (www.yaga.com) handles micropayments such as the $2.50 or so that Tribune Company and Time.com charge for archived articles. It also provides for aggregation of payments, and specializes in splitting payments among copyright holders, merchants, and affiliates.

- ✔ **PaymentOne:** This company (www.paymentone.com) has relationships with more than 1,400 Local Exchange Carriers (LECs). This enables the company to let consumers charge small online purchases to their phone bills through its PhoneBill product.

- ✔ **RedPaper.com:** This company (www.redpaper.com) lets content providers sell prose, poetry, and essays online for as little as a few cents each.

If you can link your Web site, eBay Store, or other venues to your offerings on these micropayment sites, you begin to achieve synergy: your various sales sites point to one another and build attention for your overall sales efforts.

Auctioning off your professional services

There's nothing new about making a living selling your design, consultation, or other professional services. But the Internet provides you with new and innovative ways to get the word out about your products and services. Along with having your own Web site in which you describe your experience, provide samples of your work, and make references to clients you've helped, you can find new clients by auctioning off your services in what's known as a *reverse auction*. In a reverse auction, the provider of goods or services doesn't initiate a transaction — rather, the customer does.

A reverse auction site called Elance Online (go to www.elance.com and click Elance Online) enables professional contractors to offer their services and bid on jobs. The site is ideal if you don't offer bits of content, such as stories or articles, but usually charge by the hour or by the job for your services. In this case, the customer is typically a company that needs design, writing, construction, or technical work. The company posts a description of the job on the Elance site. Essentially, it's a Request for Bids or Request for Proposals: Freelancers who have already registered with the site then make bids on the job. The company's purchasing officer can then choose the lowest bid, or choose another company based on its qualifications.

 It's free for organizations that have jobs to offer to post their projects online. However, contractors have to subscribe in order to be listed on the site and bid on those projects. You have to pay an 8.75 percent fee to Elance if you are chosen to perform a job. The least expensive package that enables you to bid on projects for which you are qualified, the Enhanced Listing package, cost $12 to $30 per month depending on the type of work you do. Find out more at

www.elance.com/c/static/main/displayhtml.pl?file=rate_card.html&rid=93G4

Exploring New Products and Services You Can Sell

E-commerce works when merchants give customers a choice. You provide information about you and your products that allows shoppers to find out more. Hopefully, they'll make the ultimate choice to purchase something from you, but that depends on choices you have made beforehand. The choices you make when you first get started in e-commerce have an impact on the success with which you reach your targeted customers. One of the main choices is determining what you plan to sell online. Because you have made the decision to sell on the Internet, chances are good that you're a technology-savvy businessperson. You're open to new technologies and new ways of selling. The twenty-first century has seen an explosion in products and services that were unheard of just a decade or so ago. If you can take advantages of one of these opportunities, you increase your potential customer base.

Providing music files and other creative work

Today's online customers are quite sophisticated about shopping online. You can make your music or audio clips available online from your Web site. The easiest option is to use your computer or a digital tape recorder to make the recording and save the file in `.wav` (Waveform Audio Format), MP3, `.ram` (RealAudio), or `.wma` (Windows Media Audio). Chances are excellent that your visitors have one or more media players that can process and play at least one of these types of files.

The rock group Wilco (which hails from my own town, Chicago) helped revolutionize the way music is sold online. When Wilco's album *Yankee Hotel Foxtrot* was rejected by their big-time record company (oddly enough, the supposedly media-savvy AOL Time Warner), the group's members took matters into their own hands and decided to sell the record on their Web site (`www.wilcoworld.net`). They also made a number of songs available online for free. Eventually, they signed with an independent record label. The fact that they made the record available online started a "buzz" for it, and this valuable word-of-mouth traffic made the album one of the best-selling albums of 2003. Since then, many other groups have decided to make their music available online.

The biggest success story, in terms of getting music online, is of course Apple's marketplace iTunes (`www.apple.com/itunes`). Groups like Wilco routinely provide links to their albums on the iTunes music site, where you can download each track separately for 99 cents each. But if you're just starting out in the biz, you can digitize your audio files and post them online so others can download them.

Groceries and other household services

Small, easily shipped merchandise like golf balls or tools are undeniably well suited to online sales. But your online business doesn't need to be restricted to such items. Even perishable items like foodstuffs can be and frequently are purchased online. Initially, the field attracted *pure plays* — companies such as Webvan that devoted their sales activities solely to the Internet. They failed to compete with brick-and-mortar stores.

The good news is that traditional brick-and-mortar grocery stores are finding success by marketing their products on the Web as a way of supplementing their traditional retail sales. Independent food producers such as Schwan's (www.schwans.com), based in Marshall, Minnesota, are now able to deliver in their local area to customers who order on their Web sites. Other food providers, such as FamilyChef.com (www.familychef.com, as shown in Figure 4-3) deliver nationwide via FedEx.

The Food Marketing Institute (www.fmi.org) has studied why shoppers decide to buy groceries online; the study showed that the main reasons are

✔ Cost savings

✔ Convenience

✔ Greater product variety

Figure 4-3: Regional grocers and food producers are widening their customer bases thanks to the Web.

If you are able to offer food items that consumers can't find elsewhere, and at a competitive price, you should consider selling food online. People hate negotiating parking lots and waiting in long lines at the checkout counters of traditional supermarkets. People who live alone and who have difficulty getting out (such as the elderly or sick) naturally turn to buying their groceries online.

Are you interested in reaching online grocery shoppers online? A paper by the online journal First Monday (`www.firstmonday.dk/issues/issue7_9/kempiak`) examines the rise, fall, and rise of the online grocery industry and provides tips on what consumers are looking for when they pick out groceries with their keyboard and mouse. Also check out the Food Marketing Institute's report "The e-Tail Experience: What Grocery Shoppers Think about Online Shopping 2000 – Executive Summary" at `www.fmi.org/e_business/etailexperience.htm`.

Exploring m-commerce

The needs and habits of consumers drive what sells best online. These days, consumers are going online in many more ways than just sitting at a computer — that is, they're branching out from e-commerce to *m-commerce* (mobile commerce). Consumers are using their cell phones, PDAs, and pocket computers to connect to cyberspace. Retailers are hungry to reach these "wired" prospects any way they can; here are just two examples:

✔ **Cell phone ring tones:** I get a very negative reaction when I receive unsolicited ads over my cell phone. What kinds of selling *do* work online? Here's an example: When I first got my spiffy new Web-enabled Nokia 6820 cell phone, I thought it would be fun to get some gimmicks for the kids (at least, I told them the gimmicks were for them; they were for me, too). I went online and downloaded a ring tone that was available on my phone, and I later purchased a game that could be played on my phone as well.

✔ **Photos and graphics:** I did a search around my own cell phone's version of the Web (mMode, the online network provided by the merger of AT&T and Cingular Wireless) and discovered that the main items you can purchase are games to play on your cell phone and ring tones that your cell phone can emit. Some hunting within the Games & Ring Tones category uncovered a group of graphic images from Wallpaper Universe by a mobile content provider called FunMail (`www.funmail.com`). If you can draw some simple graphics and format them by using Wireless Markup Language (WML) or a development tool such as the Java 2 Platform, Micro Edition (J2ME) you, too, can create content for the growing cell phone and hand-held market.

Online Content and Commentary

Plenty of traditional publications have discovered that they can supplement home delivery and newsstand sales by providing some parts of their content online on a subscription-only basis. Typically, some of the content is available for free, while other stories are designated as *premium content* that are made available only to subscribers who have paid to subscribe to the site and enter a valid username and password. The online versions of the *Wall Street Journal* (www.wsj.com) and *New York Times* (www.nytimes.com) both have premium content that is available only to paying subscribers.

Technically, it's not as difficult as you may think to make some content on your Web site publicly available and some content restricted only to those who have a username and password. Most Web server software enables Webmasters to designate certain directories as password protected and others as freely available. If you're technically savvy and decide to operate your own Web server, you can use the open-source application Apache to password-protect some parts of your Web site. The tricky part is not in restricting the content but in creating the system that enables buyers to assign themselves usernames and passwords and pay for their subscriptions in the first place. It's best to hire a Web designer or sign up with an e-commerce hosting service with support staff that can lead you through the process of setting up such systems.

Blogging to build your brand

People have been speaking their minds for fun and profit for as long as there have been media to broadcast their words. Think about comedians like Will Rogers, Richard Prior, and Lenny Bruce. What would they have done in the age of the Internet? They would have started their own blogs, that's what.

A *Web log* (*blog* for short) is a type of online journal or diary that can be frequently updated. Blogs can be about anything in particular or nothing at all: You can blog about your daily activities or travels and let your family and friends know what you've been up to lately, or you can get your views and opinions out in the world and develop a community of like-minded readers. Many blogs consist of commentary by individuals who gather news items or cool Web pages and make them available to their friends (or strangers who happen upon their blogs). This, in fact, was the original idea behind blogs, and the concept followed by many of the most popular ones: highlighting little-known Web sites or articles or stores in the media that readers are too busy to read, and providing alternative views and commentary about those Web sites, news stories, or other current events.

Is it really possible to make a living by blogging? It is certainly possible to supplement one's income this way. Andrew Sullivan, who writes Daily Dish (`www.andrewsullivan.com`), one of the most popular blogs around, reported on his site that he was getting as many as 300,000 visitors each day in the days leading up to the presidential election of 2004, when dedicated readers like me were flocking to politically oriented blogs to get opinion and analysis. After the election, visits went down, but they still hit 100,000 a day. And Sullivan could proclaim in his blog that ad revenue from an advertising service that specializes in blogs, Blogads (`www.blogads.com`), was making it possible for him to continue.

An early blogger named Rebecca Blood has written a useful history of Weblogs at `www.rebeccablood.net/essays/weblog_history.html`. The Blogads FAQ (`www.blogads.com/publisher_html`) says that bloggers who participate in the Blogads network make an average of $50 per month in ad revenue, and some even clear as much as $5,000 per month. A Los Angeles blogger named Matt Welch gets specific about his earnings on his site (`www.mattwelch.com/archives/week_2004_01_25.html#2396`). Over a 10-month period, he had an average of 5,560 weekly visitors to his blog, and earned a total over that period of $407.66.

Finding your niche

Blogging, like anything on the Web, works when you identify a niche group and target that group by providing those people with content (or goods, or services) that they are likely to want. The challenge is finding something to say and putting time and energy into saying it on a regular basis. Although I have set up my own blog at `www.gregholden.com`, I find it difficult to devote the time and commitment for daily contributions. Yet, the most successful blogs seem to be ones that are created by people who are used to writing something every day, such as journalists. Academic faculty members who are published and well regarded in their fields also run popular blogs.

What do you feel strongly about? What do you know well? Is there something you would love to communicate and discuss every day? If so, that's what you should use to organize your blog. A blog can be about anything you like — and I mean anything. A prime example: The Appliance Blog in which an appliance repairman in Springfield, Oregon, provides a daily diary of his service calls and repairs. Along the way, he provides links to the Web sites of major appliance manufacturers as well as a forum where you can ask questions about your own appliance problems. The repairman's blog isn't a place where you can find out what he had for breakfast or what he thinks about world peace; it's focused solely on what he knows, and it's a useful resource for anyone who is having a problem with an appliance.

One of the best-known blogs was the one created by an Iraqi citizen who went by the pseudonym Salam Pax. His blog — Where is Rael? — provided a compelling account of daily life in Iraq in 2002 and 2003, during the U.S. military's campaign to topple the regime of Saddam Hussein.

How, exactly, do you start a blog? Most people sign up for an account with an online service that streamlines the process. Some of the best known are

- ✔ LiveJournal (`www.livejournal.com`)
- ✔ Movable Type (`www.movabletype.org`)
- ✔ Blogger (`www.blogger.com`)
- ✔ Typepad (`www.typepad.com`)

Two of these services are in fact related. Movable Type works by providing bloggers with a computer script written in the Perl programming language. You need to copy and install the script on the Web server that hosts the site on which you want to publish the blog. If this process is too technical for you (it probably is, unless you run your own Web server) you can do one of two things: Pay Movable Type $40 to install the software for you, or pay a monthly fee to TypePad, which is Movable Type's paid service provider.

Just a few years ago, you had to be a programmer to figure out how to create a blog on your Web page. But a number of services are available online to streamline the process for nonprogrammers like you and me. Blogger (`www.blogger.com`) lets you create your own blog for free, so it's a good place to start. Google owns Blogger, so the site enables you to participate in Google's AdWords program (see Chapter 14) as well so you might gain some revenue from your blog. As with any Web-based content, you should do some planning beforehand and write down some notes, such as

- ✔ A name for your blog
- ✔ What you want to talk about
- ✔ Some ideas for your first blog

Then follow these steps:

1. **Start up your Web browser, go to the Blogger home page (`www.blogger.com`), and click Create Your Blog Now.**

   The Create Blogger Account page appears.

2. **Fill out the form with a username, password, and e-mail address; read the terms of service; select the Acceptance of Terms check box; and click Continue.**

   The Name Your Blog page appears.

3. **Come up with a short name for your blog; add that blog to the URL supplied and click Continue.**

   For instance, if your blog is called ToolTime, your URL should be `tooltime.blogspot.com`.

   The Choose a Template page appears.

4. **Click the button beneath the graphic design (or template) you want to use, and then click Continue.**

   A page appears with a light bulb icon and the notice Creating Your Blog. . . After a few seconds, a page appears with the notice Your Blog Has Been Created!.

5. **Click Start Posting.**

   A page appears in which you type a title for your first posting and then type the posting itself (see Figure 4-4).

6. **Click the Publish Post button at the bottom of the page.**

   Your blog post is published online. That's all there is to it!

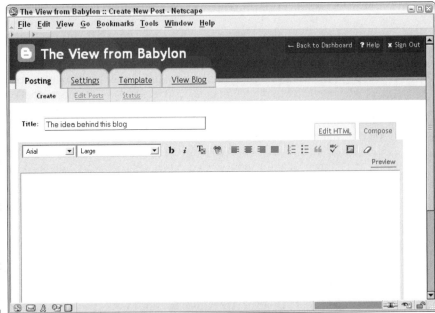

Figure 4-4:
Blogger makes it easy to create a blog for free and give it a graphic design.

Blogs that are odd, quirky, based on dramatic human-interest situations such as wartime journals, or that are politically oriented tend to be the most successful. That said, here are some ways to build up an audience for your blog:

✔ **Writing for other bloggers:** Your first audience will probably consist of family or friends, or other bloggers who live in the same geographic area or write about the same subjects you do. Contact those bloggers and ask them to exchange links with your blog; ask your other readers to spread the word about your blog, too.

✔ **Sprinkling keywords and categories:** Blogs are like other Web pages: Although their contents change frequently, search engines index them. The more keywords you include in your postings, and the greater the range of subjects you cover, the more likely you are to have your blog turn up in a set of search results.

✔ **Posting consistently:** When readers latch on to a blog they like, they visit it frequently. You need to post something — anything — on a daily basis, or at least several times a week.

✔ **Syndicating your blog:** One way of spreading the word about your blog is providing a "feed" of its latest contents, such as the headings of posts and the dates of the latest posts. This summary is automatically prepared in XML (eXtensible Markup Language) by most blogging tools. You make the feed of your blog available on its home page; sites that aggregate (in other words, collect) the feeds from many of their favorite blogs can collect them and quickly know when the blogs have been updated.

If you can make a living at blogging or at end up with some "fun money" at the end of each month, more power to you. But don't go into blogging with that attitude, or you'll lose interest right away. Look at a blog as another tool in your online business toolkit — another way of getting your message before the public, another place where you can steer visitors to your Web site or your store on eBay or Yahoo!. It makes sense to treat your blog as a venue where you talk about what you like to buy and sell online and to strike up ongoing conversations among your customers and clients. In other words, you don't generate income with a blog by selling directly to the public. You try to build up a number of loyal readers and attract advertising revenue — or simply attract more customers to your Web site.

Building Community

As an article in *E-Commerce Times* put it: "Friendship Sells." Studies consistently show that people who spend large amounts of time in community venues such as discussion forums end up spending money on the same Web site (eBay is the perfect example). It's a "value proposition," but you can't attach a specific dollar value to it.

CASE STUDY

No bells, no whistles, all trust: The beauty of Craigslist

When it comes to online communities, you'd be hard pressed to find one stronger than the devoted users who regularly post ads and respond to ads on one of the Craigslist sites around the world. Craigslist (www.craigslist.org) is a true Internet phenomenon. It was started by Craig Newmark back in 1995 as a simple e-mail newsletter announcing upcoming cultural events in Craig's hometown, San Francisco. Over time, the recipients began to use the newsletter to post notices and sell items. Then job notices were posted.

Before long, participants came to depend on Craigslist to find out what was going on in their communities, to find items for sale, or to find jobs. Newmark steadfastly refused to add flashy graphics, high-tech programming, or other features to his site. He also refused many offers to purchase his newsletter. He spent seven days a week keeping his newsletter's content reliable and free of e-mail spams and scams. His grateful visitors have since come to rely on Craigslist's content as "for real" rather than a come-on, and they faithfully trust it and use it.

The work has generated a substantial income for Craigslist. Reportedly, its annual income approaches $10 million (as reported by Newmark's assistant in an article at www.signonsandiego.com/uniontrib/20040913/news_mz1b13craig.html). That income apparently comes not from flashy banner ads or popup windows, but from users who pay to post classified ads: Employers pay from $25 to $75 to post job listings, depending on the city in which they are located. eBay recently purchased a 25 percent interest in Craigslist but has pledged not to change the design. Newmark reportedly wants eBay to help him deflect constant approaches from spammers and scammers.

What's the lesson for you? When you're just starting out, it pays to

✔ Focus on the quality of your content.

✔ Make your site useful for individuals.

✔ Develop a loyal customer or user base.

✔ Knock yourself out to keep your site up to date.

If you can turn your Web site into a resource, income will follow.

Community building on commercial Web sites doesn't necessarily involve discussion boards or chat rooms. Anything you can do to get your customers communicating with one another will do it. On Amazon.com, a kind of community feel is created by the book reviews written by individual readers and "Top 10" book lists let visitors share their views.

You can find the aforementioned *E-Commerce Times* article at `www.ecommerce times.com/story/18096.html`.

Partnerships

The notion of online community cuts both ways: It's not only for consumers who visit Web sites and join communities, but for businesspeople like you, too. Some of the liveliest and most popular online communities are eBay Groups — discussion forums started by eBay members themselves. And among those, some of the most popular are the ones in which sellers share tips and advice about boosting their online incomes, finding merchandise to sell, identifying mystery items, and so on.

Don't forget that even though you might run a business by yourself, from your home, you're not really alone. If you need some encouragement, join a discussion group, or consult the tips and resources in the Small Business Associations section of this book's Online Directory.

Market research

An estimated 135 million individuals in the U.S. are online (with an estimated 4 million new users going online for the first time in August 2004 alone, according to a Neilsen//NetRatings report summarized at

`www.clickz.com/stats/sectors/geographics/article.php/3427141`

Given the sheer number of consumers who are on the Web, it stands to reason that you can find out a lot about those individuals by going online. If you don't have any awareness of who your potential customers are and what they want, you may never get them to pull out their credit cards and make purchases from you. You can do your own market research by going online to find your customers, listen to their views in chat rooms and on discussion forums, and do some market research. Approach consumers who already buy the types of products or services that you want to sell.

Consult the Guerilla Marketing books (gmarketing.com) for insights into different ways to reach your target consumers. Also see the section about guerilla marketing and advertising strategies in Chapter 15.

The other aspect of market research that is perfectly executed with a Web browser is research into your own online competitors — businesses that already do what you hope to do. It can be discouraging, at first, to discover companies that have already cleared the trail that you hoped to blaze. But the chances of doing something absolutely unique on the Web are small or nonexistent. But use the discovery as an educational opportunity to find out whether there is a market for your product and a way to sell it that differs from existing competitors. Take note of features displayed by your competitors' Web sites, such as the following:

- ✔ **Selling:** How does the Web site do its selling? Does it sell only in one location, or does its Web site supplement eBay or Amazon.com sales or a brick-and-mortar business? Does the site make suggestions about related items that a consumer might want (a practice known as up-selling)?

- ✔ **Organization:** How is the Web site organized? Is it easy to find specific products or information about them? How many navigational aids (navigation bars, drop-down menu lists, site maps, and the like) are provided?

- ✔ **Depth:** How many levels of information are included on the Web site? The more information is offered on the site, the *stickier* (more able to hold a visitor's attention) the site becomes. Try to make your own Web site just as deep and sticky.

In your review of the competition's Web presentation, make a list of features that you can emulate as well as features you can improve on. Your goal should not be to copy the site, but to discover your own unique niche and identify customers whose needs might not be addressed by the other venue.

Don't you wish you could install a hidden microphone to eavesdrop on your customers as they surf the Web? You can do some eavesdropping, but on a different part of the Internet — namely, Usenet. *Usenet,* the part of the Internet that consists of thousands of newsgroups, is separate from the Web but can be accessed from the Web through sites such as Google Groups (groups.google.com). You can "listen in" on newsgroup discussions by finding groups that fit your type of commerce and then *lurking* — that is, reading the messages without responding to them. After acquainting yourself with the group's concerns, you can post your own newsgroup messages and begin to determine your customers' concerns more directly. Keep in mind, though, that it's important to avoid overt advertising for your business in a newsgroup, which can provoke an angry response from the group's membership.

Part II

Establishing Your Online Presence

The 5th Wave   By Rich Tennant

In this part . . .

Just as business owners in the real world have to rent or buy a facility and fix it up to conduct their businesses, you have to develop an online storefront to conduct your online business. In this part, I explain how to put a virtual roof over your store and light a cyberfire to welcome your customers. You also find out about security strategies to protect your customers' privacy. In other words, this part focuses on the nuts and bolts of your Web site itself.

The World Wide Web is the most exciting and popular place to open an online store. But merely creating a set of Web pages isn't enough to succeed online. Your site needs to be compelling — even irresistible. This part shows you how to organize your site and fill it with useful content that attracts customers in the first place and encourages them to stay to browse. I also show you how to get your pages up and running quickly, to equip your site (and yourself) to handle many different kinds of electronic purchases, and to keep improving your site so that it runs more efficiently.

Chapter 5

Giving Your Business Site Structure and Style

*N*ot so long ago, a business that was on the World Wide Web was distinctive by definition. Nowadays, it seems that every business — from the Mom and Pop corner store to the international conglomerate — is on the Web. As cyberspace fills up with small businesses trying to find their niches, standing out from the crowd and attracting attention on the Internet becomes increasingly difficult.

But the same tried and true principles apply even though Web surfers are increasingly mobile and increasingly accustomed to sophisticated content. You don't have to load your site down with scripts, animations, and flashy gimmicks. The trick is to have no trick: Keep your site simple, well organized, and content rich.

In this chapter, I present one of the best ways for a new business to attract attention online: through a clearly organized and eye-catching Web site. (Another strategy for attracting visitors — developing promotions and content that encourages interaction — is the subject of Chapter 6.)

Feng Shui Your Web Site

According to the Web site called The Geomancer (thegeomancer.netfirms. com/fengshui.htm), *Feng Shui* is the art of arranging objects in an environment to achieve (among other things) success in your career, wealth, and happiness. If that's true, you should try to practice some Feng Shui with your online business environment — that is, your Web site.

Although you may be tempted to jump right into the creation of a cool Web site, take a moment to plan. Whether you're setting off on a road trip across the nation or building a new addition for your house, you'll progress more smoothly by drawing a map of where you want to go. Do you remember when you were a tiny little nipper and did your homework with a pencil and paper? Dig down into your miscellaneous drawer until you find these ancient tools and then make a list of the elements you want to have on your site.

Look over the items on your list and break them into two or three main categories. These main categories will branch off your *home page,* which functions as the grand entrance for your online business site. You can then draw a map of your site that assumes the shape of a triangle, as shown in Figure 5-1.

Making them fall in love at first site

First impressions are critical on the Web, where shoppers have the ability to jump from site to site with a click of the mouse button. A few extra seconds of downtime waiting for complex images or mini-computer programs called *Java applets* to download can cause your prospective buyer to lose patience and you to lose a sale.

How do you make visitors to your welcome page feel like they are being greeted with open arms? Here are some suggestions:

✔ **Keep it simple:** Don't overload any one page with more than three or four images. Keep all images 20K or less in size.

✔ **Find a fast host:** Some Web servers have super-fast connections to the Internet and others use slower lines. Test your site; if

your pages take 10 or 20 seconds or more to appear, ask your host company why and find out whether they can move you to a faster machine.

✔ **Offer a bargain:** Nothing attracts attention as much as a contest, a giveaway, or a special sales promotion. If you have anything that you can give away, either through a contest or a deep discount, do it. See Chapter 6 for more ideas.

✔ **Provide instant gratification:** Make sure that your most important information appears at or near the top of your page. Readers on the Web don't like having to scroll through several screens worth of material in order to get to the information they want.

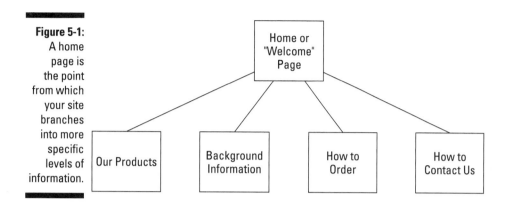

Figure 5-1:
A home
page is
the point
from which
your site
branches
into more
specific
levels of
information.

Note: The page heading "Background Information" is a placeholder for detailed information about some aspect of your online business. For my brother's audio restoration business, I suggested that he include a page of technical information listing the equipment he uses and describing the steps he takes to process audio. You can write about your experience with and love for what you buy and sell, or anything else that will personalize your site and build trust.

The preceding example results in a very simple Web site. But there's nothing wrong with starting out simple. For my brother, who is creating his first Web site and is intimidated by getting started, this simple model is working well. Many other businesses start with a three-layered organization for their Web sites. This arrangement divides the site into two sections, one about the company and one about the products or services for sale (see Figure 5-2).

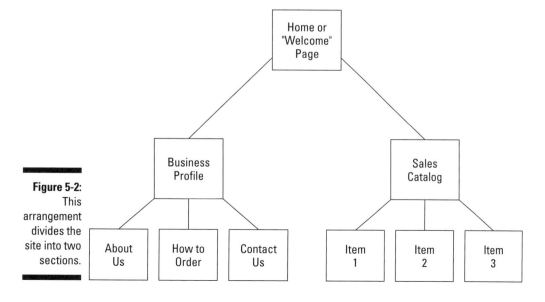

Figure 5-2:
This
arrangement
divides the
site into two
sections.

Think of your home page as the lobby of a museum where you get the help of the friendly person at the information desk who hands you a list of the special exhibits you can visit that day and shows you a map so you can begin to figure out how you're going to get from here to there. Remember to include the following items on your home page:

✔ The name of the store or business

✔ Your logo, if you have one

✔ Links to the main areas of your site or, if your site isn't overly extensive, to every page

✔ Contact information, such as your e-mail address, phone/fax numbers, and (optionally) your business address so that people know where to find you in the Land Beyond Cyberspace

Nip and Tuck: Establishing a Visual Identity

The prospect of designing a Web site may be intimidating if you haven't tried it before. But just remember that it really boils down to a simple principle: *effective visual communication that conveys a particular message.* The first step in creating graphics is not to open a painting program and start drawing, but rather to plan your page's message. Next, determine the audience you want to reach with that message and think about how your graphics can best communicate what you want to say. Some ways to do this follow:

✔ Gather ideas from Web sites that use graphics well — both award-winning sites and sites created by designers who are using graphics in new or unusual ways. To find some award winners, check out The Webby Awards (www.webbyawards.com) and The International Web Page Awards (www.websiteawards.com).

✔ Use graphics consistently from page to page to create an identity and convey a consistent message.

✔ Know your audience. Create graphics that meet visitors' needs and expectations. If you're selling fashions to teenagers, go for neon colors and out-there graphics. If you're selling financial planning to senior citizens, choose a distinguished and sophisticated typeface.

How do you become acquainted with your customers when it is likely that you will never actually meet them face to face? Find newsgroups and mailing lists in which potential visitors to your site are discussing subjects related to what you plan to publish on the Web. Read the posted messages to get a sense of the concerns and vocabulary of your intended audience.

Accommodating your viewers

Recent surveys indicate that, for the first time, the number of Web surfers with broadband connections (such as cable modem or DSL) is just beginning to outnumber those with dialup modem connections. But the many Web surfers who still have very slow Internet connections (or very low tolerances for waiting) may not have the bandwidth to display even ordinary images quickly enough. And, although it may be tempting to show off, you may as well forget about presenting such content as live video, teleconferencing, and other graphics files on the Web. After many minutes or even just seconds of waiting, the surfer is likely to hit the browser's Stop button, with the result that no graphics appear at all.

How do you prevent customers from blocking out your beautiful graphics and ruining the whole effect? Some alternatives include

✔ Creating low-resolution alternatives to high-resolution graphics, such as thumbnails (postage-stamp sized versions of larger images)

✔ Cropping images to keep them small

✔ Using line art whenever possible, rather than high-resolution photos

By using the same image more than once on a Web page, you can give the impression of greater activity but yet not slow down the appearance of the entire page. Why? If you repeat the same image three times, your customer's browser has to download the image file only once. It stores the image in a storage area, called *disk cache,* on the user's hard drive. To display the other instances of the image, the browser retrieves the file from the disk cache, so the second and third images appear much more quickly than the first one did.

Users can also disable image display altogether so they don't see graphics on any of the sites they visit. The solution: Always provide a simple textual alternative to your images so that, if the user has disabled the display of a particular image, a word or two describing that image appears in its place.

Choosing wallpaper that won't make you a wallflower

The technical term for the wallpaper behind the contents of a Web page is its *background.* Most Web browsers display the background of a page as light gray unless you specify something different. In this case, leaving well enough alone isn't good enough. If you don't choose a different color, viewers are likely to get the impression that the page is poorly designed or that the author of the page hasn't put a great deal of thought into the project. So even a neutral color, such as white, is better than gray.

You can change the background of your Web page by tinkering with the HTML source code, but why would you want to? Most Web page creation programs offer a simple way to specify a color or an image file to serve as the background of a Web page. For example, in an HTML Editor called Netscape Composer, a free and easily overlooked Web page design tool that comes with the Netscape Communicator Web browser package, you use the Page Colors and Background dialog box (see Figure 5-3) to set your Web page wallpaper.

Figure 5-3:
Most Web
page editors
let you
specify
background
image/color
options in a
dialog box
like this.

Color your Web site effective

You can use colors to elicit a particular mood or emotion and also to convey your organization's identity on the Web. The right choice of color can create impressions ranging from elegant to funky.

The basic colors chosen by the package-delivery company United Parcel Service (www.ups.com) convey to customers that it is a staid and reliable company, and the U.S. Postal Service (www.usps.gov) sticks to the patriotic choice of red, white, and blue. In contrast, the designers of the HotHotHot hot sauce site (www.hothothot.com) combine fiery colors and original art to convey a spice that sizzles.

When selecting colors for your own Web pages, consider the demographics of your target audience. Do some research on what emotions or impressions are conveyed by different colors and which colors best match the mission or identity of your business. Refer to resources such as the online essay by Noble Image Web Design (www.nobleimage.com/no_flash/articles/color_choices.htm), which examines in some detail the subject of how color choices make Web surfers react differently.

Even if you have the taste of a professional designer, you need to be aware of what happens to color on the Web. The best color choices for Web backgrounds are ones that don't shift dramatically from browser to browser or platform to platform. The best palette for use on the Web is a set of 216 colors that is common to all browsers. These are called *browser-safe colors* because they appear pretty much the same from browser to browser and on different monitors. The palette itself appears on Victor Engel's Web site (the-light.com/netcol.html).

Keep in mind that the colors you use must have contrast so that they don't blend into one another. For example, you don't want to put purple type on a brown or blue background, or yellow type on a white background. Remember to use light type against a dark background, and dark type against a light background. That way, all your page's contents will show up.

As long as your type and graphics are visible, there is no color choice that will create a magic spell. You should first pay attention to your gut reactions. Then get feedback from your colleagues and test your choice on a few sample members of your audience before you make your final decision.

Tiling images in the background

You can use an image rather than a solid color to serve as the background of a page. You specify an image in the HTML code of your Web page (or in your Web page editor), and browsers automatically *tile* the image, reproducing it over and over to fill up the current width and height of the browser window.

This isn't the time to be totally wild and crazy. Background images only work when they're subtle and don't interfere with the page contents. Be careful to choose an image that doesn't have any obvious lines that will create a distracting pattern when tiled. The effect you are trying to create should literally resemble wallpaper.

What you absolutely don't want to have happen is that the background image makes the page unreadable. Visit the Maine Solar House home page (`www.solarhouse.com`) shown later in Figure 5-8 for a rare example of a background image that is faint enough to not interfere with foreground images and that actually adds something to the page's design.

Using Web typefaces like a pro

If you create a Web page and don't specify that the text be displayed in a particular font, the browser that displays the page will use its default font — which is usually Times or Helvetica (although individual users can customize their browsers by picking a different default font).

However, you don't have to limit yourself to the same-old/same-old. As a Web page designer, you can exercise a degree of control over the appearance of your Web page by specifying that the body type and headings be displayed in a particular nonstandard font. A few of the choices available to you have names such as Arial, Courier, Century Schoolbook, and so on. But just because you fall in love with a particular typeface doesn't mean your audience will be able to admire it in all its beauty. The problem is that you don't have ultimate control over whether a given browser will display the specified typeface because you don't know for sure whether the individual user's system has access to your preferred typefaces. If the particular font you specified is not available, the browser will fall back on its default font (which, again, is probably Helvetica or Times).

That's why, generally speaking, when you design Web pages, you're better off picking a generic typeface that is built into virtually every computer's operating system. This convention ensures that your Web pages look more or less the same no matter what Web browser or what type of computer displays them.

Where, exactly, do you specify type fonts, colors, and sizes for the text on a Web page? Again, special HTML tags tell Web browsers what fonts to display, but you don't need to mess with these tags yourself if you're using a Web page creation tool. The specific steps you take depend on what Web design tool you're using. In Macromedia Dreamweaver, you have the option of specifying a group of preferred typefaces rather than a single font in the Property Inspector (see Figure 5-4). If the viewer doesn't have one font in the group, another font is displayed. Check the Help files with your own program to find out exactly how to format text and what typeface options you have.

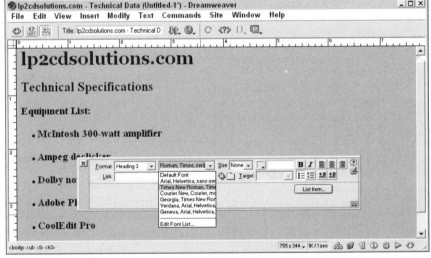

Figure 5-4: Most Web page design tools let you specify a preferred font or fonts for your Web page in a dialog box like this.

Not all typefaces are equal in the eye of the user. Serif typefaces, such as Times Roman, are considered to be more readable (at least, for printed materials) than sans-serif fonts, such as Helvetica. However, an article on the Web Marketing Today Web site (www.wilsonweb.com/wmt6/html-email-fonts.htm) found that by a whopping 2 to 1 margin, the sans-serif font Arial is considered more readable on a Web page than Times Roman.

If you want to make sure that a heading or block of type appears in a specific typeface (especially a nonstandard one that isn't displayed as body text by Web browsers), scan it or create the heading in an image-editing program and insert it into the page as a graphic image. But make sure it doesn't clash with the generic typefaces that appear on the rest of your page.

Clip art is free and fun

Not everyone has the time or resources to scan photos or create their own original graphics. But that doesn't mean you can't add graphic interest to your Web page. Many Web page designers use clip-art bullets, diamonds, or other small images next to list items or major Web page headings to which they want to call special attention. Clip art can also provide a background pattern for a Web page or highlight sales headings such as Free! New! or Special!

When I first started out in the print publications business, I bought catalogs of illustrations, literally clipped out the art, and pasted it down. It's still called clip art, but now the process is different. In keeping with the spirit of exchange that has been a part of the Internet since its inception, some talented and generous artists have created icons, buttons, and other illustrations in electronic form and offered them free for downloading.

Here are some suggestions for sources of clip art on the Web:

- ✔ Barry's Clip Art Server (www.barrysclipart.com)
- ✔ Clip Art Universe (nzwwa.com/mirror/clipart)
- ✔ The Yahoo! page full of links to clip art resources (dir.yahoo.com/ Computers_and_Internet/Graphics/Clip_Art)

If you use Microsoft Office, you have access to plenty of clip art images that come with the software. If you're using Word, just choose Insert➪Picture➪ Clip Art to view clip art images as displayed in the Insert Picture dialog box. If these built-in images aren't sufficient, you can also connect to a special Microsoft Clip Gallery Live Web site by clicking the Clips Online toolbar button in the Insert Clip Art dialog box. Web page editors — such as Microsoft FrontPage and CoffeeCup HTML Editor — come with their own clip art libraries, too.

Be sure to read the copyright fine print *before* you copy graphics. All artists own the copyright to their work. It's up to them to determine how they want to give someone else the right to copy their work. Sometimes, the authors require you to pay a small fee if you want to copy their work, or they may restrict use of their work to nonprofit organizations.

A picture is worth a thousand words

Some customers know exactly what they want from the get-go and don't need any help from you. But most customers love to shop around or could use some encouragement to move from one item or catalog page to another. This is where images can play an important role.

Even if you use only some basic clip art, such as placing spheres or arrows next to sale items, your customer is likely to thank you by buying more. A much better approach, though, is to scan or take digital images of your sale items and provide compact, clear images of them on your site. Here's a quick step-by-step guide to get you started:

1. **Choose the right image to scan.**

   After you purchase a scanner or digital camera (see the suggestions in Chapter 2), the next step is to select images (if you're going to scan) or take images (if you're using a camera) that are well illuminated, have good contrast, and are relatively small in size.

   The original quality of an image is just as important as how you scan or retouch it. Images that are murky or fuzzy in print will be even worse when viewed on a computer screen.

2. **Preview the image.**

   Most digital cameras let you preview images so that you can decide whether to keep or delete individual pictures before downloading to your computer. If you're working with a scanner, scanning programs let you make a quick *preview scan* of an image so that you can get an idea of what it looks like before you do the actual scan. When you press the Preview button, you hear a whirring sound as the optical device in the scanner captures the image. A preview image appears on-screen, surrounded by a *marquee box* (a rectangle made up of dashes), as shown in Figure 5-5.

Figure 5-5:
The marquee box lets you crop a preview image to make it smaller and reduce the file size.

3. **Crop the image.**

   Cropping an image is a good idea because it highlights the most important contents and reduces the file size. Reducing the file size of an image
   should always be one of your most important goals — the smaller the
   image, the quicker it appears in someone's browser window. *Cropping*
   means that you resize the box around the image in order to select the
   portion of the image that you want to keep and leave out the parts of the
   image that aren't essential.

   Almost all scanning and graphics programs offer separate options for
   cropping an image and reducing the image size. By cropping the image,
   you eliminate parts of the image you don't want, and this *does* reduce
   the image size. But it doesn't reduce the size of the objects within the
   image. Resizing the overall image size is a separate step, which enables
   you to change the dimensions of the entire image without eliminating
   any contents.

4. **Select an input mode.**

   Tell the scanner or graphics program how you want it to save the visual
   data — as color, line art (used for black-and-white drawings), or grayscale
   (used for black-and-white photos).

5. **Set the resolution.**

   In Chapter 2, I note that digital images are made up of little bits (dots)
   of computerized information called *pixels*. The more pixels per inch,
   the higher the level of detail. When you scan an image, you can tell the
   scanner to make the dots smaller (creating a smoother image) or larger
   (resulting in a more jagged image). This adjustment is called *setting the
   resolution* of the image. (When you take a digital photo, the resolution of
   the image depends on your camera's settings.)

   How many dots per inch (dpi) do you want your image to be? When
   you're scanning for the Web, you expect your images to appear primarily
   on computer screens. Because many computer monitors can display resolutions only up to 72 dpi, 72 dpi — a relatively rough resolution — is an
   adequate resolution for a Web image. (By contrast, many laser printers
   print at a resolution of 600 dpi.) But using this coarse resolution has the
   advantage of keeping the image's file size small. Remember, the smaller
   the file size, the more quickly an image appears when your customers
   load your page in their Web browsers.

6. **Adjust contrast and brightness.**

   Virtually all scanning programs and graphics editing programs provide
   brightness and contrast controls that you can adjust with your mouse to
   improve the image. If you're happy with the image as is, leave the brightness and contrast set where they are. (You can also leave the image as is
   and adjust brightness and contrast later in a separate graphics program,
   such as Paint Shop Pro, which you can try out by downloading it from
   the JASC Web site, www.jasc.com.)

7. **Reduce the image size.**

   The old phrase "good things come in small packages" is never more true than when you're improving your digital image. If you're scanning an image that is 8" x 10" and you're sure that it needs to be about 4" x 5" when it appears on your Web page, scan it at 50 percent of the original size. This step reduces the file size right away and makes the file easier to transport. That's really important if you have to put it on a floppy disk to move it from one computer to another.

8. **Scan away!**

   Your scanner makes a beautiful whirring sound as it turns those colors into pixels. Because you're scanning only at 72 dpi, the process shouldn't take too long.

9. **Save the file.**

   Now you can save your image to disk. Most programs let you do this by choosing File⇨Save. In the dialog box that appears, enter a name for your file and select a file format. (Because you are working with images to be published on the Web, remember to save either in GIF or JPEG format.)

 When you give your image a name, be sure to add the correct filename extension. Web browsers recognize only image files with extensions such as `.gif`, `.jpg`, or `.jpeg`. If you name your image product and save it in GIF format, call it `product.gif`. If you save it in JPEG format and you're using a PC, call it `product.jpg`. On a Macintosh, call it `product.jpeg`.

GIF versus JPEG

Web site technology and HTML may have changed dramatically over the past several years, but for the most part, there are only two types of images as far as Web pages are concerned: GIF and JPEG. Both formats use methods that compress computer image files so that the visual information contained within them can be transmitted easily over computer networks. (PNG, a third format designed a few years ago as a successor to GIF, is appearing online more and more, but it still isn't as widely used as GIF.)

GIF (pronounced either "jiff" or "giff") stands for Graphics Interchange Format. GIF is best suited to text, line art, or images with well-defined edges. Special types of GIF allow images with transparent backgrounds to be interlaced (broken into layers that appear gradually over slow connections) and animated. JPEG (pronounced "jay-peg") stands for Joint Photographic Experts Group, the name of the group that originated the format. JPEG is preferred for large photos and continuous tones of grayscale or color that need greater compression.

For more details on scanning images, check out *Scanning For Dummies,* 2nd Edition, by Mark Chambers (Wiley).

Creating a logo

An effective logo establishes your online business's graphic identity in no uncertain terms. A logo can be as simple as a rendering of the company name that imparts an official typeface or color. Whatever text it includes, a logo is a small, self-contained graphic object that conveys the group's identity and purpose. Figure 5-6 shows an example of a logo.

A logo doesn't have to be a fabulously complex drawing with drop-shadows and gradations of color. A simple, type-only logo can be as good as gold. Pick a typeface you want, choose your graphic's outline version, and fill the letters with color.

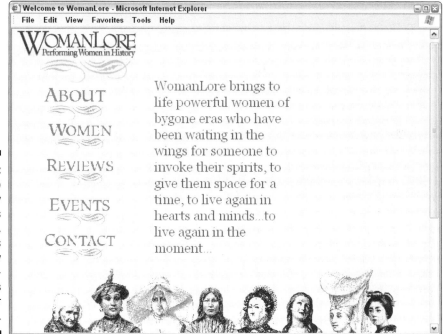

Figure 5-6: A good logo effectively combines color, type, and graphics to convey an organization's identity or mission.

Extreme Web Pages: Advanced Layouts

People who have some experience creating Web sites typically use frames and tables. On the other hand, they might be right up the alley of an adventurous type who wants to start an online business. So this section includes some quick explanations of what tables and frames are so that you know where to start when and if you decide you do want to use them.

A quick HTML primer

Thanks to Web page creation tools, you don't have to master HyperText Markup Language in order to create your own Web pages, although some knowledge of HTML is helpful when it comes to editing pages and understanding how they're put together.

HTML is a markup language, not a computer programming language. You use it in much the same way that old-fashioned editors marked up copy before they gave it to typesetters. A markup language allows you to identify major sections of a document, such as body text, headings, title, and so on. A software program (in the case of HTML, a Web browser) is programmed to recognize the markup language and to display the formatting elements that you have marked.

Markup tags are the basic building blocks of HTML as well as its more complex and powerful cousin, eXtensible Markup Language (XML). Tags enable you to structure the appearance of your document so that, when it is transferred from one computer to another, it will look the way you described it. HTML tags appear within carrot-shaped brackets. Most HTML commands require a *start tag* at the beginning of the section and an *end tag* (which usually begins with a backslash) at the end.

For example, if you place the HTML tags <B> and </B> around the phrase "This text will be bold," the words appear in bold type on any browser that displays them, no matter if it's running on a Windows-based PC, a UNIX workstation, a Macintosh, a palm device that's Web enabled, or any other computer.

Many HTML commands are accompanied by *attributes,* which provide a browser with more specific instructions on what action the tag is to perform. In the following lines of HTML, SRC is an attribute that works with the <IMG> tag to identify a file to display:

```
<IMG SRC="house.jpg">
```

Each attribute is separated from an HTML command by a single blank space. The equal sign (=) is an operator that introduces the value on which the attribute and command will function. Usually, the value is a filename or a directory path leading to a specific file that is to be displayed on a Web page. The straight (as opposed to curly) quotation marks around the value are essential for the HTML command to work.

Setting the tables for your customers

Tables are to designers what statistics are to sports fans. In the case of a Web page, they provide another means to present information in a graphically interesting way. Tables were originally intended to present "tabular" data in columns and rows, much like a spreadsheet. But by using advanced HTML techniques, you can make tables a much more integrated and subtle part of your Web page.

Because you can easily create a basic table by using Web page editors, such as HotDog, Netscape Composer, and FrontPage, starting with one of these tools makes sense. Some adjustments with HTML are probably unavoidable, however, especially if you want to use tables to create blank columns on a Web page (as I explain later in this section). Here is a quick rundown of the main HTML tags used for tables:

- ✔ `<TABLE> </TABLE>` encloses the entire table. The `BORDER` attribute sets the width of the line around the cells.

- ✔ `<TR> </TR>` encloses a table row, a horizontal set of cells.

- ✔ `<TD> </TD>` defines the contents of an individual cell. The `HEIGHT` and `WIDTH` attributes control the size of each cell. For example, the following code tells a browser that the table cell is 120 pixels wide:

  ```
  <TD WIDTH=120> Contents of cell </TD>
  ```

Don't forget that the cells in a table can contain images as well as text. Also, individual cells can have different colors from the cells around them. You can add a background color to a table cell by adding the `BGCOLOR` attribute to the `<TD>` table cell tag.

The clever designer can use tables in a hidden way to arrange an entire page, or a large portion of a page, by doing two things:

- ✔ Set the table border to 0. Doing so makes the table outline invisible, so the viewer sees only the contents of each cell, not the lines bordering the cell.

- ✔ Fill some table cells with blank space so that they act as empty columns that add more white space to a page.

An example of the first approach, that of making the table borders invisible, appears in Figure 5-7: David Nishimura's Vintage Pens Web site (`www.vintage pens.com`) where he sells vintage writing instruments.

Figure 5-7:
This page is divided into table cells, which give the designer a high level of control over the layout.

Framing your subject

Frames are subdivisions of a Web page, each consisting of its own separate Web document. Depending on how the designer sets up the Web page, visitors may be able to scroll through one frame independently of the other frames on the same page. A mouse click on a hypertext link contained in one frame may cause a new document to appear in an adjacent frame.

Simple two-frame layouts such as the one used by one of my personal favorite Web sites, Maine Solar House (see Figure 5-8), can be very effective. A page can be broken into as many frames as the designer wants, but you typically want to stick with only two to four frames because they make the page considerably more complex and slower to appear in its entirety.

Frames fit within the BODY section of an HTML document. In fact, the <FRAMESET> </FRAMESET> tags actually take the place of the <BODY> </BODY> tags and are used to enclose the rest of the frame-specific elements. Each of the frames on the page is then described by <FRAME> </FRAME> tags.

Only the more advanced Web page creation programs provide you with menu options and toolbar buttons that enable you to create frames without having to enter the HTML manually. Most of the popular Web page editors do this, including Macromedia Dreamweaver and HotDog Professional by Sausage Software. See each program's Help topics for specific instructions on how to implement framing tools.

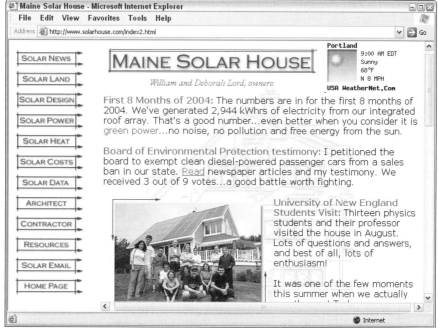

Figure 5-8:
This site
uses a
classic two-
frame layout:
A column of
links in the
narrow
frame on the
left changes
the content
in the frame
on the right.

Frames add interactivity and graphic interest to a page, but many users dis-
like the extra time they require. As a Web page designer, be sure to provide a
"no frames" alternative to a "frames" layout.

Breaking the grid with layers

Tables and frames bring organization and interactivity to Web pages, but they
confine your content to rows and columns. If you feel confined by the old up-
down, left-right routine, explore layers for arranging your Web page content.

Layers, like table cells and frames, act as containers for text and images on a
Web page. Layers are unique because they can be moved around freely on
the page — they can overlap one another, and they can "bleed" right to the
page margin.

Layers carry some big downsides: You can't create them with just any Web
editor. Macromedia Dreamweaver is the Web editor of choice, and it's not free
(at this writing, Dreamweaver MX 2004 costs $339). Layers are supported only
by versions 4.0 or later of Microsoft Internet Explorer or Netscape Navigator.
However, Dreamweaver lets you create a layout in layers and then convert it
to tables, which are supported by almost all browsers.

With Dreamweaver, you can draw a layer directly on the Web page you're creating. You add text or images to the layer, and then resize or relocate it on the page by clicking and dragging it freely. The result is some innovative page designs that don't conform to the usual grid.

Hiring a Professional Web Designer

Part of the fun of running your own business is doing things yourself. So it comes as no surprise that most of the entrepreneurs I interviewed in the course of writing this book do their own Web page design work. They discovered how to create Web sites by reading books or taking classes on the subject. But in many cases, the initial cost of hiring someone to help you design your online business can be a good investment in the long run. Keep in mind that after you pay someone to help you develop a look, you can probably implement it in the future more easily yourself. For example:

- ✒ If you need business cards, stationery, brochures, or other printed material in addition to a Web site, hiring someone to develop a consistent look for everything at the beginning is worth the money.

- ✒ You can pay a designer to get you started with a logo, color selections, and page layouts. Then you can save money by adding text yourself.

- ✒ If, like me, you're artistically impaired, consider the benefits of having your logo or other artwork drawn by a real artist.

Most professional designers charge $40 to $60 per hour for their work. You can expect a designer to spend five or six hours to create a logo or template. But if your company uses that initial design for the foreseeable future, you're not really paying that much per year.

Chapter 6

Attracting and Keeping Customers

In This Chapter

▶ Creating compelling content through links and hooks

▶ Promoting your business by providing objective, useful information

▶ Making less do more through concise, well-organized content

▶ Writing friendly, objective prose that sells your products and services

▶ Inviting customer interaction with forms, e-mail, and more

*A*s a writer, I know only too well the challenge of staring at a totally white piece of paper or a blank computer screen. It's then that I remember my writing teacher telling me to "let it flow" and worry about editing after I've unleashed my creativity. That's good advice up to a point, especially for something like a Web log. But when it comes to a business Web site, you need to present the *right* content in the *right* way to make prospective clients and customers want to explore your site the first time and then come back for more later on.

Because one of my primary points in this chapter is that you need to express your main message on your business site up front, I do the same by explaining what I consider to be the right content for an online business. The material that you include on your site should

- ✔ Remember that people who are online absorb information fast

- ✔ Make it easy for visitors to find out who you are and what you have to offer

- ✔ Be friendly and informal in tone, concise in length, and clear in its organization

- ✔ Help develop the all-important one-to-one-relationship with customers and clients by inviting dialogue and interaction, both with you and with others who share the same interests

In other words, you need to be straightforward about who you are and where you're coming from on your business site. This chapter is obviously about writing for the Web. But the idea is not to be satisfied with generating just any old text. The goal is to craft exciting, well-organized, and easily digestible information. What follows is how to put these objectives into action.

Features that Attract Customers

Half the battle with developing content for a business Web site is knowing what shoppers online want and determining strategies for providing it to them. Identifying your target audience will help you devise a message that will make each potential customer think you are speaking directly to him or her. But you also should keep in mind some general concepts that will help you market successfully to all ages, both genders, and every socioeconomic group.

Studies of how people absorb the information on a Web page indicate that people don't really read the contents from top to bottom (or left to right, or frame to frame) in a linear way. In fact, most Web surfers don't *read* in the traditional sense at all. Instead, they browse so quickly you'd think they have an itchy mouse finger. They "flip through pages" by clicking link after link. As more Internet users connect with broadband technologies, such as DSL and cable, they can absorb complex graphics and multimedia. On the other hand, lots of users are beginning to use palm devices, pocket PCs, Web-enabled cell phones, and even Internet-ready automobiles to get online. Because your prospective customers don't necessarily have tons of computing power or hours' worth of time to explore your site, the best rule is to keep it simple.

People who are looking for things on the Web are often in a state of hurried distraction. Think about a television watcher browsing during a commercial or a harried parent stealing a few moments on the computer while the baby naps. Imagine this person surfing with one hand on a mouse, the other dipping chips into salsa. This person isn't in the mood to listen as you tell your fondest hopes and dreams for success, starting with playing grocery store cashier as a toddler. Here's what this shopper is probably thinking:

> *"Look, I don't have time to read all this. My show is about to come back on and I still need to go to the bathroom."*

> *"What's this? Why does this page take so long to load? And I paid good money to get a direct connection installed. I swear, sometimes I wish the Web didn't have any graphics. Here, I'll click this. No, wait! I'll click that. On no, now the baby is fussing already."*

The following sections describe some ways to attract the attention of the distracted and get them to scroll down to exactly where you want them to go.

Don't be shy about what you have to say

Don't keep anyone in suspense about who you are and what you do. Keep in mind that people who come to a Web site give that site less than a minute (in fact, I've heard only 20 seconds) to answer their primary questions:

- ✔ Who are you, anyway?
- ✔ All right, so what is your main message or mission?
- ✔ Well then, what do you have here for me?
- ✔ Why should I choose your site to investigate rather than all the others that seem to be about the same?

This is a pretty intimidating picture, I admit. But I really believe that this is what most Web surfers are thinking as they randomly scroll through sites.

A study conducted by online advertiser DoubleClick, Inc. in the first quarter of 2004 (www.mediapost.com/dtls_dsp_news.cfm?newsID=253716&news Date=06/03/2004) found that as many as 48 percent of online shoppers abandoned their shopping carts and failed to complete purchases because pages were too slow to load. The Consumer 40 Internet Performance Index by Keynote Systems (www.keynote.com/solutions/performance_indices/ consumer_index/consumer_40.html) found in early December 2004 that, in a survey of 40 Web sites, the average site takes a full 26 seconds or more to load over a 56Kbps modem. However, Web search engine AltaVista was found to be among the fastest loading of 40 Internet sites, requiring only 5.30 seconds to appear. Other top finishers prove that just because you have a big commercial Web site, you don't need to make it complicated: Ameritrade's Web page was clocked at 12.58 seconds and CFSBDirect at 7.09 seconds.

When it comes to Web pages, it pays to put the most important components first: who you are, what you do, how you stand out from any competing sites, and contact information.

If you have a long list of items to sell, you probably can't fit everything you have to offer right on the first page of your site. Even if you could, you wouldn't want to: As in a television newscast, it's better to prioritize the contents of your site so that the "breaking stories" or the best contents appear at the top, and the rest of what's in your catalog is arranged in order of importance.

I suppose there are a few gamblers in every group, but I'm not the type that goes for all or nothing. Think long and hard before you use features that may scare people away instead of wowing them. I'm talking about those "splash pages" that contain only a logo or short greeting, and then reload automatically and take the visitor to the main body of a site. I also don't recommend loading up your home page with Flash animations or Java applets that take your prospective customers' browsers precious seconds to load.

Encourage visitors to click, click, click!

Imagine multi-tasking Web surfers arriving at your Web site with only a fraction of their attention engaged. Make the links easy to read and in obvious locations. Having a row of links at the top of your home page, each of which points the visitor to an important area of your site, is always a good idea. Such links give visitors an idea of what your site contains in a single glance and immediately encourage viewers to click a primary subsection of your site and explore further. By placing an interactive table of contents right up front, you direct surfers right to the material they are looking for.

The links can go at or near the top of the page on either the left or right side. The Dummies.com home page, shown in Figure 6-1, has a few links just above the top banner, but also sports links down *both* the left and right sides.

If you want to be ranked highly by search engines (and who doesn't) you have another good reason to place your site's main topics near the top of the page in a series of links. Some search services index the first 50 or so words on a Web page. It therefore stands to reason that if you can get lots of important keywords included in that index, the chances are better that your site will be ranked highly in a list of links returned by the service in response to a search. See Chapters 14 and 15 for more on embedding keywords.

Figure 6-1:
Putting at
least five or
six links near
the top of
your home
page is a
good idea.

Use the following steps to create links to local files on your Web site by using Netscape Composer, the free Web page editor that comes with the Netscape Communicator Web browser. The steps assume that you have started up the program and that the Web page you want to edit is already open:

1. **Select the text or image on your Web page that you want to serve as the jumping-off point for the link.**

   If you select a word or phrase, the text is highlighted in black. If you select an image, a black box appears around the image.

2. **Choose Insert⇨Link or press Ctrl+L.**

   The Link Properties dialog box appears, as shown in Figure 6-2.

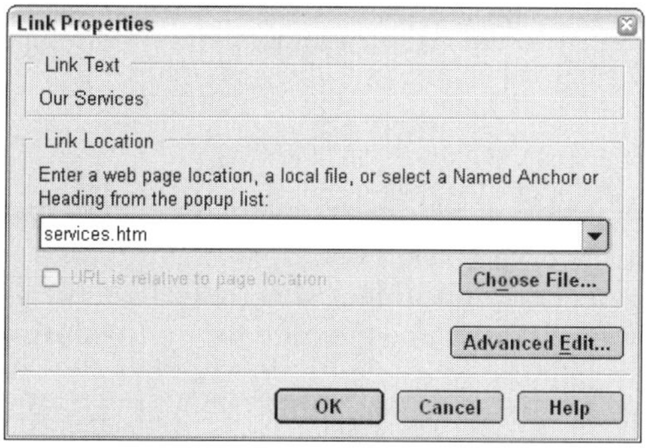

Figure 6-2:
If you keep all your related Web pages in the same directory, you have to enter only a simple filename as the link destination.

Link Properties
Link Text
Our Services
Link Location
Enter a web page location, a local file, or select a Named Anchor or Heading from the popup list:
services.htm ▼
☐ URL is relative to page location   Choose File...
Advanced Edit...
OK   Cancel   Help

3. **In the box beneath Link Location, enter the name of the file you want to link to if you know the filename.**

   If the page you want to link to is in the same directory as the page that contains the jumping-off point, you need to enter only the name of the Web page. If the page is in another directory, you need to enter a path relative to the Web page that contains the link (or click the Choose File button, locate the file in the Open HTML File dialog box, and click the Open button).

4. **Click OK.**

   The Link Properties dialog box closes, and you return to the Composer window. If you made a textual link, the selected text is underlined and in a different color. If you made an image link, a box appears around the image.

Presenting the reader with links up front doesn't just help your search engine rankings, it also indicates that your site is content rich and worthy of exploration.

Tell us a little about yourself

One thing you need to state clearly as soon as possible on your Web site is who you are and what you do. Profnet does this by condensing its mission statement into a single phrase:

Helping Business Professionals Find More Business

Can you identify your primary goal in a single sentence? If not, try to boil down your goals to two or three sentences at the most. Whatever you do, make your mission statement more specific and customer oriented than simply saying, "Out to make lots of money!" Tell prospects what you can do for them; the fact that you have three kids in college and need to make money to pay their tuition isn't really their concern.

Add a search box

One of the most effective kinds of content you can add to your site is a search box. A search box invites visitors to interact instantly with your Web site. If you can find a Web host that will help you set up a search box, you don't have to mess around with computer scripts and indexing tools. (See the section, "Make your site searchable," later in this chapter, for more information.)

Search boxes are commonly found on commercial Web sites. You usually see them at the top of the home page, right near the links to the major sections of the site. The Dummies.com Technology page, shown in Figure 6-3, includes a search box in the upper-right corner of the page.

I'm always looking for freelance writing jobs, but I have to admit that you don't really need to hire a professional to make a Web site compelling. You're not writing an essay, a term paper, or a book here. Rather, you need to observe only a few simple rules:

- ✔ Provide lots of links and hooks that readers can scan.

- ✔ Keep everything concise!

The key word to remember is "short." Keep sentences short. Limit paragraphs to one or two sentences in length. You may also want to limit each Web page to no more than one or two screens in length so that viewers don't have to scroll down too far to find what they want — even if they're on a laptop or smaller Internet appliance.

Figure 6-3:
Many
surfers
prefer using
a search box
to clicking
links.

Making your content scannable

When you're writing something on paper, whether it's a letter to Mom or your grocery list, contents have to be readable. Contents on your Web site, on the other hand, have to be scannable. This principle has to do with the way people absorb information online. Eyes that are staring at a computer screen for many minutes or many hours tend to jump around a Web page, looking for an interesting bit of information on which to rest. In this section, I suggest ways to attract those nervous eyes and guide them toward the products you have to sell or toward the services you want to provide.

I'm borrowing the term *scannable* from John Morkes and Jakob Nielsen of Sun Microsystems, who use it in their article "Concise, Scannable, and Objective: How to Write for the Web" (`www.useit.com/papers/webwriting/writing.html`). I include a link to this article in the Internet Directory on this book's Web site, along with other tips on enriching the content of your Web pages. See the section of the Directory called "Developing Compelling Content" for more information.

Point the way with headings

One hard-to-miss Web page element that's designed to grab the attention of your readers' eyes is a heading. Every Web page needs to contain headings that direct the reader's attention to the most important contents. This book provides a good example. The chapter title (I hope) piques your interest first. Then the section headings and subheadings direct you to more details on the topics you want to read about.

Most graphics designers I've worked with label their heads with letters of the alphabet: "A," "B," "C," and so on. In a similar fashion, most Web page editing tools designate top-level headings with the style Heading 1. Beneath this, you place one or more Heading 2 headings. Beneath each of those, you may have Heading 3 and, beneath those, Heading 4. (Headings 5 and 6 are too small to be useful, in my opinion.) The arrangement may look like this (I've indented the following headings for clarity; you don't have to indent them on your page):

```
Miss Cookie's Delectable Cooking School (Heading 1)
    Kitchen Equipment You Can't Live Without (Heading 2)
    The Story of a Calorie Counter Gone Wrong (Heading 2)
    Programs of Culinary Study (Heading 2)
        Registration (Heading 3)
        Course Schedule (Heading 3)
            New Course on Whipped Cream Just Added! (Heading 4)
```

You can energize virtually any heading by telling your audience something specific about your business. Instead of "Ida's Antique Mall," for example, say something like "Ida's Antique Mall: The Perfect Destination for the Collector and the Crafter." Instead of simply writing a heading like "Stan Thompson, Pet Grooming," say something specific, such as "Stan Thompson: We Groom Your Pet at Our Place or Yours."

Become an expert list maker

Lists are simple and effective ways to break up text and make your Web content easier to digest. They're easy to create and easy for your customer to view and absorb. For example, suppose that you import your own decorations and you want to offer certain varieties at a discount during various seasons. Rather than bury the items you're offering within an easily overlooked paragraph, why not divide your list into subgroups so that visitors will find what they want without being distracted by holidays they don't even celebrate?

The following example shows how easy lists are to implement if you use Macromedia Dreamweaver, a popular Web page creation tool that you can test for yourself for a 30-day trial period by downloading the program from the Macromedia Web site (`www.macromedia.com/downloads`). You have your Web page document open in Dreamweaver, and you're at that point in the page where you want to insert a list. Just do the following:

1. Type a heading for your list and then select the entire heading.

For example, you might type and then select the words **This Month's Specials**.

2. **Choose Text⇨Paragraph Format.**

   A list of paragraph styles appears as a submenu next to the Paragraph Format submenu.

3. **Click a heading style, such as Heading 3, to select it from the list of styles.**

   Your text is now formatted as a heading.

4. **Click anywhere in the Dreamweaver window to deselect the heading you just formatted.**

5. **Press Enter to move to a new line.**

6. **Type the first item of your list, press Enter, and then type the second item on the next line.**

   Repeat until you've entered all the items of your list.

7. **Select all the items of your list (but not the heading).**

8. **Choose Text⇨List⇨Unordered List.**

   A bullet appears next to each list item, and the items appear closer together on-screen so that they look more like a list. That's all there is to it! Figure 6-4 shows the result.

Most Web editors let you vary the appearance of the bullet that appears next to a bulleted list item. For example, you can make it a hollow circle rather than a solid black dot, or you can choose a rectangle rather than a circle.

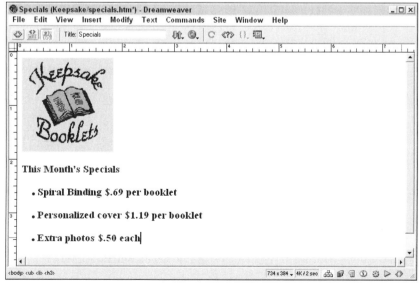

Figure 6-4: A bulleted list is an easy way to direct customers' attention to special promotions or sale items.

Lead your readers on with links

I mean for you to interpret the preceding heading literally, not figuratively. In other words, I'm not suggesting that you make promises on which you can't deliver. Rather, I mean that you should do anything you can to lead your visitors to your site and then get them to stay long enough to explore individual pages. You can accomplish this goal with a single hyperlinked word that leads to another page on your site:

More . . .

I see this word all the time on Web pages that present a lot of content. At the bottom of a list of their products and services, businesses place that word in bold type: **More . . .** I'm always interested in finding out what more they could possibly have to offer me.

Magazines use the same approach. On their covers you'll find "reefer" phrases that refer you to the kinds of stories that you'll find inside. You can do the same kind of thing on your Web pages. For example, which of the following links is more likely to get a response?

Next

Next: Paragon's Success Stories

Whenever possible, tell your visitors what they can expect to encounter as a benefit when they click a link. Give them a tease — and then a big pay-off for responding.

Enhance your text with well-placed images

You can add two kinds of images to a Web page: an *inline image,* which appears in the body of your page along with your text, or an *external image,* which is a separate file that visitors access by clicking a link. The link may take the form of highlighted text or a small version of the image called a *thumbnail.*

The basic HTML tag that inserts an image in your document takes the following form:

```
<IMG SRC="URL">
```

This tag tells your browser to display an image (`<IMG>`) here. `"URL"` gives the location of the image file that serves as the source (`SRC`) for this image. Whenever possible, you should also include `WIDTH` and `HEIGHT` attributes (as follows) because they help speed up graphics display for many browsers:

```
<IMG HEIGHT=51 WIDTH=48 SRC="target.gif">
```

Most Web page editors add the `WIDTH` and `HEIGHT` attributes automatically when you insert an image. Typically, here's what happens:

1. You click the location in the Web page where you want the image to appear.

2. Then you click an Image toolbar button or choose Insert➪Image to display an image selection dialog box.

3. Next you enter the name of the image you want to add and click OK.

   The image is added to your Web page. (For more information, see Chapter 5.)

A well-placed image points the way to text that you want people to read immediately. Think about where your own eyes go when you first connect to a Web page. Most likely, you first look at any images on the page; then you look at the headings; finally, you settle on text to read. If you can place an image next to a heading, you virtually ensure that viewers will read the heading.

Freebies: Everyone's favorite

No matter how much money you have in the bank, you're bound to respond to a really good deal. If you want surefire attention, use one of the following words in the headings on your online business site's home page:

- ✔ Free
- ✔ New
- ✔ Act (as in Act Now!)
- ✔ Sale
- ✔ Discount
- ✔ Win

Contests and sweepstakes

The word *free* and the phrase *Enter Our Contest* can give you a big bang for your buck when it comes to a business Web page. In fact, few things are as likely to get viewers to click into a site as the promise of getting something for nothing.

Giveaways have a number of hidden benefits, too: Everyone who enters sends you personal information that you can use to compile a mailing list or prepare marketing statistics. Giveaways get people involved with your site, and they invite return visits — especially if you hold contests for several weeks at a time.

Of course, in order to hold a giveaway, you need to have something to *give away*. If you make baskets or sell backpacks, you can designate one of your sale items as the prize. If you can't afford to give something away, offer a deep (perhaps 50 percent) discount.

Your Web page title: The ultimate heading

When you're dreaming up clever headings for your Web pages, don't overlook the "heading" that appears in the narrow title bar at the very top of your visitor's Web browser window: the *title* of your Web page.

The two HTML tags `<TITLE>` and `</TITLE>` contain the text that appears within the browser title bar. But you don't have to mess with these nasty HTML codes: All Web page creation programs give you an easy way to enter or edit a title for a Web page. In Dreamweaver, you follow these steps:

1. **With the Web page you're editing open in the Dreamweaver window, choose Modify⇨ Page Properties.**

   The Page Properties dialog box appears.

2. **In the Title text box, enter a title for your page.**

3. **Click OK.**

   The Page Properties dialog box closes and you return to the Dreamweaver window. The title doesn't automatically appear in the title area at the top of the window. When you view the page in a Web browser, however, the title is visible.

If you have the Toolbar open, you can also simply type the Title in the Title box and press Enter. In either case, make the title as catchy and specific as possible, but make sure that the title is no longer than 64 characters. An effective title refers to your goods or services while grabbing the viewer's attention. If your business is called Myrna's Cheesecakes, for example, you might make your title "Smile and Say Cheese! With Myrna's Cakes" (40 characters).

You can organize either a sweepstakes or a contest. A *sweepstakes* chooses its winner by random selection; a *contest* requires participants to compete in some way. The most effective contests on the Internet tend to be simple. If you hold one, consider including a "Rules" Web page that explains who is eligible, who selects the winner, and any rules of participation.

Be aware of the federal and state laws and regulations that cover sweepstakes and contests. Such laws often restrict illegal lotteries as well as the promotion of alcoholic beverages. Telemarketing is sometimes prohibited in connection with a contest. Following are some other points to consider:

- ✔ Unless you are sure that it's legal to allow Web surfers from other countries to participate, you're safest limiting your contest to U.S. residents only.

- ✔ On the contest rules page, be sure to clearly state the starting and ending dates for receiving entries. Some states have laws requiring you to disclose this information.

- ✔ Don't change the ending date of your contest, even if you receive far fewer entries than you had hoped for.

Before your contest goes online, make sure that you've observed all the legal guidelines by visiting the Arent Fox Contests and Sweepstakes News & Alerts page:

www.arentfox.com/quickGuide/businessLines/sweeps/contestsSweep
stakes/contestssweepstakes.html

If you do hold a contest, announce it at the top of your Web page, and hint at
the prizes people can win. Use bold and big type to attract the attention of
your visitors.

Expert tips and insider information

Giveaways aren't just for businesspeople in retail or wholesale salespeople
who have merchandise they can offer as prizes in a contest. If your work
involves professional services, you can give away something just as valuable:
your knowledge. Publish a simple newsletter that you e-mail to subscribers
on a periodic basis (see Chapter 13 for instructions on how to do this). Or
answer questions by e-mail. Some Web page designers (particularly, college
students who are just starting out) work for next to nothing initially, until
they build a client base and can charge a higher rate for their services.

Make your site searchable

A search box is one of the best kinds of content you can put on your Web
site's opening page. A search box is a simple text-entry field that lets a visitor
enter a word or phrase. By clicking a button labeled Go, Search, or something
of the sort, the search term or terms are sent to the site, where a script checks
an index of the site's contents for any files that contain the terms. The script
then causes a list of documents that contain the search terms to appear in
the visitor's browser window.

Search boxes let visitors instantly scan the site's entire contents for a word
or phrase. They put visitors in control right away and get them to interact
with your site. They are popular for some very good reasons.

Yes, I recommend some sort of search utility for e-commerce sites. However,
adding a search box to your site doesn't make much sense if you have only
five to ten pages of content. Add search capability only if you have enough
content to warrant searching. If your site has a sales catalog driven by a
database, it makes more sense to let your customers use the database
search tool instead of adding one of the site search tools that I describe in
this section.

The problem is that search boxes usually require someone with knowledge
of computer programming to create or implement a program called a CGI
script to do the searching. Someone also has to compile an index of the
documents on the Web site so that the script can search the documents.
An application such as ColdFusion can do this, but it's not a program for
beginners.

But you can get around having to write CGI scripts to add search capabilities to your site. Choose one of these options:

- ✔ **Let your Web host do the work:** Some hosting services will do the indexing and creation of the search utility as part of their services.

- ✔ **Use a free site search service:** The server that does the indexing of your Web pages and holds the index doesn't need to be the server that hosts your site. A number of services will make your site searchable for free. In exchange, you display advertisements or logos in the search results you return to your visitors.

- ✔ **Pay for a search service:** If you don't want to display ads on your search results pages, pay a monthly fee to have a company index your pages and let users conduct searches. FreeFind (`www.freefind.com`) has some economy packages, a free version that forces you to view ads, and a professional version including $9 per month for a site of 500 pages or less. SiteMiner (`siteminer.mycomputer.com`) charges $19.95 per month for up to 1,500 pages, but lets you customize your search box and re-index your site whenever you add new content.

Judy Vorfeld went beyond having a simple Search This Site text box on her Office Support Services Web site. She has one at (`www.ossweb.com/search.html`) which makes use of Google's search engine. But as you can see in Figure 6-5, she also provides a separate Sitemap page that provides a list of links to her site's most important contents.

Figure 6-5: A Search This Site text box or Sitemap page lets visitors instantly match their interests with what you have to offer.

You say you're up to making your site searchable, and you shudder at the prospect of either writing your own computer script or finding and editing someone else's script to index your site's contents and actually do the searching? Then head over to Atomz (www.atomz.com) and check out the hosted application Atomz Search. If your site contains 500 pages or less, you can also add a search box to your Web page that lets visitors search your site. Other organizations that offer similar services include:

- ✔ Visit FreeFind (www.freefind.com)
- ✔ PicoSearch (www.picosearch.com)
- ✔ Webinator (www.thunderstone.com/texis/site/pages/webinator.html)

Writing Unforgettable Text

Business writing on the Web differs from the dry, linear report writing one is often called upon to compose (or worse yet, read) in the corporate world. So this is your chance to express the real you: You're online, where sites that are funny, authors who have a personality, and content that's quirky are most likely to succeed.

Striking the right tone

When your friends describe you to someone who has never met you, what do they say first? Maybe it's your fashion sense or your collection of salt and pepper shakers. Your business also has a personality, and the more striking you make its description on your Web page, the better. Use the tone of your text to define what makes your business unique and what distinguishes it from your competition.

Getting a little help from your friends

Tooting your own horn is a fine technique to use in some situations, but you shouldn't go overboard with promotional prose that beats readers over the head. Web readers are looking for objective information they can evaluate for themselves. An independent review of your site or your products carries far more weight than your own ravings about how great your site is. Sure, you know your products and services are great, but you'll be more convincing if your offerings can sell themselves, or you can identify third parties to endorse them.

CASE STUDY

Building an online presence takes time

Judy Vorfeld, who goes by the *nom de Net* Webgrammar, knows all about finding different ways to attract a regular clientele. And she knows how important it is to have good content in a business Web site. She started the online version of her business Office Support Services (www.ossweb.com) from her home in Arizona in early 1998. She now has a second business site (www.editingandwritingservices.com) and a third (www.webgrammar.com), which serves as a resource for students, educators, writers, and Web developers.

Q. What would you describe as the primary goal of your online business?

A. To help small businesses achieve excellent presentation and communication by copyediting their print documents, books, and Web sites.

Q. How many hours a week do you work on your business site?

A. Three to six hours, which includes my syndicated writing tips, surveys, and newsletter, Communication Expressway (www.ossweb.com/ezine-archive-index.html).

Q. How do you promote your site?

A. Participating in newsgroups, writing articles for Internet publications, adding my URLs to good search engines and directories, moderating discussion lists and forums for others, offering free articles and tips on my sites, and networking locally and on the Web.

Q. Has your online business been profitable financially?

A. I continue to break even, and am able to upgrade hardware and software regularly. I rarely raise my rates because my skills seem best suited to the small business community, and I want to offer a fee these people can afford.

Q. Who creates your business's Web pages?

A. Basic design is done by a Web designer, and I take over from there. I want the ability to make extensive and frequent changes in text and design. I do hire someone to format my ezine pages, graphics, and programming.

Q. What advice would you give to someone starting an online business?

A. I have a bunch of suggestions to give, based on my own experience:

- **Network.** Network with small business people who have complementary businesses and with those who have similar businesses. Also, network by joining professional associations participating in the activities. Volunteer time and expertise. Link to these organizations from your site.

- **Join newsgroups and forums.** Study netiquette first. Lurk until you can adequately answer a question or make a comment. Also, keep on the lookout for someone with whom you can build up a relationship, someone who might mentor you and be willing to occasionally scrutinize your site, a news release, and so on. This person must be brutally honest, but perhaps you can informally offer one of your own services in return.

- **Learn Web development and the culture.** Even if you don't do the actual design, you have to make decisions on all the offers you receive regarding how to make money via affiliate programs, link exchanges, hosts, Web design software, etc. It's vital that you keep active online and make those judgments yourself, unless you thoroughly trust your Webmaster. Find online discussion lists that handle all areas of Web development and keep informed.

✔ **Include a Web page that shows your business biography or profile.** Mention any volunteer work you do, groups to which you belong, and anything else you do in and for the community. You need to paint as clear a picture as possible in just a few words. Avoid showcasing your talents and hobbies on a business site unless they are directly related to your business.

✔ **In *everything* you write, speak to your visitors.** Use the word "you" as much as possible. Avoid the words "I," "we," and "us." You, as a businessperson, are there to connect with your visitors. You can't give them eye contact, but you can let them know that they matter, that they are (in a sense) the reason for your being there.

✔ **Become known as a specialist in a given field.** Be someone who can always answer a question or go out and find the answer. Your aim is to get as many potential clients or customers to your site as possible, not to get millions of visitors. Forget numbers and concentrate on creating a site that grabs the attention of your target market.

✔ **Get help.** If you can't express yourself well with words (and/or graphics), and know little about layout, formatting, etc., hire someone to help you. You'll save yourself a lot of grief if you get a capable, trustworthy editor or designer.

She concludes: "Don't start such a business unless you are passionate about it and willing to give it some time and an initial investment. But when you do start, there are resources everywhere — many of them free — to help people build their businesses successfully."

What's that you say? *Wired* magazine hasn't called to do an in-depth interview profiling your entrepreneurial skills? Yahoo! hasn't graced you with the coveted "glasses" icon (indicating, in the estimation of Yahoo!'s Web site reviewers, a cool site worthy of special attention) on one of its long index pages? Take a hint from what my colleagues and I do when we're writing computer books such as the one you're reading now: We fire up our e-mail and dash off messages to anyone who may want to endorse our books: our mentors, our friends, and people we admire in the industry.

People should endorse your business because they like it, not simply because you asked for an endorsement. If they have problems with your business setup, they can be a great source of objective advice on how to improve it. Then, after you make the improvements, they're more likely than ever to endorse it.

Satisfied customers are another source of endorsements. Approach your customers and ask if they're willing to provide a quote about how you helped them. If you don't yet have satisfied customers, ask one or two people to try your products or services for free and then, if they're happy with your wares, ask permission to use their comments on your site. Your goal is to get a pithy, positive quote that you can put on your home page or on a page specifically devoted to quotes from your clients.

Don't be afraid to knock on the doors of celebrities, too. Send e-mail to an online reporter or someone prominent in your field and ask for an endorsement. People love to give their opinions and see their names in print. You just may be pleasantly surprised at how ready they are to help you.

Sharing your expertise

Few things build credibility and ensure return visits like a Web site that presents "inside" tips and goodies you can't get anywhere else. The more you can make your visitors feel that they're going to find something on your site that is rare or unique, the more success you'll have.

Tell what you know. Give people information about your field that they may not have. Point them to all sorts of different places with links.

Siteinspector.com (www.siteinspector.com) provides many services that Web site owners can access and use online for free. One utility sends your business URL to a variety of search engines and indexes. Another evaluates how highly your site is ranked by the major search services. After you have designed your pages, added your content, and gone online, check your pages with a utility such as Doctor HTML. The program costs $350 for a single computer, but the service will analyze a single Web page at a time for free. Go to www.doctor-html.com/RxHTMLpro/cgi-bin/single.cgi to make sure that everything on one of your most important pages (such as your home page) works efficiently.

Inviting Comments from Customers

Quick, inexpensive, and *personal:* These are three of the most important advantages that the Web has over traditional printed catalogs. The first two are obvious pluses. You don't have to wait for your online catalog to get printed and distributed. On the Web, your contents are published and available to your customers right away. Putting a catalog on the Web eliminates (or, if publishing a catalog on the Web allows you to reduce your print run, dramatically reduces) the cost of printing, which can result in big savings for you.

But the fact that online catalogs can be more personal than the printed variety is perhaps the biggest advantage of all. The personal touch comes from the Web's potential for *interactivity.* Getting your customers to click links makes them actively involved with your catalog.

Getting positive e-mail feedback

Playing hide and seek is fun when you're amusing your baby niece, but it's not a good way to build a solid base of customers. In fact, providing a way for your customers to interact with you so that they can reach you quickly may be the most important part of your Web site.

Add a simple *mailto* link like this:

Questions? Comments? Send e-mail to: `info@mycompany.com`

A mailto link gets its name from the HTML command that programmers use to create it. When visitors click the e-mail address, their e-mail program opens a new e-mail message window with your e-mail address already entered. That way, they have only to enter a subject line, type the message, and click Send to send you their thoughts.

Most Web page creation programs make it easy to create a mailto link. For example, if you use Dreamweaver, follow these steps:

1. **Launch and open the Web page to which you want to add your e-mail link.**

2. **Position your mouse arrow and click at the spot on the page where you want the address to appear.**

   The convention is to put your e-mail address at or near the bottom of a Web page. A vertical blinking cursor appears at the location where you want to insert the address.

3. **Choose Insert⇨Email Link.**

   The Insert Email Link dialog box appears.

4. **In the Text box, type the text that you want to appear on your Web page.**

   You don't have to type your e-mail address; you can also type **Webmaster**, **Customer Service**, or your own name.

5. **In the E-Mail box, type your e-mail address.**

6. **Click OK.**

   The Insert Email Link dialog box closes, and you return to the Dreamweaver Document window, where your e-mail link appears in blue and is underlined to signify that it is a clickable link.

Other editors work similarly but don't give you a menu command called Email Link. For example, in World Wide Web Weaver, a shareware program for the Macintosh, you choose Tags⇨Mail. A dialog box called Mail Editor appears. Enter your e-mail address and the text you want to appear as the highlighted link, and then click OK to add the mailto link to your page.

The drawback to publishing your e-mail address directly on your Web page is that you're virtually certain to get unsolicited e-mail messages (commonly called *spam*) sent to that address. Hiding your e-mail address behind generic link text (such as "Webmaster") may help reduce your chances of attracting spam.

Web page forms that aren't off-putting

You don't have to do much Web surfing before you become intimately acquainted with how Web page forms work, at least from the standpoint of someone who has to fill them out in order to sign up for Web hosting or to download software.

When it comes to creating your own Web site, however, you become conscious of how useful forms are as a means of gathering essential marketing information about your customers. They give your visitors a place to sound off, ask questions, and generally get involved with your online business.

Be clear and use common sense when creating your order form. Here are some general guidelines on how to organize your form and what you need to include:

✔ **Make it easy on the customer:** Whenever possible, add pull-down menus with pre-entered options to your *form fields* (text boxes that visitors use to enter information). That way, users don't have to wonder about things such as whether you want them to spell out a state or use the two-letter abbreviation.

✔ **Validate the information:** You can use a programming language called JavaScript to ensure that users enter information correctly, that all fields are completely filled out, and so on. You may have to hire someone to add the appropriate code to the order form, but it's worth it to save you from having to call customers to verify or correct information that they missed or submitted incorrectly.

✔ **Provide a help number:** Give people a number to call if they have questions or want to check on an order.

✔ **Return an acknowledgment:** Let customers know that you have received their order and will be shipping the merchandise immediately or contacting them if more information is needed.

As usual, good Web page authoring and editing programs make it a snap to create the text boxes, check boxes, buttons, and other parts of a form that the user fills out. The other part of a form, the computer script that receives the data and processes it so that you can read and use the information, is not as simple. See Chapter 13 for details.

Not so long ago, you had to write or edit a scary CGI script in order to set up forms processing on your Web site. A new alternative recently turned up that makes the process of creating a working Web page form accessible to non-programmers like the rest of us. Web businesses, such as Response-O-Matic (`www.response-o-matic.com`) and FormMail.To (`www.formmail.to`), will lead you through the process of setting up a form and providing you with the CGI script that receives the data and forwards it to you.

Providing a guestbook

The basic idea of a guestbook is not all that new and exciting. You probably have gone to plenty of special events where they ask you to sign in and write a little something about the guests of honor or the place where the party is being held. But a guestbook on your Web site can add a whole other dimension to your business by making your customers feel that they are part of a thriving community. When you provide a guestbook on one of your business's Web pages, your clients and other visitors can check out who else has been there and what others think about the site.

If you set out to create your own Web page guestbook from scratch, you'd have to create a form, write a script (fairly complicated code that tells a computer what to do), test the code, and so on. Thankfully, an easier way to add a guestbook is available: You simply register with a special Web business that provides free guestbooks to users. One such organization, Lycos, offers a guestbook service through its Html Gear site (`htmlgear.lycos.com/specs/guest.html`).

If you register with Html Gear's service, you can have your own guestbook right away with no fuss. (Actually, Html Gear's guestbook program resides on one of its Web servers; you just add the text-entry portion to your own page.) Here's how to do it:

1. **Connect to the Internet, start up your Web browser, and go to** `htmlgear.lycos.com/specs/guest.html`.

2. **Scroll down the page and click the Get this Gear! link.**

   You go to the Network Membership page.

3. **Click the Sign Me Up! button and follow the instructions on subsequent pages to register for the guestbook and other software on the Html Gear site.**

   The program asks you to provide your own personal information, choose a name and password for your guestbook, enter the URL of the Web page on which you want the guestbook to appear, and provide keywords that describe your page.

4. **After you've registered, a page entitled Gear Manager appears. Click Add Gear and then Get Gear next to Guest Gear.**

   After a few seconds, a page called Create Guest Gear appears. This page contains a form that you need to fill out in order to create the guestbook *text-entry fields* (the text boxes and other items that visitors use to submit information to you) to your Web page.

5. **Fill out the Create Guest Gear form.**

   The form lets you name your guestbook and customize how you want visitors to interact with you. For instance, you can configure the guestbook to send you an e-mail notification whenever someone posts a message.

6. **When you're done filling out the form, click Save & Create.**

   The Get Code page appears. A box contains the code you need to copy and add to the HTML for your Web page.

7. **Position your mouse arrow at the beginning of the code (just before the first line, which looks like this:** `<!-- \/ GuestGEAR Code by http://htmlgear.com \/ ->`**), press and hold down your mouse button, and scroll across the code to the last line, which reads:** `<!-- /\ End GuestGEAR Code /\ -->`**.**

   The code is highlighted to show that it has been selected.

8. **Choose Edit⇨Copy to copy the selected code to your computer's Clipboard.**

9. **Launch your Web editor, if it isn't running already, and open the Web page you want to edit in your Web editor window.**

   If you're working in a program (such as Dreamweaver or HotDog Pro) that shows the HTML for a Web page while you edit it, you can move on to Step 10. If, on the other hand, your editor hides the HTML from you, you have to use your editor's menu options to view the HTML source for your page. The exact menu command varies from program to program. Usually, though, the option is contained in the View menu. In FrontPage, for example, you click the HTML tab at the bottom of the window. The HTML for the Web page you want to edit then appears.

10. **Scroll down and click the spot on the page where you want to paste the HTML code for the guestbook.**

How do you know where this spot is? Well, you have to add the code in the BODY section of a Web page. This is the part of the page that is contained between two HTML tags, <BODY> and </BODY>. You can't go wrong with pasting the code just before the </BODY> tag — or just before your return e-mail address or any other material you want to keep at the bottom of the page. The following example indicates the proper placement for the guestbook code:

```
<HTML>
<HEAD>
<TITLE>Sign My Guestbook</TITLE>
</HEAD>
<BODY>
The body of your Web page goes here; this is the part
        that appears on the Web.
Paste your guestbook code here!
</BODY>
</HTML>
```

11. Choose Edit➪Paste.

The guestbook code is added to your page.

12. Close your Web editor's HTML window.

Exactly how you do this varies depending on the program. If you have a separate HTML window open, click the close box (X) in the upper-right corner of the HTML window, if you are working in a Windows environment. (If you're working on a Mac, close the window by clicking the close box in the upper-left corner of the window that displays the HTML.)

The HTML code disappears, and you return to your Web editor's main window.

13. Choose File➪Save to save your changes.

14. Preview your work in your Web browser window.

The steps involved in previewing also vary from editor to editor. Some editors have a Preview toolbar button that you click to view your page in a Web browser. Otherwise, launch your Web browser to preview your page as follows:

• If you use Netscape Navigator, choose File➪Open Page, click the name of the file you just saved in the Open Page dialog box, and then click Open to open the page.

• If you use Internet Explorer, choose File➪Open, click the name of the file you just saved in the Open dialog box, and then click Open to open the page.

The page opens in your Web browser, with a new Guestbook button added to it, as shown in Figure 6-6.

Now, when visitors to your Web page click the Sign My Guestbook link, they go to a page that has a form they can fill out. Clicking the View My Guestbook link enables visitors to view the messages that other visitors have entered into your guestbook.

The problem with adding a link to a service that resides on another Web site is that it makes your Web pages load more slowly. First, your visitor's browser loads the text on your page. Then it loads the images from top to bottom. Besides this, it has to make a link to the Html Gear site in order to load the guestbook. If you decide to add a guestbook, images, or other elements that reside on another Web site, be sure to test your page and make sure that you're satisfied with how long the contents take to appear. Also make sure to use the "Moderation" feature that enables you to screen postings to your guestbook. That way, you can delete obscene, unfair, or libelous postings before they go online.

Chit-chat that counts

You've accomplished a lot by the time you've put your business online. Hopefully, you're already seeing the fruits of your labors in the form of e-mail inquiries and orders for your products or services.

That's all good, but this is no time to rest on your laurels. After visitors start coming to your site, the next step is to retain those visitors. A good way to do this is by building a sense of community by posting a bulletin-board-type discussion area.

A discussion area takes the form of back-and-forth messages on topics of mutual interest. Each person can read previously posted messages and either respond or start a new topic of discussion. For an example of a discussion area that's tied to an online business, visit the Australian Fishing (www.ausfish.com.au) discussion areas, one of which is shown in Figure 6-7.

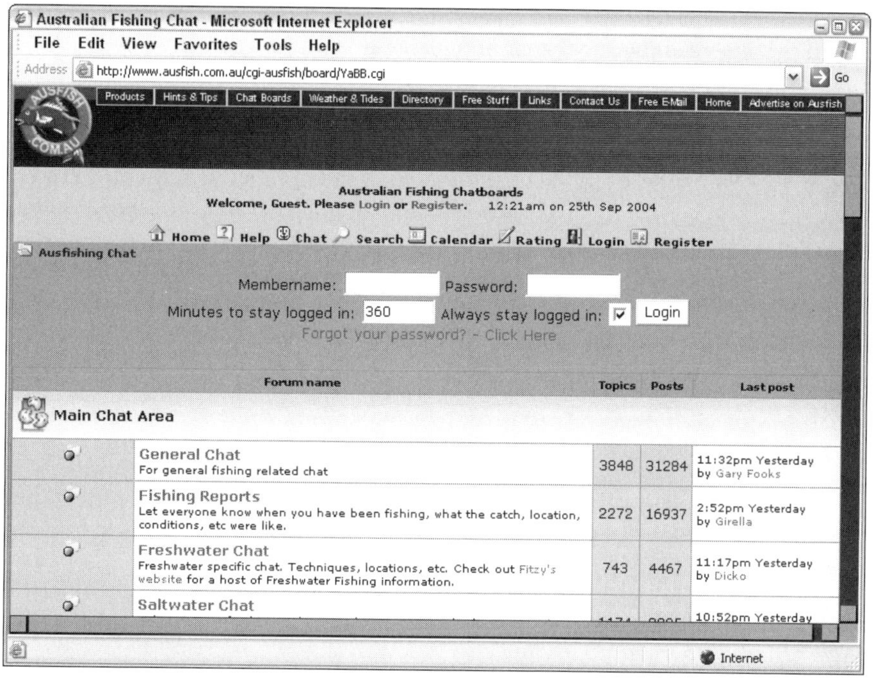

Figure 6-7:
A discussion area stimulates interest and interaction among likeminded customers.

The talk doesn't have to be about your own particular niche in your business field. In fact, the discussion will be more lively if your visitors can discuss concerns about your area of business in general, whether it's flower arranging, boat sales, tax preparation, clock repair, computers, or whatever.

How, exactly, do you start a discussion area? The basic first step is to install a special computer script on the computer that hosts your Web site. (Again, discussing this prospect with your Web hosting service beforehand is essential.) When visitors come to your site, their Web browsers access the script, enabling them to enter comments and read other messages.

Here are some specific ways to prepare a discussion area for your site:

✔ Install Microsoft FrontPage, which includes the scripts you need to start a discussion group. You can't download a trial version; you have to buy the software for $199.

www.microsoft.com/office/frontpage/howtobuy/default.mspx

✔ Copy a bulletin board or discussion-group script from either of these sites:

- Extropia.com (www.extropia.com/applications.html)
- Matt's Script Archive (www.worldwidemart.com/scripts)

✔ Start your own forum on a service such as HyperNews, by Daniel
   LaLiberte, or install the HyperNews program yourself.

   `www.hypernews.org/HyperNews/get/hypernews.html`

Because chat rooms and discussion groups are for a more advanced business
Web site, I don't discuss them in detail in this book. If you want to find out
more, please refer to my book *Small Business Internet For Dummies* (Wiley).

Chapter 7

Building in Security Up Front

*W*hether the perceived threat is from foreign terrorists or roving gangs of teenage hoodlums, everyone seems to be on heightened security alert these days. And when you're an online businessperson, you face some real concerns that involve your own equipment and data as well as the welfare of your clients. The whole idea of security can seem intimidating. After all, you need to protect your business from the viruses and other hack attacks that are proliferating along with the always-on broadband Internet connections, which are especially vulnerable to these intrusions. Fortunately, there are some down-to-earth measures you can take, most of which involve nothing more than good old common sense. You don't need to spend lots of money to make your information and that of your all-important customers secure.

In this chapter, I discuss some technologies and strategies that can keep your data secure. Some of these measures are easy to put into practice and especially important for home-based businesspeople. Others are technically challenging to implement on your own. But even if you have your Web host or a consultant do the work, it's good to familiarize yourself with Internet security schemes. Doing so gives you the ability to make informed decisions about how to protect your online data. You can then take steps to lock your virtual doors so you don't have to worry that your cyberstock is easy pickings for hackers and other boogeymen.

Practicing Safe Business

I'm not about to suggest that you buy a gun or even a guard dog to protect your home office. Yet I do need in good conscience to point out that working at home carries its own set of safety concerns for small-business owners. Luckily, these concerns tend to be easy to address. Safe computing practices, such as using password protection, making backups, and installing antivirus software, can go a long way toward keeping your data secure, even if you never have to get into more technical subjects such as public-key encryption.

When you sleep where you work

Traffic in my city has gone from bad to worse, and I remind myself every morning as I'm working on my laptop while sitting on my back porch in my pajamas how lucky I am to not have to commute. Yet I'm constantly fielding phone calls from parents of the friends of my children as well as nonprofit groups that I support who assume that because I'm home I have the whole day free to do as I please. So, knowing all too well that it's easier said than done, here are some simple steps that can help you set more clearly defined boundaries between work and domestic life, even when it all happens under the same roof.

When the computer is a group sport

Even if you're of a certain age, it's probably hard to comprehend that not so very long ago, there was one telephone per household and even that was connected to a party line shared by a number of other families. Now everyone in my family, at least, thinks they are entitled to their own computers. We haven't reached that level of paradise yet, but there is a lot to be said for having at least two separate machines — one for personal use and one for business use. The idea is that you set up your system so that you have to log on to your business computer with a username and password. (For suggestions on how to devise a good password that's difficult to crack, see the section, "Picking passwords that are hard to guess," later in this chapter.)

If you have only one computer, passwords can still provide a measure of protection. Windows gives you the ability to set up different user profiles, each associated with its own password. You can assign a different profile to each member of your family. You can even make a game out of selecting profiles: Each person can pick his or her own background color and desktop arrangement for Windows. User profiles and passwords don't necessarily protect your business files, but they convey to your family members that they should use their own software, stick to their own directories, and not try to explore your company data.

You can also set up different user profiles for your copy of Netscape Communicator. That way, your kids won't receive your business e-mail while they're surfing the Internet because you'll have different e-mail inboxes. If you're on Windows, choose Start➪Programs➪Netscape Communicator➪Utilities➪User Profile Manager. If you use Outlook Express for e-mail, choose File➪Identities . . .➪Add New Identity to create an identity and assign a password to it.

Folder Guard, a program by WinAbility Corporation (www.winability.com/folderguard), enables you to hide or password-protect files or folders on your computer. The software works with Windows 95/98/Me/2000/XP. You can choose from the Standard version, which is intended for home users, or the Professional version, which is designed for business customers. A 14-day trial version is available for download from the WinAbility Web site; if you want to keep the Standard version of Folder Guard, you have to pay $39.95 (or $59.95 for the Professional version).

One ringie dingie . . . two ringie dingies . . .

Back to the topic of telephones, even a thrifty guy like me considers it to be a necessity, not a luxury, to get a separate phone line for business use (even if it's your cell phone rather than a land line). Having a devoted phone line not only makes your business seem more serious but also separates your business calls from your personal calls. Additionally, if you need a phone line to connect to the Net, you then have a choice of which line to use for your modem.

The next step is to set up your business phone with its own answering machine or voice mail. On your business voice mail, identify yourself with your business's name. This arrangement builds credibility and makes you feel like a real business owner. You can then install privacy features, such as caller ID, on your business line as needed.

Even though I've resigned myself to paying for multiple phone lines, I'm still constantly on the lookout for the best deal possible. One place I go to for tips and news on telephone service, not only for small businesses but also for personal use, is the Telecommunications Research & Action Center (www.trac.org). This site provides suggestions of ways to cut your phone bills and make smart decisions on telephone service.

Preparing for the worst

There's an old joke about the telegram from a mother that read, "Worry. Details to follow." When you're lying awake at night, you can be anxious about all sorts of grim disasters: flood, fire, theft, computer virus, you name it. Prevention is always better than cure, so this chapter covers steps you can take to prevent problems. But, should a problem arise, there are also ways to recover more easily.

Insurance . . . the least you can do

I can think of ways to spend money that are a whole lot more fun than paying insurance premiums. Yet there I am every month, writing checks to protect myself in case something goes wrong with my house, car, body, and so on. And yes, there's another item to add to the list: protecting my business investment by obtaining insurance that specifically covers me against hardware damage, theft, and loss of data. You can also go a step further and obtain a policy that covers the cost of data entry or equipment rental that would be necessary to recover your business information. Here are some specific strategies:

✔ Make a list of all your hardware and software and how much each item cost, and store a copy of it in a place such as a fireproof safe or safe-deposit box.

✔ Take photos of your computer setup in case you need to make an insurance claim and put them in the same safe place.

✔ Save your electronic files on CD or DVD and put the disc in a safe storage location, such as a safe-deposit box.

Investigate the many options available to you for insuring your computer hardware and software. Your current homeowner's or renter's insurance may offer coverage, but make sure the dollar amount is sufficient for replacement. You may also want to look into the computer hardware and software coverage provided by Safeware, The Insurance Agency, Inc. (`www.safeware.com`).

Think ahead to the unthinkable

The Gartner Group estimates that two out of five businesses that experience a major disaster will go out of business within five years. I would guess that the three that are able to get back up on their feet and running quickly are those that already had recovery plans in place. Even if your company is small, you need to be prepared for big trouble — not only for terrorist attacks, but natural disasters such as floods, hurricanes, or tornadoes. A recovery effort might include the following strategies:

✔ **Backup power systems:** What will you do if the power goes out and you can't access the Web? Consider a battery backup system such as APC Back-UPS Office (`www.apc.com/products/back-ups_office/index.cfm`). It instantly switches your computers to battery power when the electricity goes out so you can save your data and switch to laptops. A version that runs for five to ten minutes costs $59.99. Even more important, make sure that your ISP or Web host has a backup power supply so that your store can remain online in case of a power outage.

✔ **Data storage:** This is probably the most practical and essential disaster recovery step for small or home-based businesses. Back up your files on a computer that's not located in the place where you physically work. At the very least, upload your files periodically to the Web space that your hosting service gives you. Also consider storing your files with an online storage service. (See the section on online storage space in this book's Internet Directory for suggestions, including one free storage option.)

✔ **Telecommunications:** Having some alternate method of communication available in case your phone system goes down ensures that you're always in touch. The obvious choice is a cell phone. Also set up a voice mailbox so that customers and vendors can leave messages for you even if you can't answer the phone.

Creating a plan is a waste of time if you don't regularly set aside time to keep it up to date. Back up your data on a regular basis, purchase additional equipment if you need it, and make arrangements to use other computers and offices if you need to — in other words, *implement* your plan. You owe it not only to yourself but also to your customers to be prepared in case of disaster.

Low- and high-tech locks

If you play the word game with a Web surfer or Web site and say "security," you're likely to get a response such as "encryption." But security doesn't need to start with software. The fact is, all the firewalls and passwords in the world won't help you if someone breaks into your home office and trashes or makes off with the computer that contains all your files.

Besides insuring your computer equipment and taking photos in case you need to get it replaced, you can also invest in locks for your home office and your machines. They might not keep someone from breaking into your house, but they'll at least make it more difficult for intruders to carry off your hardware.

Here are some suggestions for how to protect your hardware and the business data your computers contain:

✔ **Lock your office:** Everyone has locks on the outer doors of their house, but go a step further and install a deadbolt lock on your office door.

✔ **Lock your computers:** Innovative Security Products (www.wesecure.com) offers several varieties of computer locking systems. They also sell ultraviolet pens that you

can use to mark your equipment with your name and the serial number of your computer in case the police recover it.

✔ **Mark your modem:** Unbeknownst to someone who's up to no good, an innovative theft recovery system called CompuTrace can be installed on your hard drive. Then, if your computer is stolen, the software is activated. When the thief connects its internal modem to a phone line, the authorities are notified. The system works with other types of Internet connections as well, including DSL and cable modems. CompuTrace Plus (www.computrace.com) is offered by Absolute Software Corp. and costs home office users $49.95 for one year of monitoring.

✔ **Make backups:** Be sure to regularly back up your information on Zip drives or similar storage devices. Also consider signing up with a Web-based storage service where files can be transferred from your computer. That way, if your computers and your extra storage disks are lost for whatever reason, you'll have an online backup in a secure location. Look into @Backup (www.atbackup.com), which will give you 100MB of storage space for $99 per year.

Antivirus protection without a needle

ISCA Labs (`www.icsalabs.com/html/communities/antivirus/alerts.shtml`), which keeps track of viruses circulating around the Internet, has estimated that as many as 20,000 viruses are present online at any one time. As an online businessperson, you're going to be downloading files, receiving disks from customers and vendors, and exchanging e-mail with all sorts of people you've never met before. Surf safely by installing antivirus programs such as

- ✔ **Norton Internet Security by Symantec Corporation (`www.symantec.com/product`):** This application, which includes an antivirus program and a firewall and lists for $69.95, automates many security functions and is especially good for beginners. A standalone version, Norton Anti-Virus, is available for $49.95, but I highly recommend the more full-featured package, which includes a firewall that will block many other dangerous types of intrusions such as Trojan horses.

- ✔ **AVG AntiVirus by GriSoft (`www.grisoft.com`):** Many users who find Norton Internet Security too intrusive (it leaves lots of files on your computer and consumes a great deal of memory) turn to this product, which comes in a free version as well as a more full-featured version for $33.30.

- ✔ **AntiVir Personal Edition by H+BEDV (`www.free-av.de`):** Another popular free program. The program's home page is in German, which may turn off U.S. users.

- ✔ **VirusScan by McAfee (`www.mcafee.com/us`):** This is the leading competitor to Norton Anti-Virus, which comes bundled with Norton Internet Security. A version called VirusScan ASaP for small businesses costs $40.80. VirusScan is included in McAfee Internet Security, which includes a firewall and costs $49.99.

This is another area that demands your attention on a regular basis. Viruses change all the time, and new ones appear regularly. The antivirus program you install one day may not be able to handle the viruses that appear just a few weeks or months later. You may want to pick an antivirus program that doesn't charge excessive amounts for regular updates (for instance, you have to pay for a new version every year, as Norton Internet Security does). Also check the ICSA's monthly antivirus Product Testing Reports (`www.icsalabs.com/html/communities/antivirus/labs.shtml`).

A visible sign that you're trustworthy

Like the office assistant whose work is visible only when he or she is not doing a good job, you may be squeaky clean but nobody will know unless there's a problem . . . or unless you display a seal from TRUSTe. This nonprofit organization is seeking to boost the degree of trust that Web surfers have in the Internet. It does this through a third-party oversight "seal" program. If you demonstrate to TRUSTe that you're making efforts to keep your visitors' personal data secure, and if you pledge not to share your customers' data and to publish a privacy statement on your site, TRUSTe issues you a seal of approval that you can place on your site's home page. The TRUSTe seal is intended to function as the online equivalent of the Good Housekeeping seal of approval on a product.

By itself, the seal doesn't keep hackers from breaking into your site and stealing your data. That's still up to you. Having the seal just makes visitors feel better about using your services. The TRUSTe site provides you with a wizard that leads you through the process of generating a privacy statement for your site. The statement tells visitors how you will protect their information. Find out more by visiting the TRUSTe home page (www.truste.org) and clicking the For Businesses link.

I love gadgets, and few things get me more excited than hand-held devices, laptops, and other portable computing devices. Yet those are the items that I seem to have the most trouble keeping track of, literally and figuratively. At the very least, you should make the device's storage area accessible with a password. You can also install protection software designed especially for mobile devices, such as VirusScan PDA by McAfee (www.mcafee.com/myapps/vsw/default.asp).

Installing Firewalls and Other Safeguards

You probably know how important a firewall is in a personal sense. It filters out unwanted intrusions such as executable programs that hackers seek to plant on your file system so they can use your computer for their own purposes. When you're starting an online business, the objectives of a firewall become different: You're protecting not just your own information but also that of your customers. In other words, you're quite possibly relying on the firewall to protect your source of income as well as the data on your computers.

Just what is a firewall, exactly? A *firewall* is an application or hardware device that monitors the data flowing into or out of a computer network and that filters the data based on criteria that the owner sets up. Like a security guard at the entrance to an apartment building, a firewall scans the packets (small, uniform data segments) of digital information that traverse the Internet, making sure the data is headed for the right destination and that it doesn't match known characteristics of viruses or attacks. Authorized traffic is allowed into your network. Attack attempts or viruses are either automatically deleted or cause an alert message to appear to which you must respond with a decision to block or allow the incoming or outgoing packets.

Keeping out Trojan horses and other unwanted visitors

A *Trojan horse* is a program that enters your computer surreptitiously and then attempts to do something without your knowledge. Some folks say that such programs enter your system through a "backdoor" because you don't immediately know that they've entered your system. Trojan horses may come in the form of an e-mail attachment with the filename extension `.exe` (which stands for *executable*). For instance, I recently received an e-mail that purported to be from Microsoft Corporation and that claimed it contained a security update. The attachment looked innocent enough, but had I saved the attachment to my computer, it would have used my computer as a staging area for distributing itself to many other e-mail addresses.

I didn't run into trouble, however. A special firewall program I installed, called Norton Internet Security, recognized the attachment and alerted me to the danger. I highly recommend that anyone who, like me, has a cable modem, DSL, or other direct connection to the Internet install one right away. You can try out a shareware program called ZoneAlarm by Zone Labs, Inc. (`www.zone alarm.com`) that provides you with basic firewall protection, though more full-featured programs like Norton Internet Security (`www.symantec.com/product`) will probably be more effective.

Cleaning out spyware

You've also got to watch out for software that "spies" on your Web surfing and other activities and that reports them back to advertisers, potentially invading your privacy. Ad-Aware isn't a firewall, exactly, but it's a useful program that detects and erases any advertising programs you may have downloaded from the Internet without knowing it. Such advertising programs might be running on your computer, consuming your processing resources and slowing down operations. Some "spyware" programs track your activities as you surf the Web; others simply report that they have been installed. Many users regard these spyware programs as invasions of privacy because they install themselves and do their reporting without your asking for it or even knowing they're active.

When I ran Ad-Aware the first time, it detected a whopping 57 programs I didn't know about that were running on my computer and that had installed themselves when I connected to various Web sites or downloaded software. As you can see in Figure 7-1, when I ran Ad-Aware while I was working on this chapter, sure enough, it found four suspicious software components running.

I highly recommend Ad-Aware; you can download a version at `www.lava softUSA.com` and try it for free. If you decide to keep it, you pay a $15 shareware fee.

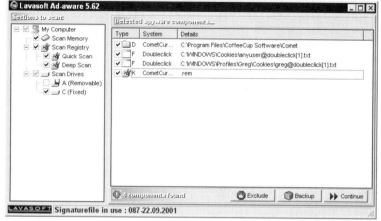

Figure 7-1:
Ad-Aware
deletes
advertising
software
that, many
users
believe, can
violate your
privacy.

Positioning the firewall

These days, most home networks are configured so that the computers on
the network can share information as well as the same Internet connection.
Whether you run a home-based business or a business in a discrete location,
you almost certainly have a network of multiple computers. A network is far
more vulnerable than a single computer connected to the Internet: A network
has more entry points than a single computer, and more reliance is placed on
each of the operators of those computers to observe good safety practices.
And if one computer on the network is attacked, there is the real potential for
the others to be attacked as well.

You probably are acquainted with software firewalls such as Norton Personal
Firewall or McAfee Firewall (www.mcafee.com/myapps/firewall/ov_
firewall.asp). Software firewalls protect one computer at a time. In a typical business scenario, however, multiple computers share a single Internet
connection through a router that functions as a gateway. Many network
administrators prefer a *hardware firewall* — a device that functions as a filter
for traffic both entering and leaving it. A hardware firewall may also function
as a router, but it can also be separate from the router. The device is positioned
at the perimeter of the network where it can protect all the company's computers at once. Examples of hardware are the Cisco PIX line (one example, which
costs about $350, is at www.cisco.com/en/US/products/hw/vpndevc/
ps2030/ps2031/index.html), and the WatchGuard Firebox SOHO 6tc,
which costs about $279, by WatchGuard (www.watchguard.com).

Companies that want to provide a Web site that the public can visit as
well as secure e-mail and other communications services create a secure
sub-network of one or more specially hardened (in other words, secured
because all unnecessary services have been removed from them) computers.
This kind of network is called a *Demilitarized Zone* or DMZ.

Keeping your firewall up to date

Firewalls work by means of attack *signatures* (also called *definitions*), which are sets of data that identify a connection attempt as a potential attack. Some attacks are easy to stop: They have been attempted for years and the amateur hackers who attempt intrusions don't give much thought to them. The more dangerous attacks are new ones. They have signatures that have emerged since you installed your firewall.

You quickly get a dose of reality and find just how serious the problem is by visiting one of the Web sites that keeps track of the latest attacks such as the Distributed Intrusion Detection System or DShield (`www.dshield.org`). On the day I visited, DShield reported that the "survival time" for an unpatched computer (a computer that has security software that has not been equipped with the latest updates called *patches*) after connecting it to the Internet was only 16 minutes. That means such a computer only has 16 minutes before someone tries to attack it. If that doesn't scare you into updating your security software, I don't know what will.

Public Keys That Provide Security

The conversations I overhear as I drive my preteen daughters and their friends to events leave no doubt in my mind that different segments of society use code words that only their members can understand. Even computers use encoding and decoding to protect information they exchange on the Internet. The schemes used online are far more complex and subtle than the slang used by kids, however. This section describes the security method that is used most widely on the Internet, and the one you're likely to use yourself: Secure Sockets Layer (SSL) encryption.

The keys to public-key/private-key encryption

Terms like SSL and encryption might make you want to reach for the remote. But don't be too quick to switch channels. SSL is making it safer to do business online and boosting the trust of potential customers. And anything that makes shoppers more likely to spend money online is something you need to know about.

The term *encryption* refers to the process of encoding data, especially sensitive data, such as credit card numbers. Information is encrypted by means of complex mathematical formulas called *algorithms.* Such a formula may transform a simple-looking bit of information into a huge block of seemingly incomprehensible numbers, letters, and characters. Only someone who has the right formula, called a *key,* which is itself a complex mass of encoded data, can decode the gobbledygook.

Here's a very simple example. Suppose that my credit card number is 12345 and I encode it by using an encryption formula into something like the following: 1aFgHx203gX4gLu5cy.

The algorithm that generated this encrypted information may say something like: "Take the first number, multiply it by some numeral, and then add some letters to it. Then take the second number, divide it by x, and add y characters to the result," and so on. (In reality, the formulas are far more complex than this, which is why you usually have to pay a license fee to use them. But this is the general idea.) Someone who has the same formula can run it in reverse, so to speak, in order to decrypt the encoded number and obtain the original number, 12345.

In practice, the encoded numbers that are generated by encryption routines and transmitted on the Internet are very large. They vary in size depending on the relative strength (or uncrackability) of the security method being used. Some methods generate keys that consist of 128 bits of data; a *data bit* is a single unit of digital information. These formulas are called *128-bit keys.*

Encryption is the cornerstone of security on the Internet. The most widely used security schemes, such as the Secure Sockets Layer protocol (SSL), the Secure Electronic Transactions protocol (SET), and Pretty Good Privacy (PGP), all use some form of encryption.

With some security methods, the party that sends the data and the party that receives it both use the same key (this method is called *symmetrical encryption*). This approach isn't considered as secure as an asymmetrical encryption method, such as public-key encryption, however. In public-key encryption, the originating party obtains a license to use a security method. (In the following section, I show you just how to do this yourself.) As part of the license, you use the encryption algorithm to generate your own private key. You never share this key with anyone. However, you use the private key to create a separate public key. This public key goes out to visitors who connect to a secure area of your Web site. As soon as they have your public key, users can encode sensitive information and send it back to you. Only you can decode the data — by using your secret, private key.

Getting a certificate without going to school

When you write a check at the grocery store, the cashier is likely to make sure you are preregistered as an approved member and also ask to see your driver's license. But on the Internet, how do you know that people are who they say they are when all you have to go on is a URL or an e-mail address? The solution in the online world is to obtain a personal certificate that you can send to Web site visitors or append to your e-mail messages.

How certificates work

A *certificate,* which is also sometimes called a Digital ID, is an electronic document issued by a certification authority (CA). The certificate contains the owner's personal information as well as a public key that can be exchanged with others online. The public key is generated by the owner's private key, which the owner obtains during the process of applying for the certificate.

In issuing the certificate, the CA takes responsibility for saying that the owner of the document is the same as the person actually identified on the certificate. Although the public key helps establish the owner's identity, certificates do require you to put a level of trust in the agency that issues it.

A certificate helps both you and your customers. A certificate assures your customers that you're the person you say you are, plus it protects your e-mail communications by enabling you to encrypt them.

Obtaining a certificate from VeriSign

Considering how important a role certificates play in online security, it's remarkably easy to obtain one. You do so by applying and paying a licensing fee to a CA. One of the most popular CAs is VeriSign, Inc., which lets you apply for a certificate called a Class 1 Digital ID.

A Class 1 Digital ID is only useful for securing personal communications. As an e-commerce Web site owner, you may want a business-class certificate called a 128-bit SSL Global Server ID (www.verisign.com/products/site). This form of Digital ID works only if your e-commerce site is hosted on a server that runs secure server software — software that encrypts transactions — such as Apache Stronghold. Check with your Web host to see if a secure server is available for your Web site.

A VeriSign personal certificate, which you can use to authenticate yourself in e-mail, news, and other interactions on the Net, costs $14.95 per year, and you can try out a free certificate for 60 days. Follow these steps to obtain your Digital ID:

1. **Go to the VeriSign, Inc. Digital IDs for Secure E-Mail page at**

```
www.verisign.com/products-services/security-
        services/pki/pki-application/email-digital-
        id/index.html
```

2. **Click the Buy Now button whether you're certain you want an ID or if you only want the trial version.**

   The Digital ID Enrollment page appears.

3. **Click Buy Now near the bottom of the page.**

   A page may appear (if you don't have JavaScript support) that asks you to identify the Web browser you use most often, and that you want to associate with the Digital ID. Click the browser you want. An application form for a Digital ID appears.

4. **Complete the application form.**

   The application process is pretty simple. The form asks for your personal information and a challenge phrase that you can use in case anyone is trying to impersonate you. It also requires you to accept a license agreement. (You don't need to enter credit card information if you select the 60-day trial option.)

5. **Click the Accept button at the bottom of the screen.**

   A dialog box appears asking you to confirm your e-mail address. After you confirm by clicking OK, a dialog box appears asking you to choose a password. When you enter a password and click OK, VeriSign uses your password to generate a private key for you. The private key is an essential ingredient in public-key/private-key technology.

6. **Click OK to have your browser generate your private key.**

   A page appears asking you to check your e-mail for further instructions. In a few minutes, you receive a message that contains a Digital ID PIN.

7. **In your e-mail program, open the new message from VeriSign Customer Support Department.**

8. **Use your mouse to highlight (select) the PIN, and then choose Edit⇨ Copy to copy the PIN.**

9. **Go to the URL for Digital ID Services that's included in the e-mail message and paste your PIN in the text box next to Enter the Digital ID Personal Identification Number (PIN).**

10. **Click Submit.**

    The certificate is generated, and the Digital IDF Installation and Registration Page appears.

11. **Click the Install button.**

    The ID from VeriSign downloads, and you're now able to view it with your browser. Figure 7-2 shows my certificate for Netscape Navigator. (Copying this ID, or anyone else's, is pointless because this is only your public key; the public key is always submitted with your private key, which is secret.)

Figure 7-2:
A personal certificate assures individuals or Web sites of your identity.

After you have your Digital ID, what do you do with it? For one thing, you can use it to verify your identity to sites that accept certificate submissions. Some sites that require members to log in use secure servers that give you the option of submitting your certificate rather than entering the usual user-name and password to identify yourself. You can also attach your Digital ID to your e-mail messages to prove that your message is indeed coming from you. See your e-mail program's Help files for more specific instructions.

You can't encrypt or digitally sign messages on any computer other than the one to which your certificates are issued. If you're using a different computer than the one you used when you obtained your certificates, you must contact your certificate issuer and obtain a new certificate for the computer you're now using. Or, if your browser allows transfers, you can export your certifi-cate to the new computer.

Keeping Other Noses Out of Your Business

Encryption isn't just for big businesses. Individuals who want to maintain their privacy, even while navigating the wilds of the Internet, can install special software or modify their existing e-mail programs in order to encode their online communications.

The Cyberangels Web site (www.cyberangels.org) presents some good tips and strategies for personal protection on the Internet.

Encryption software for the rest of us

PGP (Pretty Good Privacy), a popular encryption program, has been around about as long as the Web itself. PGP lets you protect the privacy of your e-mail messages and file attachments by encrypting them so that only those with the proper authority can decipher the information. You can also digitally sign the messages and files you exchange, which assures the recipient that the messages come from you and that the information has not been tampered with. You can even encrypt files on your own computer, too.

PGP (`web.mit.edu/network/pgp.html`) is a freely available personal encryption program. PGP is a *plug-in,* an application that works with another program to provide added functionality. You can integrate the program with popular e-mail programs such as Eudora and Microsoft Outlook (although Netscape Messenger is notably absent from the list of supported applications).

In order to use either the free version of PGP or another, commercial version called PGP Personal Privacy, the first step is to obtain and install the program. After you install the program, you can use it to generate your own private-key/public-key pair. After you create a key pair, you can begin exchanging encrypted e-mail messages with other PGP users. To do so, you need to obtain a copy of their public keys, and they need a copy of your public key. Because public keys are just blocks of text, trading keys with someone is really quite easy. You can include your public key in an e-mail message, copy it to a file, or post it on a public-key server where anyone can get a copy at any time.

After you have a copy of someone's public key, you can add it to your *public keyring,* which is a file on your own computer. Then you can begin to exchange encrypted and signed messages with that individual. If you're using an e-mail application supported by the PGP plug-ins, you can encrypt and sign your messages by selecting the appropriate options from your application's toolbar. If your e-mail program doesn't have a plug-in, you can copy your e-mail message to your computer's Clipboard and encrypt it there by using PGP built-in functions. See the PGP User's Guide files for more specific instructions.

The freeware version of PGP is distributed freely by MIT with the approval of Network Associates, which owns the rights to PGP encryption technology and has incorporated it into a variety of commercial security products. A commercial product called PGP Personal Privacy is still being sold by McAfee for $49.95 but is no longer being actively marketed. The freeware version of PGP will run on Windows 95/98/NT/2000 and the Mac OS 7.6.1 or later. (It also ran on my Windows Me computer.)

Encrypting e-mail messages

You can use your existing software to encrypt your mail messages rather than have to install a separate program such as PGP. In the following sections, I describe the steps involved in setting up the e-mail programs that come with the Big Two browser packages, Microsoft Internet Explorer and Netscape Communicator, to encrypt your messages.

If you use Outlook Express, you can use your Digital ID to do the following:

 ✔ **Send a digital signature:** You can digitally shrink-wrap your e-mail message by using your certificate in order to assure the recipient that the message is really from you.

 ✔ **Encrypt your message:** You can digitally encode a message to ensure that only the intended party can read it.

To better understand the technical details of how you can keep your e-mail communications secure, read the Digital ID User Guide, which you can access at

www.verisign.com/stellent/groups/public/documents/guides/
005326.pdf

After you have a digital ID, in order to actually make use of it, you need to follow these steps (these steps apply to Internet Explorer):

 1. **After you obtain your own Digital ID, the first step is to associate it with your e-mail account. Select Tools⇨Accounts.**

    The Internet Accounts dialog box appears.

 2. **Select your e-mail account and click Properties.**

    The Properties dialog box for your e-mail account appears.

 3. **Click the Security tab to bring it to the front.**

 4. **Click the Select button in the Signing Certificate section; then when the Select Default Account Digital ID dialog box appears, select your Digital ID.**

 5. **Click OK to close the Select Default Account Digital ID dialog box; then click OK to close the Properties dialog box, and click Close to close the Internet Accounts dialog box.**

You return to the main Outlook Express window.

6. **To send a digitally signed e-mail message to someone, click Create Message.**

   The New Message dialog box appears.

7. **Click either or both of the security buttons at the extreme right of the toolbar, as shown in Figure 7-3.**

   The Sign button enables you to add your Digital ID. The Encrypt button lets you encrypt your message.

8. **Finish writing your message and then click the Send button.**

   Your encrypted or digitally signed message is sent on its way.

Figure 7-3:
When you click the Sign and Encrypt buttons, your message goes out encrypted and with your certificate attached.

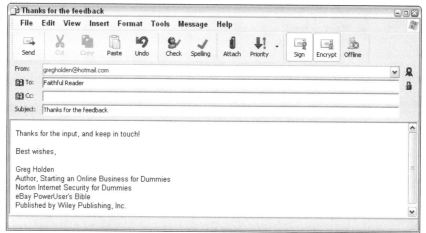

The preceding steps show you how to digitally sign or encrypt an individual message. You have to follow these steps every time you want to sign or encrypt a message. On the other hand, by checking one or more of the options (Encrypt Contents and Attachments for all Outgoing Messages and Digitally Sign all Outgoing Messages) on the Security tab of the Options dialog box, you activate Outlook Express's built-in security features for *all* your outgoing messages. (You can still "turn off" the digital signature or encryption for an individual message by deselecting the Sign or Encrypt buttons in the toolbar of the New Message dialog box.)

If you use Netscape Messenger, the e-mail application that comes with Netscape Communicator, follow these steps to encrypt your e-mail messages or include your certificate with them. (These steps apply to Netscape 7 or later.)

1. **With Messenger running, select Edit⇨Mail & Newsgroups Account Settings.**

   The Mail & Newsgroups Account Settings window appears.

2. **Click the word Security in the list of topics beneath your account name on the left side of the window.**

   The Security options appear on the right side of the window.

3. **In the Digital Signing section of the window, click Select.**

   The Select Certificate dialog box appears.

4. **Make sure the VeriSign, Inc. ID is displayed (choose this certificate from the drop-down list if it is not), and then click OK.**

   The Select Certificate dialog box closes. A dialog box appears asking if you want to use the same certificate for reading and sending messages. Click OK to return to the Security settings.

5. **Select the Digitally Sign Messages (By Default) check box, and then click OK.**

   The Mail & Newsgroups Account Settings window closes and you return to the main Messenger window.

6. **You can now address and write your message and then click the Send button in the Message Composition toolbar.**

   Your encrypted or digitally signed message is sent on its way.

By checking one or more of the options in the Security dialog box, you activate Messenger's built-in security features for all your outgoing messages. In order to actually verify or undo those features (that is, if you want a message to be unencrypted or to be sent without a digital signature), you need to follow these additional steps:

1. **With any Messenger window open (Inbox, Message Center, or Message), click the Compose toolbar button.**

   The Message Composition window appears.

2. **In the Compose window toolbar, click Security.**

   A drop-down list appears. A check mark appears next to the Encrypt This Message or Digitally Sign This Message options if you previously selected either option in the Security dialog box.

3. **If you want to undo either of these options, click the check box to deselect it.**

4. **You can now address and write your message and then click the Send button in the Message Composition toolbar.**

   Your unencrypted or digitally unsigned message is sent on its way.

Picking passwords that are hard to guess

You put a lot of effort into picking the names of your kids and pets, and now you get to choose passwords. But, whereas you want others to think the names are cool, the point of creating a password is to make it difficult for thieves to figure out what it is. That is true whether you're protecting your own computer, downloading software, subscribing to an online publication, or applying for a certificate (as I explain earlier in this chapter).

One method for choosing a password is to take a familiar phrase and then use the first letter of each word to form the basis of a password. For example, the phrase "Every Good Boy Does Fine" would be EGBDF. Then, mix upper-case and lowercase, add punctuation, and you wind up with eGb[d]f. If you *really* want to make a password that's hard to crack, add some numerals as well, such as the last two digits of the year you were born: eGb[d]f48.

Whatever you do, follow these tips for effective password etiquette:

- ✔ **Don't use passwords that are in a dictionary:** It takes time but not much effort for hackers to run a program that tries every word in an online dictionary as your password. So if it's in the dictionary, they will eventually discover it.

- ✔ **Don't use the same password at more than one site:** It's a pain to remember more than one password, not to mention keeping track of which goes with what. Plus, you tend to accumulate lots of different passwords after you've been online for a while. But if you use the same password for each purpose and your password to one site on the Internet is compromised, all your password-protected accounts are in jeopardy.

- ✔ **Use at least six characters:** The more letters in your password, the more difficult you make the life of the code-crackers.

When it comes to passwords, duplication is not only boring but also dangerous. It's especially important not to reuse the same password that you enter to connect to your account on a commercial service such as America Online or CompuServe as a password to an Internet site. If a hacker discovers your password on the Internet site, that person can use it to connect to your AOL or CompuServe account, too — and you'll have to pay for the time they spend online.

A mouthful of protection with authentication

Authentication is a fun word to try to say quickly ten times in a row, and it's also another common security technique used on the Web. This measure simply involves assigning approved users an official username and password that they must enter before gaining access to a protected network, computer, or directory.

Most Web servers allow you to set up areas of your Web site to be protected by username and password. Not all Web hosts allow this, however, because it requires setting up and maintaining a special password file and storing the file in a special location on the computer that holds the Web server software. If you need to make some content on your business site (such as sensitive financial information) available only to registered users, talk to your Web host to see whether setting up a password-protected area is possible.

Chapter 8

Monitoring and Improving Your Business

In This Chapter

▶ Obtaining a better Web address for your online store

▶ Upgrading your Web server to handle more traffic

▶ Reorganizing your e-commerce site to improve usability

▶ Managing your sales stock: Sourcing, replenishing inventory, and fulfilling orders

*O*ne of the many advantages of doing business online is the ease with which you can shift your store's focus. With a brick-and-mortar establishment, changing the business's name, address, or physical appearance can be labor intensive and expensive. On the Web, you can remake your store's *front door* (your home page) in a matter of minutes. You can revamp your sales catalog in less than an hour.

Because it's relatively easy to make changes to your Web site, you have no excuse for not making regular improvements and updates to your online store. Revising the store doesn't just mean changing the colors or the layout on your Web site, which is the part of your operation that customers notice. It also means improving back-office functions that customers don't see, such as inventory management, invoices, labels, packing, and shipping. This chapter examines different ways to test, check, and revise your Web site based on its current performance so that you can boost your revenue and increase sales as well as make your Web site more usable.

Strengthening Your Infrastructure

Every business has a foundation — some elements that give it a presence in the marketplace or in the place where it is physically located. For a traditional, brick-and-mortar business, this might be an address or phone number, or the building in which the merchandise is presented and the employees work. That's how the post office gets mail to the business, and how the customers find the business.

For an online business, your infrastructure consists primarily of the domain name that forms the main part of your Web address, and the Web server that presents your Web site files — which, in turn, present the merchandise you have for sale. Your server makes your site available, and your URL gives your customers a way to find you: Together, they're the equivalent of your street address and the physical space you rent. Over time, you may have to change your domain name if you receive complaints or comments that your site is too hard to find or your URL is too long. You may also need to find a new Web server in order to keep your business running more effectively if any of the following occurs:

- ✔ Your pages slow down.
- ✔ Customers complain that your forms don't work.
- ✔ You run out of storage space on your server and your host wants to charge you a high amount for more space.

Other regular upgrades need to be made to your domain and/or your Web server, as described in the sections that follow.

Improving your domain name

As described in Chapter 3, you have a choice of two different types of domain names: One that is relatively short (for instance, `mynewebusiness.com`) and one that is longer and more difficult to recall off the top of one's head (`myinternetprovider.com/~mynewebusiness`). Even though the first type of domain name is obviously preferable, many individuals who are creating their first Web sites start with the longer one. They get a certain amount of Web server space along with their monthly access account from their Internet Service Provider. Their natural inclination is to use the directory space they are given (which has a long URL like the one shown above) just to get the site started.

Does this sound like your story? There's nothing wrong with doing things the easiest way possible when you're a beginner. But anything you do will evolve in stages. Before long, you'll need to find a domain name that more accurately fits your business or is easier to remember, as described in the sections that follow.

Making your own name a domain

Even if you don't make it active right away, it's a good idea to lock up a name to give you the option of using it in the future. For instance, creating a personal Web site could well still be on your "to do" list. But, if your name is Joe Shmoe, you may want to purchase the domain name `joeshmoe.com` just to have it for future use. If you don't, one may eventually have to deal with one of the many domain name cybersquatters.

Cybersquatters are businesses that make money by buying up multiple domain names, knowing that people who will eventually want them will have no choice but to purchase them. If your ideal domain name is owned by a cybersquatter or by another business, you may have to tweak it a little bit. When I was looking for domain names, for instance, I was unable to find `Holden.com`. An automobile manufacturer in Australia is already using it. However, I was lucky enough to find `gregholden.com`, and I snapped it up right away — even though, at the time, I didn't have a home page of my own. You should be doing the same for your own name or your business's name right now.

Deciding which top-level domain name to use

Where does a business like yours get the easy-to-remember addresses you need? You purchase them from one of the approved domain name registrars. A registrar is a business that has been designated by the Internet Corporation for Assigned Names and Numbers (ICANN) as having the responsibility for keeping track of the names registered in one of the top-level domains. Originally, there were six domains; but as `.com` and others became crowded, alternatives were eventually approved. The domains available at this writing are shown in Table 8-1.

A *top-level domain* (TLD) is one of the primary categories into which addresses on the Internet are divided. It's the part of a domain name that comes after the dot, such as `com` in `.com`. A *domain name* includes the part that comes before the dot, such as `wiley` in `wiley.com`. A fully qualified domain name includes the host name — for example, `www.wiley.com` or `home.netscape.com`.

Table 8-1	Top-Level Domain Names		
Domain Name	*Primary Use*	*In Original Six Domains?*	*Good for Online Businesses?*
`.aero`	Companies in the aerospace and aviation industry	No	No
`.biz`	Businesses	No	Yes
`.com`	Companies or individuals involved in commerce	Yes	Yes
`.coop`	Cooperative institutions	No	No
`.edu`	Schools, colleges, and other educational institutions	Yes	No
`.gov`	Governmental agencies	Yes	No

(continued)

Table 8-1 (continued)

Domain Name	Primary Use	In Original Six Domains?	Good for Online Businesses?
.info	Sites that provide information about you, your ideas, or your organization	No	Yes
.mil	Branches of the U.S. military	Yes	No
.museum	Museums	No	No
.name	Any individual	No	No
.net	Network providers	Yes	Possibly
.org	Nonprofit organizations	Yes	No
.pro	Licensed professionals	No	Yes

Some of the newer domain names, of course, haven't really taken off. They were created in order to provide alternatives for organizations that couldn't find names in the original six domains. The new National Museum of the American Indian, for instance, has its Web site at nmai.si.edu. It's part of the Smithsonian Institution, which uses the .edu domain rather than .org or .museum. United Airlines is at www.ual.com rather than www.ual.aero. Most professional contractors try to get a name in the well-known .com domain rather than .pro or .name.

On the other hand, the .info name apparently has taken off. According to its registry service, Afilias (www.afilias.info), it is the sixth largest domain on the Internet, with 460,000 sites. Because virtually every business needs to put information about itself online, the .info domain is a good alternative if your first-choice .com domain isn't available.

The list of domains presented by ICANN (www.icann.org/registrars/accredited-list.html) indicates that certain domains are "restricted" only to certain types of individuals or organizations. For instance, .biz is restricted to businesses, .pro is restricted to licensed professionals, and so on. In actual practice, businesses don't observe such restrictions very strictly. The .net domain, which was originally intended for network service providers such as ISPs and Web hosts, is commonly used by businesses that can't find their ideal name in the .com domain, for example. You aren't necessarily limited to one domain, either.

Registering domain names related to yours

Even if you already have a domain name, it makes sense to pay a nominal fee to lock up a related name. That way, other businesses cannot attempt to register a domain that's like yours and possibly steal some of your visits. For instance, I own `gregholden.com`, but I don't own `gregholden.name`. To go about registering such a domain, you would follow these steps:

1. **Start up your Web browser and go to the `.name` domain's official registrar, Global Name Registry (GNR) at `www.nic.name`.**

   The home page for GNR Ltd. opens.

2. **Click the Registrars link, and then click the link that begins with For a Full List of All Registrars.**

   A new browser window opens with a long list of registrars — companies from which you can purchase `.name` as well as other domain names.

3. **For this example, scroll down to what is probably the best-known registrar, Network Solutions, and click the Buy Here link in its row of the table.**

   The Network Solutions home page appears.

4. **Select the .name check box and type your desired name, but without the `www` or `.name` parts (for example, type gregholden if you want `gregholden.name`). Then click the Search button.**

   A Search Results page appears. Hopefully, it will indicate that your desired name is available. (If it isn't available, you need to try another name or click one of the links under the headings View List of Expiring Domain Names or Try to Get this Domain Name Now.)

5. **Click Continue.**

   A page full of additional services appears. It's important to remember that these are all hosting, e-mail, and other services that Network Solutions offers in addition to providing you with the ownership of the domain name.

6. **If you don't need a host or e-mail and you only want to purchase the domain name, skip these options and click Continue.**

   The View Your Order page appears.

7. **Choose the length of time you want the name (you can register it for as long as 100 years). Then click Proceed.**

   The Log In/Create Account page appears. If you have an account, enter it here. If not, click Create Account and follow the steps shown on subsequent screens to pay for your order.

Network Solutions may be the best-known registrar, but it's far from the least expensive. You'll save money by shopping around for domain name registrars at www.icann.org/registrars.

Finding a new Web server

You should always consider the option of finding a new Web host if you aren't happy with the one you have. Chances are you're on a server that shares space with lots of other individuals and Web sites. If some of the organizations that share space on your server start streaming audio or video or experience heavy traffic, the performance of your Web site will likely suffer. You might well run into Web site outages, too. In either case, you should arrange with your hosting service to find a better Web server to house your site, or find another host altogether.

One upgrade you may consider is renting a dedicated computer — a computer on which yours is the only Web site. This is far more expensive than a shared hosting account, but after you have developed a customer base and have the resources, it may well be worth it. Also consider the following factors that you might find with another host:

- ✔ **File transfer capability:** The amount of data, in megabytes or kilobytes, of information that you are allowed to transfer each month before you are charged an additional fee. Successful e-commerce sites can quickly pile up thousands of page views per month, and if you go over your limit, you can get a shock when your bill arrives.

- ✔ **Marketing services:** Some Web hosting services help you advertise your online business. For instance, Hypermart (www.hypermart.net) enables customers to list their sites with 1,300 search engines for a one-time $9.99 fee. It also helps businesses optimize their exposure in search listing results (a subject explored in more detail in Chapter 14).

- ✔ **Technical support:** When you are just starting an online business, you'll probably have questions you just can't answer or problems you can't solve on your own. It's to your advantage to choose a host that will provide you with round-the-clock tech support. The Yahoo! Small Business hosting options described in Chapter 9 include a toll-free phone number you can call for support on a 24-hour basis.

Another option you have open to you, if you have a broadband Internet connection, is setting up your own Web server. This means that you have total control over the management of your Web site. That sounds really nice, but keep in mind it also means if the pages appear slowly or if your site goes down for a time, it's your responsibility to get things up and running again as soon as possible. If you are ambitious and technically able, you should consider the popular (not to mention free) Web server program Apache (www.apache.org).

Setting up and running a Web site is not for beginners. If your kids unplug or crash the computer on which your Web site is running, your business goes offline, which can cost you money. If your computer runs slowly or doesn't have enough memory, your site's performance may suffer. It's generally best for beginners to leave the hosting to professionals. Web hosts have the ability to purchase and maintain the best hardware available and have technicians on call who can solve problems round the clock. If you leave the hosting to someone else, you have more time to focus on essentials like building inventory, maintaining the content on your site, and providing good customer service.

Performing Basic Web Housekeeping

To be better prepared to maintain and improve your Web site, you should visit it yourself on a regular basis. In fact, you should be the first one to view your pages when they go online; after that, you need to revisit as often as you can to make sure that your photos display correctly and that your links take you where you want them to go. Other helpful tips are described in the following sections.

All Web browsers are not created equally in the way that they handle colors, fonts, and other Web page elements. Be sure to visit your site by using different browsers in order to confirm that things work the way you want in all cases. At the very least, check your site with Microsoft Internet Explorer and Netscape Navigator; you may also want to use a new browser called Firefox (www.mozilla.org).

Making sure your site is organized

One of the fundamental tenets of e-commerce is that products need to be easy to find. The way you organize your Web site makes sure that your customers won't end up playing hide-and-seek. The people who make a living writing about and designing Web sites call this *usability*. As long as the Web has existed, there have been experts studying what makes a Web site usable. Most agree on the following essential characteristics:

- **Keep it organized.** Create a logical path through your site that leads to your shopping cart and checkout area.

- **Keep it simple, sir . . . or madam!** Each one of your Web pages should do one thing and one thing only.

- **Keep it searchable.** Shoppers who are in a hurry want to jump past all your meticulously designed sales categories, enter a product name in a search box, and scan a page full of search results to find what they have in mind. Give them the chance to do it.

You can add a search box to your site and have your pages indexed by a service such as FreeFind (`www.freefind.com`), which is free if you consent to display ads in your search results, or as little as $5 a month for ad-free results.

Make sure that your site has a logical page flow. How many Web pages do your customers have to click through before making their purchases? The general rule "the fewer the better" applies. Your goal is to lead shoppers into your site and then encourage them to search through your sales catalog.

Make a map of your Web site

Maps are especially important when navigating the information superhighway. When it comes to your e-commerce Web site, a site map can help you make your site easier to navigate. A *site map* is a graphical representation of your Web site — a diagram that graphically depicts all the pages in the site and how they connect to one another. Some Web page editing programs, such as Microsoft FrontPage, have a site map function built into them. As you create pages and link them to one another, a site map is created. The following figure shows the site map on the left side of the window and a list of files on the right.

Keep in mind that you don't have to invest in a fancy (and expensive) software program in order to create a site map. You can also create

one the old-fashioned way, using a pencil and paper. Or you can draw boxes and arrows, using a computer graphics program you're familiar with. The point is that your site map can be a useful design tool for organizing the documents within your site.

If your sales are sluggish, make sure that your customers can actually find what they are looking for. Take a typical product in your sales catalog, and then visit your own site to see how many clicks someone would need to make in order to find it. Then see how many clicks that person would need to complete its purchase. Eliminating any unnecessary navigational layers (such as category opening pages) will make your site easier to use.

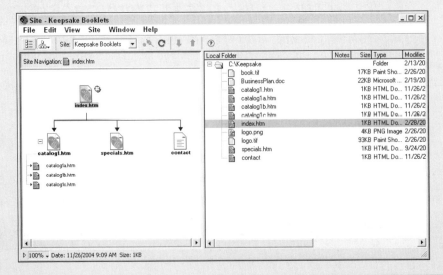

Adding navigational links

Another reason to review your existing e-commerce Web site is to evaluate the number of navigational buttons or other links you give your visitors. The most common options are a row of buttons or links across the top of the page and a column along the left side of the page. These are the most obvious places to put such links, but by no means the only types of navigational aids you can add. Your goal should be to provide three types of links when the customer is viewing a sales item:

- ✔ Links that make it easy to back out of the category the customer is in by following links to the top level

- ✔ A link to your site's home page

- ✔ Links to other parts of your site so that the shopper doesn't need to return to the home page continually when the desire to explore a new sales category arises

The MyTexasMusic.com site shown in Figure 8-1 shows two other types of useful links that appear on a catalog page. Along the top, the shopper sees a row of drop-down menu lists; choosing a menu item instantly causes the browser to jump to another part of the Web site. At the bottom of the item listing, links appear to related items and to other categories within the site.

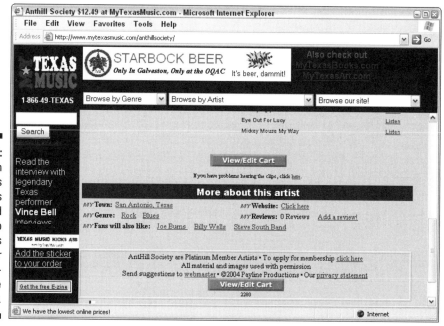

Figure 8-1: Drop-down menu lists and links to related items help shoppers explore your sales catalog more easily.

Making sure your site is searchable

The single most useful type of navigational aid is a *search box* — a text box into which visitors enter keywords to search your catalog by product name or number. Here again, there are different options for adding such a box to your site:

- ✔ **The hard way:** You create a Web page with a text box. You write a script that will process the data submitted by visitors. The server that hosts your site will need to be able to process such scripts. Usually, this means it has to have the programming language present. For instance, if a script is written in the programming language Perl, the host needs to have Perl running on the server. Not all hosts allow the execution of scripts on their servers, however; check with yours to make sure.

- ✔ **The less difficult way:** You create a Web page with a text box, but you borrow a script so you don't have to write your own. You can use the popular Simple Search form at Matt's Script Archive (www.script archive.com). Because this script is written in Perl, your host must have Perl running on the server.

- ✔ **The Microsoft way:** Most Web hosts allow the use of a set of programs called the FrontPage Server Extensions. If you have FrontPage, you can use it to create your own searchable site index.

- ✔ **The easy way:** You sign up with a service that indexes your site — in other words, scours your Web pages and records their contents — and provides you with a search box that you can add to your site.

Because the latter option is the one that doesn't require any programming and is easiest for beginners, I describe it in more detail. Services that make other peoples' Web sites searchable usually provide two options. One is free, but the results that appear when someone searches your site have advertisements displayed as well. The other isn't free, but the search results *are* ad-free. These days, shoppers are so accustomed to seeing ads displayed all over the Web that they probably won't be put off if some appear in your search results. So I wouldn't be reluctant to choose the free search option if it is available.

Picosearch (www.picosearch.com) makes it easy to place a search box on a Web site, either on a free, ad-supported basis or on a monthly subscription basis. Go to the site's home page at www.picosearch.com and follow these steps to use the free service:

1. **Type your site's URL and your e-mail address in the boxes supplied, and click Submit.**

   The Site Search New Account Setup page appears.

2. **Type your name and a password in the boxes supplied. Type the URLs for the pages you want to serve as entry points to your site. Also adjust the options for indexing and *spidering* (the amount of searching that can be done).**

   If you're in doubt about which options to choose, just leave the defaults for now; you can change them later.

3. **Scroll to the bottom of the New Account Setup page, select the check box that says you agree to the terms of the Picosearch license, and click OK, Build My FREE Search Engine!**

   A page appears informing you that your Web site is being indexed. You'll also receive at least two e-mails from Picosearch. You need to click a link in the first e-mail in order to complete the registration for your free account. (The second tells you that your site is being indexed.) A third e-mail (which can take up to 24 hours to arrive) tells you the indexing is done.

4. **Click the link supplied in the first message from Picosearch. When the Select a Plan page appears, click Subscribe next to Free Plan.**

   A page appears informing you that your registration is complete and reminding you to view another e-mail message. This message instructs you on how to add the all-important search box to your Web page.

5. **Open the message and copy the code for your search box by dragging the mouse pointer across all the following and pressing Ctrl+C:**

```
<!-- Begin Picosearch Code -->
[code follows]
<!-- End Picosearch Code -->
```

6. **Open the code for your Web page in a Web page editor or a text editor such as Notepad. Position the text cursor at the spot where you want the search box to appear, and then press Ctrl+V to paste the copied code.**

   The text is added to your Web page code.

7. **Save your Web page code and upload the new Web page to your Web server.**

After you've uploaded your page, open it in your Web browser to view the box. My own search box is shown in Figure 8-2.

Do a search on your page to see how the service works. As you can see from Figure 8-3, ads are included in a search of my own Web site. But because I searched for the term *eBay,* the ads are at least related to the topic — in other words, the ads are keyword-based.

Figure 8-2:
Free site
search
services
index your
Web site
contents
and provide
you with a
searchable
text box.

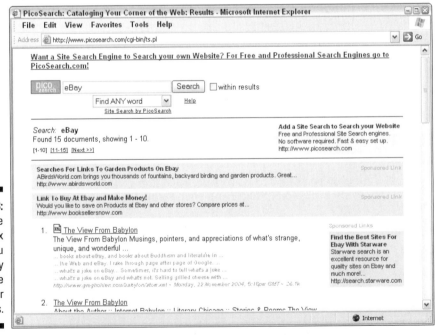

Figure 8-3:
A free
search box
requires you
to display
Google-type
ads in your
results.

A search of your Web site is only as effective as the most recent index of your pages and their contents. If you revamp or improve your Web site (as you should periodically), you need to have your site reindexed by your search service. Picosearch gives its customers the ability to reindex their site manually at any time — in other words, you go to the Picosearch Web site and request that your site be reindexed. But if you pay a monthly fee for Picosearch instead of using the free version, you can schedule automatic reindexing so that you don't have to worry about requesting a new survey of your site on your own.

Whenever you sign up for "free" services and submit an e-mail address, you are liable to receive unsolicited commercial e-mail (that is, *spam*) at that address. One solution is to not use your primary e-mail address for such registrations. Instead, set up an address specifically for this purpose and then cancel it when it becomes overrun by too much spam.

Taking your site for a test run

After you've enhanced your Web site with navigational aids, search boxes, and other changes, you need to visit it yourself to make sure everything works the way you want. You not only need to make sure that your site creates a good visual impression, but to also watch out for any problems you have to undo, such as:

- Background colors that are too similar to the color of your body text and that make your text hard to read

- Images that aren't cropped closely enough, which makes them bigger in file size than they need to be (which, in turn, makes them appear on screen too slowly)

- Pages that are overcrowded, with insufficient room between columns or between images and text

- Errors in spelling or grammar

- Type that's too small and can't be read easily by older viewers

- Copyright notices or "This site was last updated on . . ." messages that are old and out of date

- Factual statements that are no longer accurate

It makes sense to perform such evaluations when you change your site. But you should test things out whenever you move files from your computer to your Web server. In order to know how to best make improvements, it is important to continue to test and make evaluations.

If you want an entertaining rundown of bad Web design features to avoid on your own site, visit Web Pages That Suck (`www.webpagesthatsuck.com`). Author Vincent Flanders includes a feature called Mystery Meat Navigation that shows how *not* to guide visitors through your Web site.

Managing Goods and Services

Shoppers on the Web are continually in search of The New: the next new product, the latest price reduction or rebate, the latest comment in a blog, today's headlines. As a provider of content, whether it is in the form of words or images or products for sale, your job is to manage that content to keep it fresh and available. You also need to replenish stock as it is purchased, handle returns, and deal with shipping options, as described in the sections that follow.

Sourcing goods

Sourcing is a fancy term for "buying items at a really low price so that you can resell them for a profit." For a small business just starting out on the Internet, this is not an easy prospect. Lots of online businesses advertise themselves as wholesale sellers. Many say they will "drop-ship" their merchandise — in other words, ship what's purchased directly from their wholesale facility so you never actually have to handle them and may never see them.

Sound too good to be true? In many cases, it is, and you should always exercise a healthy dose of caution when you're looking for wholesale suppliers. The eBay sellers I've talked to who have faithful, reliable wholesalers guard the identities of those suppliers jealously. They usually find such suppliers only by word of mouth: Rather than answering an ad or visiting a Web site, they ask someone who knows someone who . . . you get the idea.

If you aren't in the business of selling goods or services that you manufacture yourself, you need to find a steady stream of merchandise that you can sell online. Your goal is to find a wholesaler who can supply you with good-quality items at rock-bottom prices; you can mark up the prices and make a profit while keeping the prices low enough to make them attractive. Generally, the best wholesale items are small objects that can be packed and shipped inexpensively. On eBay, things like figurines, ornaments, stationery, and other small gift items are commonly sold by PowerSellers along with the occasional antiques and collectibles. Here are a few rules of thumb for finding items you can resell:

✔ **Try them out yourself.** Purchase a few items yourself to start with, or ask the wholesaler for samples. (Resist any attempts by the wholesaler to sell you, say 10,000 items at a supposedly dirt-cheap price right off the bat.) Take a few of the items for a test drive. It's easier to convince others to buy what you like yourself.

✔ **Try to sell many small, low-priced items rather than a few large ones.**
Instead of computers or printers, consider selling computer memory
chips or printer ink cartridges, for instance.

✔ **Ask for references.** Talk to businesspeople who have already worked
with the supplier. Ask how reliable the supplier is, and whether the
prices are prone to fluctuate.

When looking for merchandise to sell, try to build on your own hobbies and
interests. If you collect model cars, try to develop a sideline selling parts,
paints, and components online. You'll find the process more enjoyable when
you are dealing in things you love and know well.

Handling returns

Your returns policy depends on the venue where you make your sales. If you
sell primarily on eBay, you should accept returns, if only because many of the
most experienced and successful sellers do, too. That doesn't mean you need
to accept every single item that is returned. Most businesses place restrictions on when they will receive a return and send a refund. The items must
be returned within 30 days; the packages must be unopened; the merchandise
must not be damaged.

Adding shipping rates

As part of creating a usable e-commerce catalog, you need to provide customers with shipping costs for your merchandise. Shipping rates can be
difficult to calculate. They depend on your own geographic location as
well as the location where you are planning to ship. If you are a small-scale
operation and you process each transaction manually, you may want to ship
everything a standard way (UPS Ground, FedEx Home Delivery, or USPS
Parcel Post). Then you can keep a copy of your shipper's charges with you
and calculate each package's shipping cost individually.

You can also save time by using the quick shipping calculator provided by
iShip (www.iship.com). Just go to the site's home page, enter the origin and
destination zip codes, and click Go. You'll get a set of shipping rates from
Airborne Express, UPS, and USPS so you can pick the most cost-effective option.
If you want some help with shipping, you can set up your site with the help of
a transaction hosting service such as ChannelAdvisor (www.channeladvisor.
com). This company has an agreement with the USPS so that it automatically
calculates shipping charges and includes those charges in the invoices it sends
to your customers.

Maintaining inventory

Shoppers on the Web want things to happen instantly. They want to get the most out of their fancy broadband connections. If they discover that you're out of stock of an item they want, they're likely to switch to another online business instead of waiting for you to restock that item. With that in mind, obey the basic principle of planning to be successful: Instead of ordering the bare minimum of this or that item, make sure you have enough to spare. Too much inventory initially is better than running out at some point, in other words.

Rely on software or management services to help you keep track of what you have. If you feel at ease working with databases, record your initial inventory in an Access or SQL database. This forces you to record each sale manually in the database so you know how many items are left. You could connect your sales catalog to your database by using a program such as ColdFusion from Macromedia. Such a program can update the database on the fly as sales are made. But you may need to hire someone with Web programming experience to set the system up for you and make sure it actually works.

If you sign up with an online store solution like Yahoo! Small Business or a sales management provider like Marketworks (www.marketworks.com), inventory is tracked for you automatically. Marketworks is popular with eBay auction sellers, but there's no reason why you can't establish an account with back-end functions such as payment, invoices, and inventory management for any online store. Whether you do the work yourself or hire an outside service, you have to be able to answer basic questions such as:

- **When should you reorder?** Establish *reorder points:* Points at which you automatically reorder supplies (when you get down to two or three items left, for instance).

- **How many do you have in stock right now?** You need to make sure that you have enough merchandise on hand not only for everyday demand but also in case a product gets hot or the holiday season brings about a dramatic increase in orders.

An e-commerce hosting service may also be able to help you with questions that go beyond the basics, such as the past purchasing history of customers. Knowing what customers have purchased in the past gives you the ability to suggest *up-sells* — additional items the person might want. But in the early stages, making sure that you have a cushion of additional inventory for the time when your site becomes a big success is your primary responsibility.

Part III
Successful Online Business Models

The 5th Wave   By Rich Tennant

FREELANCER NED WILLIS CONSULTS
WITH A MEMBER OF HIS TECHNICAL STAFF

"...and that's pretty much all there is to
converting a document to an HTML file."

In this part . . .

Going into business doesn't mean going it alone. When you're just starting out, it makes sense to sign up with a service that makes it easy for you to create a storefront, list products online, and accept electronic payments.

For one thing, you don't necessarily want to quit your day job right away. You aren't ready to start making money online 24/7 and maintain the infrastructure that goes with an online business. Signing up with a well-known hosting service is like renting office space in a mall, except that in this case, your virtual landlord gives you a jump-start. In this part, you discover how to start making money with the help of online business stalwarts such as Amazon.com, Yahoo!, PayPal, and eBay.

Chapter 9

Setting Up Amazon.com, Yahoo!, and Other Storefronts

*O*nline storefronts have always been among the most popular places to sell online. But you don't have to do all the work of creating a home page, setting up a shopping cart, and establishing a way to collect payments all by yourself. By locating your storefront on a well-established and well-known e-commerce venue, you can rack up sales without spending the big bucks on marketing and infrastructure. You can take advantage of the marketing tools the site gives you.

Other chapters in this book describe how to create a commercial Web site and an eBay store. Even if you have one of those sales venues, that doesn't mean you can't open up stores in other popular locations on the Web. In fact, the more places you "pop up" as a Web merchant, the better. Your stores can sell different products and link to one another, which boosts your business overall. This chapter examines some of the best-known alternatives for making money with well-known hosting services on the Web.

Becoming an Amazon.com Seller

Over the years, Amazon.com has become known as "Earth's biggest bookseller." It's done so by selling books on the site all by itself. Having conquered the world of online bookselling, Amazon.com is attempting to give individual entrepreneurs different options for generating revenue. You will find links leading to many of the options for selling with Amazon.com if you go to the home page (www.amazon.com) and click the See All Services link under the heading Make Money.

Amazon.com gives entrepreneurs a variety of ways to sell on its site. If you have a book or CD to sell, you are allowed to list it on Amazon.com — and not only that, but you get to place your ad alongside the listing for the same book that's being sold brand new on the site.

Become an Amazon.com Associate

You're probably already familiar with the idea of an affiliate program. The Amazon.com Associates program works like you would expect: When you become an Amazon.com Associate (in Chapter 15 is an example of a site that uses the program), you place a link to Amazon.com on your Web site. When someone makes a purchase after following the link from your site, you earn a referral fee.

If you have written or created books, CDs, or other materials that are sold on Amazon.com, you can create links to those items on your own Web site and refer your visitors to the bookseller's site so that you can potentially earn the referral fee. It so happens that I have a few books that are sold on Amazon.com, and I include images of several of these books on my own Web site (www.gregholden.com). I already had several of the ingredients for generating referral income: a Web site, books to sell, and a need for extra revenue. All that remained was to sign up with the Amazon.com Associates program and create specially formatted links that I associate with each of the book images on my home page.

Even if you haven't written books or created CDs, you can create links to books you like or recommend and use those as referrals to the Amazon.com Web site.

To get started with the program, just follow these steps:

1. **Go to the Amazon.com home page and click the Join Associates link (at the bottom of the page).**

2. **Click the Join Now button (on the left side).**

3. **Fill out the forms provided to become a member.**

   You have to tell Amazon.com whether you want to receive a check or a direct deposit into your bank account. I chose the direct deposit method, so I entered my bank account number and bank routing number. When you become a member of the program, you gain access to the Amazon.com Associates Central area.

4. **Log in as directed and access your own welcome page on the site.**

   You have to set up the Associates links according to Amazon.com's specifications so it can track when the links are clicked and determine whether purchases are subsequently made.

5. **From the Associates Central welcome page, click the Build Links link.**

A table appears describing four types of links you can make:

- **Product Links:** These are links to specific books, movies, or CDs you want to promote.

- **Recommended Product Links:** These are banner ads you display on your site that display books or other products on Amazon.com that are related to the products you sell. For instance, if you sell baby clothes, you might recommend a book on parenting that you like.

- **Search Box Links:** You put an Amazon.com search box on your site. The box lets your visitors search Amazon.com, not your own site. If someone makes a purchase after making such a search, you get a referral fee.

- **Text Links:** If the search box takes up too much graphic space on your Web pages, include a simple text link that points people to books or CDs on Amazon.com.

You can promote your friends' books and CDs, books or CDs that relate to your own goods and services, or other books and CDs you admire. By spreading the word about such materials, you can earn a few cents or perhaps a few dollars. Because I have some specific books to promote, I chose the first option, Product Links.

6. **Choose a link option, and then click Create Link.**

7. **On the next page that appears, search for the book or CD that you want to promote.**

The results of my search are shown in Figure 9-1.

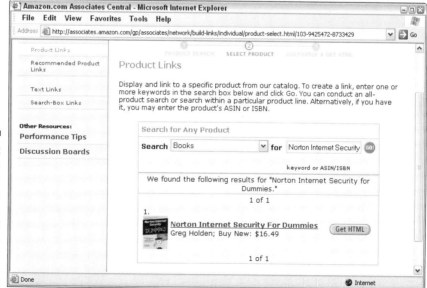

Figure 9-1:
Find the book or CD you want to promote, and then get the HTML so you can make a link.

8. **Click the Get HTML button to access some HTML code that you then copy and add to your Web page in order to display the product cover.**

This display serves as a link to the book or CD's page on Amazon.com.

I noticed that, by default, the image opened as an inline frame — a container within the Web page. This seemed too complex to me, so I clicked Customize HTML and changed the link to a simple clickable image file rather than a frame. I highlighted the HTML and pasted it into my Web page, which produced the link shown in Figure 9-2.

Figure 9-2: You can turn a book cover into a clickable link that can earn you a referral fee.

You probably won't make a fortune from Amazon.com's referral fees. You earn four to five percent of the value of the items sold, depending on the number of items you sell. If you refer someone who purchases a book for $15, for instance, you earn about 75 cents for that purchase.

Join the marketplace

Suppose you've got a pile of recently published books or CDs around (books or CDs that are being sold on Amazon.com) and you need to sell them. When you join the Amazon Marketplace, you gain the ability to sell those books yourself. Suppose you purchased a book called *eBay PowerUser's Bible,* and you were so happy with it that you just felt compelled to sell it so others could share the wisdom contained within. (You can guess who wrote this book, can't you?) Here's an example of how you would sell it:

1. **Go to the Amazon.com home page (**www.amazon.com**) and click the Marketplace link in the Make Money box.**

   The Amazon.com–Sell Your Stuff page appears.

2. **Choose the category you're interested in and enter the name or ISBN number (the number on the back cover, just above the "zebra stripe" code) of the specific item you want to see; then click the Start Selling button.**

   The sales page for the item (in this case, the book) appears.

3. **Click the Sell Yours Here button on the right side of that page.**

   The Sell Your Item – Select Condition page appears.

4. **Choose an option from the Condition drop-down list to describe the condition of your item. Add some text that describes the condition if you want, then click Continue.**

   The Sell an Item – Enter Price page appears. The instructions on this page include the important information about Amazon.com's fees: You will be charged 99 cents plus a 15 percent fee for each item you sell.

5. **Enter your price in the price box. Then click Continue.**

   Make sure your price is at or below Amazon.com's own price.

   The Sign In page appears.

6. **Enter your Amazon.com e-mail address and password. (You can use the same password you use to make purchases or sell as an Associate.) Then click Continue.**

   The Registration page appears.

7. **Choose a credit card from the list (or enter a new card name and number) to identify you. Then click Continue.**

   Another Registration page appears.

8. **Enter your nickname and a daytime phone number, and then click Continue.**

   Optionally, you have the opportunity to enter checking account information so that Amazon.com can deposit purchase money into your account. You can skip this step for now.

   A confirmation page appears.

9. **Click List Item for Sale.**

   The Your Listing Is Complete page appears. In addition, an e-mail message is sent confirming that your item is now up for sale.

If your item doesn't sell within 60 days, Amazon.com closes your listing and you pay nothing. You are sent an e-mail with details for relisting the item if you want.

Pro Merchant subscription

If you have lots of items to sell, consider becoming a Pro Merchant Subscriber. You have to pay a $39.99 monthly fee to be part of this Amazon.com program, but there are some big advantages:

- ✔ You don't have to pay the 99 cent fee.
- ✔ Your listings are not closed after 60 days.
- ✔ You can open a storefront called a zShop, as described in the next section.

It also allows you to use the powerful inventory reports to view orders, sold listings, and current open listings. You also get access to a bulk listing tool so that you can create lots of descriptions at once. You've got to sell at least a few books each month to make back your subscription fee, but if you're a bookseller by trade and have a lot of inventory to unload, this is a good alternative.

You can find out more about the Pro Merchant program at s1.amazon.com/ exec/varzea/subscription-signup/103-9425472-8733429.

Opening a zShop

zShops are Amazon.com's online shops. This is where professional and amateur sellers alike can sell items that go well beyond the things normally found on the site — everything from autographed items, vintage goods, food, wine, computer equipment, and much more.

Click the Buy It! button on the detail page of the item that interests you, and then complete your transaction with the individual seller. After you've submitted your order for an item on zShops, you'll receive an e-mail telling you how to proceed with your transaction. You'll also receive the seller's e-mail address, in case you want to contact him or her about payment and the shipping of your purchase.

zShops sellers do receive feedback from people with whom they've done business, and you can check that feedback. But the feedback system isn't nearly as well developed as the eBay feedback system because zShops just aren't that well known. However, if the seller fails to deliver after you pay for something, or if the item you receive differs substantially from what you ordered, you do have some protection in the form of Amazon.com's A-to-z Guarantee. Amazon.com will refund your loss in such cases. Find out more about the guarantee at www.amazon.com/exec/obidos/tg/browse/-/ 537868/103-9425472-8733429.

Amazon.com auctions

eBay may be the big gorilla when it comes to auctions on the Internet, but if you already sell on Amazon.com, you should consider selling on its auction site. Before you sell, be sure to have some digital photos in JPEG or GIF format ready. Here's how to get started:

1. **Go to the site's home page (www.amazon.com) and click the Auctions link under the heading Bargains on the left side of the page.**

   The Amazon.com – Auctions page appears.

2. **Click Sign In.**

   The Sign In page appears.

   If you don't have an Amazon.com account, create one by entering your e-mail address and clicking the button next to I Do Not Have an Amazon.com Password, and then clicking Continue.

   If you have an Amazon.com username and password and the site "recognizes" you by name — either because you have already logged in or because a bit of electronic data called a *cookie* was retrieved by the site from your browser's storage area — move to Step 4. If not, move to Step 3.

3. **Sign in with your Amazon.com username and password and click Continue.**

   The Amazon.com – Registration page appears.

4. **Click the Sell Items link (at the bottom of the page).**

5. **On the Make Money page that appears, click the Marketplace link (under the I Have Something to Sell heading).**

   The Sell Your Stuff form appears.

6. **Fill out the form to create your auction sale.**

It's as simple as that. Amazon.com's auction form asks for virtually the same information as eBay's Sell Your Item form, which allows members to create auction or fixed-price sales on its site. You create an auction title, a description, and upload photos of your item. One bit of information that Amazon.com's form lets you enter that eBay doesn't have is a product identification number such as the ISBN number used to identify books. You also have the option to list your auction as long as 14 days, which is longer than eBay's 10-day limit.

The tip jar

This system, also called the Honor System, gives you a way to solicit donations for your Web site or for your content. Even if someone doesn't make a purchase from you, or if you provide content that doesn't include tangible goods for sale (such as a blog), the tip jar gives you a way to make some money for your efforts.

To set up a tip jar on your own Web site, go to the Amazon Honor System home page (`s1.amazon.com/exec/varzea/subst/fx/home.html`) and click Join Now to register for the program. You verify your identity, and then enter your checking account information so that money can be deposited into your account when you receive a "tip." After that, you place HTML provided by Amazon.com into the source code for the Web page where you want the Tip Jar icon to appear. Visitors can click on a button embedded in the icon, and Amazon.com provides a form where customers enter the amount they want to pay and the account from which they want the funds to be debited. (The tippers must have a PayPal account to leave tips.) Many bloggers have gained valuable extra funds from such a tip jar, which demonstrates the value of providing useful content online.

Creating a Yahoo! Small Business

In previous editions of this book, I described the process of creating an online store by using one of the most popular and successful e-commerce hosting services around, the one managed by the longtime index and search service Yahoo!. Until recently, the service was known as Yahoo! Store. It's now called Yahoo! Small Business (`smallbusiness.yahoo.com`). Over the years, Yahoo! Store hosted many successful and well-known businesses; the site provides you with Web-based forms and tools that you access online with your browser (a page-in-progress is shown in Figure 9-3). These tools make it easy for you to create a storefront and list items for sale.

There's one significant difference between Yahoo! Store and Yahoo! Small Business. Yahoo! Store let you set up a store for free on a 30-day trial basis. With Yahoo! Small Business, you have to sign up for a hosting account and commit to pay a monthly fee before you can establish a storefront. Three hosting plans are available: Starter ($11.95 per month), Standard ($19.95 per month), and Professional ($39.95 per month). There's also a $25 setup fee, but at the time this was written, the fee was being waived as a promotion.

One of the biggest advantages for Yahoo! Small Business subscribers is toll-free, 24/7 phone support. Another is the fact that storefronts hosted with this service can make use of a built-in shopping cart and payment system. The fact that Yahoo! is so well known and has been around so long means that it is reliable: The service is not likely to go down due to technical troubles but will be there for years to come.

Yahoo! offers another Web hosting service that streamlines the process of creating personal home pages and business Web sites. It's called Yahoo! GeoCities (`geocities.yahoo.com`). The site chares a $10 setup fee plus either $4.95 or $8.95 per month for hosting.

CASE STUDY

The gift that keeps on giving — with Yahoo!'s help

Have you ever wondered what you could give a niece or nephew as a gift that would make a difference in his or her life? Jeremy G. Alicandri received a gift when he was 16 years old that had more of an impact than the giver could have possibly imagined. And it all came about because he quickly became bored with his gift. What he had unwrapped was a set of professional two-way radios. When they lost their appeal, Jeremy put them up for sale on eBay. He was pleased to be able to sell each radio for $100, which was far more than they had originally cost.

"Before I knew it, I was selling radios for profit," he says. "Within six months of selling on eBay, I'd made $800, which was enough to launch SimplyCheap.com (www.simplycheap.com) in 1999. At that point, I ran the company as a business and began offering all types of new consumer electronics and related items."

Now at the ripe old age of 22, Jeremy is running his online business full time with a Yahoo! Small Business account. He briefly considered running his own server, but he figures that the cost of doing it himself would far exceed the benefits. "For example, if a server goes down, I know I have the resources of Yahoo! to fix it. That gives me tremendous peace of mind," he says. He went on to list six reasons why he chose this particular e-commerce host:

- It is the most established e-commerce host around.

- It has the largest e-commerce platform, meaning that many companies supported its products.

- It includes integration into Yahoo! Shopping so that your store is listed in its shopping directory.

- The store builder is easy to use.

- There is a back-end processing order manager.

- You get access to 24/7 phone support.

As you can tell, Alicandri believes that being part of a big, well-known Web site with lots of other businesses helps him find customers. However, he also points out that it presents the potential customer with more competitors prior to entering his site.

When asked to identify the one or two most important features that an online storefront must have in order to succeed, Alicandri responded with the following:

- **Provide understandable content:** Products, descriptions, prices, policies, navigation, and so on.

- **Fulfillment:** Any store must be able to manage every aspect of an order, from beginning to end, in a thorough manner.

Alicandri points out that the Internet has matured significantly over the past five years, and he admits that it's now much more difficult to launch a successful store and achieve profitable sales. Here are his two major bits of advice:

- **Know your product:** Is it already being sold on the Net? Who is selling it? Where is it being sold? Can you be competitive? Who are your potential customers?

- **Be reasonable:** Don't overextend on advertising costs. Be realistic about the costs of the store. Monitor conversions. Make plans that can be reached in stages.

What's left for the boy wonder entrepreneur? Now he's launching a novel business called Inforigin. Inforigin will address the needs of businesses that currently manage or are considering launching a Web business. "We plan on managing all types of sites, ranging from e-tail sites to manufacturer's sites, at an incredible value to the client," says Alicandri.

Figure 9-3:
After you fill out a simple form, Yahoo! Small Business gives you instant results, such as this home page.

Creating Other Storefronts

Amazon.com and Yahoo! are among the best-known Web businesses. While their hosting services are reliable, they might not be ideal for your needs. If you're a creative artist and you just want to sell a few examples of your work to family and friends, CafePress might be just what you need. If you already have an account with PayPal and regularly use its payment services for sales on eBay, it makes sense to open a PayPal store. If you use Microsoft products such as FrontPage to create your Web pages, Microsoft Small Business Center is a good option for creating an online sales catalog and storefront. It's all a matter of deciding what you need. These alternatives are described in the sections that follow.

Letting CafePress sell your creative work

Creative people aren't always the best at marketing and selling their own work. There are probably millions of amateur artists out there hoping to become professionals: They have great ideas for cartoons, logos, and drawings, but the prospect of getting them printed and sold in stores is a big obstacle.

I've known one such person since she was a little girl: Her name is Kristin Lindner, and she lives in St. Louis, Missouri. She created a Web site called Elephant of Joy (www.elephantofjoy.com) to promote her line of greeting cards. When she expressed a desire to have the cards actually printed and sold at holiday time, her mother and I were faced with the prospect of sending them to a printer, with all that the process entails: minimum orders; choices of paper; proofs to review; and folding and delivery questions, not to mention the money involved.

As a cost-effective alternative, I encouraged Kristin to set up a store on CafePress.com. This service is ideally suited to artists who want to have their work printed on T-shirts, cards, and other household objects that they can sell online. The objects are only printed on demand when the order is made, so there's no question of having inventory sitting around waiting to be sold. I had Kristin send me a set of her drawings that had been scanned and saved in JPEG format. I then followed the steps detailed in Chapter 3 to create her own store on CafePress (which was assigned the URL www.cafepress.com/ elephantofjoy), along with a line of greeting cards. In a few hours, I was able to upload a number of images that she had created and assemble the product line shown in Figure 9-4.

Figure 9-4:
A Cafe
Press.com
storefront
enables you
to print and
sell your
original
artwork.

CafePress.com sets a base price for each object. For instance, a set of six greeting cards has a base price of $10.99. If you charge $14.99 for the cards, CafePress.com collects the base price, but you get the $4.99 profit. But you don't have to do the printing or shipping; CafePress.com handles all of that for you.

Launching a PayPal shop

PayPal, the online payment service, was popular long before it became part of the eBay empire. It also gives you the ability to start up a PayPal store. Because eBay and PayPal are now affiliated, this gives you the chance to create links between your eBay Store and your PayPal store. One nice feature about PayPal is that you get a Shop search box on the left side of your store.

PayPal sellers, like eBay sellers, have a numeric rating that indicates how trustworthy their performance has been. It's called the *PayPal reputation number,* and it appears next to your name on PayPal. It indicates how many Verified PayPal members have paid you.

Opening a Microsoft Small Business

Many of the successful businesspeople I've interviewed prefer to host their e-commerce Web sites with well-known companies because such companies are reliable. They have lots of technical resources, and they are likely to be around for the long haul. Microsoft certainly fits that description. Its own e-commerce hosting service, Microsoft Small Business Center (formerly known as bCentral), provides the same sorts of services as the other hosts described in this chapter. It enables you to set up an online store; it streamlines the process of setting up a sales catalog; it provides you with a payment system; it gives its members various technical support options.

Microsoft Small Business Center is more expensive than Yahoo! Small Business; the least expensive hosting option runs $12.95 per month. But it does give you a 30-day free trial period, which Yahoo! Small Business does not offer. The biggest advantage is support for Microsoft FrontPage. If you use FrontPage to create and update your Web site, you can sign up for an account with Microsoft Small Business Center and install a special piece of software called the Commerce Manager Add-In. This add-in enables you to set up a sales catalog and manage an e-commerce site from within Microsoft FrontPage. If you don't use FrontPage and you sign up for hosting with Microsoft Small Business Center, you can still use Commerce Manager, but you have to pay an additional $24.95 per month fee.

Chapter 10

Running a Business on eBay

*H*ere's a quick quiz: Throughout the ups and downs of e-commerce in the 1990s and early 2000s, what marketplace has remained strong and continued to grow at a steady rate? As you probably know already, it's eBay — I say you probably know this because chances are you've already bought or sold some things yourself on the world's most popular auction site (or maybe this chapter's title gave you a hint).

There's a difference, though, between selling occasionally in order to make a few extra bucks and doing what thousands have already done: selling on eBay as a means of self-employment. eBay itself has estimated that as many as 450,000 individuals run a business on the auction site full time. Countless others do it on a permanent part-time basis to help boost the family income. Whatever the reason, you can't overlook eBay as a way to get a first business off the ground. With eBay, you don't necessarily have to create a Web site, develop your own shopping cart, or become a credit card merchant: The auction site itself handles each of those essential tasks for you. But that doesn't mean it's easy to develop your own eBay business. It takes hard work and a commitment, combined with the important business strategies described in this chapter.

Running a business on eBay doesn't necessarily mean you depend on eBay as the sole source of your income. It might mean you sell on eBay part time for some supplementary income each month. This chapter assumes that you want to sell regularly on eBay and build up a system for successful sales that can provide you with extra money, bill-paying money, or "fun money."

Understanding eBay Auctions

In any contest, you have to know the ground rules. Anyone who has held a garage sale knows the ground rules for making a person-to-person sale. But eBay is different, and not just because auctions are the primary format. eBay gives its members many different ways to sell, and each sales format has its own set of rules and procedures. It pays to know something about the different sales so that you can choose the right format for the item you have.

This section assumes that you have some basic knowledge of eBay and that you have at least shopped for a few items and possibly won some auctions. When it comes to putting items up for sale, eBay gets more complicated. You've got the following sales options:

✔ **Standard auctions:** This is the most basic eBay auction: You put an item up for sale, and you specify a starting bid (usually, a low amount from $1 to $9.99). You don't have a reserve price; the highest bidder at the end of the sale wins (if there is a highest bidder). Standard auctions and other auctions on eBay can last one, three, five, seven, or ten days. The ending time is precise: If you list something at 10:09 a.m. on a Sunday and you choose a seven-day format, the sale then ends at 10:09 a.m. the following Sunday.

✔ **Reserve auctions:** A *reserve price* is a price you specify as a minimum in order for a purchase to be successful. Any bids placed on the item being offered must be met or exceeded; otherwise, the sale will end without the seller being obligated to sell the item. You know if a reserve price is present by the message `Reserve Not Yet Met` next to the current high bid. When a bid is received that exceeds the reserve, this message changes to `Reserve Met`. The reserve price is concealed until the reserve is met.

✔ **Multiple-item auctions:** This type of sale, also known as a Dutch auction, is used by sellers who want to sell more than one identical item at the same time. The seller specifies a starting bid and the number of items available; bidders can bid on one or more items. But the question of who wins can be confusing. The bidders who win are the ones who have placed the lowest successful bid that is still above the minimum price, based on the number of items being offered. For instance, suppose six items are offered, and ten bidders place bids. One bidder bids $20 for two items. Another bids $24 for one. Three others bid $18, two others bid $14, and three bid $10. The winners are the ones who bid $24, $20, and $18, respectively. The others lose out because only six items are available.

✔ **Fixed-price Buy It Now (BIN) sales:** A BIN price is a fixed price that the seller specifies. Fixed prices are used in all eBay Stores: The seller specifies that you can purchase the item for, say, $10.99; you click the Buy It Now button, agree to pay $10.99 plus shipping, and you instantly win the item.

✔ **Mixed auction/fixed price sales:** BIN prices can be offered in conjunction with standard or reserve auctions. In other words, even though bidders are placing bids on the item, if someone agrees to pay the fixed price, the item is immediately sold and the sale ends. If a BIN price is offered in conjunction with a standard auction, the BIN price is available until the first bid is placed; then the BIN price disappears. If a BIN price is offered in conjunction with a reserve auction, the BIN price is available until the reserve price is met. After the BIN price disappears, the item is available to the highest bidder.

Those are the basic types of sales. You can also sell automobiles on eBay Motors or even sell on eBay Live Auctions (www.ebayliveauctions.com). By knowing how eBay sales work and following the rules competently, you'll gradually develop a good reputation on the auction site.

How you sell is important, but the question of exactly *what* you should sell is one you should resolve well before you start your eBay business. Sell something you love, something you don't mind spending hours shopping for, photographing, describing, and eventually packing up and shipping. Sell something that has a niche market of enthusiastic collectors or other customers. Do some research on eBay to make sure there aren't already a thousand people peddling the same things you hope to make available.

Building a Good Reputation

In order to run a business on eBay, you need to have a steady flow of repeat customers. Customer loyalty comes primarily from the trust that is produced by developing a good reputation. eBay's feedback system is the best indicator of how trustworthy and responsive a seller is because past performance is a good indication of the kind of service a customer can expect in the future. Along with deciding what you want to sell and whether you want to sell on eBay on a part- or full-time basis, you need to have the development of a good reputation as one of your primary goals as well.

Feedback, feedback, feedback!

eBay's success is due in large measure to the network of trust it has established among its millions of members. The feedback system, in which members leave positive, negative, or neutral comments for the people with whom they have conducted (or tried to conduct) transactions is the foundation for that trust. The system rewards users who accumulate significant numbers of positive feedback comments and penalizes those who have low or negative feedback numbers. By taking advantage of the feedback system, you can realize the highest possible profit on your online sales and help get your online business off the ground.

There probably aren't any scientific studies of how feedback numbers affect sales, but I've heard anecdotally from sellers that their sales figures increase when their feedback levels hit a certain number. The number varies, but it appears to be in the hundreds — perhaps 300 or so. The inference is that prospective buyers place more trust in sellers who have higher feedback numbers because they have more experience and are presumably more trustworthy. Those who have a PowerSeller icon are even more trustworthy (see the "Striving for PowerSeller status" section later in this chapter).

Developing a schedule

One thing that can boost your reputation above all else on eBay is timeliness. If you respond to e-mail inquiries within a few hours, or at most a day or two, and if you can ship out merchandise quickly, you're virtually guaranteed to have satisfied customers who leave you positive feedback. The way to achieve timely response is to observe a work schedule.

It's tedious and time consuming to take and retake photos, edit those photos, get sales descriptions online, and do the packing and shipping that's required at the end of a sale. The only way to come up with a sufficient number of sales every week is to come up with a system. And a big part of coming up with a system is developing a weekly schedule that spells out when you need to do all of your eBay activities. A possible schedule might look like Table 10-1.

Table 10-1	eBay Business Schedule	
Day of Week	*First Activity*	*Second Activity (optional)*
Sunday	Get 7-day sales online	Send out end-of-sale notices
Monday	Packing	E-mails
Tuesday	Shipping	E-mails
Wednesday	Plan garage sales	Take photos
Thursday	Go to garage sales	Prepare descriptions
Friday	More sales	Prepare descriptions
Saturday	Respond to buyer inquiries	Get some sales online

You'll notice that there's something conspicuously missing from this proposed schedule: a day of rest. You can certainly work in such a day on Sunday (or whatever day you prefer). If you sell on eBay part time, you can probably take much of the weekend off. But most full-time sellers (and full-time self-employed people in general) will tell you that it's difficult to find a day off, especially when it's so important to respond to customer e-mails within a day or two of their receipt. You don't have to do everything all by yourself, however. You can hire full- or part-time help, which can free up time for family responsibilities.

Creating an About Me page

One of the best ways to build your reputation on eBay is to create a Web page that eBay makes available to each of its members free of charge called About Me. Your About Me page should talk about who you are, why you collect or sell what you do, and why you're a reputable seller. You can also talk about an eBay Store, if you have one, and provide links to your current auction sales. It takes only a few minutes to create an About Me page (not much longer than filling out the Sell Your Item form to get a sale online, in fact). If you want to include a photo, you should take a digital image and edit it in an image-editing program such as Paint Shop Pro or Photoshop, just as you would any other image. But a photo isn't absolutely necessary. Kimberly King, the eBay seller profiled later in this chapter, has a simple About Me page (see Figure 10-1).

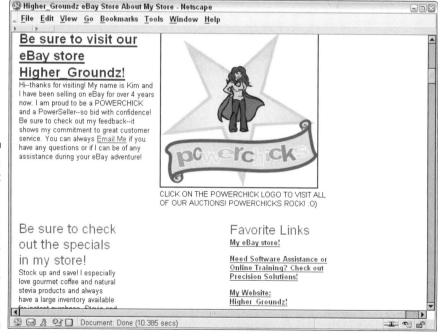

Figure 10-1:
An About Me page can be simple; it can contain links to your eBay Store and your eBay auction sales.

When you've decided what you want to say on your page, you need to save a digital photo if you want to include one. You then need to upload your photo to the Web server where you usually store your photos. Make note of the URL that identifies the location of the photo (for example, `www.myphotohost.com/mydirectory/photoname.jpg`). Then follow these steps:

1. **Click My eBay on the navigation bar near the top right corner of virtually any eBay page.**

   A login page appears.

2. **Type your User ID and password and click Sign In Securely.**

   The My eBay page appears.

3. **Click Personal Information under the My Account heading in the links on the left-hand side of the page.**

   The My eBay Account: Personal Information page appears.

4. **Scroll down to the About Me link, and click Change.**

   The About Me page appears.

5. **Scroll down to the bottom of the page and click Create My Page.**

   The Choose Page Creation Option page appears.

6. **Leave the Use Our Easy Step-By-Step Process option selected, and click Continue.**

   The About Me: Enter Page Content page appears.

7. **As indicated on the page, type a heading and text for your page. Label your photo and enter the URL for the photo in the Link to Your Picture text box. You can also type links to favorite pages and your own Web page if you have one. When you're done, click Continue.**

   The Preview and Submit page appears, as shown in Figure 10-2.

8. **Choose one of three possible layouts for your page, and preview your page content in the bottom half of the page. When you're done, click Submit.**

   Your page goes online.

Like any Web page, you can change your About Me page at any time by following the preceding steps.

Another way to ensure a good reputation as a seller is to participate actively in eBay's discussion boards. Pay special attention to boards that pertain to the type of merchandise you buy and sell. Responding to questions from new users and offering advice based on your experience will boost your standing within the user community.

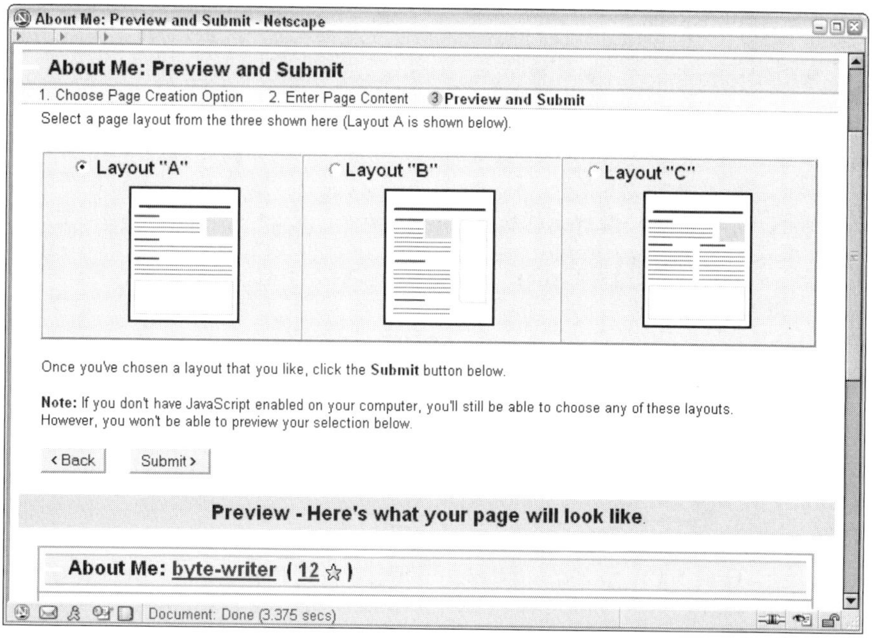

Figure 10-2:
Take a few
minutes to
proofread
your About
Me page
before you
post it
online.

Preparing Sales Descriptions That Sell

How do you actually go about selling on eBay? The aim is similar to other forms of e-commerce: You select some merchandise, take photos, type descriptions, and put the descriptions online in a catalog. But there are some critical differences as well. You don't have to specify a fixed price on eBay; as described earlier in this chapter, you can set a starting bid and see how much the market will bear. All sales descriptions are not created equal, however. Many sellers would argue that clear, sharp photos are the most important part of a description, and that, if you show the item in its best light photographically, it will practically sell itself. I'm of the opinion that a good heading and descriptions that include critical keywords are just as important as good photos. The art of creating descriptions is best discovered by inspecting other people's sales listings; the essentials are described in the sections that follow.

Details, details

The primary way of getting your sales online is eBay's Sell Your Item form. You can access this form at any time by clicking Sell on the eBay navigation bar, which appears at the top of just about any page on the eBay Web site. The Sell Your Item form is easy to use, so I don't step you through every nuance and option. In this section, however, I do point out a few features you might overlook and that can help you get more attention for your sales.

TIP

The Sell Your Item form is by no means the only way to get eBay sales online. Many full- or part-time businesspeople use special software that allows them to upload multiple images at once or schedule multiple sales so they all start and end at the same time. The auction services Andale (www.andale.com) and SpareDollar (www.sparedollar.com) offer eBay auction listing tools. In addition, eBay offers two programs you might find helpful:

- **Turbo Lister** (pages.ebay.com/turbo_lister/index.html), which is free, provides sellers with design templates that they can use to add graphic interest to their sales descriptions.

- **Selling Manager** (pages.ebay.com/selling_manager/index.html), a monthly subscription service, is sales and management software. It provides you with convenient lists that let you track what you have up for sale, which sales have ended, which items have been purchased, and what tasks you have yet to do — for instance, sending e-mails to winning bidders or relisting items that didn't sell the first time.

Choosing a second category

One of the first things you do in the Sell Your Item form is to choose a sales category in which to list your item. I highly recommend using the search box at the top of the Select Category page. Enter a keyword and click Find. You're presented with a detailed list of sales categories. The best thing about the list is that it is ranked in order of the ones that are most likely to sell items matching your desired keywords. The categories near the top of the list are the ones to choose.

I also recommend paying an extra dollar or so (when you choose a second category, your listing fee is doubled) and listing the item in a second category — especially if the second category has a percentage ranking that's almost as high as the first.

Focusing on your auction heading

The heading of an eBay sales description is the set of six or seven words that appears in a set of search results or in a set of listings in a category. In other words, it's the set of words that a potential customer initially sees when he or she is deciding whether to investigate a sale and possibly bid on it. Keep your heading short and specific. Include dates, colors, or model numbers if applicable. Try to pick one word that might attract a buyer, such as Rare, Hard-to-Find, Mint, New, or something similar.

Choosing a good ending time for your sale

With eBay sales, it's not the starting time that counts but the ending time that makes a difference. The more attention you can get at the end of a sale, the more likely you are to make a profit. Most sales get attention on weekends, when the majority of shoppers aren't working. The optimal time, in fact, is to have the sale end some time on a Saturday night or Sunday afternoon.

Of course, bidders can come from all over the world, and what's Sunday afternoon in California is Monday morning in Australia. But don't worry too much about such distinctions: Pick an ending time that's convenient for eBay shoppers in your own country to be present — not in the middle of a workday, but on the weekend.

Adding keywords

When you prepare an auction description, you don't have to make it overly lengthy. It's not the length that counts; it's the number of keywords you include. A *keyword* is a word or phrase that describes the item you have for sale and that prospective buyers are likely to enter in their eBay searches. If your description contains a keyword that someone enters, your sale will show up in search results. And just showing up in the search results is half the battle: If a buyer can find your item, he or she can then follow through with its purchase.

The more keywords you can add to your description, the more frequently that sale will be found by searchers. It's to your advantage, then, to think of all the terms that someone would use when looking for your item, and add as many of those keywords to the heading and to the body of the description as you can. If you're selling an electric drill, for example, use keywords such as *cordless, electric, 3/8-inch, Black & Decker,* or anything else a likely buyer might enter.

Upgrading your listings

Near the end of the Sell Your Item form, a series of items gives you the option to specify whether or not you want to upgrade your listings. *Upgrade,* in this case, means adding graphic highlights that are intended to help your listing stand out from those around it, either in search results or on category pages. You can choose from the options shown in Table 10-2.

Table 10-2	Listing Upgrades	
Upgrade	*Description*	*Cost*
Highlight	A colored strip is drawn across the auction title.	$5.00
Bold	The auction title is formatted in bold type.	$1.00
Gallery	A thumbnail image appears next to auction title.	$0.25
Gallery Featured	A Gallery image appears in a "feature" area at the top of Gallery pages.	$19.95
Home Page Featured	Your auction title is listed randomly along with other sales on eBay's home page.	$39.95

Of these, the single most cost-effective upgrade, in my opinion, is the Gallery thumbnail image, which costs only a quarter and calls more attention to your sales listing — especially when you consider that most other listings around yours also have Gallery images. The Home Page may be expensive, but it gives you a chance of having your sale on eBay's home page and guarantees exposure for your sale on featured areas.

In eBay's early days, if you wanted a sale to end at a particular time (say, 7 p.m. on a Sunday evening, when lots of bidders are available), you had to physically be present to create the description at a certain time. For instance, if you wanted such a sale to last seven days, you had to list it at precisely 7 p.m. the preceding Sunday. Now, you don't have to be physically present exactly a week, five days, three days, or one day before you want your sale to end: You can specify an ending time when you fill out the Sell Your Item form.

Note: Although it's free to register for an account on eBay and free to fill out the Sell Your Item form, eBay charges you an Insertion Fee when you actually put an item up for sale. The Insertion Fee is based on the starting price of the auction. The fee is only $.35 for a starting bid of $9.99 or less, which explains why most starting bids are less than $10. A Final Value Fee is also charged at the end of the auction, and it depends on the sale price. On a sale of $100, the Final Value Fee is $3.41; at $1,000, it is $28.12. For a detailed explanation of the formula used to calculate fees, see pages.ebay.com/help/sell/fees.html.

Include clear images

No matter how well written your auction's headings and description, all of your work can quickly be undone by digital images that are dark, blurry, or that load too slowly because they are too large in either physical or file size. The same principles that you use when capturing digital images for your e-commerce Web site apply to eBay images: Make sure that you have clear, even lighting (consider taking your photos outdoors); use your camera's auto-focus setting; crop your images so that they focus on the merchandise being sold; and keep the file size small by adjusting the resolution with your digital camera or your image editing software.

Some aspects to posting images along with auction descriptions are unique to eBay:

✔ **Image hosting:** If you run a business on eBay and have dozens or even hundreds of sales items online at any one time, you can potentially have hundreds of image files to upload and store on a server. If you use eBay Picture Services as your photo host, the first image for each sale is free. Each subsequent image costs 15 cents. It's worth your while to find an economical photo hosting service, such as Pixhost (www.pixhost.com) or Auction-Images (auction-images.com).

✔ **Close-ups:** If what you're selling has important details such as brand names, dates, and maker's marks, you need to have a camera that has *macro capability* — that is, the ability to get clear close-ups. Virtually all digital cameras have a macro setting, but it can be tricky to hold the camera still enough to get a clear image (you may need to mount the camera on a tripod). If you use a conventional film camera, you'll need to invest in a macro lens.

✔ **Multiple images:** You'll never hear an eBay shopper complaining that you included too many images with your auction listings. As long as you have the time and patience and an affordable image host, you can include five, six, or more views of your item (for big objects like automobiles and other vehicles, multiple images are especially important).

Be sure to crop and adjust the brightness and contrast of your images after you take them, using a program such as Paint Shop Pro by Jasc (`www.jasc.com`) or Adobe Photoshop Elements by Adobe Systems (`www.adobe.com`).

If you want to find out more about creating sales descriptions (and practically every aspect of buying or selling on eBay, for that matter) take a look at my book, *eBay PowerUser's Bible* (Wiley).

Be flexible with payment options

It might seem like payments are the most nerve-wracking part of a transaction on eBay. They have been, in the past; but as time goes on, eBay provides more safeguards for its customers. That doesn't mean you won't run into the occasional bidder who won't respond after winning your auction, or whose check bounces. But as a seller, you have plenty of protections: If someone doesn't respond, you can relist your item; if someone's check bounces, you don't lose out on your sales item because you will have held on to it during the process of having the check clear.

As an eBay seller, you should accept the basic forms of payment: personal checks, cashier's checks, and postal money orders. You can also enable your customers to pay with a credit card, either by using your merchant credit card account if you have one (see Chapter 12), or by using one of two popular electronic payment services (or both): eBay's own PayPal (`www.paypal.com`) or BidPay (`www.bidpay.com`), which is a service of Western Union. In the case of PayPal, you are charged a nominal fee (2.2 to 2.9 percent of the amount plus a 30-cent fee) when a buyer transfers money electronically to your account. In the case of BidPay, it's the buyer who pays for a paper money order, which is then mailed to you, the seller.

You should generally not accept other forms of payment from buyers. Occasionally, a buyer will insist on sending you cash in an envelope; you should insist, in turn, that the buyer sends a money order instead. COD is expensive and cumbersome; it makes the delivery service responsible for collecting your money, and if the buyer isn't home when the delivery people arrive, you might have to wait a long time to get paid.

Providing Good Customer Service

When you make the decision to sell on eBay on a regular basis, you need to develop a good reputation. Earlier in this chapter, I outline ways that you can do that. But one of the best ways to achieve that goal — providing a high level of customer service to your buyers — is an issue that warrants a separate discussion. The single best way to do *that* is to be responsive to e-mail inquiries of all sorts. This means checking your e-mail at least once a day and spending lots of time typing messages. If you take days to get back to someone who asks you about the color or the condition of an item you have for sale, it might just be too late for that person to bid. And slow response to a high bidder or buyer after the sale can make the buyer nervous and result in "neutral" feedback — not a complaint about fraud or dishonesty, but a note about poor service. Such feedback is considered as bad as a negative comment on eBay.

Setting terms of sale

One aspect of good customer service is getting back to people quickly and communicating clearly and with courtesy. When you receive inquiries, you should always thank prospective customers for approaching you and considering the sale; even if they don't end up placing bids, you will have spread goodwill.

Another way to be good to your customers is to be clear about how you plan to ship your merchandise and how much it will cost. When you fill out the Sell Your Item form (which I discuss further in the earlier section, "Details, details"), you can specify either an actual shipping cost (a cost based on weight and the buyer's residence) or a flat shipping fee (a shipping fee you charge for all of your items).

The moment you specify a shipping charge in the Sell Your Item form, you set eBay's automated Checkout system in motion. The Checkout system enables buyers to calculate their own shipping charges. The advantage to you, as the seller, is that you don't need to send your buyers a message stating how much they need to pay you.

Packing and shipping safely

One of the aspects of selling on eBay that is often overlooked (not by *buyers*) is the practice of packing and shipping. After sending out payment for something, buyers often wait on pins and needles, eagerly hoping to receive their items while dreading a unresponsive seller who refuses to ship what has been purchased. Besides the danger of fraud, there's the danger that the item you send will be damaged in transit.

Be sure to use sturdy boxes when you ship and that you take care to adequately cushion your merchandise within those boxes. I've received boxes from sellers who stuffed the insides with bubble wrap and newspaper, and I was happy for the trouble. If you are shipping something particularly fragile, consider double-boxing it: Put it in a box, place the box in a larger one, and put cushioning material between the two. Your customers will be pleased to receive the merchandise undamaged, and you'll get good feedback as a result.

 Place a thank-you note, business card, or even a small gift inside the box with your shipment. It will spread good feelings and remind buyers how to get in touch with you in the future.

Moving from Auctioneer to eBay Businessperson

eBay sellers don't start out saying, "I'm going to be a PowerSeller, and I'm going to sell full time on eBay for a living!" Rather, they typically start out on a whim. They find an object lying around in a box, in the attic, or on a shelf, and they wonder: Will anyone pay money for this?

That's what happened to Kimberly King, a housewife living in Longmont, Colorado. Back in March 2000, she was cleaning up around the house when she found an old purse. "I thought, 'Gee, should I sell this?' I didn't have enough stuff to hold a garage sale. I'd heard about eBay, so I thought I would see what it was like to sell something. I found out just how easy it was to set up an ID and to register. I ended up getting $20 for the purse, which was much more than I would have at a garage sale. I was hooked."

After she felt comfortable selling on eBay, a new thought popped up: "You start thinking, 'Let's see, that thing sold, what else do we have that we can sell?' When I really saw that I could do this on a regular basis, I thought, 'I can do this all the time; I can have some fun money.'"

Opening an eBay Store

An eBay Store is a Web site within eBay's own voluminous Web empire. It's a place where sellers can post items for sale at fixed prices. The great advantage of having a store is that it enables a seller to keep merchandise available for purchase for 30, 60, 90, or even an unlimited number of days at a time. It gives customers another way to buy from you, and it can significantly increase your sales, too. eBay itself, at a recent eBay Live event, made the claim that eBay Stores brought about a 25 percent increase in overall sales. (Kimberly King, the PowerSeller profiled below, says her store accounts for perhaps 55 to 60 percent of her sales.)

CASE STUDY

PowerSeller keeps sales going with a little help from her friends

PowerSeller status is something that many eBay sellers strive for, and Kimberly King is no exception. After she started selling on a regular basis, she decided to try for the coveted icon. "When I realized that I could do this, I had to do a little more research about what I was selling," she says. "Having not been in sales before, I found that there are some strategies you have to follow and some things you have to hunt for, like a wholesale supplier."

Having a steady stream of merchandise to buy at wholesale and then resell on eBay is important for PowerSellers, who are required to maintain at least $2,000 in gross sales each month in order to keep their PowerSeller icon. This requirement does put some pressure on a seller, King says. "I do put some pressure on myself to keep my PowerSeller status. I feel I have to list a certain number of items, and be available for people constantly. You have more people you are helping and working with."

A housewife and mother, King has to fit her eBay activities in between errands, childcare, and many other responsibilities. Still, she manages to spend as much as six hours on the auction site

each day. She takes her own photos of each of her sales items even though her wholesaler has offered stock photos because, she says, shoppers need to see exactly what they are buying. "Right now I am striving to list ten sales online per day. It's hard to remember to do this yourself, so some other sellers and I have decided to be 'listing buddies.' We remind each other every day that we need to keep up our quota; that way, we're accountable to someone."

Over the years she's had her share of great profits among her 2,000-plus sales: an autographed item by Mickey Mantle that she bought for only $5 sold for $80; some Navajo rugs sold for more than $800. More than half of her sales are antiques, coffee, and products made with the herbal sweetener Stevia sold in her Higher-Groundz eBay Store (stores.ebay.com/Higher-Groundz, shown in the following figure).

Having items up for sale for a month or more at a time helps King maintain her PowerSeller sales quotas. "If one of my kids is home from school sick and I can't do something that week, I have those sales in my store. It's not like I completely left eBay that week."

One of the best sources of support and help has been the member-created discussion forums called eBay Groups. "When you find something, you can post a message on the PowerChicks group asking, 'Hey I found this neat thing at a garage sale, does anyone know what this is?'" King says. "Those discussion boards have been so helpful because you get information from really knowledgeable sellers."

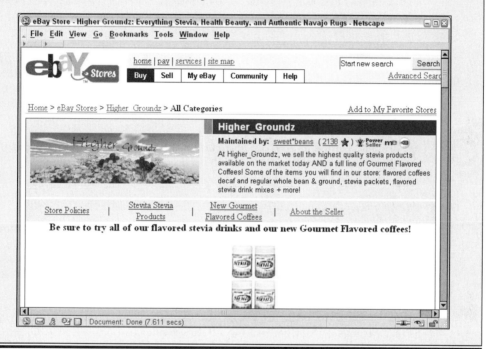

 An article in E-Commerce Times describes different strategies for getting your eBay Store listed in many of the major search engines. You can read the article at `www.ecommerce-guide.com/news/news/article.php/3385011`.

Striving for PowerSeller status

PowerSellers are among the elite on eBay. Those members who have the coveted icon next to their names feel justifiably proud of their accomplishments. They have met the stringent requirements for PowerSellers, which emphasize consistent sales, a high and regular number of completed sales, and excellent customer service. Moving from occasional seller to PowerSeller is a substantial change. Requirements include

✔ At least 100 unique feedback results — 98 percent of which are positive

✔ A minimum of $1,000 of average gross monthly sales for three consecutive months

✔ A good standing record — achieved by complying with eBay Listing Policies

✔ A current account — achieved by contacting bidders within three business days and upholding the eBay Community Values

In return for the hard work required to meet these standards, PowerSellers do get a number of benefits in addition to the icon. These include group health insurance; merchandise with a special logo on it, free banner ads, a special discussion board just for PowerSellers, and more.

The PowerSeller program isn't something you apply for. eBay reviews your sales statistics and invites you to join the program when you have met the requirements. You can find out more about the requirements and benefits of the PowerSeller program at `pages.ebay.com/services/buyandsell/welcome.html`.

Finding lots of merchandise to sell

Moving up to PowerSeller status means an ongoing commitment to conducting a large number of sales, responding quickly to customers, and shipping efficiently. It also means finding a steady and reliable stream of merchandise to sell. When you need to get 50 or more items up for sale each week, garage sales quickly become impractical for all but the most dedicated. Many PowerSellers manage to find sufficient inventory by heading to estate sales in teams, showing up in the predawn hours and waiting in line, and then buying as many things as they can grab when they scurry through a house. Others find a wholesale supplier who can provide them with low-cost items such as figurines, coffee, or holiday decorations in bulk.

Finding a wholesale supplier

All the PowerSellers I've spoken to in recent years have assured me that it's not easy to find a reputable, reliable wholesaler. They urge other sellers to do their homework by getting references and talking to satisfied customers. Many wholesalers are primarily interested in taking sellers' money and not providing good service, they say. Often, finding wholesalers is a matter of word of mouth: You ask someone who knows someone, and so on. Kimberly King (the seller I profile in the "PowerSeller keeps sales going with a little help from her friends" sidebar) used connections left over from her former management position at an herbal tea company to find a supplier.

"You're not going to find someone on eBay who is going to tell you their wholesaler," she cautions. "They're too valuable. My advice is to make sure to call and check out references; do everything you can to find out everything about a company. Some force you to make an initial order of maybe $1,000 minimum up front, knowing when you see the product you'll never order it again."

Part IV
Running and Promoting Your Online Business

The 5th Wave — By Rich Tennant

"The top line represents our revenue, the middle line is our inventory, and the bottom line shows the rate of my hair loss over the same period."

In this part . . .

*L*ike fish in the ocean, your potential customers are out there — more of them, in fact, than you can begin to count. Part III tells you everything you need to know to reel them in — hook, line, and sinker.

When you run an online business, you need to develop special strategies for getting attention and standing out from the millions of other sites that are your competitors. This means researching your market, delivering on your promises, and making sure that your customers are satisfied with your goods and services. It means exploring all the options for advertising and publicity that are available to you, optimizing your search engine visibility, making the shopping and payment experience a breeze, and choosing an effective marketing strategy that best meets your needs.

Nothing's more frustrating, after all, than feeling a nibble on your line and then having to content yourself with telling your friends about the one that got away.

Chapter 11

Easing the Shopping Experience

*N*othing can compare to the emotional thrill you feel when you start up your own new business and get it online. Nothing, that is, but the real excitement of getting paid for what you do. A pat on the back is nice, but it's even better to receive the proverbial check in the mail or have funds transferred to your business account.

When you are in an online business, there are two important components to doing financial transactions. In the first place, you have to go through some extra steps to make the customer feel secure so that you will be paid promptly and reliably. You also need to protect yourself financially. It's nice to know that, because e-commerce has been around for a few years, you have your choice of experts, services, and online tools that make your job easier. Even though independence may be one of the factors that you like most about running your own online business, you have plenty of demands on your attention and getting help is the sensible way to go.

For example, the technical side of starting up a site doesn't have to be your concern. You don't have to spend years studying to be a programmer. Plenty of utilities are available to help you create Web pages, make links, keep your books, and do other tasks online.

Time is on your side in this case because the range of software "shortcuts" is becoming larger and more user friendly. You can create forms that will process data and send it to you. You can keep track of your business expenses online, create banner ads and animations, hold videoconferences, and more. In this chapter, I suggest practices that you can implement to reduce your business time-to-market as well as ways to share information more efficiently. Every hour you save by taking advantage of these services is an hour you can spend on another part of your business, or even relaxing.

Here is a short list of what you need to do to be a successful e-commerce businessperson: set up the right atmosphere for making purchases, provide options for payment, and keep sensitive information private. Oh, and don't forget that your main goal is to get goods to the customer safely and on time. In this chapter, I describe ways in which you can implement these essential online business strategies.

Attracting and Keeping Online Customers

You've heard it before, but I can't emphasize enough the importance of understanding the needs and habits of online shoppers and doing your best to address them. When it comes to e-commerce, there is a direct correlation between meeting the needs of your customers and having a healthy balance in your bank account.

Seeing your merchandise is the first step

Customers may end up buying an item in a brick-and-mortar store, but chances are that they saw it online first. In fact, they often aren't interested until they read a detailed description. More and more shoppers are assuming that legitimate stores will have a Web site and an online sales catalog.

"It's not enough to just say we have this or that product line for sale. Until we actually add an individual item to our online store, with pictures and prices, we won't sell it," says Ernie Preston, who helped create an 84,000-item online catalog for a brick-and-mortar tool company profiled later in this chapter. "As soon as you put it in your online catalog, you'll get a call about it. Shopping on the Web is the convenience factor that people want."

Don't hesitate to post as many items as possible on your online catalog and don't scrimp on the amount of detail that you include about each item. For more and more businesses, having an online catalog is becoming an integral, not peripheral, part of their identity.

Tell me that the price is right, right now

Customers may have a lot of questions to ask you, but what they want to know first and foremost is how much an item costs. Be sure to put the cost right next to the item that you're presenting. Searching through a price list will lose the competitive edge of speed and convenience, which is what Web shoppers want most. They don't have the patience to click through several pages. Chances are that they are comparison shopping and in a hurry.

Microsoft Office 2003, the widely used suite of applications that includes Word, Excel, and PowerPoint, gives you access to some clip art images that help highlight sales items. Figure 11-1 shows an example of how you can edit an HTML Web page file with Word by inserting an image from the Clip Art pane. (You can find more clip art images at the Microsoft Office Clip Art and Media Center, office.microsoft.com/clipart/default.aspx).

Show me that I can trust you!

Trust is the foundation on which every good relationship is built, and building trust is especially important for an online business. Electronic commerce is still in its early days, and many customers still have fears like these:

- How do I know that someone won't intercept my name, phone number, or credit card information and use the data to make unauthorized purchases?

- How can I be sure that your online business will actually ship me what I order and not "take the money and run?"

- Can I count on you not to sell my personal information to other businesses that will flood me with unwanted e-mail?

Font menu   Clip Art task pane

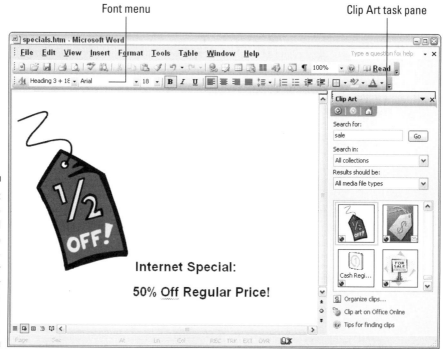

Figure 11-1: Use graphics to call attention to the information your customer wants the most: the price.

To get an in-depth look at how customers shop online and what constitutes "good" and "bad" shopping for many people, consult *Buying Online For Dummies* (Wiley), by Joseph Lowery.

How do you build trust online? If you run an eBay Store, you have the advantage of being able to display a feedback rating, and customers can look up comments left on the site by the people with whom you have done business. If you're not on eBay, you can still publish comments from satisfied customers. And you need to state your policies clearly and often. Tell people that you value their business and will do everything you can to protect their personal information. Assure them that you won't give out any customer's data without that person's consent. If you plan to accept credit card orders, be sure to get an account with a Web host that provides a *secure server,* which is software that encrypts data exchanged with a browser.

If you're a member in good standing of the Better Business Bureau (www.bbb.org), you may be eligible to join the BBBOnLine program (www.bbbonline.org) to build credibility and confidence among your clients. Businesses that participate in the BBBOnLine program show their commitment to their customers by displaying a BBBOnLine Reliability Seal or Privacy Seal on their Web sites. Consumers can click the BBBOnLine seal to view a Better Business Bureau company profile on the participating business.

Give me the essentials; show me the products

Remember that one of the big advantages of operating a business online is space. You have plenty of room in which to provide full descriptions of your sale items. You also have no reason to skimp on the details that you provide about your business, your products, and your services. Here are some suggestions of how to provide information that your customer may want:

- If you sell clothing, include a page with size and measurement charts.
- If you sell food, provide weights, ingredients, and nutritional information.
- If you sell programming, Web design, or traditional graphic design, provide samples of your work, links to Web pages you've created, and testimonials from satisfied clients.
- If you're a musician, publish a link to a short sound file of your work.

Don't be reluctant to tell people ways that your products and services are better than others. Visit the Lands' End online catalog (www.landsend.com) for good examples of how this well-established marketer describes the quality of its wares.

Looking for a Good Web Host: The 411

Time and again, I hear successful entrepreneurs extol the virtues of the companies that enable their businesses to go online. Why all the praise? Some Web hosting services or ISPs go beyond the basic tasks of providing space on a Web server and keeping the server functioning smoothly.

If you're a computer novice or just technically challenged, look for a full-service host that can help set up a Web site, make it easy to process forms or run scripts, and perform similar tasks. One of the best shortcuts to success is to find a good Web host, and then depend on that company's software tools and service reps when you need help building your Web site.

 Before you sign up with a host, check out customer service options. Specifically, find out when the service staff is available by telephone. Also ask if telephone support costs extra. If you're working alone and don't have a technical person you can call, being able to speak to a technical support person about a problem you're encountering on your site can be invaluable.

It may seem surprising to think of your Web host as one of the reasons for your success. After all, you do most of the work. At the most basic level, a hosting service is just a company that provides you with space on a server. You call them only when you have a problem or a billing question. At least, that's how most people look at their Web host.

However, whether you use the server space given to you by your ISP or sign with a full-time Web host, the relationship can be much more.

For example, pair Networks (www.pair.com), which offers a pretty typical selection of hosting options and which has been praised by some technical writers I know, offers the following kinds of e-commerce services that go above and beyond the basic hosting arrangements, which range from $9.95 to $49.95 per month:

- ✔ **Secure server:** You can pay an extra charge and have your site hosted on a secure server (a computer that encrypts traffic) so that you can protect the information that your customers send you.

- ✔ **Shopping cart:** For an extra $9.95 per month, you can add ShopSite shopping cart functionality to your site. (See Chapter 3 for more about ShopSite.)

- ✔ **Credit card authorization:** For an extra $15 per month plus a $39 setup fee, customers can set up credit card processing and address checking through the Authorize.net payment program. (See Chapter 12 for more information on setting up online credit card systems.)

✔ **Dedicated server:** The basic hosting option for almost all hosting services is to put your site on a computer that hosts many different Web sites. In other words, you're on a shared server. When traffic to your site gets really heavy, you can get your own, dedicated server. The dedicated server options that pair Networks offers start at $249 per month, but you get unlimited telephone support as well as faster access for your customers because you're running your own server.

Don't get locked in to a two- or three-year contract with a Web host. Go month to month or sign a one-year contract. Even if you're initially happy with your host, this gives you a chance to back out and go elsewhere if the company takes a turn for the worse or your needs change.

Domain name registration

People frequently get confused when I try to explain how to register a domain name and how to "point" the name at the server that hosts their Web sites. This is a perfect place for an ISP to help you. In addition to giving you an Internet connection and Web server space, some ISPs also function as domain name registrars: The ISP provides a service that enables anyone to purchase the rights to use a domain name for one, two, or more years. It's a kind of one-stop shopping: You can set up your domain name and, if the same company hosts your site, you can easily have the name associated with your site instead of having to go through an extra step or two of pointing the name at the server that holds your site.

By *pointing* your domain name at your server, I mean the following: You purchase the rights to a domain name from a registrar. You then need to associate the name with your Web site so that, when people connect to your site, they won't have to enter a long URL such as `username.home.mindspring.com`. Instead, they'll enter `www.mybusiness.com`. To do this, you tell the registrar that your domain name should be assigned to the IP address of your server. Your ISP or Web host will tell you the IP address to give to the registrar.

When you're registering your site, don't focus solely on the dot-com (`.com`) domain. Some new domains have been made available that can provide you with alternate names in case your ideal dot-com name is unavailable. Even if you do get a dot-com name (`.com` is still the most recognizable and desirable domain name extension), you may want to buy up the same name with `.biz`, `.info`, or `.tv` at the end so that someone else doesn't grab it.

Marketing utilities

Some people are great at promotion and marketing. Others excel at detail work. Only a few lucky people can do both kinds of business tasks well and enjoy it. If, like me, your promotional talents are a bit weak, find a hosting service that will help you get noticed.

Some hosts, such as Microsoft Small Business Center (`www.microsoft.com/ smallbusiness/bc/default.mspx`), give you access to a variety of marketing services if you sign with it as your host. Not all the services are free of course. For instance, the Center's optional List Builder marketing package gives you access to a selection of Web page templates that enable you to create your own newsletter and then send it to a mailing list of customers. This service costs an extra $19.95 per month (after a 30-day free trial period) in addition to the usual Small Business Center Web hosting fee of $12.95 per month. (See the section about opening a Microsoft Small Business in Chapter 9 for a brief overview about hosting solutions that Microsoft offers.)

Catalog creators

Some of the biggest Web hosts (such as Yahoo! Small Business Merchant Solutions, which I describe in Chapter 9) give you software that enables you to create an online sales catalog by using your Web browser. In other words, you don't have to purchase a Web design program, figure out how to use it, and create your pages from scratch.

On the downside, a Web-based catalog creation tool doesn't give you the ultimate control over how your pages look. You probably can't pull off fancy layout effects with tables or layers. (See Chapter 5 for more on using tables and layers to design your site's Web pages.) On the plus side, however, if you have no interest in Web design and don't want to pay a designer, you can use one of these tools to save time and money by getting your pages online quickly all by yourself.

Database connectivity

If you plan on selling only five, ten, or even twenty or so items at a time, your e-commerce site can be a *static* site, which means that every time a customer makes a sale, you have to take the time to manually adjust inventory. A static site also requires you to update descriptions and revise shipping charges or other details by hand, one Web page at a time. In contrast, a *dynamic* e-commerce site presents catalog sales items "on the fly" (dynamically) by connecting to a database whenever a customer requests a Web page. Suppose, for example, that a customer clicks a link for shoes. On a dynamic site, the customer sees a selection of footwear gathered instantly from the database server that's connected to the Web site. The Web page data is live and up-to-date because it's created every time the customer makes a request.

If you need to create a dynamic Web site, another factor in choosing a Web host is whether or not it supports the Web page and database software that you want to use. For Doug Laughter of The Silver Connection, LLC (which I profile in Chapter 3), the choice of host was essential. He wanted to develop his site himself by using technologies he was familiar with and regarded highly: Microsoft Active Server Pages (ASP) language and Macromedia UltraDev Web site creation software. If you use a database program such as MySQL, for instance, you may want to sign up with a Web host that allows you to run SQL Server on one of its servers.

Payment plans

Handling real-time online transactions is one of the most daunting of all e-commerce tasks. Some Web hosts can facilitate the process of obtaining a merchant account and processing credit card purchases made online. Yahoo! Small Business Merchant Solutions, for one, says you can receive a merchant account in just one to three days by applying through its site.

NTT/Verio, one of the best-known Web hosts/ISPs, has several hosting plans especially for e-commerce Web sites. The company's Gold Hosting Plan, which costs $50 to set up and $99.95 per month, includes access to a Merchant Payment Center as well as a shopping cart that you set up by following a tutorial. At the other end of the spectrum, a budget Web host called Webmasters.com charges $9.95 per month for a Business Hosting account if you pay for an entire year at once. The account includes access to a shopping cart and credit card payment gateway. (You have to pay an extra $5 for the use of a secure server that protects your customers' credit card information by encrypting it, however.)

In any case, you still have to set up your Web site, catalog, and shopping cart pages, and you still have to ship out your items and answer your customers' questions. But having your Web host provide you with the sales and payment tools and be available to answer your questions, removes part of the burden of setting up a payment system.

Boosting Business through Efficient Communication

In the earlier sections of this chapter, I show you how ISPs can help you create catalogs, process payments, obtain domain names, and perform other business tasks. However, sometimes the tasks that aren't directly related to marketing and sales can actually enable you to improve your profit margin by giving you more time to do marketing and sales. If you can use the Internet to communicate with vendors, co-workers, and other business partners, you increase efficiency, which, in turn, enables you to take care of business.

Efficiency involves getting everyone on the same page and working together, if not at the same time, at least at the *right* time. Standing in the hallway with a megaphone and announcing a group meeting is going to disturb people who are working — and besides, you'll miss employees who are out running errands or taking a lunch break.

A less intrusive tool for getting people together is an online *personal informa-tion manager* (PIM). An online PIM provides the tools, such as a calendar, an address book, a to-do list, and e-mail, so that members of a workgroup can coordinate their schedules.

An example of an online PIM is ScheduleOnline (www.scheduleonline.com). ScheduleOnline received high marks from the online news service CNET, par-ticularly for its calendar, which enables multiple users to share lists of tasks and meetings, as shown in Figure 11-2. Users can invite others to meetings (guests confirm with a single click), send meeting announcements by e-mail, and check for conflicts to ensure that everyone's schedule has an opening during the time selected.

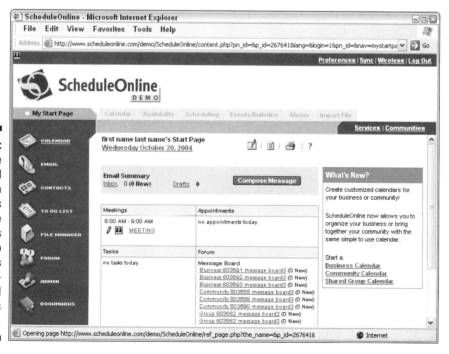

Figure 11-2:
An online personal information manager lets you share schedules and set up meetings with co-workers and customers alike.

CASE STUDY

Collaboration boosts efficiency

Health Decisions (www.healthdec.com), a clinical research and development company based in Chapel Hill, North Carolina, manages its internal operations plus an office in Oxford, England, by taking advantage of the Internet. The company posts its company's benefits, travel, and orientation information for new employees on its intranet. Staff can also purchase travel vouchers and record purchases made with company credit cards online.

Improved communication and workflow — thanks to e-mail, the intranet, and access to the wider Internet — enables the company's 80 staff members to collaborate and communicate with the aid of only two administrative staff. Health Decisions doesn't even have a receptionist.

CEO Michael Rosenberg estimates that Health Decisions would require 5–7 additional people if it used conventional communications. At an average salary of $35,000 plus benefits, he believes the company's intranet is saving them about $175,000 to $245,000 per year.

"A lot of the administrative questions you get are very predictable. How do I check the status of my 401K plan or enter time for a project? We try to put it all on our intranet. Why pay someone to do these repetitive tasks when we can put the relevant information on the intranet, and people can access the data quickly. We save time; the employee saves time. I look on it as a means of empowering people."

The Internet also enables Health Decisions to handle critical procedures far more quickly when compared with industry standards:

✔ The time required to collect and enter data into a database is only a matter of minutes, in contrast to industry averages of anywhere between several hours and several months.

✔ The error rate for databases is less than one per 10,000 database fields, compared with about 5 per 1,000 incurred by other companies.

✔ The time required to submit one 10,000-page regulatory application is three months, compared with about a year for companies that don't collaborate online.

Health Decisions conducts tests of pharmaceutical drugs. Such tests are expensive and collect an extensive amount of data. It's critical for staff to get the data in the system quickly and get the information in the field. When a study has been completed, Health Decisions uses standard forms stored on its intranet to present the data, which is then submitted via the Internet.

"We typically deal with project teams scattered around the globe, and our system is designed to collect, digest, and share information widely. While a study is still being done, we can tell how it's progressing because the data is put on the intranet in real time in a database," says Rosenberg. "We set up a Web site for each study. At other organizations, it might take a week to gather the data. On the Net, you can do it instantly. Ultimately, we have shown that we can reduce typical drug development timelines by 20 percent or more."

Making Sure Your Web Site Is Up to Snuff

It's tempting to just get your Web site online, and then forget about it. It's up to your hosting service or ISP to monitor traffic and make sure everything's up and running. That's their job, right?

It *is* their job, to be sure, but unless you keep an eye on your site and its availability to your customers, you may not be aware of technical problems that can scare potential business away. If your site is offline periodically or your server crashes or works slowly, it doesn't just waste your customers' time — it can cut into your sales directly. Luckily, some shortcuts are available to help you monitor your Web site and that don't take a lot of time and effort or technical know-how.

If your site doesn't work well, another site whose pages load more quickly can be found just a few mouse clicks away. Outages can be costly, too. Internet Week reported back in 1999 that if the Dell Computer site was down for just one minute, it would cost the hardware giant $10,000. A 90-minute outage would cost the company nearly a million dollars — and the rate is probably even higher these days.

Using software to monitor performance

A number of programs are available for between $30 and $200 that continually keep an eye on your Web site and notify you of any problems. Such programs take some effort to install. But the effort required to get them up and running has a big benefit — you know about setbacks at least as soon as your customers do, if not before.

WebCheck is a utility that monitors the performance of your Web site. It automatically checks your site and alerts you if your site goes down or if a page has been accidentally renamed or deleted. You configure WebCheck to check your site's URLs; you can have the program load the URLs once a minute, or even once every second (faster checking may slow down your site's performance, however). You can be notified by e-mail, fax, popup browser window, or taskbar icon. You can download WebCheck from the IT Utils Web site (www. itutils.com). Another application, SiteScope, by Mercury Interactive Corp (www.mercury.com/us/products/application-management/foundation/ monitors/sitescope), runs on Microsoft Windows 2003 or 2000 Server or Windows NT 4.0, and checks sites every five to ten minutes.

You don't have to install your own software in order to monitor your Web site's performance, of course. You can sign up with a company that offers such monitoring as a service. In this case, you use the company's software, which resides on its computers, not yours. For example, @Watch (www.atwatch.com) provides an online service that checks your site's images and links periodically to see if everything is working correctly. The company offers several levels of service. The @Watch Lite version costs $17.95 per month and checks your site once every 60 minutes. Other versions can check your site as frequently as every five minutes.

Dealing with service outages

Ideally, your Web host will provide a page on its Web site that keeps track of its network status and records any recent problems. *One* site monitoring notification (from a program you install yourself or one that you "rent" as a service from an ASP — see the next section "Outsourcing Your Business Needs") probably shouldn't be cause for concern. However, when you receive a *series* of notifications, call your Web hosting service and talk to its technical staff. Be courteous, but be specific. Tell technical support exactly what the problems are/were. You may even want to print out the reports you receive so that you can be aware of the exact nature of the problems. If you find that such outages are occurring on a regular basis, exercise patience but be firm in dealing with technical problems that have an impact on your business.

If the problem with your site is a slow response to requests from Web browsers rather than a complete outage, the problem may be that your server is slow because you're sharing it with other Web sites. Consider moving from shared hosting to a different option. In *co-location,* you purchase the server on which your files reside, but the machine is located at your Web host's facility rather than at your own location. Your site is the only one on your machine. You also get the reliability of the host's technical support and high-speed Internet connection.

If you really need bandwidth, consider a *dedicated server.* In this case, you rent space on a machine that is dedicated to serving your site. This arrangement is far more expensive than sharing a Web server, and you should choose it only if the number of visits to your site at any one time becomes too great for a shared server to handle. You'll know a shared server is becoming overtaxed if your site is slow to load. Discuss the situation with your host to see whether a move to a dedicated server makes sense.

Outsourcing Your Business Needs

One of the most effective ways to save time and money doing business online is to let someone else install and maintain the computer software that you use. *Outsourcing* is an increasingly common term, but in terms of e-commerce, it refers to the practice of using an online service to perform various tasks for you, such as Web hosting, form creation, or financial record keeping, rather than installing software and running it on your own computer. Outsourcing isn't anything mysterious, however: It simply refers to the practice of having an outside company provide services for your business.

Videoconferencing: Being in two places at once

One of the best and most useful types of ASP-based services you can use is videoconferencing, which can allow you to hold live meetings with your customers or business partners by using a Web-based conferencing service. It works like this: Participants need a computer that's equipped with a microphone and a camera that takes live video of them while they're sitting in front of their computers. They connect to a central location on the Web — the conferencing service — by using their Web browsers. After they're connected to the same location on the server, they can communicate in real time.

CMstat Corporation, a configuration and data management software with offices in California, Oregon, and Virginia, provides enterprise information management software to businesses around the world. Demos are essential for clients to decide if they want to make a purchase. In the past, CMstat would send a team of employees to visit each prospective customer one or more times. "We were making approximately eight trips per month for a total cost of $12,000," says Tom Tesmer, president of CMstat. "The challenge was how to increase sales, shorten the sales cycle, and reduce

expenses. Additionally, we were looking for a way to engage our customer support. CMStat estimates that it reduced travel expenses for sales and support by $26,000 the first year and, through the use of the videoconferencing service WebEx (www.webex.com) in its customer support department, reduced support calls by 50 percent after that.

What's that you say? You think that videoconferencing is too difficult to set up and expensive to use? WebEx, one of the leaders in the field of Web-based conferencing, now offers a pay-as-you-go plan. You can use the company's services for a whopping 20 cents per user per minute. It's a great way to try out the service to see how it works for you. For more about using WebEX, check out *WebEx Web Meetings For Dummies* by Nancy Stevenson (Wiley).

Keep in mind, though, that the quality of any real-time activity on the Web depends on the speed of the participants' respective Internet connections. Because of time lags, videoconferencing is really ideal for users with direct connections, such as T1 or T3 lines, cable modems, or DSL connections.

One of the companies that provides Web-based services on an outsourced basis is called an *Application Service Provider* (ASP). An ASP is a company that makes business or other applications available on the Web. You and your co-workers can then use those applications with your Web browser instead of having to purchase and install special software. For instance, when you fill out a form and create a Web page on CafePress.com (which I describe in Chapter 3), you're using CafePress.com as an ASP. Rather than create your Web page on your own computer by using a program, such as Microsoft FrontPage, you use an application on the CafePress.com site, and store your Web page information there.

How ASPs can help your company

You have to pay a monthly fee to use an ASP's services. You may incur installation fees, and you may have to sign a one- or two-year contract. In return, ASPs provide a number of benefits to your company. Here are the kinds of business processes they can help you perform:

- **Payroll and administration:** AquaPrix, Inc. (www.aquaprix.com), a small Hayward, California, water systems distribution company, outsources some of its payroll functions to a company called QuikPay. AquaPrix, which doesn't have a large administrative staff, sends payroll data to QuikPay, which calculates salary and issues checks to all employees for about $100 per month.

- **Tech support:** ComponentControl (www.componentcontrol.com), a 55-person company with offices in San Diego and New York, licenses software that enables aerospace companies to locate and trade aviation parts. Instead of having to travel all over the country to solve every problem that users encounter with its software, ComponentControl's tech support staff use an online application called DesktopStreaming that enables them to "see" the problem a customer is encountering. ComponentControl can also show customers how to use the software from its own offices, which saves on travel costs and has reduced the time to solve problems by 30 percent.

- **Online form creation:** FormSite.com (www.formsite.com) is a leader in creating a variety of forms that can help online shoppers provide such essential functions as subscribing to newsletters or other publications, asking for information about your goods and services, or providing you with shipping or billing information. The sample pizza order form shown in Figure 11-3 is an example of the type of form that this particular ASP can help you create.

✔ **Marketing and survey data gathering online:** LeadMaster (www.lead master.com) calls itself a "Web-based data mining tool." You store your customer information with LeadMaster, and LeadMaster provides you with an online database that you can access any time with your Web browser. It enables you to develop mailing lists based on your customer database. You can use LeadMaster's online tools to do sales forecasting and develop surveys that give you a better idea of what your customers need and want.

Another example of a small business that benefited from the services of ASPs can be found on e-CommerceGuide.com (www.ecommerce-guide.com/news/news/article.php/3385641). A Las Vegas-based computer seller called DiscountLaptops.com chose an ASP called CORESense to handle the processing of sales. CORESense does everything from ordering, billing, invoicing, tech support, to updating databases. With only eight employees, DiscountLaptops.com was able to triple its sales volume and boost revenues from 1.8 million in 2000 to $4.5 million in 2003.

Figure 11-3:
An ASP like FormSite. com lets you create a database-backed Web page feature such as a feedback form without having to purchase, install, and master a database program.

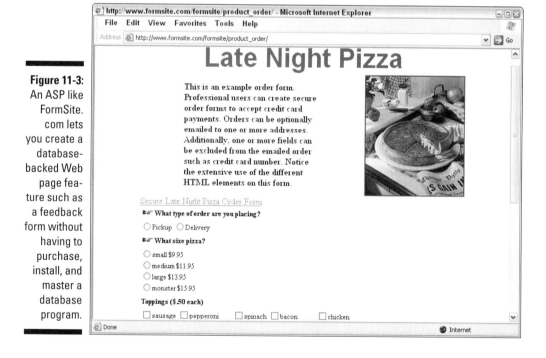

Although ASPs can help you in many ways, they require research, interviewing, contract review, and an ongoing commitment on your part. When does the extra effort make sense? I illustrate the potential pluses and minuses of outsourcing in Table 11-1.

Table 11-1	Outsourcing Benefits and Risks
Pros	*Cons*
Timesaving: Saving time can save you money in the long run.	**ASPs are relatively new:** Many are start-ups, and they may have just as little business experience as you do. Take extra care before you sign a contract for service.
Better customer service: By outsourcing scheduling or other functions, businesses give customers increased options for interacting with them online. Customers don't have to call or e-mail the company; in the case of online scheduling, customers can schedule or cancel appointments by accessing the company's online calendar.	**A contract is required:** When ASPs first began to appear in the late '90s, they spoke in terms of "renting" software. These days, ASPs usually allow customers to try out their services for a while, but then offer long-term contracts. The terms of these contracts can range from one to three years. Don't get yourself locked in to a long-term arrangement that will prevent you from trying out cheaper or better alternatives down the road.
Greater Web site functionality: ASPs enable your site to provide better service to your customers and allow you to get more work done.	**ASPs face stiff competition:** Many ASPs have failed in recent years. Make sure the companies that you sign agreements with will be around for a while by talking to current customers and reviewing resumes of senior staff and key employees. Scan the Web for any press releases or articles that serve as warning signs about the ASP's financial health.
Expanded scope: You don't have to become proficient in subjects that aren't part of your core business or expertise.	**Security risks:** The moment you hand over your business data to another online firm or give outside companies access to your internal network, you risk theft of data or virus infections from hackers. Make sure that the ASPs you work with use encryption and other Internet security measures. (See Chapter 7 for more on Web site security.)

In many cases, ASPs can provide a software solution and customize it to your needs. Outsourcing not only improves your company's bottom line, but also helps you convey your message to potential customers that you might never reach otherwise.

ASPNews.com (www.aspnews.com) provides an overview of the current state of the ASP industry. The ASPNews.com staff publishes regular articles about ASPs and industry trends. The site also includes a directory of ASPs (links manager.com/aspnews). To check out a very good ASPNews.com article on what to look for in an ASP, go to the following URL:

```
www.aspnews.com/analysis/analyst_cols/article/
0,,4431_425751,00.html
```

Before you sign on the dotted line . . .

After you try out the software or other service that you want to lease (and any reputable ASP should let you try it out first), you usually need to sign a contract to keep using the service. This is the time to slow down and read the fine print.

"It's a huge commitment for people to go into an ASP arrangement," says Dana Danley, an analyst with Current Analysis of Reston, Virginia. "The lengths of contracts can range from 12 to 50 months. Sometimes you can choose the length of a contract, but most often you're offered one contract. It's important not to get one that's too long. You don't even know for sure if the ASP will be around in three years, for instance."

Don't be in a hurry, even if you're experiencing the time-to-productivity pressures, merger upheavals, or lack of IT resources that drive many companies to outsource. In the following list, I present some suggestions to help you get the service you think you're getting:

- ✔ **Understand pricing schemes:** The pricing schemes that ASPs use to charge for their Web-based services are downright confusing. For instance, some ASPs charge on a "per-employee" basis, which means you pay according to the number of individuals in your company. But others charge "per-seat" fees based on each registered user, not every employee. Still others charge "per-CPU," which means you're charged for each machine that runs the hosted application. Make sure you understand what your prospective ASP plans to charge by asking questions and getting detailed information.

✔ **Pin down start-up fees:** Virtually all ASPs charge a start-up fee, also called a service implementation fee, when you sign the contract. Make sure the fee covers installation and any customization that you'll need.

✔ **Don't accept just any SLA:** Obtaining a *service level agreement* (SLA), a document that spells out what services you expect an ASP (or other vendor) to provide, is essential. But regard the SLA as a dynamic document. Don't stand for the boilerplate. Think of SLA as standing for Stop, Look, and Adjust.

Paula M. Hunter, vice-president of sales and marketing for cMeRun Corp (an ASP) and the president of the ASP Industry Consortium, says, "The SLA and/or hosting contract should outline additional monthly fees for data backup and recovery (often these items are included). It's also important to review the contract regarding help desk support and any fees which would be associated with placing support calls to the ASP."

✔ **Avoid "gotcha" fees:** Pricing arrangements are hardly standard with regard to ASPs. Some of the big hidden costs involve personalizing or customizing the service to adapt to legacy systems. Here are some questions you can ask in order to avoid wincing at gotchas when you open up the bill from your ASP:

   • Is there an additional cost for customizing or personalizing the application?

   • Does it cost extra to back up my company's data and recover it if one of my computers goes down?

   • Is help desk support included in my monthly fee, or will you charge me every time I call with a question or problem?

✔ **Make sure you have security:** Having information reside on someone else's system is a double-edged sword. Putting this data on the Web makes it accessible from anywhere. But some huge security risks are associated with transmitting your information across the wide-open spaces of the Net. Make sure that your ASP takes adequate security measures to protect your data by asking informed questions, such as

   • Is my data protected by SSL encryption?

   • Do you run a virtual private network?

   • How often do you back up your customers' data?

If the answer to any of these questions seems inadequate, move on to the next ASP — plenty are out there, and competition among ASPs is fierce. So right now at least, it's a buyer's market, and you should be able to get what you want.

Chapter 12

Accepting Payments

. . . .

In This Chapter

▶ Anticipating your online customers' purchasing needs

▶ Applying for credit card merchant status

▶ Finding shortcuts to processing credit card data

▶ Providing shoppers with electronic purchasing systems

▶ Delivering your products and services

. . . .

Starting up a new business and getting it online is exciting, but believe me, the real excitement occurs when you get paid for what you do. Nothing boosts your confidence and tells you that your hard work is paying off like receiving the proverbial check in the mail or having funds transferred to your business account.

The immediacy and interactivity of selling and promoting yourself online applies to receiving payments, too. You can get paid with just a few mouse clicks and some important data entered on your customer's keyboard. But completing an electronic commerce (*e-commerce* for short) transaction isn't the same as getting paid in a traditional retail store. The customer can't personally hand you cash or a check. Or, if a credit card is involved, you can't verify the user's identity through a signature or photo ID.

In order to get paid promptly and reliably online, you have to go through some extra steps to make the customer feel secure — not to mention protecting yourself, too. Successful e-commerce is about setting up the right atmosphere for making purchases, providing options for payment, and keeping sensitive information private. It's also about making sure that the goods get to the customer safely and on time. In this chapter, I describe ways in which you can implement these essential online business strategies.

Sealing the Deal: The Options

As anyone who sells online knows, the point at which payment is transferred is one of the most eagerly awaited stages of the transaction. It's also one of the stages that's apt to produce the most anxiety. Customers and merchants who are used to dealing with one another face to face and who are accustomed to personally handing over identification and credit cards suddenly feel lost. On the Web, they can't see the person they're dealing with.

For customers, paying for something purchased over the Internet is still fraught with uncertainty, even though security is improving. For merchants like you, it can still be nerve wracking; you want to make sure checks don't bounce and purchases aren't being made with stolen credit cards.

Your goal, in giving your customers the ability to provide payments online, should be to accomplish the following:

- **Give the customer options.** Online shoppers like to feel that they have some degree of control. Give them a choice of payment alternatives: phone, fax, check, and credit cards are the main ones.

- **Keep it secure.** Pay an extra fee to your Web host in order to have your customers submit their credit card numbers or other personal information to a secure server — a server that uses Secure Sockets Layer (SSL) encryption to render it unreadable if stolen.

- **Make it convenient.** Shoppers on the Web are in a hurry. Give them the Web page forms and the phone numbers they need so that they can complete a purchase in a matter of seconds.

Though the goals are the same, the options are different if you sell on eBay or on a Web site other than eBay's. If you sell on eBay, either through an auction or an eBay Store, you can take advantage of eBay's fraud protection measures: a feedback system that rewards honesty and penalizes dishonesty; fraud insurance; an investigations staff; and the threat of suspension. These safeguards mean that it's feasible to accept cash and personal checks or money orders from buyers. If you don't receive the cash, you don't ship. If you receive checks, you can wait until they clear before you ship.

On the Web, you don't have a feedback system or an investigations squad to ferret out dishonest buyers. You can accept checks or money orders, but credit cards are the safest and quickest option, and accordingly, they're what buyers expect. It's up to you to verify the buyer's identity as best you can in order to minimize fraud.

Enabling Credit Card Purchases

Having the ability to accept and process credit card transactions makes it especially easy for your customers to follow the impulse to buy something from you. You stand to generate a lot more sales than you would otherwise.

But although credit cards are easy for shoppers to use, they make *your* life as an online merchant more complicated. I don't want to discourage you from becoming credit card ready by any means, but you need to be aware of the steps (and the expenses) involved, many of which may not occur to you when you're just starting out. For example, you may not be aware of one or more of the following:

- ✔ **Merchant accounts:** You have to apply and be approved for a special bank account called a *merchant account* in order for a bank to process the credit card orders that you receive. If you work through traditional banks, approval can take days or weeks. However, a number of online merchant account businesses are providing hot competition, which includes streamlining the application process.

- ✔ **Fees:** Fees can be high but they vary widely, and it pays to shop around. Some banks charge a merchant application fee ($300 to $800). On the other hand, some online companies such as 1st American Card Service (`www.1stamericancardservice.com`) or Merchants' Choice Card Services (`www.vmc123.net`) charge no application fee.

- ✔ **Discount rates:** All banks and merchant account companies (and even payment companies like PayPal) charge a usage fee, deceptively called a *discount rate*. Typically, this fee ranges from 1 to 4 percent of each transaction. Plus, you may have to pay a monthly premium charge in the range of $30–70 to the bank. Although 1st American Card Service saves you money with a free application, it charges Internet businesses a 2.29 percent fee that it calls a discount rate, plus 25 cents for each transaction, a $9 monthly statement fee, and a minimum charge of $20 per month.

- ✔ **American Express and Discover:** If you want to accept payments from American Express and Discover cardholders, you must make arrangements through the companies themselves. You can apply online to be an American Express card merchant by going to the American Express Merchant Homepage (`www.americanexpress.com/homepage/merchant.shtml`) and clicking the Apply to Accept the Card link. At the Discover Card merchant site (`www.discoverbiz.com`), click the Become a Merchant link, which leads you to the application for credit card merchants.

✔ **Software and hardware:** Unless you depend on a payment service such as PayPal, you need software or hardware to process transactions and transmit the data to the banking system. If you plan to accept credit card numbers online only and don't need a device to handle actual "card swipes" from in-person customers, you can use your computer modem to transmit the data. 1st American Card Service lets you use software called PCCharge Express for processing transactions with your browser, but you have to either purchase the software for $295 or lease it for rates that vary from $22 to $34 per year. The hardware involved is a terminal or phone line, which you can either purchase for $229 or lease for anywhere from $17 to $26 per month, depending on the length of the lease.

You also need to watch out for credit card fraud, in which criminals use stolen numbers to make purchases. You, the merchant, end up being liable for most of the fictitious transactions. Cardholders are responsible for only $50 of fraudulent purchases. To combat this crime, before completing any transaction, verify that the shipping address supplied by the purchaser is the same (or at least in the same vicinity) as the billing address. If you're in doubt, you can phone the purchaser for verification — it's a courtesy to the customer as well as a means of protection for you. (See the later section, "Verifying credit card data.") You can do this check yourself or pay a service to do the checking.

Setting up a merchant account

The good news is that getting merchant status is becoming easier, as more banks accept the notion that businesses don't have to have an actual, physical storefront in order to be successful. Getting a merchant account approved, however, still takes a long time, and some hefty fees are involved as well. Banks look more favorably on companies that have been in business for several years and have a proven track record.

Traditional banks are reliable and experienced, and you can count on them being around for a while. The new Web-based companies that specialize in giving online businesses merchant account status welcome new businesses and give you wider options and cost savings, but they're new; their services may not be as reliable and their future is less certain.

You can find a long list of institutions that provide merchant accounts for online businesses at one of the Yahoo! index pages:

```
dir.yahoo.com/Business_and_Economy/Business_to_Business/
Financial_Services/Transaction_Clearing/Credit_Card_
Merchant_Services
```

The list is so long that knowing which company to choose is difficult. I recommend visiting Wells Fargo Bank (www.wellsfargo.com), which has been operating online for several years and is well established. The Wells Fargo Web site provides you with a good overview of what's required to obtain a merchant account.

MyTexasMusic.com, the family-run business I profile in Chapter 1, uses a Web-based merchant account company called goemerchant.com (www.goemerchant.com) to set up and process its credit card transactions. This company offers a shopping cart and credit card and debit card processing to businesses that accept payments online. MyTexasMusic.com chose to use goemerchant after an extensive search because it found that the company would help provide reliable processing, while protecting the business from customers who purchased items fraudulently.

One advantage of using one of the payment options set up by VeriSign Payment Services (www.verisign.com/products/payment.html) is that the system (which originated with a company called CyberCash) was well known and well regarded before VeriSign acquired it. I describe the widely used electronic payment company in the section, "Online Payment Systems," later in this chapter.

In general, your chances of obtaining merchant status are enhanced if you apply to a bank that welcomes Internet businesses, and if you can provide good business records proving that you're a viable, moneymaking concern.

Be sure to ask about the discount rate that the bank charges for Internet-based transactions before you apply. Compare the rate for online transactions to the rate for conventional "card-swipe" purchases. Most banks and credit card processing companies charge 1 to 2 extra percentage points for online sales.

Do you use an accounting program such as QuickBooks or MYOB Accounting? The manufacturers of these programs enable their users to become credit card merchants through their Web sites. See the "Accounting Software" section of this book's online Internet Directory for more information.

Finding a secure server

A *secure server* is a server that uses some form of encryption, such as Secure Sockets Layer, which I describe in Chapter 7, to protect data that you receive over the Internet. Customers know that they've entered a secure area when the security key or lock icon at the bottom of the browser window is locked shut.

Keeping back-office functions personal

Mark Lauer knows the importance of credit card verification and order processing. Yet he tries to make these functions as personal as possible in keeping with the spirit of online business.

Mark is president of General Tool & Repair, Inc., a power tool supplier based in York, Pennsylvania. General Tool has been in business for ten years, but seven years ago, General Tool & Repair created a simple Web page on America Online to help promote the company. Within two weeks, an order was received from a customer in Florida.

Since then, Mark has expanded his e-commerce Web site with Microsoft Commerce Server, and he set up shop at www.gtr.com.

Mark estimates that General Tool's Web site receives between 10 and 40 orders each day, and average online sales amount to $35,000 to $45,000 per month. He believes the site takes the place of 50 salespeople. "This is all business we never had until two years ago, so it's basically all extra sales for us," he notes happily.

Q. How do you process credit card orders?

A. Our customers send us the credit card information through our Web site, and our secure server encrypts the data. But we don't process orders online. We first check to see if we have the item in stock, and, if we do, we process the order the next business day. That way, we don't "slam" the customer's credit card without having the item ready to ship out.

Q. How do you verify the identity of customers who submit credit card numbers to you?

A. We use a program called Authorizer by Atomic Software. The program lets you check the shipping address against the address of the credit card owner. If the two addresses are in the same state, you're pretty sure that you can ship the item. Otherwise, you know that you'd better e-mail the card owner and tell the person there's a problem. Sometimes, a customer will want to purchase a gift and have it shipped out of state to a family member, and in this case you should also e-mail the customer just to be sure. We have since upgraded to the multi-merchant version of Authorizer, which lets us accept several different types of credit cards.

Q. Do you get many fraudulent credit card orders?

A. We don't get too many bogus orders. Normally, you can tell because they don't have the correct "ship to" address. If we suspect something, we e-mail or call the customer to confirm. Additionally, Authorizer will detect fraudulent credit card orders. Customers don't mind you being extra careful when dealing with their credit card protection, by confirming that it is a legit order. This extra step has gained us many repeat customers.

Q. Whom do you use for shipping?

A. We get orders from countries like Japan and Finland, and all over the United States, too. If the customer is affiliated with the military, you're required to use the U.S. Postal Service for shipping. If we're shipping to a business address, such as an office in New York City, we use United Parcel Service because they give the option of sending a package "signature required" which, as it implies, requires someone to sign for an item before they deliver it. We add the UPS charge for "signature required" to the shipping charge, but we feel that it's worth it because we don't want any items to get lost because they were left without a signature. There have been many instances where a customer's neighbor, employee, or landlord have signed for their package without the customer's knowledge, so it really provides protection for all involved.

Q. How do you tell your customers about shipping options?

A. We offer customers three choices during the purchase process: UPS ground, second-day air, and next-day air. We also provide a comment area where shoppers can make shipping requests or provide us with special instructions regarding their orders. That way, they can choose. We don't add on flat-rate shipping or handling charges that might be excessive. There are only five of us here, and I can't justify charging someone $25 shipping and handling for a $3 part for a power tool. Our products vary a great deal in price and weight, and we haven't found a way to provide a flat rate for shipping that is fair to everyone, so each order is treated individually. This flexibility in shipping has proven to be a service that sets us apart from the "Big Box" online power tool providers, and customers shop our Web site because of it.

If you plan to receive credit card payments, you definitely want to find a Web hosting service that will protect the area of your online business that serves as the online store. In literal terms, you need secure server software protecting the directory on your site that is to receive customer-sent forms. Some hosts charge a higher monthly fee for using a secure server; with others, the secure server is part of a basic business Web site account. Ask your host (or hosts you're considering) whether any extra charges apply.

Verifying credit card data

Unfortunately, the world is full of bad people who try to use credit card numbers that don't belong to them. The anonymity of the Web and the ability to shop anywhere in the world, combined with the ability to place orders immediately, can facilitate fraudulent orders, just as it can benefit legitimate orders.

Protecting yourself against credit card fraud is essential. Always check the billing address against the shipping address. If the two addresses are thousands of miles apart, contact the purchaser by phone to verify that the transaction is legit. Even if it is, the purchaser will appreciate your taking the time to verify the transaction.

You can use software to help check addresses. Here are three programs that perform this service:

✔ ClearCommerce (www.clearcommerce.com) sells both an automated payment system and payment authentication software that work with credit cards and banks.

✔ PCCharge by GO Software Inc. (`www.gosoftinc.com/products/`
`index.htm`).

✔ IC*VERIFY*, which you can purchase from IC*VERIFY* at `www.icverify.com`
(call 1-800-666-5777 for current pricing on IC*VERIFY*).

Processing the orders

When someone submits credit card information to you, you need to transfer
the information to the banking system. Whether you make this transfer yourself or hire another company to do it for you is up to you.

Do-it-yourself processing

To submit credit card information to your bank, you need POS (point of sale)
hardware or software. The hardware, which you either purchase or lease
from your bank, is a *terminal* — a gray box of the sort you see at many local
retailers. The software is a program that contacts the bank through a modem.

The terminal or software is programmed to authorize the sale and transmit the
data to the bank. The bank then credits your business or personal checking
account, usually within two or three business days. The bank also deducts the
discount rate from your account weekly, monthly, or with each transaction.

One payment processing program, PCCharge Express, can be obtained from
the GO Software Web site (`www.gosoftware.com`). You can install it on your
computer or use the online version. PCCharge for Windows 98 or later is
available for $295 or $34 per month for 12 months.

If you have a small-scale Web site — perhaps with only one item for sale — you
can use an online payment gateway, which enables you to add a "Pay Button"
to a catalog page that securely processes a customer's payment information.
When you receive the information, you can manually submit it for payment by
using a program such as LinkPoint Central. The transaction is then processed
on one of LinkPoint's secure servers. Both you and your customer receive
e-mail notifications that the transaction has been completed. You can find out
more on the Cardservice International Web site at `www.aboutcsi.com/`
`secure-transaction-processing.html`.

Automatic processing

You can hire a company to automatically process credit card orders for you.
These companies compare the shipping and billing addresses to help make
sure that the purchaser is the person who actually owns the card and not
someone trying to use a stolen credit card number. If everything checks out,
they transmit the data directly to the bank.

You can look into the different options provided by VeriFone, Inc. (www.verifone.com) or AssureBuy (www.otginc.com) for such services.

Automatic credit card processing works so fast that your customer's credit card can be charged immediately, whether or not you have an item in stock. If a client receives a bill and is still waiting for an item that is on back order, the person can get very unhappy. For this reason, some business owners, such as Mark Lauer (profiled in the sidebar, "Keeping back-office functions personal"), chose not to use them.

Online Payment Systems

A number of organizations have devised ways to make e-commerce secure and convenient for shoppers and merchants alike. These alternatives fall into one of three general categories:

- ✔ Organizations that help you complete credit card purchases (for example, VeriSign Payment Services).

- ✔ Escrow services that hold your money for you in an account until shipment is received and then pay you, providing security for both you and your customers.

- ✔ Organizations that provide alternatives to transmitting sensitive information from one computer to another. A number of attempts to create "virtual money" have failed. However, companies like Electracash (www.electracash.com) let customers make payments by directly debiting their checking accounts.

In order to use one of these systems, you or your Web host has to set up special software on the computer that actually stores your Web site files. This computer is where the transactions take place. The following sections provide general instructions on how to get started with setting up each of the most popular electronic payment systems.

To work smoothly, some electronic payment systems require you to set up programming languages such as Perl, C/C++, or Visual Basic on your site. You also have to work with techy documents called *configuration files.* This is definitely an area where paying a consultant to get your business set up saves time and headaches and gets your new transaction feature online more efficiently than if you tackle it yourself. VeriSign, for instance, provides support in setting up systems for its merchants; you can find an affiliate to help you or call the company directly. Visit the VeriSign Payment Processing page (www.verisign.com/products/payment.html) for links and phone numbers.

Shopping cart software

When you go to the supermarket or another retail outlet, you pick goodies off the shelves and put them in a shopping cart. When you go to the cash register to pay for what you've selected, you empty the cart and present your goods to the cashier.

Shopping cart software performs the same functions on an e-commerce site. Such software sets up a system that allows online shoppers to select items displayed for sale. The selections are held in a virtual shopping cart that "remembers" what the shopper has selected before checking out.

Shopping cart programs are pretty technical for nonprogrammers to set up, but if you're ambitious and want to try it, you can download and install a free program called PerlShop (`www.perlshop.org`). Signing up with a Web host that provides you with shopping cart software as part of its services, however, is far easier than tackling this task yourself.

A shopping cart is often described as an essential part of many e-commerce Web sites, and Web hosts usually boast about including a cart along with their other businesses services. But the fact is that you don't *have* to use a shopping cart on your site. Many shoppers are put off by them; they're just as likely to abandon a purchase than follow through by submitting payment. Plenty of other e-businesses have users phone or fax in an order or fill out an online form instead.

VeriSign payment services

The security company VeriSign, which is best known for selling certificates that consumers can use to shop online, offers small businesses a variety of online payment solutions.

VeriSign's Payment Services page (`www.verisign.com/products/payment.html`) includes services such as Payflow, which lets your company accept payments online, and Commerce Site Services, which places your site on a server that uses SSL encryption as well as certificates. (See Chapter 7 for more detailed explanations of these security features.)

There's no cost to try out one of the Payflow options for 30 days to see how it works with your own business, but both options require that you have a merchant account. (If you don't have one, VeriSign suggests several financial institutions to which you can apply.) The Payflow services do carry some charges and require you to do some work, however:

✔ **Payflow Link:** The smallest and simplest of the VeriSign payment options, Payflow Link is intended for small businesses that process 500 transactions or fewer each month. You add a payment link to your online business site, and you don't have to do programming or other site development to get the payment system to work. Payflow Link requires that you use either Internet Explorer 3.0 (or later) or Netscape Navigator 4.0 (or later). You pay a $179 setup fee and a $19.95 monthly fee.

✔ **Payflow Pro:** With this service, you can process up to 1,000 transactions per month, and any additional transactions cost 10 cents each. To use this option, you begin by installing the Payflow software on the server that runs your Web site. The customer then makes a purchase on your site, and the Payflow software sends the information to VeriSign, which processes the transaction. Payflow Pro carries a $249 setup fee and costs $59.95 per month.

You can sign up for a trial of either Payflow Link or Payflow Pro on the VeriSign Payment Services page (`www.verisign.com/products/payment.html`).

PayPal

PayPal was one of the first online businesses to hit on the clever idea of giving business owners a way to accept credit and debit card payments from customers without having to apply for a merchant account, download software, apply for online payment processing, or some combination of these steps.

PayPal is essentially an *escrow service:* it functions as a sort of financial middleman, debiting buyers' accounts and crediting the accounts of sellers — and, along the way, exacting a fee for its services, which it charges to the merchant receiving the payment. The accounts involved can be credit card accounts, checking accounts, or accounts held at PayPal into which members directly deposit funds. In other words, the person making the payment sets up an account with PayPal by identifying which account (credit card or checking, for example) a payment is to be taken from. The merchant also has a PayPal account, and has identified which checking or credit card account is to receive payments. PayPal handles the virtual "card swipe" and verification of customer information; the customer can pay with a credit card without the merchant having to set up a merchant account.

PayPal is best known as a way to pay for items purchased on eBay. eBay, in fact, owns PayPal. But the service is regularly used to process payments both on and off the auction site. If you want to sell items (including through your Web site), you sign up for a PayPal Business or Premier account. You get a PayPal button that you add to your auction listing or sales Web page. The customer clicks the button to transfer the payment from his or her PayPal account to yours and you're charged a transaction fee.

Setting up a PayPal account is free. Here's how you can set up a PayPal Business account:

1. **Go to the PayPal home page (`www.paypal.com`), and click the Sign Up Now button.**

   You go to the PayPal Account Sign Up page.

2. **Click the button next to Business Account, choose your country of residence, and click Continue.**

   The Business Account Sign Up page appears.

3. **Follow the instructions on the registration form page, and set up your account with PayPal.**

   After you've filled out the registration forms, you receive an e-mail message with a link that takes you back to the PayPal Web site to confirm your e-mail address.

4. **Click the link contained in the e-mail message.**

   You go to the PayPal — Password page.

5. **Enter your password (the one you created during the registration process) in the Password box, and then click the Confirm button.**

   You go to the PayPal — My Account page.

6. **Click the Merchant Tools tab at the top of the My Account page.**

   If you want to create a shopping cart, click the Shopping Cart link. For the purposes of this exercise, click Buy Now Buttons.

7. **Provide some information about the item you're selling:**

   • Enter a brief description of your sales item in the Item Name/ Service box.

   • Enter an item number in the Item ID/Number Box.

   • Enter the price in the Price of Item/Service box.

   • Choose a button that shoppers can click to make the purchase. (You can choose either the PayPal logo button or a button that you've already created.)

8. **When you're done, click the Create Button Now button.**

   You go to the PayPal — Web Accept page shown in Figure 12-1.

9. **Copy the code in the For Web Pages box and paste it onto the Web page that holds your sales item.**

   That's all there is to it.

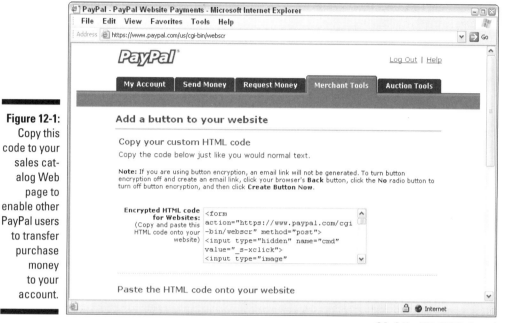

Figure 12-1:
Copy this code to your sales catalog Web page to enable other PayPal users to transfer purchase money to your account.

The nice thing about using PayPal is that the system enables you to accept payments through your Web site without having to obtain a merchant account. It does put a burden on your customers to become PayPal users, but chances are those who buy or sell on eBay already have one. The thing to remember is that both you and your customers place a high level of trust in PayPal to handle your money. If there is a problem with fraud, PayPal will investigate it — hopefully. Some former PayPal users detest PayPal due to what they describe as a lack of responsiveness, and they describe their unhappiness in great detail on sites like www.paypalsucks.com. You should be aware of such complaints in order to have the full picture about PayPal and anticipate problems before they arise.

Micropayments

Micropayments are very small units of currency that are exchanged by merchants and customers. The amounts involved may range from one-tenth of one cent (that's $.001) to a few dollars. Such small payments enable sites to provide content for sale on a per-click basis. In order to read articles, listen to music files, or view video clips online, some sites require micropayments in a special form of electronic cash that goes by names such as *scrip* or *eCash*.

Reach for your wallet!

One of the terms commonly thrown around in the jargon of e-commerce is *wallet*. A wallet is software that, like a real wallet that you keep in your purse or pocket, stores available cash and other records. You reach into the cyberwallet and withdraw virtual cash instead of submitting a credit card number.

Wallets looked promising a few years ago, but they have never really taken off. The idea is that a cybershopper who uses wallet software, such as Microsoft .NET Passport (www.passport.com), is able to pay for items online in a matter of seconds, without having to transfer credit card data. What's more, some wallets can even "remember" previous purchases you have made and suggest further purchases.

The problem with wallets is that shoppers just aren't comfortable with them. Credit cards are quick and convenient, and they've proven to be secure enough for most consumers. Consumers who are committed to using Microsoft's services can use .NET Passport, which offers a "single sign-in" to register or make purchases on sites that support this technology. It also enables consumers to create a wallet that stores their billing and shipping information. (Credit card numbers are stored in an offline database when users sign up for a .NET Passport.) Customers can then make purchases at participating sites with the proverbial single mouse click. In order for your online business Web site to support .NET Passport, you need to download and install the .NET Passport Software Development Kit (SDK) on the server that runs your Web site. You may need some help in deploying this platform; a list of consultants as well as a link to the SDK is included on the .NET Passport home page (www.passport.net/Consumer/Default.asp).

Micropayments seemed like a good idea in theory, but they've never caught on with most consumers. On the other hand, they've never totally disappeared, either. The business that proved conclusively that consumers are willing to pay small amounts of money to purchase creative content online is none other than the computer manufacturer Apple, which revolutionized e-commerce with its iPod music player and its iTunes music marketplace. Every day, users pay $.99 to download a song and add it to their iPod selections. But they make such payments with their credit cards, using real dollars and cents.

In other words, iTunes payments aren't true micropayments. The micropayment system is supposed to work like this:

1. As a vendor, you authorize a broker such as BitPass (www.bitpass.com) to sell content to your customers by using its payment system.

   Typically, BitPass content is creative: cartoons, audiobooks, craft projects, and music. If a customer goes to your site and wants to purchase articles or other content, the customer has to follow a few steps.

2. The customer first purchases a prepaid card that contains a certain amount of virtual money (say, $10) at face value from the broker. (The purchase is made through PayPal, interestingly.)

3. The broker then pays you, the merchant, the $10 purchase of virtual money that the customer made, minus a service fee.

4. The customer is then free to make purchases from your site by clicking items that have been assigned a certain value (say, one or two cents).

5. The micropayment service's software causes the few cents to be automatically subtracted from the user's supply of scrip. No credit card numbers are exchanged in these micropayment transactions.

Other payment options

A number of new online payment options have appeared that let people pay for merchandise without having to submit credit card numbers or mail checks. Here are some relatively new options to consider:

- ✔ **iBill** (www.ibill.com): A service of Internet Billing Corp., iBill provides Web sites with a number of ways to accept online payments, including an innovative system called Web900 (part of its iBillComplete service, www.ibill.com/Services/iBillComplete) that enables customers to have a transaction billed to their phone bills rather than their credit cards.

- ✔ **ClearTran** (www.cleartran.com): This service enables shoppers to make purchases by sending online checks to merchants. The shopper notifies the seller about the purchase and then contacts a special secure Web site to authorize a debit from his or her checking account. The secure site then transmits the electronic check to the merchant, who can either print out the check on paper or save the check in a special format that can be transmitted to banks for immediate deposit.

Which one of these options is right for you? That depends on what you want to sell online. If you're providing articles, reports, music, or other content that you want people to pay a nominal fee to access, consider a micropayment system (see the preceding section). If your customers tend to be sophisticated, technically savvy individuals who are likely to embrace online checks or billing systems, consider iBill or ClearTran. The important things are to provide customers with several options for submitting payment and to make the process as easy as possible for them.

Fulfilling Your Online Orders

Being on the Internet can help when it comes to the final step in the e-commerce dance: order fulfillment. *Fulfillment* refers to what happens after a sale is made. Typical fulfillment tasks include the following:

- Packing up the merchandise
- Shipping the merchandise
- Solving delivery problems or answering questions about orders that haven't reached their destinations
- Sending out bills
- Following up to see whether the customer is satisfied

Order fulfillment may seem like the least exciting part of running a business, online or otherwise. But from your customer's point of view, it's the most important business activity of all. The following sections suggest how you can use your presence online to help reduce any anxiety your customers may feel about receiving what they ordered.

The back-end (or, to use the Microsoft term, BackOffice) part of your online business is where order fulfillment comes in. If you have a database in which you record customer orders, link it to your Web site so that your customers can track orders. Macromedia Dreamweaver or ColdFusion can help with this. (The most recent versions, Dreamweaver MX and Dreamweaver MX 2004, contain built-in commands that let you link to a ColdFusion database.)

Provide links to shipping services

One advantage of being online is that you can help customers track packages after shipment. The FedEx online order-tracking feature, shown in Figure 12-2, gets thousands of requests each day and is widely known as one of the most successful marketing tools on the Web. If you use FedEx, provide a link to its online tracking page.

The other big shipping services have also created their own online tracking systems. You can link to these sites, too:

- United Parcel Service (www.ups.com)
- U.S. Postal Service Express Mail (www.usps.gov)
- DHL (www.dhl-usa.com/home/home.asp)

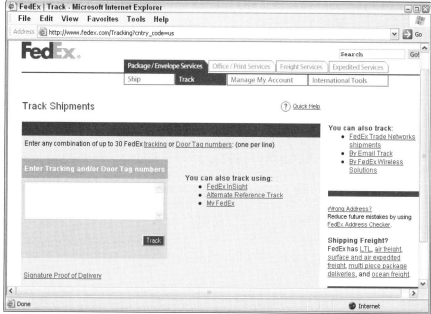

Figure 12-2:
Provide links
to online
tracking
services so
that your
customers
can check
delivery
status.

Present shipping options clearly

In order fulfillment, as in receiving payment, it pays to present your clients with as many options as possible and to explain the options in detail. Because you're online, you can provide your customers with as much shipping information as they can stand. Web surfers are knowledge hounds — they can never get enough data, whether it's related to shipping or other parts of your business.

When it comes to shipping, be sure to describe the options, the cost of each, and how long each takes. (See the sidebar called "Keeping back-office functions personal," earlier in this chapter, for some good tips on when to require signatures and how to present shipping information by e-mail rather than on the Web.) Here are some more specific suggestions:

✓ **Compare shipping costs:** Make use of an online service such as InterShipper (www.intershipper.net), which allows you to submit the origin, destination, weight, and dimensions of a package that you want to ship via a Web page form and then returns the cheapest shipping alternatives.

✔ **Make sure that you can track:** Pick a service that lets you track your package's shipping status.

✔ **Be able to confirm receipt:** If you use the U.S. Postal Service, ship the package "return receipt requested" because tracking isn't available — unless you use Priority Mail or Express Mail. You can confirm delivery with Priority Mail (domestic) and Parcel Post.

Many online stores present shipping alternatives in the form of a table or bulleted list of options. (*Tables,* as you probably know, are Web page design elements that let you arrange content in rows and columns, making them easier to read; refer to Chapter 3 for more on adding tables to your site.) You don't have to look very far to find an example; just visit the John Wiley & Sons Web site (www.wiley.com) and order a book from its online store. When you're ready to pay for your items and provide a shipping address, you see the bulleted list shown in Figure 12-3.

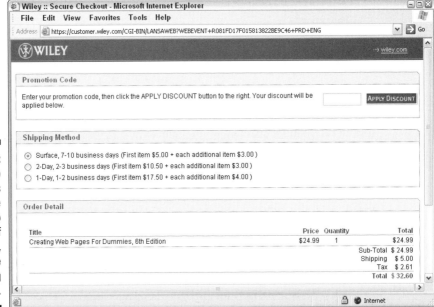

Figure 12-3: Tables help shoppers calculate costs, keep track of purchases, and choose shipping options.

Chapter 13

Service with a Virtual Smile

*I*t's only human nature: Customers often wait until the last minute to request a gift or other item for a specific occasion, and that leads to an emergency for you. It may not seem fair, but a delay in responding to your customers can lead to lost business. These days everything seems to be instant, from your oatmeal to your Internet connection. Some shoppers still like to spend hours or even days milling around the mall, browsing and lunching at their leisure. But chances are that your customer is coming to you in the first place to save time as well as money.

Customer service is one area in which small, entrepreneurial businesses can outshine brick-and-mortar stores and even larger online competitors. It doesn't matter whether you're competing in the areas of e-trading, e-music, or e-tail sales of any sort. Tools such as e-mail and interactive forms, coupled with the fact that an online commerce site can provide information on a 24/7 basis, give you a powerful advantage when it comes to retaining customers and building loyalty.

What constitutes good online customer service, particularly for a new business that has only one or two employees? Whether your customers are broadband or dialup, you need to deal with them one at a time and connect one to one. But being responsive and available is only part of the picture. This chapter presents ways to succeed with the other essential components: providing information, communicating effectively, and enabling your clientele to talk back to you online.

The Best Customer Is an Informed Customer

In a manner of speaking, satisfaction is all about expectations. If you give your customers what they are expecting or even a little bit more, they will be happy. But how do you go about setting their level of expectation in the first place? Communication is the key. The more information you can provide up front, the fewer phone queries or complaints you'll receive later. Printed pamphlets and brochures have traditionally described products and services at length. But online is now the way to go.

Say you're talking about a 1,000-word description of your new company and your products and/or services. If that text were formatted to fit on a 4-x-9-inch foldout brochure, the contents would cover several panels and take at least a few hundred dollars to print.

On the other hand, if those same 1,000 words were arranged on a few Web pages and put online, they'd probably be no more than 5K to 10K in size. The same applies if you distribute your content to a number of subscribers in the form of an e-mail newsletter. In either case, you need pay only a little, or at least next to nothing, to publish the information.

And online publishing has the advantage of easier updating. When you add new products or services or even when you want a different approach, it takes only a little time and effort to change the contents or the look.

Why FAQs are frequently used

It may not be the most elegant of concepts, but it has worked for an infinite number of online businesspeople and it will work for you. A set of *frequently asked questions* (FAQs) is a familiar feature on many online business sites — so familiar, in fact, that Web surfers expect to find a FAQ page on every business site.

Even the format of FAQ pages is pretty similar from site to site, and this predictability is itself an asset. FAQ pages are generally presented in Q-and-A format, with topics appearing in the form of questions that have literally been asked by other customers or that have been made up to resemble real questions. Each question has a brief answer that provides essential information about the business.

Just because I'm continually touting communication doesn't mean I want you to bore your potential customers with endless words that don't apply to their interests. To keep your FAQ page from getting too long, I recommend that you list all the questions at the top of the page. This way, by clicking a hyperlinked item in the list, the reader jumps to the spot down the page where you present the question that relates to them and its answer in detail.

Just having a FAQ page isn't enough. Make sure that yours is easy to use and comprehensive. Take a look at one of the most famous of the genre, the venerable World Wide Web FAQ by Thomas Boutell (`www.boutell.com/newfaq`) to get some ideas.

Sure, you could compose a FAQ page off the top of your head, but sometimes getting a different perspective helps. Invite visitors, customers, friends, and family to come up with questions about your business. You may want to include questions on some of the following topics:

- ✔ **Contact information:** If I need to reach you in a hurry by mail, fax, or phone, how do I do that? Are you available only at certain hours?

- ✔ **Instructions:** What if I need more detailed instructions on how to use your products or services? Where can I find them?

- ✔ **Service:** What do I do if the merchandise doesn't work for some reason or breaks? Do you have a return policy?

- ✔ **Sales tax:** Is sales tax added to the cost I see on-screen?

- ✔ **Shipping:** What are my shipping options?

You don't have to use the term FAQ, either. The retailer Lands' End, which does just about everything right in terms of e-commerce, uses the term Fact Sheet for its list of questions and answers. Go to the Lands' End home page (`www.landsend.com`) and click the General Information link to see how Lands' End presents the same type of material.

Writing an online newsletter

You may define yourself as an online businessperson, not a newsletter editor. But sharing information with customers and potential customers through an e-mail newsletter is a great way to build credibility for yourself and your business.

For added customer service (not to mention a touch of self-promotion), consider producing a regular publication that you send out to a mailing list. Your mailing list would begin with customers and prospective customers who visit your Web site and indicate that they want to subscribe.

An e-mail newsletter doesn't happen by magic, but it can provide your business with long-term benefits that include:

- ✔ **Customer tracking:** You can add subscribers' e-mail addresses to a mailing list that you can use for other marketing purposes, such as promoting special sales items for return customers.

- ✔ **Low-bandwidth:** An e-mail newsletter doesn't require much memory. It's great for businesspeople who get their e-mail on the road via laptops, palm devices, or appliances that are designed specifically for sending and receiving e-mail.

- ✔ **Timeliness:** You can get breaking news into your electronic newsletter much faster than you can put it in print.

The fun part is to name your newsletter and assemble content that you want to include. Then follow these steps to get your publication up and running:

1. **Create your newsletter by typing the contents in plain-text (ASCII) format.**

   Optionally, you can also provide an HTML-formatted version. You can then include headings and graphics that will show up in e-mail programs that support HTML e-mail messages.

   If you use a plain-text newsletter, format it by using capital letters; rules that consist of a row of equal signs, hyphens, or asterisks; or blank spaces to align elements.

2. **Save your file with the proper filename extension:** `.txt` **for the text version and** `.htm` **or** `.html` **if you send an HTML version.**

3. **Attach the file to an e-mail message by using your e-mail program's method of sending attachments.**

4. **Address your file to the recipients.**

   If you have lots of subscribers (many newsletters have hundreds or thousands), save their addresses in a mailing list. Use your e-mail program's address book function to do this.

5. **Send out your newsletter.**

If you have a large number of subscribers, I recommend sending your publication late at night. It's also a good idea to send it in several stages — that is, to only so many subscribers at once — rather than all at one time. Those are two good ways to help your words reach their destination quickly and reliably.

Managing a mailing list can be time consuming. You have to keep track of people who want to subscribe or unsubscribe, as well as those who ask for more information. You can save time and trouble by hiring a company such as SkyList (`www.skylist.net`) to do the day-to-day list management for you.

Mixing bricks and clicks

If you operate a brick-and-mortar business as well as a Web-based business, you have additional opportunities to get feedback from your shoppers. Take advantage of the fact that you meet customers personally on a regular basis, and ask them for opinions and suggestions that can help you operate a more effective Web site, too.

When your customers are in the checkout line (the real one with a cash register, not your online shopping cart), ask them to fill out a questionnaire about your Web site. Consider asking questions like the following:

✔ Have you visited this store's Web site? Are you familiar with it?

✔ Would you visit the Web site more often if you knew there was merchandise or content there that you couldn't find in our physical location?

✔ Can you suggest some types of merchandise, or special sales, you'd like to see on the Web site?

Including your Web site's URL on all the printed literature in your store is a good idea. The feedback system works both ways, of course: You can ask online customers for suggestions of how to run your brick-and-mortar store better, and what types of merchandise they'd like to see on your real as opposed to your "virtual" shelves.

Helping Customers Reach You

I'm the type of person who has an unlisted home phone number. But being anonymous is not the way to go when you're running an online business. (I use a different number for business calls, by the way.) Of course, you don't have to promise to be available 24/7 to your customers in the flesh. But they need to believe that they will get attention no matter what time of day or night. When you're online, contact information can take several forms. Be sure to include

✔ Your snail mail address

✔ Your e-mail address(es)

✔ Your phone and fax numbers, and a toll-free number (if you have one)

Most Web hosting services (such as the types of hosts that I describe in Chapter 3) give you more than one e-mail inbox as part of your account. So it may be helpful to set up more than one e-mail address. One address can be for people to communicate with you personally, and the other can be where people go for general information. You can also set up e-mail addresses that respond to messages by automatically sending a text file in response. (See the "Setting up autoresponders" section, later in this chapter.)

Even though you probably won't meet many of your customers in person, you need to provide them with a human connection. Keep your site as personal and friendly as possible. A contact page is a good place to provide some brief biographical information about the people visitors can contact, namely you and any employees or partners in your company.

Not putting your contact information on a separate Web page has some advantages, of course. Doing so makes your patrons have to wait a few seconds to access it. If your contact data is simple and your Web site consists only of a few pages, by all means put it right on your home page.

Going upscale with your e-mail

These days nearly everyone I know, including my parents, has an e-mail account. But when you're an online businessperson, you need to know more about the features of e-mail than just how to ask about the weather or exchange a recipe. The more you discover about the finer technical points of e-mail, the better you're able to meet the needs of your clients. The following sections suggest ways to go beyond simply sending and receiving e-mail messages, and utilize e-mail for business publishing and marketing.

Setting up autoresponders

An *autoresponder,* which also goes by the name *mailbot,* is software that you can set up to send automatic replies to requests for information about a product or service, or to respond to people subscribing to an e-mail publication or service.

You can provide automatic responses either through your own e-mail program or through your Web host's e-mail service. If you use a Web host to provide automatic responses, you can usually purchase an extra e-mail address that can be configured to return a text file (such as a form letter) to the sender.

Look for a Web host that provides you with one or more autoresponders along with your account. Typically, your host assigns you an e-mail address that takes the form info@mycompany.com. In this case, someone at your hosting service configures the account so that when a visitor to your site sends a message to info@yourcompany.com, a file of your choice, such as a simple text document that contains background information about you and your services, automatically goes out to the sender as a reply. My own Web host and ISP, XO Communications, lets me create and edit an autoresponse message for each of my e-mail accounts. First, I log on to my host's gateway, which is the service it provides customers for changing their e-mail settings. I click the link Edit E-mail Settings to go to the page called E-mail Settings shown in Figure 13-1. I check the Auto Respond box to turn the feature on and then click Edit Autoresponse Message to set up my autoresponse text.

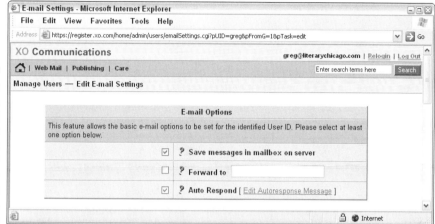

Figure 13-1:
Many Web hosts and ISPs enable users to create their own auto-response messages.

If the service that hosts your Web site does not provide free autoresponders, look into SendFree, an online service that provides you with autoresponder service for free but that requires you to display ads along with your automatic response. (An ad-free version is available for $19.97 per month.) Read about it at www.sendfree.com.

Noting by quoting

Responding to a series of questions is easy when you use *quoting* — a feature that lets you copy quotes from a message to which you're replying. Quoting, which is available in almost all e-mail programs, is particularly useful for responding to a mailing list or newsgroup message because it indicates the specific topic being discussed.

How do you tell the difference between the quoted material and the body of the new e-mail message? The common convention is to put a greater-than (>) character in the left margin, next to each line of the quoted material.

When you tell your e-mail software to quote the original message before you type your reply, it generally quotes the entire message. To save space, you can *snip* (delete) out the part that isn't relevant. However, if you do so, it's polite to type the word <snip> to show that you've cut something out. A quoted message looks something like this:

```
Mary Agnes McDougal wrote:
>I wonder if I could get some info on <snip>
>those sterling silver widgets you have for sale...
Hi Mary Agnes,
Thank you for your interest in our premium collector's line
of widgets. You can place an order online or call our toll-
free number, 1-800-WIDGETS.
```

Attaching files

A quick and convenient way to transmit information from place to place is to attach a file to an e-mail message. In fact, attaching files is one of the most useful things you can do with e-mail. *Attaching,* which means that you send a document or file along with an e-mail message, allows you to include material from any file to which you have access. Attached files appear as separate documents that recipients can download to their computers.

Adding the personal touch that means so much

Sarah-Lou Reekie started her business out of an apartment in London, England in 1997. She developed an herbal insect repellent called Alfresco while working in a botanical and herbal research center. Since then, sales have grown quickly — often doubling each year. One key to Reekie's quick success is that there were no products in direct competition with her lotion. Another key component is her personal approach to serving her customers, who include movie stars on location and other prominent entertainers like Sir Paul McCartney.

Reekie's Web site (www.alfresco.uk.com), shown in the accompanying figure, nearly doubled sales, but she stuck to basic business practices and focused on cultivating the customer base she had already developed through selling her product by word of mouth. (The trendy term for this type of publicity is "viral marketing"; see Chapter 15 for more on this topic.) She started a fan club for Alfresco, and she has personally visited some of her best customers.

Q. How have you been able to keep a steady flow of business amid the ups and downs of the world economy?

A. We have built up a bigger and bigger customer base by constantly giving good service to customers. We send out special editions for frequent buyers, have a fan club, and encourage customers to make recommendations. We bring out new and exciting products; we care and look after our customers. We are about to do a major refit on our site, as well.

Q. What are the one or two most important things people should keep in mind if they are starting an online business these days?

A. It is not necessary to spend fortunes to set it up. Find a host that has been in business a number of years. (There *are* experts now.) A clean database that really works for you is vital, as your customers are the most precious things a business can have. Keep in touch with them. Treat them with care and respect.

Q. What's the single best improvement you've made to your site to attract more customers or retain the ones you've had?

A. Putting on a special code that only special customers or fan club members can access for discounts, etc. For example, Royal Bank of Scotland employees have a special code dedicated to them.

Q. Is this a good time to start an online business?

A. I actually feel it is a great time to start an e-commerce biz for a number of reasons, not least being that the technical support is now well and truly in place. Let's just say more people know what they are doing than in earlier years. Secondly, most new customers are not as concerned about credit card security, as there really has been hardly any fraud.

Q. What advice would you give to someone thinking of starting a new business on the Web?

A. Your customer is King, Queen, Prince, and Princess. Whatever you would like yourself is what you should aim to offer. "Do as you would like to be done by" should be your motto. Expose yourself any which way and as often as is acceptable to as many well-targeted customers as possible. Most of all, keep a positive attitude. Sir Paul McCartney once said to me when I felt depressed and almost ready to give up, "Always have faith." I'm glad I listened to him!

Many e-mail clients allow users to attach files with a simple button or other command. Compressing a lengthy series of attachments by using software such as StuffIt or WinZip conserves bandwidth. Using compression is also a necessity if you ever want to send more than one attached file to someone whose e-mail account (such as an AOL account) doesn't accept multiple attachments.

Protocols such as MIME (Multipurpose Internet Mail Extensions) are sets of standards that allow you to attach graphic and other multimedia files to an e-mail message. Recipients must have an e-mail program that supports MIME (which includes almost all the newer e-mail programs) in order to download and read MIME files in the body of an e-mail message. In case your recipient has an e-mail client that doesn't support MIME attachments, or if you aren't sure whether it does, you must encode your attachment in a format such as BinHex (if you're sending files to a Macintosh) or UUCP (if you're sending files to a newsgroup).

Creating a signature file that sells

One of the easiest and most useful tools for marketing on the Internet is called a signature file, or a sig file. A *signature file* is a text blurb that your system automatically appends to the bottom of your e-mail messages and newsgroup postings. You want your signature file to tell the readers of your message something about you and your business; you can include information such as your company name and how to contact you.

Creating a signature file takes only a little more time than putting your John Hancock on the dotted line. First, you create the signature file itself, as I describe in these steps:

1. **Open a text-editing program.**

   This example uses Notepad, which comes built in with Windows. If you're a Macintosh user, you can use SimpleText. With either program, a new blank document opens on-screen.

2. **Press and hold down the hyphen (–) or equal sign (=) key to create a dividing line that will separate your signature from the body of your message.**

   Depending on which symbol you use, a series of hyphens or equal signs forms a broken line. Don't make this line too long or it will run onto another line, which doesn't look good; 30 to 40 characters is a safe measure.

3. **Type the information about yourself that you want to appear in the signature, pressing Enter after each line.**

   Include such information as your name, job title, company name, e-mail address, and Web site URL, if you have one. A three- or four-line signature is the typical length.

   If you're feeling ambitious at this point, you can press the spacebar to arrange your text in two columns. My agent (who's an online entrepreneur himself) does this with his own signature file, as shown in Figure 13-2.

Figure 13-2:
A signature file often uses divider lines and can be arranged in columns to occupy less space on-screen.

Always include the URL to your business Web site in your signature file and be sure to include it on its own line. Why? Most e-mail programs will recognize the URL as a Web page by its prefix (http://). When your reader opens your message, the e-mail program displays the URL as a clickable hyperlink that, when clicked, opens your Web page in a Web browser window.

4. **Choose File⇨Save.**

   A dialog box appears, enabling you to name the file and save it in a folder on your hard drive.

5. **Enter a name for your file that ends in the filename extension** .txt.

   This extension identifies your file as a plain text document.

6. **Click the Save button.**

   Your text file is saved on your computer's hard drive.

Now that you've created a plain-text version of your electronic signature, the next step is to identify that file to the computer programs that you use to send and receive e-mail and newsgroup messages. Doing so enables the programs to make the signature file automatically appear at the bottom of your messages. The procedure for attaching a signature file varies from program to program; the following steps show you how to do this by using Microsoft Outlook Express 6:

1. **Start Outlook Express and choose Tools⇨Options.**

   The Options dialog box opens.

2. **Click the Signatures tab.**

3. **Click New.**

   The options in the Signatures and Edit Signature sections of the Signatures tab are highlighted.

4. **Click the File button at the bottom of the tab, and then click Browse.**

   The Open dialog box appears. This is a standard Windows navigation dialog box that lets you select folders and files on your computer.

5. **Locate the signature file that you created in the previous set of steps by selecting a drive or folder from the Look In drop-down list. When you locate the file, click the filename, and then click the Open button.**

   The Signature File dialog box closes, and you return to the Options dialog box. The path leading to the selected file is listed in the box next to File.

6. **Click the Add Signatures to All Outgoing Messages check box, and then click OK.**

   The Options dialog box closes, and you return to Outlook Express. Your signature file will now be automatically added to your messages.

To test your new signature file, choose File➪New➪Mail Message from the Outlook Express menu bar. A new message composition window opens. Your signature file should appear in the body of the message composition window. You can compose a message by clicking before the signature and starting to type.

Creating forms that aren't formidable

In the old days, people who heard "here's a form to fill out" usually started to groan. Who likes to stare at a form to apply for a job or for financial aid or, even worse, to figure out how much you owe in taxes? But as an online businessperson, forms can be your best friends because they give customers a means to provide you with feedback as well as essential marketing information. Using forms, you can find out where customers live, how old they are, and so on. Customers can also use forms to sound off and ask questions.

Forms can be really handy from the perspective of the customer as well. The speed of the Internet enables them to dash off information right away. They can then pretty much immediately receive a response from you that's tailored to their needs and interests.

The two components of Web page forms

Forms consist of two parts, only one of which is visible on a Web page:

- ✔ The visible part includes the text-entry fields, buttons, and check boxes that an author creates with HTML commands.
- ✔ The part of the form that you don't see is a computer script that resides on the server that receives the page.

The aforementioned script, which is typically written in a language such as Perl, AppleScript, or C++, processes the form data that a reader submits to a server and presents that data in a format that the owner or operator of the Web site can read and use.

How the data gets to you

What exactly happens when customers connect to a page on your site that contains a form? First, they fill out the text-entry fields, radio buttons, and other areas you have set up. When they finish, they click a button, often marked Submit, in order to transmit, or *post,* the data from the remote computer to your Web site.

A computer script called a Common Gateway Interface (CGI) program receives the data submitted to your site and processes it so that you can read it. The CGI may cause the data to be e-mailed to you or it may present the data in a text file in an easy-to-read format.

Optionally, you can also create a CGI program that prompts your server to send users to a Web page that acknowledges that you have received the information and thanks them for their feedback. It's a nice touch that your customers are sure to appreciate.

Writing the scripts that process form data is definitely in the province of Webmasters or computer programmers and is far beyond the scope of this book. But you don't have to hire someone to write the scripts: You can use a Web page program (such as Microsoft FrontPage or Macromedia Dreamweaver) that not only helps you create a form but also provides you with scripts that process the data for you. (If you use forms created with FrontPage, your Web host must have a set of software called FrontPage Server Extensions installed. Call your host or search the host's online Help files to see if the extensions are present.)

Some clever businesspeople have created some really useful Web content by providing a way for nonprogrammers such as you and me to create forms online. Appropriately enough, you connect to the server's Web site and fill out a form provided by the service in order to create your form. The form has a built-in CGI that processes the data and e-mails it to you. See the "Free Forms Online" section of the Internet Directory (on this book's Web site) to find some free form creation and processing services.

Using FrontPage to create a form

You can use the Form Page Wizard that comes with Microsoft FrontPage to create both parts of forms: the data-entry parts (such as text boxes and check boxes), as well as the behind-the-scenes scripts, called *WebBots,* that process form data. Creating your own form gives you more control over how it looks and a greater degree of independence than if you use a ready-made forms service.

The first step in setting up a Web page form is determining what information you want to receive from someone who fills out the form. Your Web page creation tool then gives you options for ways to ask for the information you want. Start FrontPage and choose Insert⇨Form, and a submenu appears with many options; the most commonly used options are the following:

- ✔ **Textbox:** This creates a single-line box where someone can type text.
- ✔ **Text Area:** This creates a scrolling text box.
- ✔ **File Upload:** This lets the user send you a text file.
- ✔ **Checkbox:** This creates a check box.
- ✔ **Option Button:** This creates an option button, sometimes called a radio button.
- ✔ **Drop-Down Box:** This lets you create a drop-down list.
- ✔ **Picture:** This lets you add a graphic image to a form.

Figure 13-3 shows the most common form fields as they appear in a Web page form that you're creating.

Forms submenu

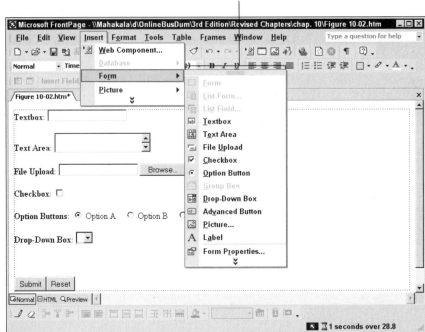

Figure 13-3:
FrontPage
provides you
with menu
options for
creating
form
elements.

When you choose Insert⇨Form, FrontPage inserts a dashed, marquee-style box in your document to signify that you're working on Web page form fields rather than normal Web page text.

The Form Page Wizard is a great way to set up a simple form that asks for information from visitors to your Web site. It lets you concentrate on the type of data you want to collect rather than on the buttons and boxes needed to gather it. I show you how to create such a form in the following steps. (These steps are for FrontPage 2002; version 2003 requires similar steps, but provides you with more options.)

1. **Choose Start⇨Programs⇨Microsoft FrontPage.**

   FrontPage starts and a blank window appears.

2. **Choose File⇨New⇨Page or Web.**

   The New Page or Web task pane appears.

3. **Click Page Templates.**

   The Page Templates dialog box appears.

4. **Double-click Form Page Wizard.**

   The first page of the Form Page Wizard appears. (You can click Finish at any time to see your form and begin editing it.)

5. **Click Next.**

6. **Follow the instructions presented in succeeding steps of the wizard to create your form.**

   a. **Click Add, and then select from the set of options that the wizard presents you with for the type of information you want the form to present.**

      This may include account information, ordering information, and so on.

   b. **Select specific types of information you want to solicit.**

   c. **Choose the way you want the information to be presented.**

      You have options such as a bulleted list, numbered list, and so on.

   d. **Identify how you want the user-submitted information to be saved.**

      You can choose to save information as a text file, a Web page, or with a custom CGI script if you have one.

7. **Click Finish.**

   The wizard window closes and your form appears in the FrontPage window.

When you finish, be sure to add your own description of the form and any special instructions at the top of the Web page. Also add your copyright and contact information at the bottom of the page. Follow the pattern you've set on other pages on your site. You can edit the form by using the Forms sub-menu options if you want to.

Be sure to change the background of the form page from the boring default gray that the wizard provides to a more compelling color. See Chapter 5 for more specific instructions on changing the background of Web pages you create.

Making Customers Feel That They Belong

In the old days, people went to the market often, sometimes on a daily basis. The shopkeeper was likely to have set aside items for their consideration based on individual tastes and needs. More likely than not, the business transaction followed a discussion of families, politics, and other neighborhood gossip.

Good customer service can make your customers feel like members of a community that frequent a Mom-and-Pop store on the corner of their block — the community of satisfied individuals who regularly use your goods and services. In the following sections, I describe some ways to make your customers feel like members of a group, club, or other organization who return to your site on a regular basis and interact with a community of individuals with similar interests.

Putting the "person" into personal service

How often does an employee personally greet you as you walk through the door of a store? On the Web as well as in real life, people like a prompt and personal response. Your challenge is to provide someone on your Web site who's available to provide live customer support.

Some Web sites do provide live support so that people can e-mail a question to someone in real-time (or close to real-time) Internet technologies, such as chat and message boards. The online auction giant eBay has a New Users Board, for example, where beginners can post questions for eBay support staff, who post answers in response.

An even more immediate sort of customer support is provided by *chat,* in which individuals type messages to one another over the Internet in real time. One way to add chat to your site is to start a Yahoo! Group, which I describe later in this chapter.

LivePerson (`www.liveperson.com`) provides a simpler alternative that allows small businesses to provide chat-based support. LivePerson is software that enables you to see who is connected to your site at any one time and instantly lets you chat with them, just as if you're greeting them at the front door of a brick-and-mortar store.

LivePerson works like this: You install the LivePerson Pro software on your own computer (not the server that runs your site). With LivePerson, you or your assistants can lead the customer through the process of making a purchase. For instance, you might help show customers what individual sale items look like by sending them an image file to view with their Web browsers. You can try out LivePerson Pro for free for 30 days, and then pay $99 per month thereafter.

Not letting an ocean be a business barrier

You're probably familiar with terms such as "global village" and "international marketplace." But how do you extend your reach into the huge overseas markets where e-commerce is just beginning to come into its own? Making sure that products are easily and objectively described with words as well as clear images and diagrams, where necessary, is becoming increasingly important. There are other ways to effectively overcome language and cultural barriers, some of which are common sense while others are less obvious.

Keep in mind the fact that shoppers in many developing nations still prefer to shop with their five senses. So that foreign customers never have a question on how to proceed, providing them with implicit descriptions of the shopping process is essential. You should make information on ordering, payment, execution, and support available at every step.

Customer support in Asia is, in many ways, a different creature than in the West. While personalization still remains critical, language and translation gives an e-commerce site a different feel. A Western site that might work well by looking clean and well organized might have to be replaced with the more chaotic blitz of characters and options that's often found more compelling by Eastern markets. In Asia, Web sites tend to place more emphasis on color and interactivity. Many e-commerce destinations choose to dump all possible options on the front page, instead of presenting them in an orderly, sequential flow.

Having a discussion area can enhance your site

Can we talk? Even my pet birds like to communicate by words as well as squawks. A small business can turn its individual customers into a cohesive group by starting its own discussion group on the Internet. Discussion groups work particularly well if you're promoting a particular type of product or if you and your customers are involved in a provocative or even controversial area of interest.

The three kinds of discussion groups are

- ✔ **A local group:** Some universities create discussion areas exclusively for their students. Other large companies set aside groups that are restricted to their employees. Outsiders can't gain access because the groups aren't on the Internet but rather are on a local server within the organization.

- ✔ **A Usenet newsgroup:** Individuals are allowed to create an Internet-wide discussion group in the `alt` or `biz` categories of Usenet without having to go through the time-consuming application and approval process needed to create other newsgroups.

- ✔ **A Web-based discussion group:** Microsoft FrontPage includes easy-to-use wizards that enable you to create a discussion area on your business Web site. Users can access the area from their Web browsers without having to use special discussion-group software. Or, if you don't have FrontPage, you can start a Yahoo! Group, which I describe in the section named (surprise!) "Starting a Yahoo! Group."

Of these three alternatives, the first isn't appropriate for your business purposes. So what follows focuses on the last two types of groups.

In addition to newsgroups, many large corporations host interactive chats moderated by experts on subjects related to their areas of business. But small businesses can also hold chats, most easily by setting up a chat room on a site that hosts chat-based discussions. But the hot new way to build goodwill and establish new connections with customers and interested parties is an interactive Web-based diary called a *blog* (short for Web log); find out more about blogs in Chapter 4.

Starting an alt discussion group

Usenet is a system of communication on the Internet that enables individual computer users to participate in group discussions about topics of mutual interest. Internet newsgroups have what's referred to as a hierarchical structure. Most groups belong to one of seven main categories: comp, misc, news, rec, sci, soc, and talk. The name of the category appears at the beginning of the group's name, such as rec.food.drink.coffee. In this section, I discuss the alt category, which is just about as popular as the seven I just mentioned and which enables individuals — like you — to establish their own newsgroups.

In my opinion, the biz discussion groups aren't taken seriously because they are widely populated by unscrupulous people promoting get-rich-quick schemes and egomaniacs who love the sound of their own voices. The alt groups, although they can certainly address some wild and crazy topics, are at least as well known and often address serious topics. Plus, the process of setting up an alt group is well documented.

The prefix alt didn't originally stand for *alternative,* although it has come to mean that. The term was an abbreviation for Anarchists, Lunatics, and Terrorists, which wasn't so politically incorrect back in those days. Now, alt is a catchall category in which anyone can start a group, if others show interest in the creator's proposal.

The first step to creating your own alt discussion group is to point your Web browser to Google Groups (groups.google.com) or launch your browser's newsgroup software. To start up Netscape's newsreader, choose Window⇨ Mail & Newsgroups, and then click the down arrow next to the name of your newsgroup server. To start the Outlook Express newsgroup software, click the plus sign next to the name of the newsgroup software in the program's Folders pane (both options assume you've already configured Outlook Express to connect to your ISP's newsgroup server) and access the group called alt.config.newgroups. This area contains general instructions on starting your own Usenet newsgroup. Also look in news.answers for the message "How to Start a New Usenet Newsgroup."

To find out how to start a group in the alt category, go to Google (www.google.com), click Groups, and search for the message "How to Start an Alt Newsgroup." (You can also find this message at www.visi.com/~barr/alt-creation-guide.html.) Follow the instructions contained in this message to set up your own discussion group. Basically, the process involves the following steps:

1. **You write a brief proposal describing the purpose of the group you want to create and including an e-mail message where people can respond with comments.**

   The proposal also contains the name of your group in the correct form (`alt.groupname.moreinfo.moreinfo`). Try to keep the group name short and official looking if it is for business purposes.

2. **You submit the proposal to the newsgroup** `alt.config`.

3. **You gather feedback to your proposal by e-mail.**

4. **You send a special message called a** *control message* **to the news server that gives you access to Usenet.**

   The exact form of the message varies from server to server, so you need to consult with your ISP on how to compose the message correctly.

5. **Wait a while (a few days or weeks) as news administrators (the people who operate news servers at ISPs around the world) decide whether to adopt your request and add your group to their list of newsgroups.**

Before you try to start your own group, look through the Big 7 categories (`comp`, `misc`, `news`, `rec`, `sci`, `soc`, and `talk`) to make sure that someone else isn't already covering your topic.

Starting a Yahoo! Group

When the Internet was still fresh and new, Usenet was almost the only game in town. These days, the Web is pretty much (along with e-mail) the most popular way to communicate and share information. That's why starting a discussion group on the Web makes perfect sense. A Web-based discussion group is somewhat less intimidating than others because it doesn't require a participant to use newsgroup software.

Yahoo! Groups are absolutely free to set up. (To find out how, just go to the FAQ page, `help.yahoo.com/help/us/groups/index.html`, and click the How Do I Start a Group? link.) They not only enable users to exchange messages, but they can also communicate in real time by using chat. And as the list operator, you can send out e-mail newsletters and other messages to your participants, too.

Simply operating an online store isn't enough. You need to present yourself as an authority in a particular area that is of interest. The discussion group needs to concern itself primarily with that topic and give participants a chance to exchange views and tips on the topic. If people have questions about your store, they can always e-mail you directly — they don't need a discussion group to do that.

Creating a Web discussion area with FrontPage

The reason that Microsoft FrontPage is such a popular tool for creating Web sites is that it enables you to create Web page content that you would otherwise need complicated scripts to tackle. One example is the program's Discussion Group Wizard, which lets you create Web pages on which your members (as opposed to customers, remember?) can exchange messages and carry on a series of back-and-forth responses (called *threads*) on different topics. Newcomers to the group can also view articles that are arranged by a table of contents and accessible by a searchable index.

Creating the discussion area

Follow these steps to set up your own discussion group with Microsoft FrontPage:

1. **Start FrontPage by choosing Start⇨All Programs⇨Microsoft FrontPage.**

   The FrontPage window opens.

   You can create a new discussion *web* (that is, a group of interlinked documents that together comprise a Web site) of Web pages by using one of the built-in wizards that comes with FrontPage.

2. **To use the FrontPage Discussion Group Wizard, choose File⇨New⇨Page or Web.**

   The New Page or Web task pane appears.

3. **Click Web Site Templates.**

   The Web Site Templates dialog box appears.

4. **Select Discussion Web Wizard and then click OK.**

   A dialog box appears, stating that the new discussion web is being created. Then the first of a series of Discussion Web Wizard dialog boxes appears.

5. **Click Next.**

   The second dialog box lets you specify the features you want for your discussion web. If this is the first time you've created a group, leave all the options checked.

6. **Click Next.**

   A dialog box appears that lets you specify a title and folder for the new discussion web. Enter a title in the box beneath Enter a descriptive title for this discussion. You can change the default folder name _disc1 if you want.

7. **Click Next.**

   The dialog box that appears lets you choose one of three options for the structure of your discussion:

   - Select Subject, Comments if you expect visitors to discuss only a single topic.

   - Select Subject, Category, Comments if you expect to conduct discussions on more than one topic.

   - Select Subject, Product, Comments if you want to invite discussions about products you produce and/or sell.

   After you select one of these options, the next Discussion Web Wizard dialog box appears. Go through this and the subsequent dialog boxes, answering the questions they present you with in order to determine what kind of discussion group you're going to have. At any time, as you go through the series of Discussion Web Wizard pages, you can click the Finish button to complete the process.

8. **When you're done, the preset pages for your discussion web appear in the FrontPage Explorer main window.**

The middle column of the FrontPage window shows the arrangement of the discussion documents. The right side of the window is a visual map that shows how the discussion group is arranged and how the pages are linked to each other.

When you set up a discussion area with FrontPage, you have the option of designing your pages as a *frameset,* or a set of Web pages that has been sub-divided into separate frames. To find out more about frames, see Chapter 5.

Editing the discussion pages

After you use the Discussion Group Wizard to create your pages, the next step is to edit the pages so that they have the content you want. With your newly created pages displayed in the FrontPage window, you can start editing by double-clicking the icon for a page (such as the Welcome page, which has a filename such as `disc_welc.htm`) in your discussion web. Whatever page you double-click opens in the right column of the FrontPage window.

For instance, you might add a few sentences to the beginning of the Welcome page that you have just created in order to tell participants more about the purpose and scope of the discussion group. You can add text by clicking anywhere on the page and typing.

To edit more pages in your discussion group, choose File⇨Open. The Open File dialog box appears with a list of all the documents that make up your discussion group. You can double-click a file's name in order to edit it. When you finish editing files, choose File⇨Save to save your work.

To see how your discussion pages look, use the FrontPage Preview feature. Choose File⇨Preview in Browser, and the page you've been editing appears in your browser window.

Posting your discussion area

The final step is to transfer your discussion web of pages from your own computer to your Web host's site on the Internet. Many Web hosting services support one-step file transfers with Microsoft FrontPage. If you plan to use FrontPage often, I recommend locating a host that offers this support. (If your host doesn't support such transfers, you need to use an FTP program such as Fetch or WS_FTP to transfer your files.)

With one-step file transfers, you simply connect to the Internet, choose File⇨Publish Web from the FrontPage menu bar, and enter the URL of your directory on your host's Web server where your Web pages are published. Click OK, and your files are immediately transferred.

Chapter 14

Search Engine Placement

The other day, I took some old radios to a local repair shop. The store has been in business for more than three decades but never seemed to be busy. This time, however, the owner told me he was overwhelmed with hundreds of back orders and wouldn't be able to get to my jobs for several weeks. His store had just been featured on a local public television show, and now people were driving long distances to bring him retro audio equipment to fix.

If you can get your business mentioned in just the right place, customers will find you more easily. On the Web, search engines are the most important places to get yourself listed. One of the key requirements for any business is the ability to match up your products or services with potential customers and to ensure that your company will show up in lots of search results and that your site will be near the top of the first page. You do have a measure of control over the quality of your placement in search results, and this chapter will describe strategies for improving it.

The Web analytics firm WebSideStory reported in 2003 (`www.websidestory.com/pressroom/pressreleases.html?id=181`) that 13.4 percent of traffic to Web sites came from search engines, up from 7.1 percent the year before.

Understanding How Search Engines Find You

Have you ever wondered why some companies manage to find their way to the top of a page of search engine results — and occasionally pop up several times on the same page — while others get buried deep within pages and pages of Web site listings? In an ideal world, search engines would rank e-commerce sites by how well designed they are and how responsive their owners are. But with so many millions of Web sites crowding the Internet, the job of processing searches and indexing Web site URLs and contents has to be automated. Because it's computerized, you can perform some magic with the way your Web pages are written that can help you improve your placement in a set of search results.

Your site doesn't necessarily need to appear right at the top of the first search results page. The important thing is to ensure that your site appears before that of your competition. In this chapter, you'll discover different ways to use search engines to your advantage. To begin, you need to think like a searcher, which is probably easy because you probably do plenty of Web-based searches yourself. How do you find the Web sites you want? Two things are of paramount importance: keywords and links.

Keywords are key

A *keyword* is a word describing a subject that you enter in a search box in order to find information on a Web site or on the wider Internet. Suppose you're trying to find a source for an herbal sweetener called Stevia that low-carb dieters like. You'd naturally enter the term **Stevia** in the search box on your search service of choice, click a button called Search, Search Now, Go, or something similar, and wait a few seconds for search results to be gathered.

When you send a keyword to a search service, you set a number of possible actions in motion. One thing that will happen for sure is that the keyword will be processed by a script on a Web server that is operated by the search service. The script will make a request (which is called, in computerspeak, a *query*) to a database file. The database contains contents culled from millions (even billions, depending on the service) of Web pages.

The database contents are gathered from two sources. In some cases, search services employ human editors who record selected contents of Web pages and write descriptions for those pages. But Web pages are so ubiquitous and changeable that most of the work is actually done by computer programs that automatically scour the Web. These programs don't record every word on every Web page. Some take words from the headings; others index the first 50 or 100 words on a Web site. Accordingly, when I did a search for Stevia on Google, the sites that were listed at the top of the first page of search results had two attributes:

✔ Some sites that had the word Stevia in the URL, such as `www.stevia.net` or `www.stevia.com`.

✔ Other sites had the word Stevia mentioned several times at the top of the home page.

A service called Wordtracker (wordtracker.com) does daily surveys of the keyword queries made to various search engines. It creates lists of what it finds to be the most popular search terms. It's not likely those terms apply to your own e-commerce Web site, of course. But if you want to maximize the number of visits to your site, or just to make your site more prominent in a list of search results, you may do well to know what's trendy and write your text accordingly.

Adding your site's most important keyword to the URL is one solution to better search placement. But you can't always do this. When it comes to keywords, your job is to load your Web site's headings with as many words as you can find that are relevant to what you sell. You can do this by:

- Registering your site with one or more of the services (see the "Registering your site with Google" section, later in this chapter).

- Burying keywords in the <META> tag in the HTML for your home page so they won't be visible to your visitors but will appear to the spider programs that index Web pages (see the "Adding keywords to your HTML" section, later in this chapter).

- Adding keywords to the headings and initial body text on your pages, as described in the "Adding keywords to key pages" section, later in this chapter.

A keyword doesn't have to be a single word. You can also use a phrase containing two or more words. Think beyond single words to consider phrases people might enter when they're trying to find products or services you're offering.

Links help searchers connect to you

Keywords aren't the only things that point search services to Web sites. Services like Google keep track of the number of links that point to a site. The greater the number of links, the higher that site's ranking in a set of Google search listings. It's especially good if the URLs that form the links make use of your keywords. Suppose your ideal keywords are "Greg's Shoe Store." The ideal URL would be www.gregsshoestore.com, www.gregsshoestore.biz, and so on. You could create the following HTML link to your e-commerce Web site on a personal Web page, an eBay About Me page (see Chapter 10), or a zShop on Amazon.com (see Chapter 9):

```
<a href="http://www.gregsshoestore.com"> Visit Greg's Shoe
        Store </a>
```

Such a link would be doubly useful: A search service such as Google would find your desired keywords ("Greg's Shoe Store") in the visible, clickable link on your Web page, as well as in the HTML for the link.

Don't forget the human touch

I don't want to suggest that search engines work solely by means of computer programs that automatically scour Web pages and by paid advertisements. Computer programs are perceived to be the primary source, but the human factor still plays a role. Yahoo!, one of the oldest search engines around, originally compiled its directory of Web sites by means of real live employees. These days, its Web directory (`dir.yahoo.com`) isn't as easy to find on Yahoo! as it once was. But editors still index sites and assign them to a category called New and Notable Sites, which includes sites that are especially cool in someone's opinion.

There's almost no way to make sure that a human editor indexes your Web site. The only thing you can do is to make your site as unique and content rich as possible. And that will help your business not only show up in directories and search results but also drum up more paying customers for you, too.

Taking the initiative: Paying for ads

You can't get much better placement than right at the top of the first page of a set of search results, either at the top of the page or in a column on the right side. It's even better if your site's name and URL are highlighted in a color. The only way to get such preferred treatment is to pay for it. And that's just what a growing number of online businesses are doing — paying search engines to list their sites in a prominent location. See the "Paying for search listings can pay off" sidebar, later in this chapter, for more information.

Knowing who supplies the search results

Another important thing to remember about search engines is that they often gather results from *other* search services. You may be surprised to find out that, if you do a search of the Web on America Online, your search results are primarily gathered from Google. That's because AOL has a contract from Google to supply such results. Not only that, but many search services are owned by parent search services. Just what are the most popular search services, and where do they get their results? A rundown appears in Table 14-1. The services are presented in rank order, beginning in the first row with Google, which is number 1. Rankings were reported by comScore Media Metrix in May 2004.

Table 14-1	Internet Search Services			
Parent Company	**Its Search Services**	**URLs**	**Source (Search Results)**	**Source (Paid Listings)**
Google	Google	`www.google.com`	Google	Google
Yahoo!	AltaVista, AllTheWeb, Overture	`www.yahoo.com,` `www.altavista.com,` `www.overture.com`	Yahoo!	Overture
MSN	MSN Search	`search.msn.com`	Yahoo!	Overture
AOL	AOL Search, Netscape Search	`search.aol.com`	Google	Google
Excite (owned by Ask Jeeves)	Excite, iWon, MyWay.com	`www.excite.com,` `home.iwon.com,` `www.myway.com`	Google	Google
Ask Jeeves	Ask Jeeves, Teoma	`www.ask.com,` `www.teoma.com`	Teoma	Google
InfoSpace	Dogpile, WebCrawler	`www.dogpile.com,` `www.webcrawler.com`	Lycos	Enhance Interactive
Lycos	Lycos, Hotbot	`www.lycos.com,` `www.hotbot.com`	LookSmart, Yahoo!	Google

The important thing to note about this table is that many of the most popular search engines receive their listings not from their own database of Web sites, but from other search services. If you pay for a listing with Google, in other words, your ad is likely to appear not only on Google but also on HotBot, Lycos, Teoma, AOL Search, and other places. By getting your site in the Yahoo! database, you'll appear in Yahoo! search results as well as MSN Search.

These are by no means the only search services around. Other search engines focus on Web sites and Internet resources in specific countries. You can find more of them at `www.searchenginewatch.com/links/` `article.php/2156121`.

Going Gaga over Google

When it comes to search engines, Google is at the top of the heap. In fact, StatMarket (www.statmarket.com) reported in late 2004 that fully 41 percent of all search referrals were being done by Google. The next highest competitor, Yahoo!, had about 27 percent of the search market business.

Google is a runaway success thanks to its effectiveness. You're simply more likely to find something on Google, more quickly, than you are on its competitors. Any search engine placement strategy has to address Google first and foremost. But that doesn't mean you should ignore Google's competitors. Not long before this book was published, Microsoft came out with its own Internet search engine, MSN Search.

Googling yourself

If you want to evaluate the quality of your search results placement on Google, you have to start by taking stock of where you currently stand. That's easily done: Just go to Google's home page (www.google.com) and Google yourself. (In other words, do a search for your own name or your business's name — a pastime that has also been called *egosurfing*.) See where your Web site turns up in the results, and also make note of which other sites mention yours.

Next, click Advanced Search or go directly to www.google.com/advanced_search?hl=en. Under the heading Page-Specific Search, enter the URL for your e-commerce site in the Links text box, and then click Search. The results that appear in a few seconds consist of Web sites that link to yours. The list should suggest to you the kinds of sites you should approach to solicit links. It should also suggest the kinds of informational Web sites you might create for the purpose of steering business to your Web site. (See the "Maximizing links" section, later in this chapter, for a specific example.)

Playing Google's game to reach #1

Not long ago, some bloggers got together and decided to play a game called *Google bombing*. The game is simple: It consists of making links to a particular Web site in an attempt to get that site listed on Google. The more links the site has pointing to it, the higher that site will appear in a set of search results. Of course, the links that are made all have to be connected with a particular keyword or phrase. In the game I'm recalling, one phrase used was "miserable failure." The words "miserable failure" were hyperlinks pointing to the Web site of the White House. The story went that if you went to Google, typed the words **miserable failure** and clicked the I'm Feeling Lucky button, you would be taken to President Bush's biography on the White House Web site. (Incidentally, if you type those words and click Google Search rather than I'm Feeling Lucky, the number two hit takes you to Jimmy Carter's biography on the White House Web site; the number three hit takes you to Michael Moore's Web site.) You can find out more about this interesting pastime on a Web site called The Word Spy (www.wordspy.com/words/Googlebombing.asp).

The Google game applies to your e-commerce Web site, too. Suppose you sell yo-yos, and your Web site URL is www.yoyoplay.com. (This is actually one of the sites run by Lars Hundley, the entrepreneur profiled in the "Paying for search listings can pay off" sidebar, later in this chapter.) The game is to get as many other Web sites as possible to link to this URL. The terms that a visitor clicks to get to this URL can be anything: *Yo-Yos, Play Yo-Yos,* and so on. The more links you can make, the better your search results will be.

Leaving a Trail of Crumbs

In order to improve your site's search placement, you need to make it easy for searchers to find you. You leave a trail of digital crumbs. You add keywords to the HTML for your Web pages, and you make sure that your site is included in the databases of the most popular services.

Keep in mind that most Web surfers don't enter single words in search boxes. They tend to enter phrases. Combinations of keywords are extra effective. If you sell tools, don't just enter *tools* as a keyword. Enter keywords such as *tool box, power tool, tool caddy, pneumatic tool, electric tool,* and so on.

Adding keywords to your HTML

What keywords should you add to your site? Take an old-fashioned pencil and paper and write down all the words you can think of that are related to your site, your products, your services, or you — whatever you want to promote, in other words. You may also enlist the help of a printed thesaurus or the one supplied online at Dictionary.com (www.dictionary.com). Look up one term associated with your goods or services, and you're likely to find a number of similar terms.

Some search services, such as AltaVista and Overture, provide you with keyword suggestions. Go to Overture's Keyword Selector Tool (inventory.overture.com/d/searchinventory/suggestion), type a word or phrase in the box labeled Get Suggestions For:, and click the arrow next to the box. A set of suggested terms should appear in less than a minute. This utility is intended to help potential advertisers select keywords so that they can pay for ads that will appear when someone searches for those words. But they can be used to suggest keywords for your <META> tags, too.

After you have a set of keywords, you need to add them to the HTML for your Web pages. Keywords and Web site descriptions are contained within HTML commands that begin with <META>. If you type the commands by hand using a text editor, you need to locate the commands in between the <HEAD> and </HEAD> tags at the head of the document. They look like this:

```
<META NAME="description">
<META NAME="keywords">
```

Some Web page editors make this user friendly for you: You can type your information in specially designated boxes. Figure 14-1 shows Macromedia Dreamweaver's commands, which are accessed by opening the Objects panel, clicking Keywords, and then typing the words in the Keywords dialog box.

Keywords already present in HTML   Click here to add keywords.

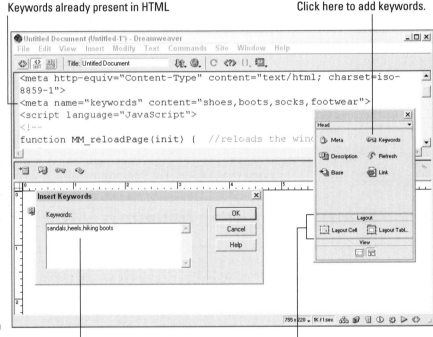

Figure 14-1:
Some Web page editors make it easy to add keywords and descriptions for search services to find.

Type keywords here.   Objects panel

You can also spy on your competitors' Web sites to see if they have added any keywords to their Web pages by following these steps:

1. **Go to your competitor's home page and choose View⇨Source if you are using Internet Explorer, or choose View⇨Page Source if you use Netscape Navigator.**

   A new window opens with the page source supplied.

2. **Scroll through the code, looking for the ⟨META⟩ tags if they are present. (Press Ctrl+F, enter META, and click the Find button if you can't find them on your own.)**

   If the page's author used ⟨META⟩ tags to enter keywords, you'll see them on-screen.

3. **Make note of the keywords supplied and see if any might be applied to your own Web site.**

Keywords, like Web page addresses, are frequently misspelled. Make sure that you type several variations on keywords that might be subject to typos: for instance, **Mississippi, Misissippi, Mississipi**, and so on. Don't worry about getting capitalization just right, however; most searchers simply enter all low-ercase characters and don't bother with capital letters at all.

Besides keywords, the ⟨META⟩ tag is also important for the Description com-mand, which enables you to create a description of your Web site or Web page that search engines can index and use in search results. Some search services also scan the description for keywords, too, so make sure that you create a description at the same time you type your keywords in the ⟨META⟩ tags.

Registering your site with Google

Google has a program that automatically indexes Web pages all over the Internet. The program actually has a name: Googlebot. However, you don't have to wait for Googlebot to find your site: You can fill out a simple form that adds your URL to the sites that are indexed by this program. Go to www.google.com/addurl.html, enter your URL and a few comments about your site, and click the Add URL button. That's all there is to it. Expect to wait a few weeks for your site to appear among Google's search results if it doesn't appear there already.

Getting listed in the Yahoo! index

If you want to get the most bang for your advertising buck, get your site listed on the most popular locations in cyberspace. For several years now, the many sites owned by Yahoo! have been ranked in the top three most popular sites on the Internet in the Media Metrix Top 50 list of Web Properties published by comScore Media Metrix (www.comscore.com/press/release.asp? press=372). Although many people think of Yahoo! primarily as a search engine, it's also a categorical index to Web sites. Getting listed on Yahoo! means being included on one of its index pages. An *index page* is a list of Web sites grouped together by category, much like what you'd find in a traditional yellow-pages phone book.

Aside from its steadily increasing size and popularity, one thing that sets Yahoo! apart is the way in which it evaluates sites for inclusion on its index pages. For the most part, real human beings do the Yahoo! indexing; they read your site description and your own suggested location and then determine what category to list your site under. Usually, Yahoo! lists sites in only one or two categories, but if Yahoo! editors feel that a site deserves its own special category, they create one for it.

The Yahoo! editors don't even attempt to process all the thousands of site applications they receive each week. Reports continue to circulate on the Web as to how long it takes to get listed on Yahoo! and how difficult it is to get listed at all. The process can take weeks, months, or even years. Danny Sullivan, the editor of *Search Engine Watch*, estimates that only about a quarter of all sites that apply get listed. That's why Yahoo! has now instituted an Express listing system — your business site will get reviewed in exchange for a $299, nonrefundable annual fee, though you *still* aren't guaranteed that you'll get listed. Find out more at help.yahoo.com/help/us/bizex/index.html.

Spying on the Web searchers

If you have ever wondered what people search for every day on the Internet, you're in luck. A site called Metaspy (www.metaspy.com) lets visitors look "behind the scenes" at a list of keywords that visitors to its search service, MetaCrawler, are entering in near-real time. (The list of search services is refreshed every 15 seconds.) It doesn't help you make your e-commerce site more visible, but it does tell you how diverse the topics are that are searched on Web sites. If nothing else, it makes you aware that some of your keywords need to be general and universal as well as topic specific.

Search Engine Watch (`searchenginewatch.com`) is a great place to go for tips on how search engines and indexes work, and how to get listed on them. The site includes an article about one company's problems getting what it considers to be adequate Yahoo! coverage (`searchenginewatch.com/sereport/9801-miningco.html`).

What can you do to get listed on Yahoo!? I have a three-step suggestion:

1. **Make your site interesting, quirky, or somehow attention grabbing.**

   You never know; you may just stand out from the sea of new Web sites and gain the attention of one of the Yahoo! editors.

2. **Go ahead and try applying to the main Yahoo! index.**

   You can at least say you tried!

   a. **Go to `www.yahoo.com`, find the category page that you think should list your site, and click the Suggest a Site link at the very bottom of the page.**

      The Yahoo! Suggest a Site page appears.

   b. **Click the Standard Consideration button.**

   c. **Verify that the Yahoo! category shown is the one in which you want to be included, and then click Continue.**

   d. **On the form that appears, provide your URL and a description for your site.**

      Make your description as interesting as possible while remaining within the content limit. (If you submit a description that's too long, Yahoo! asks you to revise it.)

3. **Try a local Yahoo! index.**

   Major metropolitan areas around the country, as well as in other parts of the world, have their own Yahoo! indexes. Go to `local.yahoo.com` and click the Browse By City link. Find the local index closest to you and apply as I describe in the preceding step. Your chances are much better of getting listed locally than on the main Yahoo! site.

You can improve your listing on Yahoo! by shelling out anywhere from $25 to $300 or more per year to become a sponsored Web site. Your site is listed in the Sponsored Sites box at the top of a Yahoo! category. The exact cost depends on the popularity of the category. There is life beyond Yahoo!, too. Several Web-based services are trying to compete by providing their own way of organizing and evaluating Web sites. Try submitting a listing to Best of the Web (`http://botw.org`) or contact one of the guides employed by About.com (`www.about.com`).

Getting listed with other search services

Search services can steer lots of business to a commercial Web site, based on how often the site appears in the list of Web pages that the user sees and how high the site appears in the list. Your goal is to maximize your site's chances of being found by the search service.

Not so long ago, search services allowed you to list your site for free, and you could be reasonably certain of getting your site included. Not so any more. Most sites guarantee that you'll be listed in their index only if you pay a subscription fee. The fee and the terms vary from service to service. I did a quick survey of the major search sites to see what the current status is. Check out Table 14-2 to see what I discovered.

Table 14-2	Search Service Listing Policies	
Service	*Free Option*	*Paid Options*
AltaVista	Submit up to five URLS for consideration; results in 4–6 weeks	Submit one URL for $39 for six-month subscription, or 2–10 URLS for $29 each for six months
Google	Submit one URL at a time to Open Directory (www.dmoz.org) for consideration; results in "several weeks"	N/A
HotBot, Lycos	Submit one URL for consideration; results in 4–6 weeks	Guaranteed listing if you pay $18 membership fee plus $12 per URL per year to join InSite Select
Overture, WebCrawler	N/A	Minimum bid of $0.05 per click-through per listing plus $20/month

Some search services are part of the Overture network, but they still allow individuals to submit their sites for consideration. Here's a quick example that shows how to submit your site (for consideration) to one of the search engines that still gives you the do-it-yourself option:

1. **Connect to the Internet, start your Web browser, and go to AltaVista at** www.altavista.com.

    The AltaVista home page appears.

2. **Click the Submit a Site link.**

    The AltaVista Submit a Site page appears.

3. **Click the Click Here link (under the heading Basic Submit).**

The Yahoo! Search Sign In page appears. Confused? Remember those interconnections between search services in Table 14-1: AltaVista gets its search results from Yahoo!. Therefore, you have to register Yahoo! in order to have people find you on AltaVista.

4. **Enter your Yahoo! ID and password. (If you don't have them yet, click the Sign Up Now link on the same page to obtain them.) Then click Sign In.**

   The Yahoo! Submit Your Site page appears.

5. **In the box labeled Enter the URL, type the URL for your site's home page, and then click the Submit URL button.**

   Your page is added to the list of pages that Yahoo!'s "crawler" program indexes. As the note on the Submit Your Site page says, you can expect the process to take several weeks.

Businesses on the Web can get obsessed with how high their sites appear on the list of search results pages. If a Web surfer enters the exact name of a site in the Excite search text box, for example, some people just can't understand why that site doesn't come back at the top — or even on the first page — of the list of returned sites. Of the millions of sites listed in a search service's database, the chances are good that at least one has the same name as yours (or something close to it) or that a page contains a combination of the same words that make up your organization's name. Don't be overly concerned with hitting the top of the search-hit charts. Concentrate on creating a top-notch Web site and making sales.

Adding keywords to key pages

Earlier in this chapter, I show you how to add keywords to the HTML for your Web pages. Those keywords aren't ones that visitors normally see, unless they view the source code for your Web page. Other keywords can be added to parts of your Web page that are visible — parts of the page that those programs called *crawlers* or *spiders* scan and index:

- ✔ **The title:** Be sure to create a title for your page. The title appears in the title bar at the very top of the browser window. Many search engines index the contents of the title because it appears not only at the top of the browser window, but at the top of the HTML, too.

- ✔ **Headings:** Your Web page's headings should be specific about what you sell and what you do.

- ✔ **The first line of text:** Sometimes, search services index every word on every page, but others limit the amount of text they index. So the first lines might be indexed while others are not. Get your message across quickly; pack your first sentences with nouns that list what you have for sale.

CASE STUDY

Paying for search listings can pay off

As you can see in Table 14-1, listing with search sites is growing more complex all the time. Many sites are owned by other sites. Two search services, Yahoo! and MSN Search, are part of the Overture search network. You tell Overture how much you'll pay if someone clicks your listing when it appears in a list of search results. The higher you bid, the better your ranking in the results. In exchange for the fees you pay to Overture, your search listings appear in multiple search sites.

Overture (formerly called GoTo.com) has lots of options for paid listings. You can create your own listing and then pay $20 per month. You can also pay a $99 fee to have Overture write up to 20 listings for you; a $199 option is also available for which Overture will write up to 100 listings for you. In each case, you need to spend a minimum of $20 per month to be listed. You bid a

minimum of five cents per click on how much you want to pay for *clickthroughs* — each time someone clicks your listing and goes to your site, you pay Overture. You can tell Overture that you want to have a Premium Listing at the top of the search results, but remember that the more clickthroughs you get, the higher fees you pay. Find out more at www.overture.com.

Lars Hundley, who in 1998 started his first online store, Clean Air Gardening (shown in the following figure), has received lots of publicity thanks to energetic marketing and good use of search engine resources, including the Overture search network. He hosts Clean Air Gardening and other e-commerce sites with Yahoo! Small Business, a storefront solution described in Chapter 9. Other informational sites are hosted on his own Web server.

Hundley uses many of the search engine place-ment tools mentioned in this chapter, such as Google's AdWords and Overture. "I also use things like Wordtracker and the Overture search term suggestion tool to make sure that I use important keywords in all my product descrip-tions. I always try to name and describe things in the words that people are searching for, and I think that really pays off over time."

Not only that, but he uses his previous journal-ism experience to write and distribute his own press releases and pitch articles to magazines such as *U.S. News and World Report,* the *Wall Street Journal, This Old House,* and others. It's hard to argue with success: Hundley reports that Clean Air Gardening brought in gross rev-enues of more than $800,000 in 2004.

The best way to ensure that your site gets indexed is to pack it with useful content. I'm talking about textual content: Search programs can't view photos, animations, or sounds. Make sure that your pages contain a significant amount of text as well as these other types of content.

Web sites that specialize in search engine optimization talk about something called *keyword density:* the number of keywords on your page, multiplied by the number of times each one is used. Keyword density is seen as a way to gain a good search engine ranking. In other words, if you sell shoes and you use ten different terms once, you won't get as good of a ranking compared to the use of six of seven words that appear twice, or a handful of well-chosen keywords used several times each.

Don't make your pages hard to index

Sometimes, the key to making things work is simply being certain that you aren't putting roadblocks in the way of success. The way you format Web pages can prevent search services from recording your text and the keywords you want your customers to enter. Avoid these obvious hindrances:

- ✔ **Your text begins too far down the page.** If you load the top of your page with images that can't be indexed, your text will be indexed that much slower, and your rankings will suffer.

- ✔ **Your pages are loaded with Java applets, animations, and other objects that can't be indexed.** Content that slows down the automatic indexing programs will reduce your rankings, too.

- ✔ **Your pages don't actually include the ideal keyword phrase you want your searchers to use.** If you have a business converting LP records to CDs, you want the phrase "LP to CD" or "convert LPs to CDs" somewhere on your home page and on other pages as well.

Every image on your Web page can potentially be assigned a textual label (also known as *ALT text* because the ALT element in HTML enables it to be used). The immediate purpose of the label is to tell visitors what the image depicts in case it cannot be displayed in the browser window. As a trick to produce more keyword density, you can assign keywords or keyword phrases to these names instead.

Maximizing links

Along with keywords, hyperlinks are what search engines use to index a site and include it in a database. By controlling two types of links, you can provide search services with that much more information about the contents of your site:

 ✔ The hyperlinks contained in the bodies of your Web pages

 ✔ The links that point to your site from other locations around the Web

The section, "Links help searchers connect to you," earlier in this chapter, mentions the links in the bodies of your own Web pages. One of the most effective tricks for increasing the number of links that point to your online store is to create several different Web sites, each of which points to that store. That's just what Lars Hundley did with his main e-commerce site, Clean Air Gardening (www.cleanairgardening.com).

"Creating my own network of gardening sites that provide quality information helps me rise to the top of the search engines in many categories," says Lars. "People find the content sites sometimes and click through to Clean Air Gardening to buy related products."

It's true: Do an Advanced Search on Google for sites that link to www.cleanairgardening.com, and you'll find links in the following locations. First, the ones that are run by Lars:

 ✔ Organic Pest Control (www.organicgardenpests.com)

 ✔ Guide to Using a Reel Mower (www.reelmowerguide.com)

 ✔ Organic Garden Tips (www.organicgardentips.com)

 ✔ CompostGuide.com (www.compostguide.com)

 ✔ Rain Barrel Guide (www.rainbarrelguide.com)

Next, just a sampling of the many sites that link to Clean Air Gardening that aren't run by Lars:

✔ National Gardening Association (garden.garden.org)

✔ GardenToolGuide.com (www.gardentoolguide.com)

✔ Master Composter (www.mastercomposter.com)

✔ Organic Gardening (www.organicgardening.com)

For the sites that Lars doesn't run himself, he solicits links. "I also exchange links with other high-ranking related sites, both in order to improve my rankings, and to provide quality links for my visitors. If you stick with quality links, you can never go wrong." For more about Lars and how he uses the Overture search network to help users find him on the Web, see the "Paying for search listings can pay off" sidebar, earlier in this chapter.

A program called Search Engine Optimizer (www.searchengineoptimizer.com) by Planet Ocean evaluates the contents of your Web pages for mistakes that can keep your site from appearing high in a list of search results. You can download and try the software for 30 days; if you decide to keep it, you pay $149.

Monitoring Traffic: The Science of Webanalytics

How do you improve the number of times your site is found by search engines? One way is to analyze the traffic that comes to your site, a practice often called *Webanalytics*. When it comes to search engine placement, the type of research you need to perform is called *log file analysis,* which can tell you exactly what keywords already have been used to find your site. You can then combine those words into new keyword phrases, hopefully helping even more people find your site. You can get software that will do the analysis for you, or you can do it yourself. I briefly describe each way in this section.

Software options

Some software options are specifically designed to help improve search engine optimization. OptiLink (www.optilinksoftware.com/download.html) counts the number of keywords on a Web page. It analyzes the links that point at the page, and helps you analyze what the best keywords are, where they need to be located, and what specific text will make the links rank higher in Google's search results.

Do-it-yourself options

The other, more labor-intensive way to analyze what drives visitors to your Web site is through analysis of log files. A *log file* is an electronic document that a Web server compiles as a record of every visit made to a Web page, image, or other object on a site. Most Web hosting services let you look at the log file for your Web site. The log file gives you a rough idea of where your visitors are from and which resources on your Web site are the most visited. By focusing on particular types of log file data, you can evaluate how visitors find your site and which search services are doing the best job of directing visitors to you.

If you look at log file information in its raw text form, you're probably mystified by page after page of numbers and techie gibberish. Log files typically record information such as the IP address and the domain name of the computer that accesses a Web page. They don't tell you the name and address of the person using the machine at the time. They give you an idea of where the computer is located geographically, based on the suffix at the end of a domain name (such as .de for Germany or .fr for France). You'll probably need to make use of a log file analyzer such as IndexTools.com (www.indextools.com) or WebTrends (www.webtrends.com), which present the data in a format that is easy to interpret.

When you're viewing log files, one important thing to track is *referrer reporting*, which gives you the site the visitor was viewing just before coming to yours. This tells you what sites are directing visitors to yours. Make note of the search engines that appear most frequently; these are the ones you need to work on when it comes to improving your placement in sets of search results.

Chapter 15

Advertising and Publicity

· ·

In This Chapter

▶ Finding free advertising for businesses on a budget

▶ Making the most of newsgroups and mailing lists

▶ Maintaining an electronic address book

▶ Hooking up with business partners

▶ Banner ads — placing yours and displaying those of others

▶ Broadening your customer base by shipping overseas

· ·

*E*ver heard of a low-budget movie that came out in 1999 called *The Blair Witch Project*? The cost to create this horror film was less than $100,000, and yet the movie made more than $120 million at the box office. Most of the movie's popularity was generated by word of mouth, but initially, the low-budget project got a high-tech boost thanks to some clever marketing on the Web. The film's promoters knew they would be able to use the Web to reach their target audience of young people who spend a lot of time online. A Web site featured "discovered footage" and chat rooms that enabled people to talk about the movie. The result was a Net buzz that helped draw viewers to the box office.

Even if your own "project" is less dramatic than a motion picture, the Web can be a cost-effective way for a small business owner such as yourself to get a potential customer's attention. In fact, the most successful advertising strategies often involve one individual connecting with another. Targeted, personalized public relations efforts work online because cyberspace is a personal place where intimate communication is possible. Blanketed advertising strategies of the sort you see in other media (most notably, display ads, commercials, or billboards) are expensive and don't always work for online businesses. Why? E-commerce is a very personal, one-to-one communications medium. Successful e-commerce sites, such as eBay, thrive not just because you can find bargains there but also because it promotes community through features such as its newsletters and message boards.

Internet advertising is becoming big business, but entrepreneurs like you can benefit from it as well. In this chapter, I describe cost-effective, do-it-yourself advertising techniques for the online entrepreneur who has a fledgling business on a tight budget. Usually, the more effort you put into attracting attention to your business, the more visits you receive. So remember that if you don't toot your own horn, there's a danger that it may not get tooted at all.

Coming Up with a Marketing Strategy

In case you haven't figured it out by now, half the battle with running a successful online business is developing a plan for what you want to do. The next step is to get noticed. The following sections describe two strategies for making your company name more visible to online customers.

A brand that speaks for you

In business-speak, branding has nothing to do with cattle roundups and everything to do with jacking up your profits. *Branding* is the process of raising awareness of a company's name and logo through advertising, public relations, or other means.

Despite the recent economic slowdowns, the Web is still a great place for developing a business brand. A November 2004 study by the Interactive Advertising Bureau (www.iab.net) reported that in the third quarter of that year online, advertising revenue (the amount businesses spend to advertise online) rose for the eighth consecutive quarter. Internet advertising revenues for the first nine months of 2004 ($7 billion) was reported to be almost as much as that for all of 2003 ($7.3 billion).

For one thing, you don't have to get your shopper to dress up, drive across town, and find a parking spot. Web users sit only a foot or two from the screen (or only inches away, if they're using a handheld device), which means that your Web page can easily get a user's undivided attention — if your content is compelling enough, that is. Don't be shy about providing links to click, thumbnail images to view, and the like. Previous studies have found that Web advertising that doesn't seem like advertising — that is interactive and entertaining — is supported and liked by consumers, and that brands advertised on the Web were seen as being forward thinking.

But don't rely on your Web page alone to spread your name. Make use of the whole Internet, including e-mail, online communities, contests, and promotions. These days, you've got plenty of options, such as the following, to get the word out about your online business:

- ✔ **Banner ads:** This type of ad is similar to the traditional print ads that you can place in a newspaper. See the "Waving a banner ad" section, later in this chapter, for more information.

- ✔ **Classifieds:** You can advertise your goods on a classified ad site such as AOL ClassifiedPlus (ClassifiedPlus.aol.com).

- ✔ **Interstitials:** These are popup ads that appear in a separate window while a Web page is loading.

- ✔ **Keyword searches:** You can pay search services to make your site appear more prominently in search results. See the "Paid search and keyword analysis" section, later in this chapter, for more information.

- ✔ **Newsletters:** You can generate goodwill and drive business to your Web site by distributing an e-mail newsletter.

- ✔ **Partnerships:** Find businesses whose goods and services complement yours and create links on each other's Web sites. See the "Partners make the profits go around" section, later in this chapter, for further discussion of this tactic.

Remember that on the Net, your goal is to promote your brand in many different ways. For example, in early 2002, a Web site was launched to advertise Poland Spring bottled water. The site not only talks about the history of the water itself, but it functions as an interactive portal to the state of Maine, where the water comes from. Visitors can sign up to receive Maine escape postcards and forward them to friends. Poland Spring thus takes advantage of *viral marketing* — word-of-mouth advertising that works well online. Many of the most popular Web logs (blogs) do the same thing: They provide links to one another's content, which helps drive up visits.

A Web site can also promote a brand that has already become well known through traditional sales and marketing strategies. The click-and-mortar version of the Gap (Gap.com, www.gap.com) works in conjunction with the clothing retailer's brick-and-mortar stores. The Web site provides a selection of styles and sizes that's generally greater than what customers can find in stores. The National Retail Federation's Stores magazine (www.stores.org) estimates that, even though the Gap foundered financially in the fiscal year ending on July 31, 2000, customers still purchased $13 billion worth of goods from the Gap.com site, which was 17.5 percent up from the previous year. At the end of 2003, Stores ranked the Gap number 2 among all specialty stores, and reported that the Gap racked up 54 percent in profits during the year.

You may not have thousands of dollars to spend on banner ads, but you can start with simple things: Make sure that your signature files, your domain name, and your e-mail address all refer to your company name as closely as possible. It may take a long time to develop name awareness, but this is a perfect place to start.

But remember that spellings that differ from the common English, such as `niteline.com`, are difficult for people to remember, and people who only hear the name spoken won't know how to type it in or search for it properly. You should also avoid hyphens, such as in `WBX-TV-Bozo@somestation.com`, because, again, their placement isn't obvious.

If the perfect domain name for your business is already taken, consider adding a short, easy-to-remember prefix or suffix to your existing company name. For example, if your company name is something common, such as Housing Services, try fairly recognizable names such as `housing.com` and `housingservices.com`. That way, the Web address is still easy to recall and associate with your business. Or create a "cyber" name that's related to your real name; the Art Institute of Chicago can't use `www.artinstitute.edu` because it's already taken by a group of Art Institutes to which it belongs. So the Art Institute of Chicago created the short abbreviation `www.artic.edu` that I, for one, find easy to remember.

Being selective about your audience

Traditional broadcast advertising, such as commercials or radio spots, are like standing on top of a tall building and screaming, "Hey everyone, come to my store." They deliver short bits of information to huge numbers of people — everyone in their coverage areas who happens to be tuned in at a particular time. The Internet has its own form of broadcasting — getting your company mentioned or advertised on one of the sites that draws millions of visitors each day.

But where the Internet really excels is in one-to-one communication of the kind that TV and radio can't touch. I suggest that you try your own personalized forms of online advertising before you attempt to blanket cyberspace with banner ads. Often, you can reach small, *targeted* groups of people — or even one prospect at a time — through free, do-it-yourself marketing strategies.

Publicity Strategies That Are Free

In the following sections, I describe some ways that you can publicize your online business yourself for free. Prepare, however, to devote several hours a week to corresponding by e-mail and applying to have your business listed in search services, Internet indexes, or Web sites that have a customer base similar to yours.

The best way to generate first-time and return visits to your business site is to make yourself useful as well as ornamental. The longer people are inclined to stay on your Web site, the more likely they are to acquire your goods or services. See Chapter 6 for some specific suggestions on generating compelling, useful content.

Keywords are the key

To maximize your Web site's chances of being listed in response to queries to the Internet search services, you can add special code to the underlying HTML (HyperText Markup Language) source code for your home page.

The *source code* for a Web page is the set of HTML commands that actually make the words, images, links, and other content appear correctly in a Web browser window. Every Web page has HTML source code, and all Web browsers let you take a peek behind the curtain of a Web page to study the source code. To do so, Netscape Navigator users choose View➪Page Source; Internet Explorer users choose View➪Source.

SoftBear Shareware LLC (a company that I profile in the section, "A contest where everyone's a winner," later in this chapter) uses this strategy to draw search engines to its Doctor Puck Web site. If you look at the source code for the Doctor Puck home page, you see the following <META> tags:

```
<META NAME="description" CONTENT="Doctor Johnny Puck founder
          of Ice Puck University invites you to shop the
          Pucktasm store with Ingrid.">
<META NAME="keywords"
          CONTENT="hockey,johnny,ice,puck,university,movies,
          model,models,free,software,shop">
```

<META> is an HTML instruction, or *tag,* that contains descriptive information about the contents of a Web page or Web site. Many search services, such as Excite and AltaVista, use computer programs that scan a Web page's <META> tags in the course of indexing that page's contents. You can include important information in <META> tags to give your site a better chance of being indexed more effectively. In the preceding example, the "description" portion of the <META> tag provides a standard site synopsis for search engines to display when they provide a link to your site. The "keywords" portion of the <META> tag includes words that users can enter into a search engine in order to find your site.

Managing your mailing list

When you make the decision to host and run your own mailing list, you assume the responsibility of processing requests to subscribe and unsubscribe from the list. This venture can start eating into the time that you need to spend on your other business activities. When mailing lists get to be too much to handle yourself, you have a couple of options to make life easier:

✔ **Purchase special mailing-list software:** This type of program automatically adds or subtracts individuals from a mailing list in response to special e-mail messages that they send to you. You can usually manage the mailing list from your home computer. If you're a Windows 95 or later user, check out

Mailing List Express by Mail-List-Software. com (`www.mail-list-software.com`). Mac users can try ListSTAR by MCF Software (`www.liststar.com`).

✔ **Hire a company to run your mailing list for you:** Even though mailing-list software can help reduce the work involved in maintaining a list, you still have to install and use the software on a regular basis. So if you're really strapped for time, hiring a company to take care of your mailing list may be the way to go. Check out SKYLIST, Inc. (`www.skylist.net`) and Lyris ListHosting (`www.lyris.com/products/listhosting`) for pricing information.

Most `<META>` tags use two attributes, `NAME` and `CONTENT`. The `NAME` attribute identifies the property and the `CONTENT` attribute specifies the property's value. *Attributes* are terms that provide a Web browser with more specific instructions about the command it is being given and how to act on that command.

Where to put the <META> tag

Every Web page is enclosed by the two tags `<HTML>` and `</HTML>`. These tags define the page as being an HTML document. The `<HTML>` tag goes at the beginning of the document and `</HTML>` goes at the end.

Within the `<HTML>` and `</HTML>` tags reside two main subdivisions of a Web page:

✔ **The header section:** This section, enclosed by the tags `<HEAD>` and `</HEAD>`, is where the `<META>` tags go.

✔ **The body section:** This section, enclosed by the tags `<BODY>` and `</BODY>`, is where the contents of the Web page — the part you actually see on-screen — go.

You don't have to include `<META>` tags on every page on your site; in fact, your home page is the only page where doing so makes sense.

How to create a <META> tag

The following steps show how to add your own <META> tags to a Web page by using Microsoft FrontPage 2002. (The steps are similar for other Web page editors.) These steps presume that you've already installed Internet Explorer and FrontPage 2002, created your Web site's home page, and saved it on your computer with a name like index.htm or index.html. To add <META> tags to your site's home page, start FrontPage and follow these steps:

1. **Open the Web page document to which you want to add <META> tags by choosing File⇨Open. (Alternatively, if you already have your Web site open, double-click the page in the FrontPage Folder List.)**

   The Open File dialog box appears.

2. **If the file resides on your computer's hard drive, locate the Web page file in the standard Windows navigation dialog box, and then click the Open button.**

3. **If the file resides on the Web, you can edit it by entering the URL for the page in the Location box of the Open File dialog box and then clicking OK. (You must be connected to the Web to display the file.)**

   The Web page opens in the Normal pane of the FrontPage window, as shown in Figure 15-1. To add the <META> tags, you must type them directly into the HTML source code for the page.

Figure 15-1:
FrontPage may look complex, but it really streamlines the process of editing Web pages.

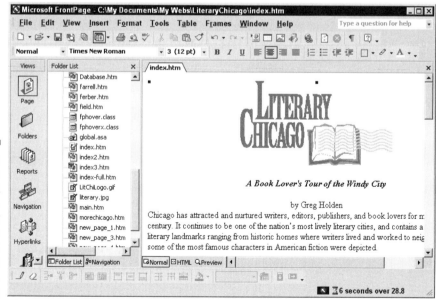

4. Click the HTML tab near the bottom of the FrontPage window.

FrontPage displays the HTML source code for your Web page.

5. Scroll to the top of your page's HTML source code, between the `<HEAD>` and `</HEAD>` tags, and enter your keywords and description by using the following format:

```
<META NAME="description" content="Your short Web site
        description goes here.">
<META NAME="keywords" content="keyword1, keyword2, key-
        word3, and so on">
```

The output appears in the View HTML window, as shown in Figure 15-2.

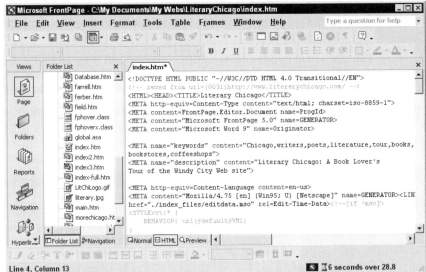

Figure 15-2:
Insert your
`<META>`
tags in
the HEAD
section of
your HTML
document.

6. Click the Normal tab to close the View HTML window.

The View HTML window closes, and you return to the FrontPage window. Your additions aren't visible on the Web page because they're intended for search engines, not visitors to your site.

Note: If you use FrontPage 2003, you view HTML code in the Code or Code and Design pane instead of clicking the HTML tab.

7. You can now make more changes to your page, or you can save your Web page and then close FrontPage.

Enter the text for your ⟨META⟩ tags in exactly the format shown in the preceding steps. (FrontPage documents come with several ⟨META⟩ tags already inserted; you can just follow the same format for your own tags.) Be sure to insert a single blank space between the words META and NAME and between "description" and CONTENT. Separate each keyword with a comma and a blank space. Also be sure to use straight double quotation marks (double-primes) both before and after the words "keywords" and "description". Finally, don't forget to enter the greater-than symbol (⟩) after each command. If you don't, the text will end up in the body of your Web page where everyone can see it.

A newsletter for next to nothing

It used to be said that the pen is mightier that the sword, but these days nothing beats a well-used mouse. No longer do you have to spend time and money to print a newsletter on actual paper and distribute it around the neighborhood. Now that you're online, you can say what you want as often as you want with your own publication. Online newsletters also help meet your clients' customer service needs, as I discuss in Chapter 13.

Publish or perish

The work of producing an online newsletter is offset by the benefits you get in return. You may obtain hundreds or even thousands of subscribers who find out about you and your online business.

In order for your publishing venture to run smoothly, however, you have some areas to consider:

- ✔ **Topics:** If you run out of your own topics to write about, look to others for inspiration. Identify magazines in your field of business so that you can quote articles. Get on the mailing list for any press releases that you can use.

- ✔ **Staff:** You don't have to do it all. Delegate the editing function to someone else, or line up colleagues to function as contributors.

- ✔ **Design:** You have two choices: You can send a plain-text version that doesn't look pretty but that everyone can read easily, or you can send a formatted HTML version that looks like a Web page but that only people who can receive formatted e-mail can read. Keep in mind, though, that many users are on corporate e-mail systems that either discourage or prohibit HTML-formatted e-mail. Others don't like HTML e-mail because it takes longer to download the graphics files.

- ✔ **Audience:** Identify your readers and make sure that your content is useful to them.

Newsletters work only if they appear on a regular basis and if they consistently maintain a high level of quality. Whether yours comes out every week, every month, or just once a year, your subscribers will expect you to re-create your publication with every new issue. Keep your newsletter simple and make sure that you have the resources to follow through.

Extra! Read all about it!

After you do your planning, the actual steps involved in creating your newsletter are pretty straightforward. I suggest that, because you're just starting out, you concentrate on producing only a plain-text version of your newsletter. Later on, you can think about doing an HTML version as well.

People are satisfied with receiving inside tips and suggestions and are happy that they don't have to wait for graphics files to download. The small Chicago publishing house that published my book *Literary Chicago* uses a typical plain-text arrangement for its newsletter, which is shown in Figure 15-3.

Before you do anything, check with your ISP to make sure that you're permitted to have a mailing-list publication. Even if your newsletter is a simple announcement that you send out only once in a while (in contrast to a discussion list, which operates pretty much constantly), you're going to be sending a lot more e-mail messages through your ISP's machines than you otherwise would.

Figure 15-3:
A plain-text newsletter typically begins with a heading, a horizontal divider, and a table of contents.

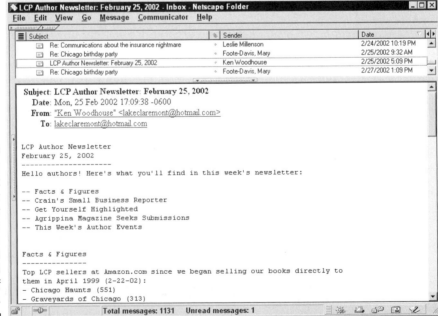

Keep your newsletters small in size; about 30K is the biggest e-mail file you can comfortably send to your recipients. If you absolutely must have a larger newsletter, break it into two or three separate e-mail messages. Reducing the file size of your newsletter keeps your readers from getting irritated because your message takes so long to download or to open. And keeping your customers happy should be one of your highest business priorities.

When you're all set with the prep work, follow these general steps for an overview of how to create and distribute your publication:

1. **Open a plain-text editor, such as Notepad (Windows) or SimpleText (Mac).**

2. **Start typing.**

   Just because your newsletter is in plain text doesn't mean that you can't spice it up. Consider the following low-tech suggestions for emphasizing text or separating one section from another:

   - **All caps:** Using ALL CAPITAL LETTERS is always useful for distinguishing the name of the newsletter or heads from subheads.

   - **Rules:** You can create your own homemade horizontal rules by typing a row of equal signs, hyphens, or asterisks to separate sections.

   - **Blank spaces:** Used carefully, that lowly spacebar on your keyboard can help you center plain text or divide it into columns.

   Be sure to proofread the whole newsletter before sending it out. Better yet, enlist the help of an objective viewer to read over the text for you. Ask him or her to make suggestions on content, organization, and format, as well as to look for typos.

3. **Save your file.**

4. **Open your e-mail program's address book, select the mailing list of recipients, and compose a new message to them.**

5. **Attach your newsletter to the message, or paste it into the body of the message, and send it away.**

If you're sending many e-mail messages simultaneously, be sure to do your mailing at a time when Internet traffic isn't heavy. Many popular newsletters, such as *eWeek News* and *HotWired*, go out on weekends, for example.

Don't flood your Internet service provider's mail server with hundreds or thousands of messages at one time; you may crash the server. Break the list into smaller batches and send them at different times. That's what Debbie Redpath Ohi did with her newsletter, *Inklings*, which attracted more than 46,000 subscribers before she decided to sell it. Inklings is no more, but you can still be inspired by the story of *Inklings* at www.globetechnology.com/woman/archive/20010322.html.

Be sure to mention your newsletter on your Web page and to provide an e-mail address where people can subscribe to it. In the beginning, you can ask people to send subscription requests to you. If your list swells to hundreds of members, consider automated mailing-list software or a mailing-list service to manage your list.

Participating in mailing lists and newsgroups

Many areas of the Internet can provide you with direct access to potential customers as well as a chance to interact with them. Two of the best places to market yourself directly to individuals are mailing lists and newsgroups. Mailing lists and newsgroups are highly targeted and offer unprecedented opportunities for niche marketing. Using them takes a little creativity and time on your part, but the returns can be significant.

Get started by developing a profile of your potential customer. Then join and participate in lists and newsgroups that may provide customers for your online business. For example, if you sell memorabilia of movie stars to fans online, you may want to join some newsgroups started by the fans themselves.

Where can you find these discussion forums? Topica (`www.topica.com`) maintains a mailing-list directory that you can search by name or topic and that includes thousands of mailing lists. (Topica also helps you create your own e-mail newsletter, by the way.) Refdesk.com (`www.refdesk.com`) maintains links to Web sites, organized by category, that help you locate and participate in lots of newsgroups, mailing lists, and Web forums.

Mailing lists

A *mailing list* is a group of individuals who receive communications by e-mail. Two kinds of mailing lists are common online:

- ✔ **Discussion lists:** These are lists of people interested in a particular topic. People subscribe to the list and have messages on the topic delivered by e-mail. Each message sent to the list goes to everyone in the group. Each person can reply either to the original sender or to everyone in the group, too. The resulting series of messages on a topic is called a *thread*.

- ✔ **Announcement lists:** These lists provide only one-way communication. Recipients get a single message from the list administrator, such as an attached e-mail newsletter of the sort that I describe earlier in this chapter.

Discussion lists are often more specific in topic than newsgroups. These lists vary from very small lists to lists that include thousands of people. An example of a discussion list is ROOTS-L, which is a mailing list for individuals who are researching family history. People on this list exchange inquiries about ancestors that they're seeking and announce family tree information they've posted online.

By making contributions to a mailing list, you establish a presence, so when members are looking to purchase the kind of goods or services you offer, they're likely to come to you rather than to a stranger. By participating in the lists that are right for you, you also find out invaluable information about your customers' needs and desires. Use this information to fine-tune your business so that it better meets those needs and desires.

Marketing through lists and newsgroups requires a low-key approach. Participating by answering questions or contributing your opinion to ongoing discussion topics is far more effective than blatant self-promotion.

Always read the welcome message and list guidelines that you receive upon joining a mailing list. Figure out the rules before you post. Lurk in the background for a few weeks to get a feel for the topics and participants before you contribute. Let your four- to six-line signature file establish your identity without selling your wares directly. Also, don't forget to spell check and proofread your messages before you send them.

Profiting from someone else's banner ads

Banner ads may be out of favor, but they're not dead by any means. When used economically and targeted to the right audience, banner ads can help you achieve one of your goals: attracting visitors to your Web site. Attract enough visitors, and banner ads can help you achieve another, even more important goal: making money.

If you attract thousands or (if you're lucky) even millions of visitors to your site each month, you become an attractive commodity to advertisers looking to gain eyespace for their own banner advertisements. By having another business pay you to display their ads, you can generate extra revenue with very little effort.

Of course, the effort involved in soliciting advertisers, placing ads, keeping track of how many visitors to your site click ads, and getting paid *is* considerable — but you don't have to manage ads yourself.

For John Moen, owner of a pair of map-related Web sites (including Graphic Maps, which I profile in Chapter 1), the move from marketing his own Web site to becoming an advertiser came when his worldatlas.com (www.worldatlas.com) site began to attract 3 million hits per month. He turned to advertising giant DoubleClick (www.doubleclick.com) to serve the ads and handle the maintenance.

"We place their (DoubleClick's) banner code on our pages, and they pay us monthly for page impressions, direct clicks, page hits, and the like," says John. "They (DoubleClick) also provide a daily report on site traffic. With their reports, I can tell which page gets the most hits and at what time of day. Banner advertising now pays very well."

Newsgroups

Newsgroups, which are often simply called discussion groups, provide a different form of online group discussion. On the Internet, you can find discussion groups in an extensive network called Usenet. America Online and CompuServe also have their own systems of discussion groups that are separate from Usenet. One of the easiest ways to access newsgroups, however, is with your Web browser. Just point it to Google Groups (`groups.google.com`). Many large corporations and other organizations maintain their own internal discussion groups as well. In any case, you access discussion groups with your Web browser's newsgroup software. The program that comes bundled with Netscape Communicator is called Netscape Collabra; Microsoft Outlook Express has its own newsgroup software, too.

You can promote yourself and your business in discussion groups the same way that you can make use of mailing lists: by participating in the group, providing helpful advice and comments, and answering questions. Don't forget that newsgroups are great for fun and recreation, too; they're a good way to solve problems, get support, and make new friends. For more information on newsgroups, see Chapter 2.

The power of an address book

If you already keep important contact information in a daily planner or other book, setting up an electronic address book on the Internet will be easy. Any good e-mail program has an address book where you can quickly record the e-mail addresses of people with whom you correspond. Every time someone sends you an inquiry, save that person's address in your online address book.

Before you know it, you'll have a mailing list of customers who have contacted you. Programs such as Microsoft Outlook Express, Netscape Messenger, and Eudora all let you collect a bunch of e-mail addresses into a single mailing list. You can then send an announcement or a newsletter to everyone on your list at one time.

After you go through the effort of assembling a mailing list, you need to remember to back it up on a regular basis. Losing a list that contains hundreds or possibly thousands of names can be a significant setback in business terms.

Linking for fun and profit

Hypertext links to your respective Web sites are personal recommendations that can carry more weight than a banner advertisement. Simply call or e-mail the owner of another Web site and ask to exchange links with that person.

Approaching your fiercest competitors to exchange links is probably not a good business practice. Rather, try to find a complementary business or group or organization that covers every business in your field.

Partners make the profits go around

The idea here is to team up with another online company whose products or services complement your own. The Big Guys do this all the time: Microsoft signs an agreement with NBC; Yahoo! joins Viacom; Viacom joins CBS.

On a smaller scale, the Gustobene site, where lovers of Italian food can go to purchase gourmet specialty items, includes a full page of links to partner Web sites that bring Italians together, such as Italmatch, a site for Italian singles (see Figure 15-4). Conversely, if you visit Italmatch (`www.italmatch.com/home.htm`), you see a referral to Gustobene on its home page.

Figure 15-4: By partnering with another organization, your small business can get more attention and reach the audience you want.

Often, you find that two businesses that have this type of symbiotic relationship are more than partners; they may be branches of the same company, or perhaps the same people created both sites. But the principle is the same: Two related businesses help one another by promoting each other's Web sites.

Trapezo (www.brightwire.com/trapezo) is in the business of setting up partnerships between related companies on the Internet. Trapezo arranges partnerships between online businesses and displays one company's content on another's Web site through a *Display Case* (a small, banner ad-type area placed in each partner's Web site).

A contest where everyone's a winner

In Chapter 1, I describe how cartographer John Moen uses contests and other promotions to attract attention to his online business. Remember that everyone loves to receive something for free. Holding a contest can attract visitors to your Web site, where they can find out about the rest of your offerings — the ones you offer for sale, that is.

You don't have to give away cars or trips around the world to get attention. SoftBear Shareware LLC, a company located both on America Online and the Web, gives away teddy bears and other simple items on its Web site (www. 799bear.com). As you can see in Figure 15-5, its Teddy Bear contest has attracted more than 20,000 visitors over several years, and was about to be discontinued as I was revising this chapter. When I asked SoftBear's owner, John Raddatz, whether contests had helped gain attention for his business, he responded as follows:

> "YES, YES, YES. Contests have increased traffic to my site. The response averages about 350 entries per month. I offer contests, free screensavers and software, which still attracts quite a few people from all over the world. My number one contest draw is at Ice Puck University (www.ipucku.com), where I offer a free hockey diploma every month. My Johnny Puck Web site (www.johnnypuck.com) has spawned a local UHF TV show here in Muskegon, Michigan. All of this started with the Teddy Bear contest on my software and screensaver site (www.jrsoftbear.com). You must offer something for free to draw people in to your site. Then you can draw their attention to your main offerings."

Elsewhere on the SoftBear Shareware site, you can see that SoftBear is enrolled in the Amazon.com Associates Program. This is another kind of cooperative link partnership you can consider for your small business. SoftBear recommends some Amazon.com books on its site and, in return, receives referral fees. Find out more by visiting www.amazon.com and clicking the Join Associates link at the bottom of the page.

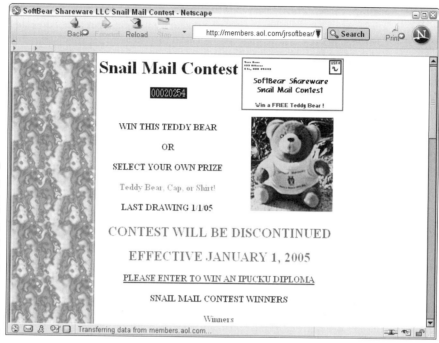

Figure 15-5:
Holding
regular
contests
attracts
attention to
the rest of
your online
business,
too.

Waving a banner ad

I'm not as big a fan of traditional banner ads as I am of the other strategies that I discuss in this chapter, especially where small entrepreneurial businesses are concerned. And indications are that banner ads are dwindling online in favor of *targeted ads* — that is, ads that appear when specified keyword searches are conducted on sites such as Google (www.google.com) and AskJeeves (www.askjeeves.com).

Banner ads are like the traditional print ads you might take out in local newspapers. In some limited cases, banner ads are free, as long as you or a designer can create one. Otherwise, you have to pay to place them on someone else's Web page, the same way you pay to take out an ad in a newspaper or magazine.

However, many commercial operations *do* use banner ads successfully on the Web. Banner ads can be effective promotional tools under certain circumstances:

- ✔ If you pay enough money to keep them visible in cyberspace for a long period of time
- ✔ If you pay the high rates charged by the most successful Web sites, which can steer you the most traffic

Banner ads differ from other Web-specific publicity tactics in one important respect: They publicize in a one-to-many rather than a one-to-one fashion. Banner ads broadcast the name of an organization indiscriminately, without requiring the viewer to click a link or in some respect choose to find out about the site.

Anteing up

You have to pay the piper in order to play the banner ad game. In general, Web sites have two methods of charging for banner ads:

- **CPM, or Cost Per Thousand:** This is a way of charging for advertising based on the number of people who visit the Web page on which your ad appears. The more visits the Web site gets, the higher the ad rates that site can charge.

- **CTR, or Clickthrough Rate:** A *clickthrough* occurs when someone clicks a banner ad that links to your (the advertiser's) Web site. (Virtually all banner ads are linked this way.) In this case, you are billed after the ad has run for a while and the clicks have been tallied.

Say 100,000 people visit the site on which your banner runs. If the site charges a flat $20 CPM rate, your banner ad costs $2,000 (100 × $20). If the same site charges a $1 per clickthrough rate, and 2 percent of the 100,000 visitors click through to your site (the approximate average for the industry), you pay the same: $2,000 (2,000 × $1).

Obviously, the more popular the site on which you advertise, the more your ad costs. Back in 1999, when Yahoo! was still publishing its advertising rates online, it charged a CPM rate of $20 to $50 for each 1,000 visits to the Yahoo! page on which the banner ad appears. If the page on which your banner runs received 500,000 visits, such ads could cost $10,000 to $25,000. Not all advertising sites are so expensive, of course.

CPM rates are difficult to calculate because of the number of repeat visitors a site typically receives. For example, a Web page designer may visit the same site a hundred times in a day when testing scripts and creating content. If the site that hosts your ad charges a rate based on CPM, make sure that they weed out such repeat visits. In general, you're better off advertising on sites that charge not only on a CPM basis, but on a cost-per-click basis as well — or, better yet, *only* on a clickthrough basis. The combination of CPM and CTR is harder for the hosting site to calculate but ultimately fairer for you, the advertiser.

Positioning banner ads can be a substantial investment, so be sure that your ad appears on a page whose visitors are likely to be interested in your company. If your company sells automotive parts, for example, get on one of the Yahoo! automotive index pages.

An article on ClickZ (www.clickz.com/news/article.php/1564281) reports that the popular search site AskJeeves has banned banner ads in favor of targeted, "branded response" ads that appear in response to search queries, and text-based ads that work similarly.

Designing your ad

The standard "medium rectangle" and "large rectangle" banner ads are by far the most popular ones. Some standard square configurations or small button-like shapes are common, too. The numeric measurements for ads usually appear in pixels. An inch contains roughly 72 pixels, so a 468-x-60-pixel ad (the most common size) is about 6.5 inches wide and about 0.875 inch in height.

The rectangular ads appear most often at the top of a Web page, so they load first while other page contents have yet to appear; smaller ads may appear anywhere on a page. (Ensuring that your ad appears at the top of a Web page is always a good idea.)

Many banner ads combine photographic images, type, and color in a graphically sophisticated way. However, simple ads can be effective as well. You can create your ad yourself if you have some experience with a graphics program such as Paint Shop Pro. (You can download a trial copy of Paint Shop Pro at www.jasc.com.)

Need some help in creating your own banner ad? If you have only a simple, text-only ad in mind and you don't have a lot of money to spend on design, try a create-your-own-banner-ad service or software program. I've had mixed results with the online banner-ad services such as The Banner Generator, provided for free by Prescient Code Solutions (www.coder.com/creations/banner). See Figure 15-6 for an ad that I created in just a couple of minutes by using a shareware program called Banner Maker Pro (www.bannermakerpro.com).

Figure 15-6:
With the right choice of color, a text-only banner ad can look good.

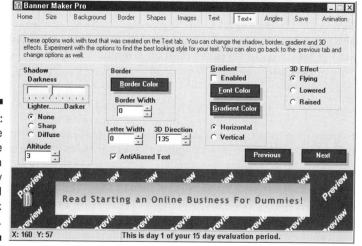

Guerrilla Marketing and Advertising Strategies

I didn't make up the term *guerilla marketing*. As you may already know, the term appears in the titles of a series of popular books by Jay Conrad Levinson and Michael McLaughlin. It appears to be a buzzword that encompasses many sensible marketing techniques, from providing good customer service to knowing what your competition is doing. It also means going beyond the passive placement of ads on Web pages or other venues, and taking a proactive, aggressive approach to getting your business name and brand out there in the marketplace. With competition growing all the time among online businesses, it pays to know all the options when it comes to online advertising, including the ones that I describe in this section.

Popup (and under, and over) ads

The moment you connect to the guerilla marketing site (www.gmarketing.com) a window pops up on your computer, urging you to subscribe to a newsletter. Anything you can do to induce your visitors to identify themselves and provide contact information, from an e-mail address to a street address, is to your advantage.

Popup ads are the bane of many Web surfers, and utilities like the Google add-on browser toolbar and firewalls like Norton Internet Security have the ability to block them from appearing in the first place. But they can still get through to some individuals who don't have software configured to block them. And if your Web site becomes popular enough, you'll be approached by a company that wants to place its ad on your page, either as a banner ad that is part of the page or a window that does one of several things:

- **Pops up:** This type of ad window is probably the most common one. It appears when a page is viewed and pops up atop the page you want to view. These ads work best when their content is related to the page you've opened: Subscribe to our newsletter, buy our book, attend our seminar, or other supplementary information.

- **Pops under:** When you open Web pages on many sites that display ads, a new window opens. But this window, which contains an ad unrelated to maps or clip art, opens underneath the primary window. Its content is only visible when the user specifically tries to close it, or closes or minimizes the other window(s) atop it.

- **Pops on top:** These ads, also called *interstitials,* totally replace the content you want to view. You are forced to look at them for a period of time and close them before you can view the page you wanted to see. I see these ads used on the online magazine *Slate* (slate.msn.com). When you click on an article, a totally new window appears, with animated content, and it is big enough that it completely covers the article you want to read. You need to close the ad window in order to keep reading. You can read about interstitials at `ecommerce.internet.com/ solutions/ectips/article/0,1467,6311_771181,00.html`.

John Moen told me that he has received criticism for popup and other ads on his clip art site. But the ad revenue makes it possible for him to keep creating the art and giving it away for free. In the end, there's a benefit for the consumer, who gets the free art and only has to click the close box to delete the window that pops under.

Adding life to your ads

Ads on billboards, the sides of buildings, the sides of buses, the lights on top of cabs, and the pages of a newspaper and magazine have one thing in common: They basically sit there and don't do anything. They can have lights pointed at them, and magazine ads for perfumes can be given their own scent.

On the Web, ads can get interactive in several different ways. The aim is to gain more attention from the jittery, hurried Web surfer who is, after all, looking for something else on the current Web page. You see several examples of interactive ads on the Graphic Maps clip art pages I mention in the previous section. The ad at the top of the page appears to "shiver" as it moves around, and the ad near the bottom of the page seems to blink on and off. (Not only that, but there's a pop-under ad, which you can see peeking out of the corner of the clip art page.)

It's easier than you think to create ads that appear to move around. You need software that's used to create animated GIF images, such as GIF Construction Set Professional, a Windows-only program available for $24.99 from Alchemy Mindworks (`www.mindworkshop.com/alchemy/gifcon.html`), or the Macintosh application GIF.gIf.giF, available for $28 from Pedagoguery Software (`www.peda.com/ggg`). When you create the initial ad image and save it in GIF format, you create a series of variations and string them together to create the animation. The animation software leads you through the process.

Paid search and keyword analysis

Suppose your Web business gains some revenue, and you decide to take things a step further by placing banner ads on the Web pages of businesses that sell products and services that complement yours. How do you know for sure which ads are bringing you business, or at the very least, visitors? Overture Services provides a variety of tools that can help small businesses gain ad revenue and track which of their ads get the most exposure.

Overture's Market Console is intended to help its network of advertisers track who views their ads and how many visitors click through to their Web sites. Overture is a pioneer in the field of sponsored search.

One of the easiest ways to gain exposure for your Web site is to identify some AdWords on Google (www.google.com), the wildly popular search engine. You pay a small fee to have a link to your site displayed on the right side of a page of Google search results. You identify some keywords that determine when Google displays your ad. Find out more in Chapter 14.

Minding Your Ps and Qs (Puns and Quips)

What is it that attracts shoppers to your business and encourages them to place orders from thousands of miles away? It's what you have to sell and how you present it. But how can customers understand what you're selling if they speak a different language? You must make your site accessible to *all* your potential customers.

Speaking their language

Put yourself in your customer's place. Suppose that you're from Spain. You speak a little English, but Spanish is your native tongue, and other Romance languages, such as French or Italian, are definitely easier for you to understand than English. You're surfing around an Internet shopping mall and you come across sentences such as

> Hey, ratchet-jaws. Shoot me some e-mail with your handle, and steer clear of Smokeys with ears.

> Whatever. All you home boys will be down with my superfly jive.

> Like, this cable modem is totally awesome to the max.

Get the picture? Your use of slang and local dialect may have customers from your own hometown or region in stitches, but it can leave many more people scratching their heads and clicking to the next site. The first rule in making your site accessible to a worldwide audience is to keep your language simple so that people from all walks of life can understand you.

Good manners and good business practices are both important in Japan. You'll find tips covering both subjects at the Gateway Japan Web site (www.gwjapan.com).

Using the right salutations

First impressions mean a lot. The way you address someone can mean the difference between getting off on the right foot and stumbling over your shoelaces. The following useful tidbits are from the International Addresses and Salutations Web page (`www.bspage.com/address.html`), which, in turn, borrowed them from Merriam Webster's *Guide to International Business Communication*:

- ✔ In Austria, address a man as *Herr* and a woman as *Frau*; don't use *Fräulein* for business correspondence.

- ✔ In southern Belgium, use *Monsieur* or *Madame* to address someone, but the language spoken in northern Belgium is Flemish, so be sure to use *De heer* (Mr.) when addressing a man, or *Mevrouw*, abbreviated to *Mevr.* (Mrs.), when addressing a woman.

- ✔ In India, use *Shri* (Mr.) or *Shrimati* (Mrs.). Don't use a given name unless you're a relative or close friend.

- ✔ In Japan, given names aren't used in business. Use the family name followed by the job title. Or, add *-san* to the family name (for example, Fujita-san), or the even more respectful *-sama* (Fujita-sama).

Adding multilingual content to your Web site is a nice touch, particularly if you deal on a regular basis with customers or clients from a particular area. Regional differences abound, so it's prudent to find a person familiar with the area you are trying to target to read your text before you put it up on the Web. Let a friend, not the absence of orders, tell you that you've committed a cultural *faux pas*.

Making your site multilingual

One of the best ways to expand your business to other countries is to provide alternate translations of your content. You can either hire someone to prepare the text in one or more selected languages or use a computer program to do the work for you. Then provide links to the Web pages that contain the translated text right on your site's home page, like this:

```
Read this page in:
French
Spanish
German
```

One translation utility that's particularly easy to use — and, by the way, free — is available from the search service AltaVista. Just follow these steps to get your own instant translation:

1. **Connect to the Internet, launch your Web browser, and go to** babelfish.altavista.com.

   The AltaVista: World/Translate page appears.

2. **If you have a specific bit of text that you want to translate, click in the text box on this page and either type in the text or paste it from a word processing program. If you want the service to translate an entire Web page, enter the URL in the text box.**

   Be sure to include the first part of the URL (for example, http:// www.mysite.com rather than just mysite.com).

   Obviously, the shorter and simpler the text, the better your results.

3. **Choose the translation path (that is, *from* what language you want to translate) by clicking the Select From and To Languages drop-down list.**

   At this writing, the service offers translation to or from Chinese, English, French, Korean, Spanish, German, Italian, Japanese, Portuguese, and Russian.

4. **Click the Translate button.**

   Almost as fast as you can say "Welcome to the new Tower of Babel," a new Web page appears on-screen with the foreign language version of your text. (If you selected a Web page to translate, the Web page appears in the new language. The title of the page, however, remains in the original language.)

A computer can never be as good as a human being when it comes to language translation. I once tried to translate my own Web page into French, showed it to a friend who is a native speaker, and she laughed at the results. If you try a computer translation, only attempt the simplest of sentences. And get someone who understands the language to proofread the results.

Instead of creating a foreign-language version of your Web page, you can provide a link to the AltaVista translation page on your own page. That way, your visitors can translate your text for themselves.

You can download the software behind the AltaVista translation service, Systran Personal, from the Systran Software, Inc. Web site (www.systransoft. com). The $59 program is available for Windows only and requires at least 128MB of RAM and 599MB of hard drive space. If you need translation to or from Japanese, Chinese, or Korean (or from Russian to English), look into Systran Professional Premium, which costs $760. This program has the same software requirements as the Personal package, as well as an Asian font display driver for Asian language translation.

You don't have to translate your entire Web site. In fact, just providing an alternate version of your home page may be sufficient. The important thing is to give visitors an overview of your business and a brief description of your products and services in a language they can understand easily. Most important, include a `mailto:` link (see Chapter 6) so that people can send mail to you. However, if you aren't prepared to receive a response in Kanji or Swahili, request that your guests send their message in a language that you can read.

Although you probably don't have sufficient resources to pay for a slew of translation services, having someone translate your home page so that you can provide an alternate version may be worthwhile — especially if you sell products that are likely to be desirable to a particular market. Plenty of translation services are available online. Yahoo! has an index of translation services at

```
dir.yahoo.com/Business_and_Economy/Business_to_Business/
Translation_Services/Web_Site_Translation
```

Using the right terms

Sometimes, communicating effectively with someone from another country is a matter of knowing the terms used to describe important items in that language. The names of the documents you use to draw up an agreement or pay a bill are often very different in other countries than they are in your own. For example, if you're an American merchant and someone from Europe asks you to provide a *proforma invoice,* you may not know what the person wants. You're used to hearing the document in question called a *quote.*

When you and your European buyer have come to terms, a Commercial Invoice is an official form you may need to use for billing purposes. Many of these forms have to do with large-scale export/import trade, and you may never have to use them. But if you do undertake trade with people overseas, be aware that they may require you to use their own forms, not yours, in order to seal the deal. To avoid confusion later on, ask your overseas clients about any special requirements that pertain to business documents before you proceed too far with the transaction.

Joining the International Trade Brigade

International trade may seem like something that only multinational corporations practice. But the so-called little guys like you and me can be international traders, too. In fact, the term simply refers to a transaction between two or more individuals or companies in different countries. If you're a designer living in the U.S. and you create some stationery artwork and Web pages for someone in Germany, you're involved in international trade.

Keeping up with international trade issues

If you really want to be effective in marketing yourself overseas and become an international player in world trade, you need to follow the tried-and-true business strategies: networking, education, and research. Join groups that promote international trade, become familiar with trade laws and restrictions, and generally get a feel for the best marketing practices around the world.

Here are some suggestions for places you can start:

- ✔ **The Market Access Unit page of the Irish government's Department of Enterprise, Trade, and Employment Web site:** This page contains links to the European Union's Commercial Policy as well as requirements governing Export Licensing and Import Licensing.

  www.entemp.ie/trade/marketaccess

- ✔ **Small Business Exporters Association:** A group of small- and mid-size business exporters devoted to networking, assistance, and advocacy.

  www.sbea.org

- ✔ **globalEDGE:** This site is published by Michigan State University and includes hundreds of international trade links.

  globaledge.msu.edu/ibrd/ibrd.asp

The Newsletter Access Web site (www.newsletteraccess.com/subject/intertrade.html) has information on how to subscribe to hundreds of different newsletters that discuss international trade issues.

Researching specific trade laws

Instead of waiting for overseas business to come to you, take a proactive approach. First, do some research into the appropriate trade laws that apply to countries with which you might do business. The Internet has an amazing amount of information pertaining to trade practices for individual countries.

You can seek out international business by using one or more message boards designed specifically for small business owners who want to participate in international trade. These message boards let users post *trade leads,* which are messages that announce international business opportunities.

For example, at the ECCommerce.com B2B trade bulletin board (www.eceurope.com), you may find a message from a Finnish company selling surplus paint, a United States company that needs office equipment, or a British company offering X-Ray equipment for export. Advertisements on this site typically include the URL for the business's Web site. The site charges a fee to post your own notices.

If you're in the business of creating computer software or hardware, you need to be aware of restrictions that the U.S. government imposes on the export of some computer-related products. In fact, you may incur a fine of more than $100,000 from the U.S. Treasury Department and the U.S. State Department for exporting to a Denied Person, Specially Designated National, or Restricted Country. The list of these people and countries changes frequently. Look for links to the current ones at www.treas.gov/ofac/index.html.

The Buy & Sell Exchange site of the Federation of International Trade Associations (www.worldbid.com) lets you post your own trade leads or search for other leads by keyword. The Trade Leads page of the extensive globalEDGE site (globaledge.msu.edu/ibrd/busresmain.asp?Resource CategoryID=13), includes links to sites that post trade leads in countries such as Egypt, India, and Taiwan.

Exploring free trade zones

A *free trade zone* (FTZ) is an officially designated business or industrial area within a country where foreign and domestic goods are considered to be outside of the territory covered by customs. You don't have to pay customs duty, taxes, or tariffs on merchandise brought into, handled, or stored in an FTZ. You can find FTZs in many countries as well as in many U.S. states.

The purpose of FTZs is to reduce customs costs and make it easier for businesses to send goods into a country. You can store your items there for a while, exhibit them, and, if necessary, change them to comply with the import requirements of the country in question, until the time comes when you want to import them into the country.

Shipping Overseas Goods

It never hurts to state the obvious, so here goes: Don't depend on ground mail (appropriately nicknamed *snail mail*) to communicate with overseas customers. Use e-mail and fax to get your message across and, if you have to ship information or goods, use airmail express delivery. Surface mail can take weeks or even months to reach some regions of some countries — if it gets there at all.

Your customer may ask you to provide an estimate of your export costs by using a special set of abbreviations called incoterms. *Incoterms* (short for *international commercial trade terms*) are a set of standardized acronyms that were originally established in 1936 by the International Chamber of Commerce. They establish an international language for describing business transactions to prevent misunderstandings between buyers and sellers from different countries. Incoterms thus provide a universal vocabulary that is recognized by all international financial institutions.

Incoterms are most likely to apply to you if you're shipping a large number of items to an overseas factory rather than, for example, a single painting to an individual's home. But just in case you hit the big time, you should be aware of common incoterms, such as

- ✔ **EXW (Ex Works):** This term means that the seller fulfills his or her obligation by making the goods available to the buyer at the seller's own premises (or *works*). The seller doesn't have to load the goods onto the buyer's vehicle unless otherwise agreed.

- ✔ **FOB (Free on Board):** This term refers to the cost of shipping overseas by ship — not something you're likely to do in this high-tech day and age. But if you sell a vintage automobile to a collector in France, who knows?

- ✔ **CFR (Cost and Freight):** This term refers to the costs and freight charges necessary to transport items to a specific overseas port. CFR describes only costs related to items that are shipped by sea and inland waterways and that go to an actual port. Another incoterm, CPT (Carriage Paid To) can refer to any type of transport, not just shipping, and refers to the cost for the transport (or *carriage*) of the goods to their destination.

You'll find a detailed examination of incoterms at the International Chamber of Commerce Web site (www.iccwbo.org/index_incoterms.asp).

If the item you're planning to ship overseas by mail is valued at more than $2,500, the U.S. requires you to fill out and submit a Shipper's Export Declaration (SED) and submit it to a U.S. customs agent. The SED requires you to provide your name, address, and either your Social Security number or your Internal Revenue Service Employer Identification Number (EIN). You also have to describe what's being sent, where it's being sent from, and its ultimate destination. You can purchase an SED from your local U.S. customs office or from the Government Printing Office (www.access.gpo.gov), 202-783-3238. Detailed instructions on how to fill out the SED are available on the U.S. Census Bureau's Web site (www.census.gov/foreign-trade/www/correct.way.html). You can file the SED through the U.S. Customs Service's Web site (www.cbp.gov/xp/cgov/export/aes/easy_steps.xmlAES).

Some nations require a certificate of origin or a signed statement that attests to the origin of the exported item. You can usually obtain such certificates through a local chamber of commerce.

Some purchasers or countries may also ask for a certificate of inspection stating the specifications met by the goods shipped. Inspections are performed by independent testing organizations.

Wherever you ship your items, be sure to insure them for the full amount they are worth. Tell your customers about any additional insurance charges up front. Finally, choose an insurance company that is able to respond quickly to claims made from your own country and from your customers' country.

Getting Paid in International Trade

Having an effective billing policy in place is especially important when your customers live thousands of miles away. The safest strategy is to request payment in U.S. dollars and to ask for cash in advance. This approach prevents any collection problems and gets you your money right away.

CASE STUDY

Marketing through global networking

Jeffrey Edelheit knows the potential for making connections around the world by taking advantage of the networking value of the World Wide Web. Edelheit, a business planning and development consultant based in Sebastopol, California, supports fledgling entrepreneurs' dreams of getting their businesses off the ground. He also helps established businesspeople extend their reach by looking at ways of gaining greater market exposure — including going online. In addition, Jeffrey works closely with management and staff to develop the internal systems necessary to build a strong operational base for the company.

Edelheit provides the following guidance:

✔ **Be deliberate in the creation of your Web site:** "I've worked with clients who are able to attract overseas customers and express themselves through creating their own Web sites," he says. A well thought out Web site can create a relationship between you and your customers; in other words, the stronger the relationship, the greater the opportunity for sales.

✔ **Know your market:** Jeffrey goes on to say, "The most important suggestion I can make is to know the overseas market that you want to reach and be aware of the issues associated with doing business there. I recommend getting contact information for an international trade group from the country's consulate."

✔ **Research shipping costs and regulations:** Shipping costs and restrictions are among the most common problems new businesspeople encounter when dealing with foreign customers, he says. "Check with the U.S. Customs Service and find out what the duty charges are before you ship overseas. Once, in the '80s, a company I was working with shipped an IBM computer to Sweden, but because there were still restrictions on exporting high-tech equipment, I nearly got arrested by the U.S. Customs for not having received the required special clearance."

✔ **Avoid being ethnocentric:** Also be aware of how consumers in other cultures regard your products, he suggests. Make sure that nothing about your products would be considered offensive or bad luck to someone from another part of the world.

✔ **Be visible:** Edelheit emphasizes that after you figure out the inside tricks to the search engines and cooperative links, you have unlimited potential to reach people. He believes that one of the keys to a successful Web site is providing information that your targeted market would find useful and then providing product offerings as an attractive supplement.

"The average consumer, whether in this country or overseas, wants to know who they are doing business with, and to develop a relationship with that person. A commercial Web site not only enables you to express yourself, but lets you create a 'value-added' experience for your customers," he concludes.

What happens if you want to receive payment in U.S. dollars from someone overseas but the purchaser is reluctant to send cash? You can ask the purchaser to send you a personal check — or, better yet, a cashier's check — but it's up to the buyer to convert the local currency to U.S. dollars. You can also suggest that the buyer obtain an International Money Order from a U.S. bank that has a branch in his or her area, and specify that the money order be payable in U.S. dollars. Suggest that your customers use an online currency conversion utility, such as the Bloomberg Online Currency Calculator (www.bloomberg.com/analysis/calculators/currency.html), to do the calculation.

You can also use an online escrow service, such as Escrow.com (www.escrow.com) or Moneybookers.com (www.moneybookers.com), which holds funds in escrow until you and your customer strike a deal, or Secure-Commerce (www.secure-commerce.com.au), which specializes in transactions with Australian companies. An escrow service holds the customer's funds in a trust account so that the seller can ship an item knowing that he or she will be paid. The escrow service transfers the funds from buyer to seller after the buyer has inspected the goods and approved them.

Escrow services usually accept credit card payments from overseas purchasers; this is one way to accept credit card payments even if you don't have a merchant account yourself. The credit card company handles conversion from the local currency into U.S. dollars.

If you're going to do a lot of business overseas, consider getting export insurance to protect yourself against loss due to damage or delay in transit. Policies are available from the Export-Import Bank of the United States (www.exim.gov) or from other private firms that offer export insurance.

Part V
The Necessary Evils: Law and Accounting

The 5th Wave   By Rich Tennant

"Ms. Lamont, how long have you been sending out bills listing charges for 'Freight', 'Handling', and 'Sales Tax', as 'This', 'That', and 'The Other Thing'?"

In this part . . .

Before you can start raking in the big (or at least moderate) bucks on the Web, you've got to get your ducks in a row. Along with the flashy parts of an online business — the ads, the Web pages, the catalog listings — you have to add up numbers and obtain the necessary licenses.

This part addresses the aspects of doing business online that have to be covered in order to pay taxes, take deductions, and observe the law. You might think of them as necessary evils that help you avoid trouble. But they're also ways to help you boost your bottom line and help you stand out from your competitors, too. In this part, you read about taxes, licensing, accounting, copyright, and other scintillating legal and financial must-haves for your online business.

Chapter 16

Making It All Legal

*A*s the field of e-commerce becomes more competitive, e-litigation, e-patents, e-trademarks, and other means of legal protection multiply correspondingly. The series of antitrust suits against Microsoft are only the most notable examples. The courts are increasingly being called upon to resolve smaller e-squabbles and, literally, lay down the e-law.

For instance, in April 2002, the popular search service Overture sued another popular search service, Google, for allegedly stealing its patented system of presenting search results based on bids placed by advertisers and Web sites. In 2003, the WIPO Arbitration and Mediation Center was confronted with 1,100 domain name disputes — an average of three per day. Many of these were filed by large corporations seeking to gain control over domain names that were allegedly being held by small business cybersquatters that hold on to multiple domain names in the hope of selling them. In summer 2004, Microsoft settled a lawsuit it had filed in U.S. District Court by paying $20 million to stop a company called Lindows.com from infringing on its trademarked name Windows.

As a new business owner, you need to remember that ignorance is not an excuse. This area may well make you nervous because you lack experience in business law and you don't have lots of money with which to hire lawyers and accountants. You don't want to be discovering for the first time about copyright law or the concept of intellectual property when you're in the midst of a dispute. In this chapter, I give you a snapshot of legal issues that you can't afford to ignore. Hopefully, this information will help you head off trouble before it occurs.

Note: This chapter was reviewed for accuracy by David M. Adler of the Chicago law firm David M. Adler, Esq. & Associates, PC (`www.ecommerceattorney.com`). Adler and his firm specialize in legal issues facing businesses that want to conduct e-commerce. Adler advises: "This chapter is a good starting point. But it cannot begin to explain all the issues in the level of complexity to which they exist, and [it] should be regarded as just the beginning of a discussion with a competent lawyer who will look in detail at your individual facts and situation."

Trade Names and Trademarks

A *trade name* is the name by which a business is known in the marketplace. A trade name can also be *trademarked,* which means that a business has taken the extra step of registering its trade name so that others can't use it. At the same time, it's important to realize that a trade name can be a trademark even though it hasn't been registered as such. The United States Patent and Trademark Office defines a trademark as "a word, phrase, symbol, or design, or a combination of words, phrases, symbols, or designs, that identifies and distinguishes the source of the goods of one party from those of others." Big corporations protect their trade names and trademarks jealously, and sometimes court battles erupt over who can legally use a name.

Although you may never get in a trademark battle yourself, and you may never trademark a name, you need to be careful which trade name you pick and how you use it. Choose a trade name that's easy to remember so that people can associate it with your company and return to you often when they're looking for the products or services that you provide. Also, as part of taking your new business seriously and planning for success, you may want to protect your right to use your name by registering the trademark, which is a relatively easy and inexpensive process.

You can trademark any visual element that accompanies a particular tangible product or line of goods, which serves to identify and distinguish it from products sold by other sources. In other words, a trademark is not necessarily just for your business's trade name. In fact, you can trademark letters, words, names, phrases, slogans, numbers, colors, symbols, designs, or shapes. For example, take a look at the cover of the book you're reading right now. Look closely and see how many ™ or ® symbols you see. The same trademarked items are shown at the Dummies Web site, as you can see in Figure 16-1. Even though the *For Dummies* heading doesn't bear a symbol, it's a trademark — believe me.

The ™ mark can be used with items that may have been registered with a particular state but not with the U.S. Patent and Trademark Office. The ® symbol means the item has been registered with the aforementioned office.

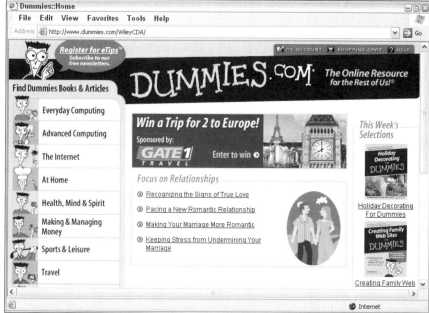

Figure 16-1:
You don't
have to
use special
symbols to
designate
logos or
phrases on
your Web
site, but you
may want to.

For most small businesses, the problem with trademarks is not so much protecting your own as it is stepping on someone else's. Research the name you
want to use to make sure that you don't run into trouble.

Determining whether a trademark is up for grabs

To avoid getting sued for trademark infringement and having to change your
trade name or even pay damages if you lose, you should conduct a trademark
search before you settle on a trade name. The goal of a trademark search is to
discover any potential conflicts between your trade name and someone else's.
Ideally, you conduct the search before you actually use your trade name or
register for an official trademark.

"If you don't have a registered trademark, your trade name becomes very difficult to protect," comments David Adler. "It's a good idea to do a basic search
on the Internet. But keep in mind that just because you don't find a name on
the Internet doesn't mean it doesn't exist. Follow that up with a trademark
search. You don't want to spend all the money required to develop a brand
name only to find that it isn't yours."

The following list details three ways that you can do a trademark search:

- ✔ **Search the old-fashioned manual way by visiting one of the Patent and Trademark Depository Libraries:** They are listed online at `www.uspto.gov/go/ptdl/ptdlib_1.html`. While time consuming, this approach doesn't cost anything.

- ✔ **Pay a professional search firm to do the research for you:** Look for professional search firms in the Yellow Pages under Trademark Consultants or Information Brokers. You can expect to pay between $25 and $50 per trademark searched. More complete searches that cover registered and unregistered marks that are similar to the one you want to use can cost several hundred dollars.

- ✔ **Conduct a search online:** Alternatively, you can use the Web and your own computer to help you conduct a trademark search. The best place to go is TESS, the United States Patent and Trademark Office's federal trademark database. This is the same as doing a search at a depository library, but it's convenient and also free. Just go to `www.uspto.gov/main/trademarks.htm` and click the SEARCH Trademarks link.

Cyberspace goes beyond national boundaries. A trademark search in your own country may not be enough. Most industrialized countries, including the United States, have signed international treaties that enable trademark owners in one country to enforce their rights against infringement by individuals in another country. Conducting an international trademark search is difficult to do yourself, so you may want to pay someone do the searching for you.

The consequences of failing to conduct a reasonably thorough trademark search can be severe. In part, the consequences depend on how widely you distribute the protected item — and on the Internet, you can distribute it worldwide. If you attempt to use a trademark that has been federally registered by someone else, you could go to court and be prevented from using the trademark again. You may even be liable for damages and attorney's fees. So it's best to be careful.

Protecting your trade name

The legal standard is that you get the rights to your trade name when you begin using it. You get the right to exclude others from using it when you register. But when you apply to register a trademark, you record the date of its first use. Effectively, then, the day you start using a name is when you actually obtain the rights to use it for trade.

In addition to a federal trademark law, each state has its own set of laws establishing when and how trademarks can be protected. You can obtain trademark rights in the states in which the mark is actually used, but attorney Adler says a federally registered trademark can trump such rights. It's important, then, to also file an application with the United States Patent and Trademark Office.

After researching your trade name against existing trademarks, you can file an application with the Patent and Trademark Office online by following these steps:

1. **Connect to the Net, start up your browser and go to the Trademark Electronic Application System (TEAS) home page** (www.uspto.gov/teas/index.html, **as shown in Figure 16-2).**

   This page includes a two-column table: The left column contains instructions on how to fill out your application online and pay by credit card; the right column explains how to print out the application form and mail it with a check to the Patent and Trademark Office.

2. **Click the Apply for a NEW Mark link under Forms to file online.**

   A page with a list of application forms appears.

3. **Click the Trademark/Servicemark Application, Principal Register link.**

   The Trademark/Service Mark Application Form Wizard page appears.

4. **Select the appropriate radio buttons and menu options on this page (note that you're asked whether anyone else is already using the desired trademark because the program assumes that you've done a trademark search), and click Next at the bottom of the page.**

   An application form page appears.

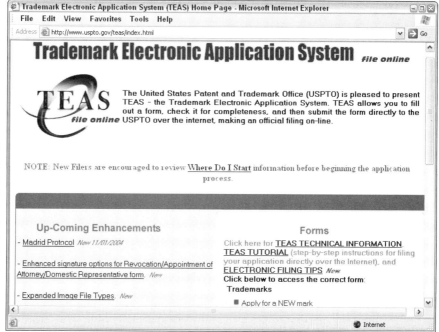

Figure 16-2: You can quickly apply for your own federally registered trademark online by using this site.

5. **Fill out the required forms in the application, including your credit card data (so that you can pay the $335 per application fee) and the electronic signature fields at the bottom of the application.**

6. **You can attach a GIF or JPEG image of a symbol or logo that you want to trademark by clicking the Attach an Image link.**

   A new page appears that lets you specify the image. Even though the image you want to trademark may be in color, the image you submit with your application must be in black-and-white form.

7. **Click the Validate Form button at the bottom of the form.**

   If you filled out all the fields correctly, a Validation screen appears. If not, you return to the original form page so that you can correct it.

8. **Print the special declaration to support the adoption of the electronic signature and retain it for your records, and then click the Submit button.**

   You receive a confirmation screen if your transmission is successful. Later, you will receive an e-mail acknowledgment of your submission.

Generally, each state has its own trademark laws, which apply only to trademarks to be used within a single state. Products that may be sold in more than one state (such as those sold on the Internet) can be protected under the federal Lanham Act, which provides for protection of registered trademarks. In order to comply with the Lanham Act, you register your trademark as described in the preceding series of steps.

Be prepared for a lengthy approval process after you file your application. Trademark registration can take 18 to 24 months. It's not uncommon to have an application returned. Often, an applicant will receive a correspondence called an *Office Action* that either rejects part of the application or raises a question about it. If you receive such a letter, don't panic. You need to go to a lawyer who specializes in or is familiar with trademark law and who can help you respond to the correspondence. In the meantime, you can still operate your business with your trade name. You can also apply a form that communicates your intent to use a trademark, which enables you to use a trademark before it is registered.

Trademarks are listed in the trademarks register, last for 15 years, and are renewable. You don't have to use the ™ or ® symbol when you publish your trademark, but doing so impresses upon people how seriously you take your business and its identity.

Making sure your domain name stays yours

The practice of choosing a domain name for an online business is related to the concept of trade names and trademarks. By now, with cybersquatters and other businesspeople snapping up domain names since 1994 or so, it's unlikely that your ideal name is available in the popular `.com` domain. It's also likely that another business has a domain name very similar to yours or to the name of your business. There are two common problems:

- Someone else has already taken the domain name related to the name of your existing business.

- The domain name you choose is close to one that already exists or to another company with a similar name. (Remember the Microsoft Windows/Lindows.com dispute that I mention at the beginning of this chapter?)

If the domain name that you think is perfect for your online business is already taken, you have some options. You can contact the owner of the domain name and offer to buy it. Alternatively, you can choose a domain name with another suffix. If a dot-com name isn't available, try the old standby alternatives, `.org` (which, in theory at least, is for nonprofit organizations) and `.net` (which is for network providers).

You can also choose one of the new Top-Level Domains (TLDs), a new set of domain name suffixes that have been made available, which include the following:

- `.biz` for businesses
- `.info` for general use
- `.name` for personal names

You can find out more about the new TLDs at the InterNIC Web site, `www.internic.net/faqs/new-tlds.html`, and in Chapter 8.

You can always get around the fact that your perfect domain name isn't available by changing the name slightly. Rather than `treesurgeon.com`, you might choose `tree-surgeon.com` or `treesurgery.com`. But be careful, lest you violate someone else's trademark and get into a dispute with the holder of the other domain name. A court may order you to stop using the name and pay damages to the other domain name's owner.

On the other hand, if you have been doing business for a while and have a trademarked name, and you find someone else owns the domain name, you can assert your rights and raise a dispute yourself. To resolve the dispute, you would go to a group like the WIPO Arbitration and Mediation Center (`arbiter.wipo.int/center/index.html`) or ICANN, the Internet Corporation for Assigned Names and Numbers (`www.icann.org`). But first, find out more about what constitutes trademark infringement and how to enforce a trademark. Go to Nolo.com's Legal Encyclopedia (`www.nolo.com/lawcenter/ency/index.cfm`), scroll down and click the Trademarks link, and then click the Using and Enforcing Trademarks FAQ link.

Practicing Safe Copyright

What's the difference between a trademark and a copyright? Trademarks are covered by trademark law and are distinctive words, symbols, slogans, or other things that serve to identify products or services in the marketplace. *Copyright*, on the other hand, refers to the creator's ownership of creative works, such as writing, art, software, video, or cinema (but not names, titles, or short phrases). Copyright also provides the owner with redress in case someone copies the works without the owner's permission. Copyright is a legal device that enables the creator of a work the right to control how the work is to be used.

Although copyright protects the way ideas, systems, and processes are embodied in the book, record, photo, or whatever, it doesn't protect the idea, system, or process itself. In other words, if Abraham Lincoln were writing the Gettysburg Address today, his exact words would be copyrighted but the general ideas he expressed would not be.

Even if nobody ever called you a nerd, as a businessperson who produces goods and services of economic value, you may be the owner of intellectual property. *Intellectual property* refers to works of authorship as well as certain inventions. Because intellectual property may be owned, bought, and sold just like other types of property, it's important that you know something about the copyright laws governing intellectual property. Having this information maximizes the value of your products and keeps you from throwing away potentially valuable assets or finding yourself at the wrong end of an expensive lawsuit.

Copyright you can count on

These days, the controversy regarding copyright on the Web centers on the Digital Millennium Copyright Act (DMCA), which calls for Internet radio stations to pay high royalty fees to record labels for music they play. The DMCA contains at least one provision that has implications for all online businesses: Internet service providers are expected to remove material from any customer Web sites that appears to constitute copyright infringement. So it pays to know something about copyright.

Everything you see on the Net is copyrighted, whether or not a copyright notice actually appears. Copyright exists from the moment a work is fixed in a tangible medium, including a Web page. For example, plenty of art is available for the taking on the Web, but look before you grab. Unless an image on the Web is specified as being copyright free, you'll be violating copyright law if you take it. HTML tags themselves aren't copyrighted, but the content of the HTML-formatted page is. General techniques for designing Web pages are not copyrighted, but certain elements (such as logos) are.

Fair use . . . and how not to abuse it

Copyright law doesn't cover everything. One of the major limitations is the doctrine of *fair use,* which is described in Section 107 of the U.S. Copyright Act. The law states that fair use of a work is use that does not infringe copyright "for purposes such as criticism, comment, news reporting, teaching (including multiple copies for classroom use), scholarship, or research." You can't copy text from online magazines or newsletters and call it fair use because the text was originally news reporting.

Fair use has some big gray areas that can be traps for people who provide information on the Internet. Don't fall into one of these traps. Shooting off a quick e-mail asking someone for permission to reproduce his or her work isn't difficult. Chances are, that person will be flattered and will let you make a copy as long as you give him or her credit on your site. Fair use is entirely dependent on the unique circumstances of each individual case, and this is an area where, if you have any questions, you should consult with an attorney.

Keep in mind that it's okay to use a work for criticism, comment, news reporting, teaching, scholarship, or research. That comes under the "fair use" limitation. (See the nearby sidebar, "Fair use . . . and how not to abuse it" for more information.) However, I still contend that it's best to get permission or cite your source in these cases, just to be safe.

Making copyright work for you

A copyright — which protects original works of authorship — costs nothing, applies automatically, and lasts more than 50 years. When you affix a copyright notice to your newsletter or Web site, you make your readers think twice about unauthorized copying and put them on notice that you take copyright seriously. You can go a step further and register your work with the U.S. Copyright Office.

Creating a good copyright notice

Even though any work you do is automatically protected by copyright, having some sort of notice expresses your copyright authority in a more official way. Copyright notices identify the author of a given work (such as writing or software) and then spell out the terms by which that author grants others the right (or the license) to copy that work to their computer and read it (or use it). The usual copyright notice is pretty simple and takes this form:

```
Copyright 2005 [Your Name] All rights reserved
```

You don't have to use the © symbol, but it does make your notice look more official. In order to create a copyright symbol that appears on a Web page, you have to enter a special series of characters in the HTML source code for your page. For example, Web browsers translate the characters © as the copyright symbol, which is displayed as © in the Web browser window. Most Web page creation tools provide menu options for inserting special symbols such as this one.

Copyright notices can also be more informal, and a personal message can have extra impact. The graphic design company Echoed Sentiments Publishing (www.espconcepts.com) includes both the usual copyright notice plus a very detailed message about how others can use its design elements (www.espconcepts.com/gratis_design_elements.html).

Protection with digital watermarks

In traditional offset printing, a *watermark* is a faint image embedded in stationery or other paper. The watermark usually bears the name of the paper manufacturer, but it can also identify an organization for whom the stationery was made.

Watermarking has its equivalent in the online world. Graphic artists sometimes use a technique called *digital watermarking* to protect images they create. This process involves adding copyright or other information about the image's owner to the digital image file. The information added may or may not be visible. (Some images have copyright information added, not visible in the body of the Web page but in the image file itself.) Other images, such as the one shown in Figure 16-3, have a watermark pasted right into the visible area, which makes it difficult for others to copy and reuse them.

Figure 16-3:
If your products are particularly precious, such as unique works of art, assert your copyright over them on your Web site.

Digimarc (www.digimarc.com), which functions as a plug-in application with the popular graphics tools Adobe Photoshop (www.adobe.com) and Paint Shop Pro 7 (www.jasc.com), is one of the most widely used watermarking tools.

Doing the paperwork on your copyright

You have copyright over the materials you publish on the Web, but there's a difference between having copyright and having a *registered copyright*. Registering your copyright is something I recommend for small businesses because it's inexpensive and easy to do, and it affords you an extra degree of protection. Having registered your copyright gives your case more weight in the event of a copyright dispute; it enables you to claim statutory damages of $150,000 if you can prove that there has been an infringement. You don't need to register, but doing so shows a court how serious you are about obtaining protection for your work.

Registering copyright is a breeze compared to the process of registering a trademark. To register your work, you can download a short application form from the U.S. Copyright Office Web site at www.loc.gov/copyright/forms. This form is in Adobe Acrobat PDF format, so you need Acrobat Reader to view it. (Adobe Acrobat Reader is a free application that you can download from the Adobe Systems Incorporated Web site at www.adobe.com.) You can then send the form by snail mail, along with a check for $35 and a printed copy of the work you are protecting, to Library of Congress, Copyright Office, 101 Independence Avenue, S.E., Washington, DC 20559-6000.

At this writing, the Copyright Office's online registration system (which is called CORDS) is still being tested and is not yet widely available.

Restrictions Such as Licensing

Another set of legal concerns that you must be aware of when you start an online business involves any license fees or restrictions that are levied by local agencies. Some fees are specific to businesses that have incorporated, which brings up the question of whether you should consider incorporation for your own small business. (I discuss the legal concerns and pros and cons of incorporation in the upcoming section, "Your Business in the Eyes of the Law.")

Local regulations you should heed

Before you get too far along with your online business, make sure that you have met any local licensing requirements that apply. For example, in my county in the state of Illinois, I had to pay a $10 fee to register my sole proprietorship. In return, I received a nice certificate that made everything feel official.

Other localities may have more stringent requirements, however. Check with city, county, and state licensing and/or zoning offices. Trade associations for your profession often have a wealth of information about local regulations as well. Also, check with your local chamber of commerce. If you fail to apply for a permit or license, you may find yourself paying substantial fines.

The kinds of local regulations to which a small business may be susceptible include the following:

- ✔ **Zoning:** Your city or town government may have *zoning ordinances* that prevent you from conducting business in an area that is zoned for residential use, or they may charge you a fee to operate a business out of your home. This policy varies by community; even if your Web host resides in another state, your local government may still consider your home the location of your business. Check with your local zoning department.

- ✔ **Doing Business As:** If your business name is different from your own name, you may have to file a Doing Business As (DBA) certificate and publish a notice of the filing in the local newspaper. Check with your city or county clerk's office for more information.

- ✔ **Taxes:** Some states and cities levy taxes on small businesses, and some even levy property tax on business assets such as office furniture and computer equipment.

Restrictions that may restrict your trade

If you are planning to sell your goods and services overseas, you need to be aware of any trade restrictions that may apply to your business. In particular, you need to be careful if any of the following applies:

- ✔ You trade in foodstuffs or agricultural products.

- ✔ You sell software that uses some form of encryption.

- ✔ Your clients live in countries with which your home country has imposed trade restrictions.

For more detailed suggestions of how to research international trade law, see Chapter 15.

The Arent Fox Web site, which is run by a Washington, D.C.-based law firm, has lots of good legal information for people who want to do business online. Of particular interest is its E-TIPSheet (www.arentfox.com/publications/E-TIPSheet/e-tipsheet.html), which publishes news about trademark, licensing, and doing business internationally on the Internet.

Your Business in the Eyes of the Law

Picking a legal form for your online business enables you to describe it to city and county agencies as well as to the financial institutions with which you deal. A legal type of business is one that is recognized by taxing and licensing agencies. You have a number of options from which to choose, and the choice can affect the amount of taxes you pay and your liability in case of loss. The following sections describe your alternatives.

If you're looking for more information, Eric Tyson and Jim Schell explore the legal and financial aspects of starting and operating a small business in *Small Business For Dummies,* 2nd Edition (Wiley).

Sole proprietorship

In a *sole proprietorship,* you're the only boss. You make all the decisions and you get all the benefits. On the other hand, you take all the risk, too. This is the simplest and least expensive type of business because you can run it yourself. You don't need an accountant or lawyer to help you form the business, and you don't have to answer to partners or stockholders, either. To declare a sole proprietorship, you may have to file an application with your county clerk.

Partnership

In a *partnership,* you share the risk and profit with at least one other person. Ideally, your partners bring skills to the endeavor that complement your own contributions. One obvious advantage to a partnership is that you can discuss decisions and problems with your partners. All partners are held personally liable for losses. The rate of taxes that each partner pays is based on his or her percentage of income from the partnership.

If you decide to strike up a partnership with someone, drawing up a *Partnership Agreement* is a good idea. Although you aren't legally required to do so, such an agreement clearly spells out the duration of the partnership and the responsibilities of each person involved. In the absence of such an agreement, the division of liabilities and assets is considered to be equal, regardless of how much more effort one person has put into the business than the other.

Advantages of a statutory business entity

A *statutory business entity* is a business whose form is created by statute, such as a corporation or a limited liability company. If sole proprietorships and partnerships are so simple to start up and operate, why would you consider incorporating? After all, you almost certainly need a lawyer to help you incorporate. Plus, you have to comply with the regulations made by federal and state agencies that oversee corporations. Besides that, you may undergo a type of *double taxation:* If your corporation earns profits, those profits are taxed at the corporate rate, and any shareholders have to pay income tax at the personal rate.

Despite these downsides, you may want to consider incorporation for the following sorts of reasons:

- ✔ If you have employees, you can deduct any health and disability insurance premiums that you pay.
- ✔ You can raise capital by offering stock for sale.
- ✔ Transferring ownership from one shareholder to another is easier.
- ✔ The company's principals are shielded from liability in case of lawsuits.

If you offer services that may be susceptible to costly lawsuits, incorporation may be the way to go. You then have three options: a C corporation, a subchapter S corporation, or a limited liability corporation (LLC). The LLC is the best choice for many small businesses. But you have to designate officers, hold shareholders' meetings, and have an attorney keep the minutes of those meetings. Although it's more expensive to create, the LLC is simpler to operate and more suitable for lone entrepreneurs.

Subchapter S corporations

One benefit of forming a subchapter S corporation is liability protection. This form of incorporation enables start-up businesses that encounter losses early on to offset those losses against their personal income. Subchapter S is intended for businesses with fewer than 75 shareholders. The income gained by an S corporation is subject only to personal tax, not corporate tax.

You might designate that you are the president, your cousin Nick is the secretary, and other relatives serve as your shareholders and officers. Many corporations that are run by only one or two people have only one make-believe meeting a year; the attorney has a quick phone call to record what "happened" at the meeting and files the appropriate papers.

Sounds great, doesn't it? Before you start looking for a lawyer to get you started, consider the following:

✔ Incorporation typically costs several hundred dollars.

✔ Corporations must pay an annual tax.

✔ Attorneys' fees can be expensive.

✔ Filing for S corporation status can take weeks or months to be received and approved. (You need to meet your state's requirements for setting up a corporation, and then file Form 2553 to elect S corporation status.)

All these facts can be daunting for a lone entrepreneur who's just starting out and has only a few customers. But my brother Mike, who is mentioned in Chapter 1 and who is just starting up an audio restoration business called lp2cdsolutions (www.lp2cdsolutions.com), did create an S corporation, so his liability is limited: In case of a lawsuit, assuming there is no illegal conduct on the part of the owner, the corporation is sued, not him personally. I recommend that you wait until you have enough income to hire an attorney and pay incorporation fees before you seriously consider incorporating, even as an S corporation.

C corporations

Many big businesses do not meet the strict requirements to become C corporations. In fact, everything about C corporations tends to be big — including profits, which are taxed at the corporate level as well as at the shareholder level — so I mention this legal designation only in passing because it's probably not for your small entrepreneurial business.

C corporations tend to be large and have lots of shareholders. In order to incorporate, all stockholders and shareholders must agree on the name of the company, the choice of the people who will manage it, and many other issues. The issue of double taxation in connection with C corporations means that you need to contact a tax professional if you have questions about this business entity or are thinking of creating one.

Limited liability corporations

The limited liability corporation (LLC) is a relatively new type of corporation that combines aspects of both S and C corporations. The forms required to create LLCs cost $500, and that doesn't include an attorney's fees. However, limited liability corporations have a number of attractive options that make them good candidates for small businesses. Benefits include the following:

✔ Members have limited liability for debts and obligations of the LLC.

✔ LLCs receive favorable tax treatment.

✔ The individual investors, who are called members, share income and losses.

An LLC can be a sole proprietorship, corporation, or a partnership. A similar entity, a Limited Liability Partnership (LLP) needs to be a partnership. The responsibilities of LLP members are spelled out in an operating agreement, an often complex document that should be prepared by a knowledgeable attorney.

Keeping Out of Legal Trouble

A big part of keeping your online business legal is steering clear of so-called business opportunities that can turn into big problems. You can run into trouble both at the federal or the local level. In the following sections, I highlight some areas to watch out for.

Get it in writing!

Perhaps the most important way to avoid legal trouble is to get all of your agreements in writing. Even if the parties involved type up and sign a simple one-page sheet describing what is to be done and what is to be paid, that's far better than a verbal agreement. It's also better than an e-mail message — an e-mail doesn't enable signatures, and a single message doesn't clearly point out that both parties have actually agreed to something. A qualified lawyer can help you prepare contracts that you can send to both suppliers and customers who engage your services.

The other important things to get in writing are *policy statements:* statements that spell out how a customer is to use your goods or services, or statements as to how you manage your customers' personal information. Such statements build trust among your clientele. But remember that, when you publish a policy statement on your Web site, you need to actually follow what it prescribes; you can be sued if you violate it.

Is multilevel marketing worth it?

Be careful if you undertake *multilevel marketing* (MLM), also known as *network marketing.* Multilevel marketing /network marketing is a strategy used by many reputable firms, such as Amway: You recruit some people to help you, and those people, in turn, recruit others to help them. No doubt, some network marketers are on the up and up. But other companies (many of which you can find online) use MLM to run an old-fashioned pyramid scheme in which the participants recruit other investors. I'm not saying that you shouldn't look into network marketing at all; I'm saying that you should be very careful about how much money you have to commit in order to play the game.

A potty mouth can flush your business down the toilet

Ever heard of the "seven dirty words" made famous in a routine by comedian George Carlin? The Federal Communications Commission (FCC) has banned them from being uttered on TV and radio broadcasts. However, the FCC does not regulate the Internet. The U.S. Supreme Court struck down the Communications Decency Act, which sought to regulate "obscene" communications on the Internet. Then Congress passed the Child Online Protection Act (COPA), but it was struck down in federal court.

Now, there's the Children's Internet Protection Act (CIPA), which was signed into law by President Bill Clinton in late 2000. It requires schools and libraries to filter pornography, obscenity, and other material deemed offensive to children. At this writing it, too, is being challenged in court.

It might seem like you can say whatever you want online. But you might get your site filtered out, not only by a librarian but also by a parent using child-safety software. So use your judgment as a businessperson. You don't want to turn away potential customers by your choice of language. Also, make sure you don't violate your ISP's terms of use, lest you find your Web site suddenly offline.

The U.S. Postal Service treats MLM businesses as lotteries; go to `www.usps.gov/websites/depart/inspect/pyramid.htm` to read the warning about them. Fraudulent pyramid schemes typically violate the Postal Lottery Statute (Title 18, United States Code, Section 1302). Yahoo! also maintains a list of Web pages that warn against MLM schemes, which you can find at `dir.yahoo.com/Business_and_Economy/Business_to_Business/Business_Opportunities/Network_Marketing`. Don't be taken in by someone who wants you to participate in a questionable MLM-type scheme.

Adult content is risky business

Be careful if you provide so-called adult content. There's no doubt about it: Cyberspace is full of X-rated sites, some of which do make money. But this is a risky area. Congress continues to debate legislation that may legally require online vendors of adult material to restrict access to sites by persons less than 17 years of age. Additionally, many ISPs prohibit you from publishing Web pages that contain adult content.

If you do sell adult items online, consider working with a blocking company, such as CyberPatrol (`www.cyberpatrol.com`) or Net Nanny (`www.netnanny.com/home/home.asp`) that can prevent minors from visiting your site.

What you don't know about acceptable use policies can hurt you

Be aware of acceptable use policies set up by agencies that control what goes out online. Usually, the company that hosts your Web site has a set of acceptable use guidelines spelling out what kind of material you can and can't publish. For example, America Online has its own policies for its members who create home pages through AOL.

Another important kind of acceptable use policy that you need to know about is the acceptable use policy issued by your Internet service provider. The most common restriction is one against *spamming* (sending out unsolicited bulk mailings). Not following your Web host's or your ISP's guidelines can get you kicked off the Internet, so make sure that you're aware of any restrictions by reading the guidelines posted on your ISP's or Web host's site.

The tax man cometh

Sales tax varies from state to state. Your job as an online storeowner is to charge the sales tax rate applicable in the state in which the purchase is made — that is, the state where your customer lives, not where you live. (See Chapter 17 for a more detailed examination of the sales tax situation.)

Luckily, computer software is available to help you calculate sales taxes for every state. Many Web hosting services or ISPs also help with sales tax collection, among their other services. Shopping cart programs and some electronic storefront programs, such as the ones that I discuss in Chapter 9, help you calculate sales tax, too.

If you don't have a hosting service or ISP to provide you with e-commerce software, however, you have to download software or look up sales tax rates on your own. A wonderful utility called Online Sales Tax Calculator, provided by the Sales Tax Clearinghouse, will do the work for you. Just access the calculator at `thestc.com/RateCalc.stm`. Enter your home state and the city and state where your customer resides. Click the Lookup button, and the calculator will not only look up the county where the customer resides but also report any applicable local sales taxes and calculate them for you. If you need to calculate Canadian sales taxes, you can download a shareware application called Sales Tax Calculator, by Carter Computer Solutions (`www.niagara.com/~mcarter/taxw.htm`). You can download and try the program for 30 days; if you want to keep Sales Tax Calculator, you need to pay a modest $10 fee.

Chapter 17

Online Business Accounting Tools

Some people have a gift for keeping track of expenses, recording financial information, and performing other fiscal functions. Unfortunately, I'm not one of those people. Yet I know well the value of accounting procedures, especially those that relate to an online business.

Without having at least some minimal records of your day-to-day operations, you won't have any way — other than the proverbial "gut feeling" — of knowing whether your business is truly successful. Besides that, banks and taxing authorities don't put much stock in gut feelings. When the time comes to ask for a loan or to pay taxes, you'll regret not having records close at hand.

In this chapter, I introduce you to some simple, straightforward ways to handle your online business's financial information — and all business-people know that accurate record keeping is essential when revenues dwindle and expenses must be reduced. Read on to discover the most important accounting practices and find out about software that can help you tackle the essential fiscal tasks that you need to undertake to keep your new business viable.

ABCs: Accounting Basics for Commerce

The most important accounting practices for your online business can be summarized as follows:

- ✔ **Deciding what type of business you're going to be:** Are you going to be a sole proprietorship, partnership, or corporation? (See more about determining a legal form for your business in Chapter 16.)

- ✔ **Establishing good record keeping practices:** Record expenses and income in ways that will help you at tax time.

- ✔ **Obtaining financing when you need it:** Although getting started in business online doesn't cost a lot, you may want to expand someday, and good accounting can help you do it.

There's nothing sexy about accounting (unless, of course, you're married to an accountant; in that case, you have a financial expert at hand and can skip this chapter anyway!). Then again, there's nothing enjoyable about unexpected cash shortages or other problems that can result from bad record keeping.

Good accounting is the key to order and good management for your business. How else can you know how you're doing? Yet many new businesspeople are intimidated by the numbers game. Use the tool at hand — your computer — to help you overcome your fear: Start keeping those books!

Choosing an accounting method

Accepting that you have to keep track of your business's accounting is only half the battle; next, you need to decide how to do it. The point at which you make note of each transaction in your books and the period of time over which you record the data make a difference not only to your accountant but also to agencies such as the Internal Revenue Service. Even if you hire someone to keep the books for you, it's good to know what options are open to you.

You don't have to take my word for all this. Consult the Internal Revenue Service Publication 334, Tax Guide for Small Businesses (www.irs.gov/pub/irs-pdf/p334.pdf). Review section 2, Accounting Periods and Methods, which explains how to do everything right when tax time comes. Also check out the Accounting System section of the CCH Business Owner's Toolkit site (www.toolkit.cch.com/text/P06_1300.asp).

Cash-basis versus accrual-basis accounting

Don't be intimidated by these terms: They are simply two methods of totaling up income and expenses. Exactly where and how you do the recording is up to you. You can take a piece of paper, divide it into two columns labeled *Income* and *Expenses,* and do it that way. (I describe some more high-tech tools later in this chapter.) These are just two standard ways of deciding when to report them:

- **Cash-basis accounting:** You report income when you actually receive it and write off expenses when you pay them. This is the easy way to report income and expenses, and probably the way most new small businesses do it.

- **Accrual-basis accounting:** This method is more complicated than the cash-basis method, but if your online business maintains an inventory, you must use the accrual method. You report income when you actually receive the payment; you write down expenses *when services are rendered* (even though you may not have made the cash payment yet). For example, if a payment is due on December 1, but you send the check out on December 8, you record the bill as being paid on December 1, when the payment was originally due. Accrual-basis accounting creates a more accurate picture of a business's financial situation. If a business is experiencing cash flow problems and is extending payments on some of its bills, cash-basis accounting provides an unduly rosy financial picture, whereas the accrual-basis method would be more accurate.

Choosing an accounting period

The other choice you need to make when it comes to deciding how to keep your books is the accounting period you're going to use. Here, again, you have two choices:

- **Calendar year:** The calendar year ends on December 31. This is the period with which you're probably most familiar and the one most small or home-based businesses choose because it's the easiest to work with.

- **Fiscal year:** In this case, the business picks a date other than December 31 to function as the end of the fiscal year. Many large organizations pick a date that coincides with the end of their business cycle. Some pick March 31 as the end, others June 30, and still others September 30.

 If you use the fiscal-year method of accounting, you must file your tax return three and a half months after the end of the fiscal year. If the fiscal year ends on June 30, for example, you must file by October 15.

Knowing what records to keep

When you run your own business, it pays to be meticulous about recording everything that pertains to your commercial activities. The more you understand what you have to record, the more accurate your records will be — and the more deductions you can take, too. Go to the office supply store and get a financial record book called a *journal,* which is set up with columns for income and expenses.

Tracking income

Receiving checks for your goods or services is the fun part of doing business, and so income is probably the kind of data that you'll be happiest about recording.

You need to keep track of your company's income (or, as it is sometimes called, your *gross receipts*) carefully. Not all the income your business receives is taxable. What you receive as a result of sales (your *revenue*) is taxable, but loans that you receive aren't. Be sure to separate the two and pay tax only on the sales income. But keep good records: If you can't accurately report the source of income that you didn't pay taxes on, the IRS will label it *unreported income,* and you'll have to pay taxes and possibly fines and penalties on it.

Just how should you record your revenue? For each item, write down a brief, informal statement. This is a personal record that you may make on a slip of paper or even on the back of a canceled check. Be sure to include the following information:

- ✔ Amount received
- ✔ Type of payment (credit card, electronic cash, or check)
- ✔ Date of the transaction
- ✔ Name of client or customer
- ✔ Goods or services you provided in exchange for the payment

Collect all your check stubs and revenue statements in a folder labeled *Income* so that you can find them easily at tax time.

Assessing your assets

Assets are resources that your business owns, such as your office and computer equipment. *Equity* refers to your remaining assets after you pay your creditors.

Any equipment you have that contributes to your business activities constitutes your assets. Equipment that has a life span of more than a year is expected to help you generate income over its useful life; therefore, you must spread out (or, in other words, *expense*) the original cost of the equipment over its life span. Expensing the cost of an asset over the period of its useful life is called *depreciation.* In order to depreciate an item, you estimate how many years you're going to use it and then divide the original cost by the number of years. The result is the amount that you report in any given year. For example, if you purchase a computer that costs $3,000 and you expect to use it in your business for five years, you expense $600 of the cost each year.

You need to keep records of your assets that include the following information:

✔ Name, model number, and description

✔ Purchase date

✔ Purchase price, including fees

✔ Date the item went into service

✔ Amount of time the item is put to personal (as opposed to business) use

File these records in a safe location along with your other tax-related information.

Recording payments

Even a lone entrepreneur doesn't work in a vacuum. An online business owner needs to pay a Web host, an ISP, and possibly Web page designers and other consultants. If you take on partners or employees, things get more complicated. But in general, you need to record all payments such as these in detail as well.

Your accountant is likely to bring up the question of how you pay the people who work for you. You have two options: You can treat them either as full- or part-time employees or as independent contractors. The IRS uses a stringent series of guidelines to determine who is a contractor and who is a full-time employee. Refer to the IRS Publication 15A (www.irs.gov/pub/irs-pdf/p15a.pdf), which discusses the employee/independent contractor subject in detail.

Hiring independent contractors rather than salaried workers is far simpler for you: You don't have to pay benefits to independent contractors, and you don't have to withhold federal and state taxes. Just be sure to get invoices from any independent contractor who works for you. If you have full-time employees whom you pay an hourly wage, things get more complicated, and you had best consult an accountant to help you set up the salary payments.

Listing expenses

When you break down business expenses on Schedule C (Profit or Loss from Business) of your federal tax return, you need to keep track of two kinds of expenses:

✔ The first type of expenses (simply called "Expenses" in Part II of Schedule C) includes travel, business meals, advertisements, postage, and other costs that you incur in order to *produce revenue.*

✔ The second kind of expenses (grouped under "Other Expenses" in Part V of Schedule C) includes instances when you're just exchanging one asset (cash) for another (a printer or modem, for example).

The difference between "Expenses" and "Other Expenses" lies in how close the relationship is between the expense and revenue produced. In the case of the Part II "Expenses," your expenditure is directly related — you wouldn't take out an advertisement or take a business trip if you didn't expect it to produce revenue. In the second case, the act of spending money doesn't directly result in more revenue for you. You would purchase a modem, for instance, to help you communicate and get information online, not just to boost your bottom line. You do *hope,* though, that the equipment being purchased will *eventually* help you produce revenue.

Get a big folder and use it to hold any receipts, contracts, canceled checks, credit card statements, or invoices that represent expenses. It's also a great idea to maintain a record of expenses that includes the following information:

- ✔ Date the expense occurred
- ✔ Name of the person or company that received payment from you
- ✔ Type of expense incurred (equipment, utilities, supplies, and so on)

Recalling exactly what some receipts were for is often difficult a year or even just a month after the fact. Be sure to jot down a quick note on all canceled checks and copies of receipts to remind you of what the expense involved.

Understanding the Ps and Qs of P&Ls

You're likely to hear the term *profit-and-loss statement* (also called a P&L) thrown around when discussing your online business with financial people. A P&L is a report that measures the operation of a business over a given period of time, such as a week, a month, or a year. The person who prepares the P&L (either you or your accountant) adds up your business revenues and subtracts the operating expenses. What's left are either the profits or the losses.

Most of the accounting programs listed later in this chapter (and in the Internet Directory on this book's Web site) include some way of presenting profit-and-loss statements and enable you to customize the statements to fit your needs.

Accounting Software for Your Business

The well-known commercial accounting packages, such as Quicken, Microsoft Money, QuickBooks, and MYOB, let you prepare statements and reports and even tie into a tax preparation system. Stick with these programs if you like setting up systems such as databases on your computer. Otherwise, go for a simpler method and hire an accountant to help you.

Whatever program you choose, make sure that you're able to keep accurate books and set up privacy and backup schemes that prevent your kids from zapping your business records.

If your business is a relatively simple sole proprietorship, you can record expenses and income by hand and add them up at tax time. Then carry them through to Schedule C or IRS Form 1040. Alternatively, you can record your entries and turn them over to a tax advisor who will prepare a profit-and-loss statement and tell you the balance due on your tax payment.

If you're looking to save a few dollars and want an extra-simple accounting program that you can set up right now, look no farther than Owl Simple Business Accounting 2, available for Windows 95 or later. Mac users can try WhereDidAllMyMoneyGo? by Bert Torfs (`users.pandora.be/bert.torfs/ WhereIst.html`).

Simple Business Accounting 2, by Owl Software (`www.owlsoftware.com/ sba.htm`), really lives up to its name. It's so simple that even a financially impaired person like yours truly can pick it up quickly. Owl Simple Business Accounting 2 (SBA) is designed to enable people with no prior accounting experience to keep track of income and expenses, and it uses the single-entry accounting system favored by the IRS. You can try the program for 30 days, and then pay $39 to keep it.

The following steps illustrate how easy it is to start keeping books with SBA. These instructions assume that you have downloaded and installed the software from the Owl Software Web site.

1. **Choose Start⇨All Programs⇨OWL Business Apps⇨SB Accounting 2.**

   The main Owl Simple Business Accounting window appears, as shown in Figure 17-1.

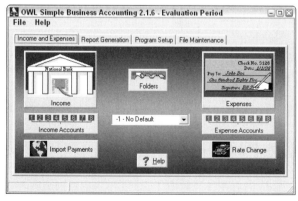

Figure 17-1: SBA uses folders to contain income and expense data that you report.

The program comes with a set of sample data already entered to help you get accustomed to its features. Choose Help➪Help to open the SBA User's Guide help files. Click the topic Getting Started if you want an overview of how the program operates.

2. **Click the Program Setup tab to bring it to the front, and make any custom changes you may want:**

   • If you want to operate in a fiscal year different from the pre-entered January 1, enter the number for the new month that you want to set as the beginning of your fiscal year.

   • If you want your on-screen and printed reports to be in a different font than the preselected one (MS Sans Serif), click the Report Font button, choose the font you want, and then click OK to close the Font dialog box. Times New Roman is usually a good choice because it's relatively compact.

3. **Click the File Maintenance tab to bring it to the front, and then click the Erase Data button. When asked if you want to erase expense data or other information, click OK.**

   This step erases the sample data that was pre-entered to show you how the program works.

4. **Select the Income and Expenses tab to bring it to the front, and then click the Folders button to create folders for your business data.**

   The PickFol dialog box appears, as shown in Figure 17-2. This dialog box lists any folders that have been created.

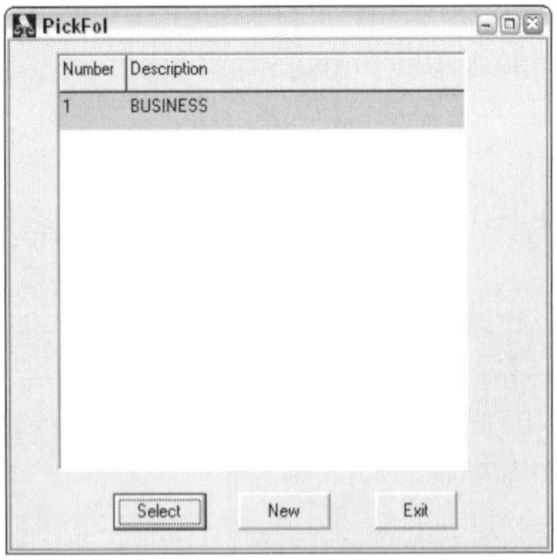

Figure 17-2:
Use this dialog box to add, delete, or edit folders that hold your business data.

Number	Description
1	BUSINESS

PickFol

Select   New   Exit

5. **Click New.**

   The Folder Definition dialog box appears.

6. **Enter a new name in the Description box and click Save.**

   A Confirm dialog box appears asking if you want to add another folder.

7. **If you do, click Yes and repeat Step 6; when you're done, click No.**

   The Folder Definition dialog box closes, and you return to the PickFol dialog box, where your renamed folder or folders appear.

   You may want to create separate folders for your personal or business finances, for example. After your folders are set up, you can record data as the following steps describe.

8. **Click Exit.**

   The PickFol dialog box closes and you return to the main OWL Simple Business Accounting window.

9. **Select the Income and Expenses tab to bring it to the front and then click either the Income Accounts or Expense Accounts button to create an Income or Expense Account.**

   The Select Account dialog box appears.

10. **Click New.**

    The Account Definition dialog box appears.

11. **Enter a name for the account in the Description dialog box, and then click Save.**

    A dialog box appears asking if you want to create another account.

12. **If you do, click Yes and repeat Step 11; when you're done, click No.**

    The Select Account dialog box appears, listing the items you just created.

13. **Click Exit.**

    You return to the main OWL Simple Business Accounting window.

14. **When you've created Income and Expense Accounts, click either the Income button or the Expense button, depending on the type of data you want to enter.**

    Depending on the button you clicked, the Select Income or Select Expense dialog box appears.

15. **Click New to enter a new item.**

    A dialog box named either Income or Expense appears, depending on the button you selected in Step 14.

16. **Enter the amount and description in the appropriate fields and click Save.**

    The Confirm dialog box appears asking you to confirm that you either want to add or delete a record.

17. **Click No.**

    You return to the Income or Expense dialog box, where you can make more entries.

18. **When you finish, click Save.**

    You return to the Select Item dialog box, where you can review your changes.

19. **Click Exit.**

    You return to the Income and Expenses options.

20. **When you're all finished, choose File⇨Exit to exit the program until your next accounting session.**

After entering some data, you can select the Report Generation tab, run each of the reports provided by SBA, and examine the output. SBA can generate the following reports: Expense Reports, Income Reports, Profit Reports, a General Ledger Report, and a Check Register. When running the reports, be sure to select a reporting period within the current calendar year.

The Tax Man Cometh: Concerns for Small Business

After you make it through the start-up phase of your business, it's time to be concerned with taxes. Here, too, a little preparation up front can save you lots of headaches down the road. But as a hard-working entrepreneur, time is your biggest obstacle.

In an American Express survey, 26 percent reported that they wait until the last minute to start preparing their taxes, and 13.9 percent said that they usually ask for an extension. Yet advance planning is really important for taxes. In fact, Internal Revenue Code Section 6001 mandates that businesses must keep records appropriate to their trade or business. The IRS has the right to view these records if they want to audit your business's (or your personal) tax return. If your records aren't to the IRS's satisfaction, the penalties can be serious.

Should you charge sales tax?

This is one of the most frequently asked questions I receive from readers: Should I charge sales tax for what I sell online? The short answer is that it depends on whether or not your state collects sales tax at all. There's no single regulation that applies to all states equally.

If your state doesn't collect sales tax (at this writing, five states — Montana, Alaska, Delaware, New Hampshire, and Oregon — do not), you don't need to, either. However, if your state requires it, yes, you need to collect sales tax — but only from customers who live in the same state where your company has a "physical presence." A state's tax laws apply only within its own borders. If you're located in Ohio, for instance, your business is subject to Ohio sales tax regulations, but only for transactions that are completed in Ohio. If you sell to someone in, say, California, you don't need to collect sales tax from that California resident. But because tax laws change frequently, the safest thing I can tell you is to check with your own state's department of revenue to make sure.

The nature of what constitutes a "physical presence" varies. Some states define it as an office or warehouse. If you take orders only by phone or online, you don't have to collect sales tax. But again, check with your state. Also, most states require that their merchants charge sales tax on shipping and handling charges as well as the purchase price.

One good piece of news is that the president signed the Internet Tax Non-Discrimination Act, an extension of the Internet Tax Freedom Act, which calls for a freeze on new taxes on Internet access and e-commerce until 2007. You can read the text of the bill at www.theorator.com/bills108/s150.html.

The Internet Tax Freedom Act does *not* mean that Internet sales are free from sales tax. It means only that states can't impose any new sales tax requirements on Internet merchants over and above what other merchants already have to collect in sales tax. To deal with this supposed loophole, most states charge a "use" tax in addition to a sales tax: If a resident of the state makes a purchase from another state, the transaction is still subject to use tax. But one state can't compel a merchant located in another state to collect its use tax — only merchants located within its own borders.

Sales tax varies from state to state, city to city, and county to county. Some states tax only sales of tangible personal property, while others tax services as well. Not only that, but some counties and municipalities levy local taxes on sales. Check with your local comptroller or department of revenue to find out for sure what your requirements are.

Federal and state taxes

Although operating a business does complicate your tax return, it's something you can handle if your business is a simple one-person operation, if you're willing to expend the time, and finally, if you have kept the proper business records.

If you have a sole proprietorship, you need to file IRS form Schedule C along with your regular form 1040 tax return. If your sole proprietorship has net income, you're also required to file Schedule SE to determine any Social Security and FICA taxes that are due.

State taxes vary depending on where you live. You most likely need to file sales tax and income tax. If you have employees, you also need to pay employee withholding tax. Contact a local accountant in order to find out what you have to file, or contact the state tax department yourself. Most state tax offices provide guidebooks to help you understand state tax requirements.

When you start making money for yourself independently, rather than depending on a regular paycheck from an employer, you have to start doing something you've probably never done before: You have to start estimating the tax you will have to pay based on the income from your own business. You're then required to pay this tax on a quarterly basis, both to the IRS and to your state taxing agency. Estimating and paying quarterly taxes is an important part of meeting your tax obligations as a self-employed person.

A page full of links to state tax agencies is available at `www.tannedfeet.com/state_tax_agencies.htm`.

Deducing your business deductions

One of the benefits of starting a new business, even if the business isn't profitable in the beginning, is the opportunity to take business deductions and reduce your tax payments. Always keep receipts from any purchases or expenses associated with your business activities. Make sure that you're taking all the deductions for which you're eligible. I mention some of these deductions in the following sections.

Your home office

If you work at home (and I'm assuming that, as an entrepreneur, you probably do), set aside some space for a home office. This isn't just a territorial thing. It can result in some nifty business deductions, too.

Taking a home office deduction used to be difficult because a 1993 Supreme Court decision stated that, unless you met with clients, customers, or patients on a regular basis in your home office, you couldn't claim the home-office deduction. However, the 1997 tax law eliminates the client requirement and requires only that the office be used "regularly and exclusively" for business.

What you deduct depends on the amount of space in your home that's used for your business. If your office consumes 96 square feet of a house with 960 square feet of living/working space, you can deduct 10 percent of your utilities, for example. However, if you have a separate phone line that's solely for business use, you can deduct 100 percent of that expense.

Your computer equipment

Computer equipment is probably the biggest expense related to your online business. But taking tax deductions can help offset the cost substantially. The key is showing the IRS (by reporting your income from your online business on your tax return) that you used your PC and related items, such as modems or printers, for business purposes. You track what you spend on computer equipment in the "Other Expenses" section, which is Part V of Schedule C in your federal tax return.

In case you're ever audited, be sure to keep some sort of record detailing all the ways in which you have put your computer equipment to use for business purposes. If less than half of your computer use is for your business, consider depreciating its cost over several years.

Other common business deductions

Many of the business-related expenses that you can deduct are listed on IRS form Schedule C. The following is a brief list of some of the deductions you can look for:

- Advertising fees
- Internet access charges
- Computer supplies
- Shipping and delivery
- Office supplies
- Utilities fees that pertain to your home office

Part VI
The Part of Tens

The 5th Wave
By Rich Tennant

"This is a 'dot-com' company, Stacey. Risk-taking is a given. If you're not comfortable running with scissors, cleaning your ear with a knitting needle, or swimming right after a big meal, this might not be the place for you."

In this part . . .

1f you're like me, you have one drawer in the kitchen filled with utensils and other assorted objects that don't belong anywhere else. Strangely enough, that's the place I can almost always find something to perform the task at hand.

Part VI of this book is called "The Part of Tens" because it's a collection of miscellaneous secrets arranged in sets of ten. Filled with tips, cautions, suggestions, and examples of new ways to make money online, this part presents many kinds of information that can help you plan and create your own business presence on the Internet.

You can find another Part of Ten chapter on this book's Web site at www.dummies.com/go/onlinebusinessfd.

Chapter 18

Ten Must-Have Features for Your Web Site

* *

*Y*ou can put any number of snazzy features on your Web site. If you ever meet with a Web design firm, you're sure to hear about all the cool scripts, animations, and other interactive add-ons that can go on your pages. Some pizzazz isn't a bad thing, especially if you are just starting out and need to set yourself apart from the competition. Interactive features and a well-designed Web site give you an air of competence and experience, even if your online business is brand new.

But the Web site features that count toward your bottom line are the ones that attract and retain customers and induce them to return to you regularly. Along with the bells and whistles, your business home on the Web needs to have some basic must-haves that shoppers expect. Make sure your site meets the minimum daily requirements: It needs to be easy to find, loaded with content, include content and background information about you, and include features that make shopping easy and secure. This Part of Tens chapter describes ten specific features that will help you achieve these objectives.

Secure some easy-to-remember URLs

Names are critical to the success of any business. A name becomes identified with a business, and people associate the name with its products and its level of customer service. When a small company developed a software product called Lindows, giant Microsoft sued and eventually paid $20 million to stop the infringement on its well-known trademarked product Windows.

Write down five or six names that are short and easy to remember and that would represent your business if included in an URL. Do a domain name search and try to find the one you want. (A good place to search is Whois.net, `www.whois.net`). Try to keep your site's potential name as short and as free of elements like hyphens as possible. A single four- to ten-character name in between the `www.` and the `.com` sections of the URL will be easy to remember.

Domain names are cheap, especially if you are able to lock them up for several years at a time. A name in the `.com` domain is still the most desirable type of URL suffix because it's the one that most consumers expect to see when they're trying to find your Web site's URL. Even if you are able to get a `.com` name, you should purchase domain names in other, popular domains such as `.net` and `.org`. That way, you protect your URL from being "poached" by competitors who are trying to copy you. If your URL is easily misspelled, consider purchasing a domain name that represents a common misspelling. That way, if shoppers make a typing error, they'll still be directed to your site.

Provide a convenient payment method

Shoppers go online for many reasons, but those reasons don't include a desire for things to be complex and time consuming. No matter how technically complex it may be to get one's computer on the Internet, shoppers still want things to be quick and "seamless." At the top of the list of seamless processes is the ability to pay for merchandise purchased online.

You don't have to get a merchant account from a bank to process your own credit card payments. You don't need to get point-of-sale hardware, either. The other day, I paid for a heater from a company that sent me to PayPal's Web site. PayPal (`www.paypal.com`) began as an independent company, but it became so popular among members of the auction site eBay that eBay eventually purchased it. Chances are that many of your prospective customers already have accounts with PayPal if they use eBay. I did, so my purchase process was completed in less than a minute. Set yourself up as a seller with PayPal and BidPay and accept money orders, personal checks, and cashier's checks. If you can take the additional step of getting a shopping cart and a credit card payment system, so much the better.

Promote security, privacy, and trust

Even shoppers who have been making purchases online for years at a time still feel uncertainty when they type their credit card number and click a button labeled Pay Now, Purchase, or Submit to a commercial Web site. I'm speaking from personal experience.

What promotes trust? Information and communication. Shoppers online love getting information that goes beyond what they can find in a printed catalog. Be sure to include one or more of the following details that can make shoppers feel good about pressing your Buy Now button:

> ✔ An endorsement from an organization that is supposed to promote good business practices, such as TRUSTe (www.truste.org)
>
> ✔ A privacy statement that explains how you are going to handle customers' personal information
>
> ✔ Detailed product descriptions that show you are knowledgeable about a product

Another thing that promotes trust is information about who you are and why you love what you do, as described in the "Blow your own horn" section, later in this chapter.

Choose goods and services that buyers want

Every merchant would love to be able to read the minds of his or her prospective customers. On the Internet, you have as much chance of reading someone's mind as you have of meeting that person face to face. Nevertheless, the Internet does give potential buyers several ways to tell you what they want:

> ✔ Come right out and ask them. On your Web site, invite requests for merchandise of one sort or another.
>
> ✔ After a purchase, ask customers for suggestions of other items you would like them to buy from you.
>
> ✔ Visit message boards, newsgroups, and Web sites related to the item you want to sell.
>
> ✔ Make a weekly (remember that Saturdays and Sundays are the best days for auctions to end) search of eBay's completed auctions to see what has sold, and which types of items have fetched the highest prices.

An article called "The art of online merchandising" (techupdate.zdnet.com/techupdate/stories/main/0,14179,2592389-1,00.html) gets highly technical, but it contains lots of best practices: Decide why you want to sell something online; identify what constitutes success for your sales efforts; back your decisions with information; run promotions and launch sales that are intended to achieve your goals; track the way customers use your site; evaluate what works and what doesn't, and adjust your sales effort accordingly.

Have a regular influx of new products

With a printed catalog, changes to sales items can be major. The biggest problem is the need to physically reprint the catalog when inventory changes. One of the biggest advantages associated with having an online sales catalog is the ability to alter your product line in a matter of minutes, without having to send artwork to a printer. You can easily post new sales items online each day, as soon as you get new sales figures.

One reason to keep changing your products on a regular basis is that your larger competitors are doing so. Lands' End, which has a well-designed and popular online sales catalog (www.landsend.com), puts out new products on a regular basis and announces them in an e-mail newsletter to which loyal customers can subscribe.

Be current with upkeep and improvements

Do you have a favorite blog, comic strip, or newspaper columnist that you like to visit each day? I certainly do. If these content providers don't come up with a new material on a regular basis, you get discouraged. Your loyal customers will hopefully feel the same way about your Web site, eBay Store, Amazon shop, or other sales venue.

I know what you're thinking: You've got so many things to do that you can't possibly be revisiting your Web site every day and changing headings or putting new sales online. You have to get the kids off to school, pack up some merchandise, run to the post office, clean up the house — the list goes on and on. You can't be two places at once. But two people can. Hire a student or friend to run your site and suggest new content for you. In a five-minute phone conversation, you can tell your assistant what to do that day, and you can go on to the rest of your many responsibilities.

Personally interact with your customers

The fact that personal touch counts for so much in Internet communication is a paradox. With rare exceptions, you never meet face to face with the people with whom you exchange messages. Maybe it's the lack of body language and visual clues that make shoppers and other Web surfers so hungry for attention. But the fact is that impersonal, mass e-mail marketing messages (in other words, "spam") are reviled while quick responses with courteous thank-yous are eagerly welcomed.

You can't send too many personal e-mail messages to your customers, even when they're only making an inquiry and not a purchase. Not long ago, I asked some questions about a heater I was thinking of buying online. I filled out the form on the company's Web site and submitted my questions. The representative of the company got right back to me.

"First of all, let me thank you for your interest in our product," the letter began. She proceeded to answer my questions, and then finished with another thank-you, and "If you have any further questions, please don't hesitate to ask." I didn't hesitate: I asked some more, she answered, and again said "don't hesitate to ask" at the end. It's possible this is all "form letter" material, added to the beginning and end of every inquiry, but it makes a difference. I eventually purchased the item. Don't be afraid to pour on the extra courtesy and provide complete answers to every question: Just tell yourself each answer is worth an extra dollar or two in sales. It probably is.

Post advertisements in the right places

When most people think about advertising on the Internet, they automatically think about banner advertisements placed on someone else's Web page. This is only one kind of online ad, and possibly the least effective. Make use of all the advertising options going online brings you, including the following:

- ✔ **Word of mouth:** Bloggers do this all the time: One person mentions something in another blog, that blogger mentions someone else, and so on.

- ✔ **Link exchanges:** "You link to my Web site and I'll link to yours," in other words. This is especially effective if you are linking to a business whose products and services complement your own.

- ✔ **Multiple Web sites:** If you have three Web sites, you immediately have two sites linking to each one of yours. Your ability to exchange links with other Web sites triples, too.

- ✔ **Search engines:** Make sure that your site is listed in the databases maintained by Google and the other search engines (see Chapter 14 for more information).

 Make sure that your home page contains keywords in text and headings that search engines can use to index it and add it to your database. The more keywords you add, the better your chances of having your site turn up in search results.

Blow your own horn

Sam Walton founded Wal-Mart, and the Walton family still runs it, but 99 percent of the shoppers who flock to the megastores every day don't know or care about that fact. Wal-Mart is a well-established brand with a physical presence. Your fledgling online business has neither of those advantages. You need to use your Web site to provide some essential background about you, why you started your business, and what your goals are.

Your immediate aim is to answer the question that naturally arises when a consumer visits your online business: "Who are these people?" or "Who is this guy (or woman)?" The indirect goal is to answer a question that the shopper doesn't necessarily ask consciously, but that is present nonetheless: "Why should I trust this place?" Be sure to tout your experience, your background, your family or hobbies — anything to reassure online shoppers that you're a reputable person who is looking out for their interests.

Create a well-organized Web site

This isn't quite as essential as it used to be, because you can establish a regular income on eBay without having any Web site at all. But even if you become a well-established eBay seller, you're going to want a Web site at some point or another. How do you make your site well organized? Make sure your site incorporates these essential features:

- ✔ **Navigation buttons:** Consumers who are in a hurry (in other words, almost all consumers) expect to see a row of navigation buttons along the top or one of the sides of your home page. Don't make them hunt; put them there.

- ✔ **A site map:** A page that leads visitors to all areas of your site can prevent them from going elsewhere if they get lost.

- ✔ **Links that actually work:** Nothing is more frustrating than clicking on a link that's supposed to lead to a photo and/or a bit of information that you really want and to come up with the generic "Page not found" error message.

- ✔ **Links that indicate where you are on the site:** Such links are helpful because, like a trail of breadcrumbs, they show how the customer got to a particular page. Here's an example:

```
Clothing > Men's > Sportswear > Shoes > Running
```

When your site grows to contain dozens of pages and several main categories, links that look like this can help people move up to a main category and find more subcategories.

Be the first to visit your Web site, and test it to make sure that the forms, e-mail addresses, and other features function correctly. If someone sends you and e-mail message only to have it "bounce back," you'll probably lose that customer, who might well conclude that you aren't monitoring your Web site or your business. At the very least, open your site in both Microsoft Internet Explorer and Netscape Navigator (as well as the popular new browser Firefox) to make sure that your text and images load correctly.

Chapter 19

Ten Hot New Ways to Be an Ontrepreneur

···

Not so long ago, starting an online business primarily meant creating a Web site and organizing it in a businesslike manner. You would create a catalog, add a shopping cart and payment system, and hope customers would find you. You might be in an online shopping mall with other online businesses.

These days, you don't have to create a full-fledged Web site to sell online. The hottest ways to make money are to sign up with an online service that helps individuals get their content online and market themselves or their products and services before the public. You might have to pay a small monthly hosting fee; you might have to pay a sales commission. But the benefits are huge: You don't have to do all the work of creating a catalog and payment system because your host will do the work for you. It might mean signing up with a company that streamlines the process of setting up an online blog; it might mean creating a store on eBay or Amazon.com.

This chapter presents ten innovative approaches to making money online. By following one or more of these relatively simple options, you can start generating income quickly and painlessly. You might not make a fortune, but you focus attention on yourself and your business that can brighten your life even as it puts some extra cash in your pocket.

Starting a blog

Adding the personal touch has always separated the Mom and Pop stores from the soulless warehouses. Nowadays, however, you're likely to be greeted with a cheery hello even when you wander into a discount mall. So the precedent has definitely been set for mixing the family into business. With a blog of the sort described in Chapter 4, you can combine the personal and business areas of your life into a single Web page.

The advantage of a blog is that you can give customers a window into your soul. That can build trust, which in turn, can build business. You might not want to define yourself with your strong religious preferences or passionate view on the results of the latest election, but it could be a definite asset to post a few photos of your children or pets. You might also include a narrative of your latest family vacation. On a slightly more businesslike side, it would be really great to have a link to the text of a paper you presented at the latest professional conference you attended. Of even more relevance might be a series of photos showing the happy day that the new press was delivered to your printing plant, accompanied by examples of new brochures that feature the results of its bells and whistles. Whatever the subject, the goal is to keep the tone of the text upbeat and breezy, friend to friend.

A woman named Julie Powell decided to methodically work her way through all the recipes in Julia Child's classic *Mastering the Art of French Cooking*. She started a blog called The Julie/Julia Project (blogs.salon.com/0001399/) in which she described her attempts to create each dish in the book, chronicling her successes and failures. Because of the popularity of her Web site, she landed a deal for a real book that, she reports, enabled her to leave her day job as a secretary.

Turning your hobby into a business

I'm a perfect example of a person who was able to start a new career thanks to the Internet. I started when the World Wide Web was new, and lots of folks who were previously not all that comfortable with the computer were trying to go online. Nowadays, there's not such a need for beginner's books, especially now that modern babies seem to be born with computer mice in their hands. So I'm not recommending that you follow in my exact footsteps. But the point is that you should take anything you love and are good at and turn it into a Web site.

I once wrote about a woman named Kim Corbin who loves to skip. She started a Web site called iSkip.com (www.iskip.com). She now goes around the country, giving seminars on skipping and inspiring others to improve their mood and get some exercise by doing the same. The gothic rock star Marilyn Manson sells his artwork on his Web site (www.marilynmansonartworkonline.com). One of my favorite online people, a Wisconsin woman who calls herself The Butter Cow Lady and who has gained local fame through her butter sculptures, sells her life story on her site (www.thebuttercowlady.com). On the Web, you're limited only by your imagination as to what you can sell. Take what you know and love and run with it.

Getting other people to contribute

Many Web sites work by soliciting contributions from interested visitors. If you build a Web site, others will come. The most obvious example is eBay: The site's success is due almost entirely to content submitted by sellers around the world.

You can emulate eBay's success on a smaller scale. Say you'd like to sell greeting cards. You might post the images of folks who take photographs of scenery, make block prints of jungle animals, or collect drawings of preschoolers. Or quilting might be your passion. Why not set up a Web site that offers the work of those who create different patterns, use different fabrics, collect antique quilts, or do repair? The Web is the perfect place to bring like-minded individuals together, and contributions from others can keep your site current and successful while giving you time to focus on design and marketing issues.

Sites like PoetsPassion.com (`www.poetspassion.com`) solicit poems from artists on many different topics, and they display ads provided by Google. Slashdot (`slashdot.org`), a popular news-and-views site for computer nerds, depends on those very same nerds for many of its stories and reviews, and gains credibility for welcome opinions from far and wide.

Inspiring others with your thoughts

Sometimes, you end up making a huge change in your life without really trying. You put something online that's sincere, heartfelt, and that you think might help some other people. You find out that there are tons of people out there who feel the same way.

I am reminded of the story of Reata Strickland, a Webmaster and Sunday school teacher in Tuscaloosa, Alabama. She was touched by a short story called "Interview with God." She spent a couple of days turning the story into a Web page presentation. She put the pages online, felt good that she had done so, and moved on to other things. In the meantime, the site took on a life of its own. Reata was soon notified by her church's Internet Service Provider that her site had attracted 500,000 visitors. Before long, the site was getting two million visitors a month. Reata has since made herself into a marketable personality, giving talks, creating new presentations, and selling merchandise related to the short story "Interview with God" and similar products. She also wrote a 64-page book called *Interview with God*. It was all unplanned, but she embraced her success and made the most of it: You can, too.

You'll find the original Interview with God presentation and more about Reata Strickland at Moments with God (`www.momentswithgod.com`).

Offering your services on eLance

If you say the phrase "making money online," what would come to the minds of most people is selling small, easily transportable objects. But merchandise is only one type of product you can make available in the marketplace; you can also market your services and your knowledge. Put out an ad on your local version of Craigslist (www.craigslist.org). Then register with eLance (www.elanceonline.com) as a professional contractor.

Simply purchasing a domain name for your Web site and then creating a simple one-page advertisement that points people to your offices and explains your qualifications will help. Check out e-commerce attorney David Adler's page (www.ecommerceattorney.com).

Opening the PayPal tip jar

Chapter 9 addressed several different ways to make money with the help of the biggest of all online booksellers, Amazon.com, including Amazon's tip jar feature. PayPal has its own tip jar button, and you can add it to your blog or Web site in an effort to solicit donations from faithful visitors who find value in what you do.

First, you need to apply for a PayPal account if you don't have one already by going to the PayPal home page (www.paypal.com) and clicking Sign Up Now. It's free to obtain an account and to set up the Tip Jar service. Go to the Pay-Pal - Directory of Features page (www.paypal.com/us/cgi-bin/webscr?cmd=p/mer/directory_intro) and click Get Started in the row labeled Donations. Follow the steps on subsequent screens to set up the button, which enables individuals to send payments to your PayPal account.

Giving out not-so-free advice

The Internet has always been a great place to get questions answered. Over the years, the newsgroups that populate Usenet have been the primary resources for answers and support. You can also start a Web site on which you offer your consulting services. If you know something about computers or the repair and maintenance of other objects, you can answer questions and earn a few bucks on the Google Answers site (answers.google.com). At the time this was written, the program had all the Researchers (registered question answerers) it needed, but predicted that more would be hired in the near future; check back to see if you can join the team. You can also gather tips, tricks, and instructions pertaining to your field of interest: Rod Stephens does just that on his VB Helper site (www.vb-helper.com) where he gathers information on the programming language Visual Basic. He also solicits donations via the Amazon.com tip jar (see the preceding section).

Turning to your pets for help

I'm not kidding. As an online businessperson, you are looking for something you are passionately interested in and that other people love just as much. Practically everybody has a pet of some sort that they love. Pets, pet care, and related products and services abound on the Web. If you breed pets, you can start up a Web site and take orders; you can create pet toys and sell them online; if you're a photographer, you can take photos of pets; if you're a Web site designer, you can create Web sites for pampered pets that describes training. Just think about the animals you love and that live close to you, and you're bound to come up with some ideas that will have them and their owners eating out of your hand.

Becoming a storehouse of information

What's that you say? You don't have a pet, you can't draw, you don't have any products to sell, and you aren't a professional contractor. Never fear. On the Web, information sells. Chances are you have a storehouse of information about one topic in particular. You know a lot about your family history, you know everything there is to know about collecting coins, you are a genius with identifying rocks, or you are an avid birdwatcher. Create a Web site in which you put every bit of information you have online. Make your site the one and only, all greatest resource ever devoted to this topic. Follow the example of the Urban Legend Reference Pages (`www.snopes.com`), a Web site started back in 1995 by a husband-and-wife team living in California. The site collects urban legends of all sorts and reports on whether or not they're actually true; it makes enough money from ads to keep it going. But the main thing is that it's a labor of love for its creators.

Need income? Just ask!

It sounds odd, but if you present yourself in the right way on the Web, and you simply ask for money, you just might get it. The most famous case is that of Karyn Bosnak. When she found herself buried in $20,000 of credit card debt, she created a Web site called SaveKaryn.com (`www.savekaryn.com`). She asked for donations to help her out of debt. In just 20 weeks, her site received nearly two million visits, and she wasn't in debt anymore — especially since her book *Save Karyn* was published in several languages, too.

When blogger Andrew Sullivan was in need of funds to keep his blog online, faithful readers donated more than $70,000. Sullivan was well established by that time; people knew he would use the money to keep providing them with the opinions and insights they were used to. Present yourself in an open, positive manner, and readers will respond to you, too.

Be advised that the field of virtual panhandling is already very crowded. Just check the Google directory at `directory.google.com/Top/Society/People/Requesting_Help/Debt_Reduction`. These folks have created Web sites seeking donations so they can get out of debt. You'll have to find a way to distinguish yourself from the crowd if you want attention for your financial needs.

Expanding your existing business to the Web

Expanding your business to the Web isn't new, of course. But a surprising number of established businesspeople haven't done it yet. Many of the lawyers I know have no idea what to do with the Web. The same goes for other service providers, such from dentists to plumbers to auto mechanics. It can be as simple as listing a fee chart, your hours, and where to park when customers come to your facility. Or you can expand a bit to include references from satisfied customers.

The point is that these days a large percentage of the population is sitting at the computer already hooked up to the Internet. When they suddenly realize that they need their suit pressed for a meeting the next day or that their kids need school supplies, they are more likely to call up information on service providers by using a search engine than they are to flip through the phone book and make a call to find out locations and hours.

Index

Notes